THE ROAD HOME

Published in the United States by
Beckham Publications Group, Inc.
ISBN: 0-931761-73-5
10 9 8 7 6 5 4 3 2 1

The Road Home

A Spiritual Autobiography

Nadine Louise

Silver Spring

To God

and to my

soul friends

with whom and through whom

all things are possible

CONTENTS

INTRODUCTION

SOME time ago a friend sent me a tape of a song he had written, a guitar instrumental called "The Road Home." He chose that title because, it was a "traveling" song, and he asked me to tell him what I thought of it. I told him that the song was great, but that the title also had a special meaning for me. It really struck a personal chord. I could really say a lot about the road home.

Not long after, I realized that that was exactly what I was supposed to do. I had been given my creative marching orders—"It's time to write"—some months earlier. I had an idea of *what* I was supposed to share, but the *how* had not come to me. The *what* was a group of short essays defining my personal spiritual beliefs and the lessons I've learned in the process of reclaiming my authentic, or true, self and my life after a devastating loss. And the *how* had just been given to me through a special friend. I was to write about "The Road Home"—my road home, my life. Not the *story* of my life, but the *lessons* of my life.

This is not an autobiography of accomplishments and events. This is an autobiography of spiritual beliefs, attitudes, principles, and truths, with the events of my life interwoven throughout. This is a spiritual autobiography because my road home had to be miraculously transformed into a spiritual journey before I could find my way. This is a journey that has taken me down a mystical path. It first led me to a God outside of myself, then to a God within myself and others, and, ultimately, to my true self and unique path. This is a journey that is taking and will take me beyond this life into another, the place from which I came: the road home.

So this is, without question, a spiritual experience; but it is not a religious experience in the traditional sense, at least it has not been for me. When I refer to my spiritual guide as

God, understand that I refer to a God of *my* understanding. And *my* understanding of God may be very different from the God of *your* understanding, as you will see when you read about him. He is, above all, a power greater than myself who expresses through me as love. He is one whom I choose to call God. I use that term and the male gender only because I am used to it and have no personal objections to doing so. God is neither male nor female, spirit nor flesh, personal nor impersonal, but all things at once.

My personal brand of spirituality is grounded in the philosophies of twelve step recovery programs, because it was addictive behaviors (my own and others') that literally brought me to my knees and forced me to establish a personal relationship with God. But, my spiritual curiosity goes beyond program. My concept of God and my personal belief system have been formulated, augmented, and strengthened through many diverse sources. God speaks to me through whatever medium I am tuned in to, and these are both traditional and nontraditional. So, for me, there is no right or wrong way to travel the road home. These are the principles and philosophies that have worked for me, and that is what I have been told to share with you. As we say in the program, "Take what you like and leave the rest."

There is also no right or wrong way to approach reading about my spiritual journey and the principles and philosophies I have discovered along the way. The first five segments of the book provide the framework for what follows and, as such, ought to be read continuously. The spiritual essays categorized as gifts, rewards, principles, practices, and road hazards may be read either continuously or randomly selected according to your interest in a particular principle. They are meant to be self-contained, with excerpts from my personal story woven throughout to illustrate the principle being discussed.

The journey itself is a process of continuous change, continuous growth, and continuous healing. Writing this spiritual autobiography is a part of my process, so the changes, growth, and healing I am experiencing are reflected in my writing. As I open my heart more to God, I also open my heart more to you. The shift is subtle, but if you read this with an open heart you will sense it. I have purposely tried to not rewrite these pages for fear of eliminating the shift, as it is an important part of my message.

Finding my personal truth, my true self, and following my unique path are not always easy, even with a spiritual guide. But the road home is never dull and boring, the rewards are great, and it is never too late to begin. My prayer is that some part of my experience may help you in your own process of self-discovery and make your personal journey a bit easier. Or, if you have not consciously begun this process, that it may inspire you to do so. That is my purpose and God's intent. So bon voyage, my friend. May your road home be loving, joyous, truthful, and serene. None of us deserves anything less.

Namaste.

Chapter I

THE JOURNEY

ON the day I was born, I began a journey. The purpose of this journey was to take me back to the place I came from on a path designed to be uniquely mine. But, very soon I left my path and began following the path that others wanted me to walk, in order to earn their love and approval. I became what they wanted me to be and did what they wanted me to do. As a child, I followed the approved path blindly; as an adult, I became more cautious in choosing a fellow traveler to follow, but, I still followed until I learned that the path was not right for me, that it did not fit. Then I would leave and try, for a time, to find my way alone, without a guide, a map, or a fellow traveler. Occasionally, I caught sight of my unique path and claimed it as mine; but, without a guide, I soon lost my way again. Weary and alone, I would find someone else to follow, and again I would lose my way.

Then one day, quite by accident, I discovered that I had a guide and that this guide had always been with me. Always, since my birth. My aloneness had been an illusion. This guide loved me unconditionally and unwaveringly. I did not have to do anything to earn love—simply being Nadine was good enough. This guide knew what my unique path was because he had created it. All I had to do was walk with him, and he was more than willing, even overjoyed, to show me the way.

At first, although I welcomed his company, I did not trust him to guide me, to show me the way. Not only did I not trust him to show me my unique path, I didn't trust myself to recognize it! To recognize my unique path I had to recognize and own my authentic, or true, self, and I really was not sure just who or what that was! After all, I was fifty-three years old. I had been lost and wandering about for a very long time. Also, at the time I discovered the presence of my guide, I was with a fellow traveler, one whom I loved very much. So I chose to keep on walking with him, following his path, even though his path was the path of an addict and was subsequently difficult to follow.

For five more years I followed, ever aware that the guide was with me, waiting for me to call on him. Occasionally I would call on him to help me over a particularly difficult stretch of road. But then, when the path got smoother again, I'd say, "Thank you very much," and forge ahead on my own again, but still always on the path of my traveling companion. Others came too—fellow travelers who recognized my pain because they had walked similar paths. They walked with me as well, but always at a distance. They would have come closer, but I would not let them. I was too used to being alone and too afraid to let them come close.

Then, one day, my companion came to the end of his journey and left me stranded, heartbroken, and alone on a path that was not mine. In desperation, I turned to my guide and begged him to help me. He smiled, took me in his arms, and simply loved me as he always had. The others came as well and held me and loved me as they always had. Then, slowly, one step at a time, my guide and fellow travelers helped me find my way—the way back to both my true self and my unique path. At sixty, I finally began to walk the path designed to be uniquely mine, my very own road home.

My guide and I walk together now; in fact, you might say that we are inseparable. Over time I have learned to have faith and trust in his guiding abilities, mostly through trial and error. It seems that every time I try to do his job, to take over as guide, I get lost again! So I turn around and he is right there, patiently waiting, infinitely loving, and always ready to show me the way. But only when I am willing to allow him to do so.

My unique path is very different than the ones I have walked before. It is exciting, challenging, meaningful, wondrous, and, with my guide lighting the way with love, my path leads only to my highest good. I walk with many fellow travelers now. We are all on different paths, but we are all connected and I am never alone, even in solitude. My path is filled with love, truth, joy, serenity, and a passion for a life that is truly mine. True, my path is not smooth and free from pain, but no one's is. Inescapably, there are bumps in the road. But my guide is there to comfort me and give me what I need when the going gets rough. He is my source of strength, hope, wisdom, courage, and love; and as long as I allow him to guide me, all is well. As long as I humbly ask him for help, it is given to me.

The road home is, of course, my life. The path I walk now, my unique path, is a spiritual path, and my guide is the God of my understanding. Through him and with him, I have learned much and have been given many gifts. Some of these gifts I brought with me at birth, and they were either forgotten in the process of self-discovery, or they were discarded or discounted because they did not fit someone else's path. Some of these gifts were given to me by him through fellow travelers. Some of these gifts are the rewards that come from allowing my guide to chart the course of my life. Some of these gifts are principles and practices that I've acquired more recently. These gifts are the tools that, when used, make my journey easier and more pleasant. Some of these gifts are the challenges of life, the bumps in the road, those aspects of being human that can make my journey difficult and painful and lead me off on a detour. I call these challenges the road hazards. The gifts, the rewards, the principles, the practices, the road hazards—these are the things that I have been commissioned by my guide to share with you. You see, my guide is also my co-author and co-creator. In this, as with all other things, I am no longer alone. My loving guide is ever with me.

Chapter II

THE PATH

I believe that each of us has a path, which is uniquely ours, that we were meant to walk. It is a path designed to lead us to our highest good and bring the highest good to those who walk with us. This path is shaped by the unique gifts that each of us possesses—those qualities, attributes, talents, strengths, weaknesses, and vulnerabilities that define who we are. These are the gifts we bring with us to this life, and often the process of living deludes us into distorting or disowning these gifts. So we wander through our lives, not quite knowing what to do with them, searching for a path that eludes us. And elude us it will, until we reclaim our truth. To find our unique path, we must first find ourselves. Once we know who we are, we can create the details of our lives according to the path's direction.

I believe that my true self has five components: spiritual, emotional, physical, mental, and creative. My spiritual self, or soul, is who I am—my true essence, the God within—and is my connection to Universal truth. When I follow my unique path, my spiritual self serves as the foundation upon which all my other selves rest, and it is the inner guide that shapes my thoughts, feelings, and creations. My physical self then reflects and expresses my spiritual self, and all are in balance and harmony. This is the ideal that I strive for now, but it is an ideal that I have only recently begun to understand. For most of my life, the components of my true self were drastically unbalanced. I have lived mostly in my head, denying emotions that created undesirable behaviors, caught up in the physical world, with my creative and spiritual components either ignored or purposely rejected. To know who I am, I must find all the parts, claim them, love them, reunite them, and bring them into harmony. And it was in the process of attempting to find all my missing parts that I found my spirituality and, ultimately, the God of my understanding.

For most of my life I have been a follower, at first through necessity and later by choice. One of the gifts I brought with me into this life is intelligence, and I learned that my needs would only be met if I behaved in a certain way. Love was not freely given, or so I believed; it had to be earned. And I earned love, first from my parents and later from others, by being and doing what I believed they wanted me to be and do. Now, this may not have been truth, but it was my perception and thus became my belief.

So that is what I did. As a child, I did and behaved as my parents wanted and expected me to do and behave. And what they wanted and expected was a perfect child. They wanted and expected me to excel in whatever I did so they could be proud of me. So I did that. I excelled at everything I did. My method was simple. If I could not excel, I did not do it. What I could not do well, I did not do at all.

As a child, I was still me; my true self was still pretty much intact and my unique gifts were still owned and used. But they were used according to my parents' desires and needs. My mother told me once that I was always well behaved, that I never got into mischief or trouble or had to be punished, which means I did not learn how to explore, to satisfy my curiosity, to reach out beyond the safety of their world. I was gifted with intelligence and musical and artistic ability, but again, these gifts were used to fulfill their expectations. I was expected to get good grades, so I did—always the highest in my class. I learned how to memorize and chose courses that weren't challenging to me. But I did not learn how to question or formulate my own beliefs. I accepted whatever was taught me and did not go beyond into what was not taught. I was being perfectly trained to be a follower.

I was expected to excel musically, and I did. I learned how to read music and play the piano, and I took voice lessons and gave solo recitals and played and sang in band and chorus. When I graduated from high school, I won three of the five awards given to graduating seniors—for scholarship, music, and activities. But none of it meant very much, because it was all expected of me. And who I was did not mean very much either, because who I was was unlovable. That was the message I had mistakenly received as an infant, and that was the message my life experiences were conveying. I may have excelled in scholarship, music, and activities, but I had failed miserably in relationships. Female friendships were unreliable; male friendships were nonexistent. I didn't date because no one asked me out. My teenage romances were all fantasy relationships. So it is little wonder that I married the first man who cared about me, whom I'll call the Rescuer. The Rescuer was eleven years older than I; we began dating when I was a senior in high school and married three years later. And in nineteen years, this was my first act of rebellion—the first thing I ever did in my life that was against my parents' wishes.

I wish I could say that I stopped being a follower then, but, of course, I did not. I just switched paths—the Rescuer's life became my life, his path became my path, and it was the first of many such paths that I would follow. The next path took me 1,500 miles across the country to a new life in Idaho. This path led me to a brief encounter with God and my spiritual self through a religion that I could not follow perfectly, and, thus, eventually rejected. And because I believed God and the religion to be one and the same, I turned my back on both and told myself I did not need either of them in my life. I believe it was then that I began to consciously seek my sense of personal worth through others. Obviously who I was was not worth very much. So my idea was that if I found a person who was valued by others and I was with him and became like him, then I would be valued by others. Of course, this idea was wrong. But it took me two more marriages, several lovers, a tremendous amount of pain, and about forty years to figure that out!

So I kept trying on other people's personalities and lives, trying to make them fit me, and none of them ever did. Not entirely, so I bent myself to fit them. I cast aside the parts of my true self that did not fit a particular relationship, filed them away in some dark corner of my soul. Many of my greatest gifts were casually discarded in that way. I was married to my second husband, whom I will refer to as the Skier/Climber, for ten years, and he never heard me play the piano. My third husband, whom I will refer to as the Piano Player, was aware of my musical gifts but never understood the depth of my intelligence and sensitivity because I never shared it with him. Gifts, likes, preferences, these I could discard, bend, mold to fit. But I never did learn how to bend me, those innate qualities and personal characteristics that were uniquely mine. So I could only follow and be someone else for so long. Then it became too painful, too uncomfortable, too restrictive, and I had to leave. I placed the shackles around my true self, and then had to break free.

When I left my second marriage, I felt like I'd just been let out of prison. The freedom was exhilarating! I had just turned forty, and life had finally begun, or so I thought. I was no longer a follower. The course I charted would be mine, not someone else's. I also, at that time, hadn't a clue as to what that course would be because I hadn't a clue who I really was. So I began to search. I reclaimed cast-off gifts, like music and writing, dusted them off, began using them again. A brief encounter with a fellow traveler I refer to as the Marlboro Man ended so painfully that for the first time I began to look at my part in my unsuccessful relationships. I began to read again—psychologically based self-help books that gave me tools and techniques to change behaviors and, hopefully, avoid repeating past mistakes. During that time, I did a lot of psychological work and thought I had cured myself of my emotional maladies. Note I said "thought." Everything was still a mind trip, a do-it-yourself mental project. I would, by hell, find my way without any help from anyone or anything else!

One of the psychological tools I used for self-analysis was a personality profile done by a local counselor. What she told me revealed an apparent contradiction. I exhibited a strong need for independence coupled with a strong need to belong. With time, the latter need prevailed. I got tired of walking alone and married again. The Piano Player was a man blessed with wonderful musical gifts and cursed with the disease of alcoholism. Once more I became a follower, only in a strangely distorted way. True, I followed his path, not only personally, but professionally as well. My musical gifts augmented his, and we performed his music together as a duo. But, I could not follow him. His disease caused him to make too many wrong turns, so I took over the lead. Sometimes the Piano

Player followed willingly, sometimes he ran away. Sometimes I dragged him along, sometimes I carried him. But, for a long time, as long as I could stand it, I kept on doing it alone, without help from anyone or anything else. I loved him, and I knew he loved me, so while my head said leave, my heart said stay. And even though I was bruised, battered, and bleeding, I would not let him go.

The Piano Player died of alcohol-induced liver failure at fifty-nine. Once more, I began to search—to reclaim myself, my gifts, my desires, my needs, my dreams. Only this time things were different. This time my search included a lot of grieving and letting go of dreams that died with the Piano Player, those things that were a unique part of our life together. And this time I was no longer alone. The effect his disease had on me literally brought me to my knees and back to God. My awareness of his disease also brought me an awareness of my own addictive use of certain foods, over which I was as powerless as he was over his use of alcohol. And, by surrendering to my powerlessness over both alcohol and addictive foods, I became spiritually empowered. I reclaimed my spiritual self and found a God who had never abandoned me. I had abandoned him. And in abandoning him, I had abandoned myself.

Today I walk my path with a guide, but the one who guides me is spiritual, not human, and the path we walk together is the path that is uniquely mine. Rediscovering and reclaiming my true self is a continuing process. I am a work in progress, and I do mean *work.* This is not an easy process by any means. Simple, yes; easy, no. It takes courage and strength and a lot of self-love to seek out and examine all parts of me, to own, accept, and love the dark side that we all have. It takes courage, strength, love, and self-forgiveness to acknowledge, reclaim, and begin to use the strengths that have not been owned and developed, the gifts that have not been used and shared. It takes courage, strength, love, and perseverance to sort through piles of beliefs, attitudes, behaviors, thoughts, feelings, dreams, and fears, to examine them and discard those that no longer fit or are misperceptions, to become willing to allow damaging behaviors to be changed into constructive ones. It takes courage and love to face my fears and move through and beyond them.

It takes courage, strength, and love to clear out the debris from the past, to open old emotional wounds so they may be cleansed and properly healed. It takes courage, strength, and love to go back and properly grieve past losses so they can be put to rest. It takes courage, strength, love, and forgiveness to let go of the excess baggage that I carry around with me, the burden of guilt, resentment, and regret that weighs me down and makes walking my path so much harder than it needs to be.

It should be clear by now that this is *not* a do-it-yourself project. I cannot do all this by myself, nor was I ever expected to. In truth, I cannot do most of this work myself; I only do the footwork, and God does the rest. The process of self-discovery is one I can handle as long as I remember to receive the spiritual help and guidance that is there for me. For me, learning how to trust and have faith in my spiritual guide, and learning how to humbly receive his help have been my hardest lessons since I began walking with God. Still, learning these lessons has been the key to my being able to find my path and keep on course. I do not do it perfectly and probably never will, but I do it well enough to know that I am heading in the right direction. I can also usually tell, now, when I have wandered off course by the discomfort and pain I feel. Now that I have found it, walking my unique path just feels right. It is natural, comfortable, joyful, and serene and worth every ounce of effort I have put into it.

My guide provides wisdom, and I provide the willingness to hear his wise counsel and act (or not act) accordingly. Our path may not always be to my liking, but it will always bring me the lessons I need in order to heal and grow spiritually. And that is, after all, the reason I am walking it in the first place!

Chapter III

THE GUIDE

MY spiritual guide, the God of my understanding, has many aliases, and his form is continuously changing. The more I think I know about him, the less I really *do* know. God is a glorious mystery, never to be completely defined or understood. I have come to know God primarily as love, but also as life, as light, as truth, as healing, as my co-creator, as my higher power, as the universal force, and as the spirit within. God is all of these things; they are all the same. God is, at once, both within and outside of myself. God is within you; God is everywhere, present in all of creation. And because God is within myself and you and all creation, we are all connected and interdependent, both to each other and to God. Our souls are spiritually linked. Separation is a self-induced illusion. No one is ever alone unless they choose to see themselves as alone. Everything, absolutely everything, in our world that is real is a part of God. Everything, absolutely everything, sourced and created in love is a part of God. Anything not sourced in God is an illusion.

I'm sure that as an infant and as a very young child I had the same sense of connection to God that all very young children so delightfully exhibit. However, since I have no direct recollection of any event before the age of five, I have no memory of that early sense of connection. I do know that I have always believed in the existence of God, but my perception of him has changed drastically over the course of my life. The God of my childhood and youth was a very wise old man who had created all things. He sat way off somewhere in some obscure place called Heaven, and was sort of an overseer, a king on a throne. He was very impersonal and very unreachable. He was not mean, punishing, or judgmental, so I was not afraid of him. But he was not particularly loving either, and he certainly was not at all interested in me in any personal way.

My childhood concept was my personal interpretation of the tenets of Methodist Christianity. My parents were neither religious nor openly spiritual, but I was sent to Sunday school and went to church with my mother and grandmother. So I learned about the bible, Jesus, and love, but I never really understood any of it and I certainly never felt it. I could vaguely see the God outside of me, but I could not feel the God within. And religion was certainly not a real part of my life then. I, like my parents, was neither religious nor spiritual.

When I was a young woman, my perceived God acquired some new traits. I had fallen in love with a man of Roman Catholic faith, so, of course, I had to become Catholic as well. Now God was both king and judge. He had a list of rules I was to follow and a procedure through which he meted out forgiveness when those rules were violated. Forgiveness and salvation were both very conditional, and my romance with both the Catholic man and Catholicism ended at about the same time. I found I could not follow the rules perfectly, so I chose not to follow them at all. I left the church; and since I had accepted the belief that theirs was the only true path to God, I chose to leave him behind as well. I still believed in him, but I decided I did not need him in my life. I could find my way quite well by myself.

Still, Catholicism had given me a gift that I would not fully appreciate for many years. This was the time when the Catholic Mass was performed entirely in Latin. The services were very quiet, very reverent, and very introspective. And I felt something there I had never felt before. I felt the God within myself. I felt a connection to my soul, to the spiritual component of my true self. At the time, I did not understand what this feeling was. It would be more than thirty years before I felt, understood, and embraced that connection again.

For most of those thirty years, I ignored both the God outside of me and the God within myself. For the first fifteen years or so, my soul was nurtured through nature. I lived a very outdoor life—hiking, backpacking, mountaineering, camping, skiing, and kayaking. Although I didn't know it and probably would have denied it if I did, my spirituality came to me from the outside through osmosis. And every once in awhile a particularly awesome sight would strike a chord so deep that I would feel it from the inside, feel my soul in rapture. I can still recall those experiences. A full moon casting a shimmering reflection of the peaks surrounding a high mountain lake, giving it an ethereal, otherworldly glow. The magnificence of a 20,000-foot Himalayan peak, the presence of which completely filled my view down an immense valley, towering above everything majestically, silently, peacefully, as if it were God. The views from the tops of mountain peaks where, so high above everything else, I felt like I was God. Later, after I had left that life behind, similar experiences came to me through music. The simple beauty of my soon-to-be husband's piano rendition of "Misty." The truth found in the words of his bandleader's songs, and the honesty with which he sang them. All these things, and many more, touched my soul enough to keep my spiritual self alive until I would be led to finding it and reclaiming it.

It was through addiction that I reconnected with God and allowed him to come back into my life. The Piano Player, who played "Misty" so beautifully, destroyed himself with alcohol, and it was through him that I found the twelve steps of Alcoholics Anonymous. The first time I heard the steps read was at an AA meeting, and I recall being very suspicious and decidedly uncomfortable. What was all this God stuff? Still, I had called out in anguish and despair to a God I barely believed in for him to help the Piano Player, for something to happen that would stop his drinking, and it did. I had cried out for help, and God had heard me and responded. But I had asked for help for someone else, not for me. Once that help was received, I turned away from God again. The Piano Player quit drinking. He was cured, and all was perfect in my world. Or so I deluded myself into believing.

Three and a half years later, the Piano Player began to drink again. And when this perfect world crashed and shattered, I crashed and shattered as well. This is one of the hazards of living someone else's life, of following someone else's path. When they go down, they take you with them! One early morning, after I had spent several minutes crying, pleading with, yelling at, and lecturing this man, he looked up at me, bleary-eyed, unshaven, and hung over, and said, "You know, you've got a problem." He was right, but the problem was not him. It was me. I had become a victim of his disease, and this time I cried out for God to help me.

God guided me to a counselor who taught me about the twelve steps, as they applied to me. For those of you not familiar with them, the twelve steps are a spiritual philosophy of life. Although the path was created for people with, or affected by, addictions, the philosophy can work for anyone. Accepting this philosophy brought a God of my understanding back into my life. Oddly, this God was not at all like the God I had turned my back on years earlier. He was, first and foremost, a power greater than myself, someone I could depend on to handle those things I knew I could not. He was personal, not distant and remote, and he cared about me. This God was more like a father than a king or a judge, but still not someone I could trust completely as required by Step Three, which says: “Made a decision to turn my will and my life over to the care of God *as we understood him.*”

I had turned my husband's disease over to God, but I had not turned his life over to him. And it would be many years before I would trust God enough to surrender my personal addictions to him and make the decision to turn my will and my life over to his care. It would be even more years before I would be able to do this consistently and completely.

Of course, eventually I did, or I would not be writing this today. And when I did, when I began to let God guide my life, some amazing things began to happen. The God, who I used to believe lived light-years away, led me to the God that lives within myself, and gradually I began to connect more and more with the God within myself through heart-directed intuition and meditative practice. And as I did this, I became more and more aware of who and what I am and came to trust the guidance that I received from the God within. I learned that there were certain things I innately know, and that following my unique path requires me to trust in my knowing and act on that guidance. Now when my soul speaks to me through my heart, I listen. I no longer have to acquire my spirituality externally through osmosis. It is alive and well, within myself, acknowledged and accepted. And the more intimate my relationship with God becomes, the easier it becomes to be who I am, to become a living expression of the God force within myself.

Now the God of my understanding is a living and constant part of my life. My understanding of God has gradually evolved and expanded as I have gotten to know him better, and I have come to realize how limitless he is and how limited my perception of him has been. To me, God is a spirit who possesses all the very best qualities of a father, mother, best friend, guide, teacher, and mentor. He neither judges nor punishes. Instead, he gently guides me in the direction of my highest good, encourages me to follow his guidance, and is infinitely patient when I lose my way. He is always there for me, always caring, always concerned about my well-being. Nothing about my life is too unimportant to bring to him. No problem is unworthy of his attention, no question too stupid or naive to ask. He is vitally interested in every aspect of my being, as he is vitally interested in every aspect of your being. God does not play favorites; he is totally impartial and impersonal in the distribution of his gifts. We are all equally blessed by his grace. But, there is one catch. God has given us free will so he cannot help us unless we allow him to. God is always there, but we have to acknowledge his presence and be willing to accept his gifts.

Chapter IV

THE FELLOW TRAVELERS

FOR many years, the only contact God had with me was through external sources. Because I had rejected him and would not either talk or listen to him directly, he came to me in disguise, sneaked up on me when I was not looking. He nurtured my soul through external stimuli (music, art, nature) and guided and shaped me as best he could through other people: my fellow travelers, the few select people whose lives I shared and whose paths I followed. And "few" is the right word here. I had many casual acquaintances, but few friends; and there was no one (including myself) who really knew who Nadine was. Sharing myself with someone might draw them close, and I could not do that. If they really saw who I was, they would see my flaws and imperfections and they would leave. If I wanted them to stay, I tried to hold them there by doing for them, not attracting them by sharing who I was with them. And, mostly, I did not let them anywhere near me. Physically and mentally, perhaps, but never emotionally or spiritually.

My physical and emotional isolation began very early on my journey. I am an only child, born to parents who did not let anyone get close to them, not even their child, whom they adored. I know now that both of them loved me very much, but neither of them knew how to show it in a way I could feel or understand. Our nuclear family was quite small, and my parents had few close friends. I was born in Chicago, but later moved from the city to my grandparents' small farm in north-central Illinois. Now I was an only child living on a farm and going to a one-room school with a maximum of four to six other students! So being alone came natural to me; being with others did not. After the one-room school closed, I was abruptly cast into a world with lots of kids, a world I had no skills to cope with. At ten, I was overweight, unusually tall, and fully developed physically. Emotionally, I was as underdeveloped as I was physically overdeveloped. So I became the favorite target of two older kids who bolstered their egos by picking on those who did not know how to fight back.

The next two years were my "lost" years. Who I was crawled inside of myself and hid to escape the pain. Eventually, my need to please my parents forced the artistic and musical parts of me out of hiding, but still I was very isolated. My female friends in high school periodically and without warning would shut me out of their lives for an indeterminate period of time. I was not popular, never dated, and I hid behind a facade of activities and excess weight. No one ever got close. No one, that is, until my first husband-to-be, the Rescuer, introduced me to sex. Physical closeness then became a substitute for emotional closeness, and I alternated between sex and food as substitutes for love and intimacy for many, many years. Both of these served to isolate, to keep me from having to share the real me with anyone. It is ironic but true that physical closeness can be used to create emotional distance.

I traveled my road as an adult with no more than two "close" female friends at one time. There was also a progression of male companions and lovers, both real and fantasized, none of whom ever knew me completely. These are the men whose paths I walked for a time and then separated from. These were the shapers, the ones who God used to gently nudge me back to him and to owning and reclaiming my true self. Each of them gave me at least one gift and led me to where I needed to go.

Following the Rescuer's path took me into a world of science and education and led me to the Catholic man I followed to Idaho. This man's unavailability led me to another man, whose path took me into the world of nature, of hikers, backpackers, skiers, and mountaineers. In this world I found the Skier/Climber, whose gifts were a college education and the tenacity, perseverance, and physical stamina required to follow his path. He gave me a broader view of the world through foreign travel, Himalayan treks, and many, many summits. My college education led me to a wonderful professional mentor, whose gifts were self-esteem, gentleness, unconditional love, and the courage to leave my oppressive marriage and strike out by myself to try and find my own path. That process led me to two more men—the first taught me about impenetrable emotional walls and introduced me to the Westbank Lounge, where first we and later I went to "meet people." The second man, the Marlboro Man, drew me very close to him, and when I fell in love with him, he bolted and ran. This man took me to the heights of passion and ecstasy and the depths of despair. His gift to me was the gift of self-examination, of finally being willing to look for and own *my* part in the collapse of my personal relationships.

At the Westbank Lounge, I heard and was touched by the voice and songs of the Songteller, one of the bandleaders who played there regularly and who would ultimately become a soul friend. I became a follower of this man and his music and was led through him to my relationship with the Piano Player. Now, this was possibly God's smartest move, because the Piano Player's gifts were the ones that would lead me home. He gave me the music that we played together for seventeen years, which was a marvelous gift and was also the bond that kept me around long enough to receive his other gifts. He gave me the opportunity to walk the final steps of his journey with him, to be with him when he died. He gave me my recovery from addiction, because it was through his addiction that I finally became able to see my own addictive behavior and to seek help. And last, but certainly not least, he gave me my relationship with God.

The gifts of recovery are what this book is about, so I won't go into them again here. It's enough to say that now I have many fellow travelers who walk their paths beside me—sometimes a little ahead, sometimes a little behind, sometimes side by side. I am very connected now to all my fellow travelers, even the ones I do not know personally, and my sense of connection is very strong. Strong enough that I can also feel when the connection is blocked by fear, either theirs or mine. Feeling secure in this sense of connection allows me to travel the road home either alone or with someone, because I am never alone even when I am by myself.

Now, of course, the progression of my life events is no longer linear and related to a single fellow traveler. With God as my guide and co-creator, the path is uniquely mine. Each of my fellow travelers makes his or her own unique contribution to what I call the big picture of my life. It doesn't matter whether the interaction is brief or prolonged, casual or intimate. Each fellow traveler has a part to play, a gift or a lesson to give me, and their roles are varied and diverse.

Some are healers, sent to bring me awareness of old emotional wounds that need to be reopened and purged of pain so that they may heal properly. Healers may or may not have anything to do with the original wound, but their presence takes me back into the place I need to go to release buried pain, anger, or fear. Some are mirrors, sent to help me to know and understand myself better. Mirrors show me my strengths and weaknesses, because what I recognize in others is in me as well. I cannot see something in others if it is not, or has not been, a part of my experience or myself. Mirrors accurately reflect my truth back to me, and if the truth is painful—if I see a part of me that I do not like and have disowned—mirrors can be healers as well. Healers and mirrors are often the most challenging fellow travelers in my life.

Some are messengers, sent to give me guidance that I cannot see or do not believe when it comes to me through contact with the God within. Some are guides, sent to teach me how to read the road map that helps me find my way on my path. When I first reconnected with God, most of his guidance came through messengers and guides. Later, when I discovered the God within me and began to trust my inner guidance, more and more of God's messages came through my heart-directed intuition. Still, there are times when I just don't quite trust my inner guidance, and I am unsure which is talking, my mind or my heart. That is when a validator usually appears. The validators, often authors, serve to strengthen and confirm what I *believe* to be my truth but do not yet *know* to be my truth.

Some are carriers, who either directly or indirectly provide me with a physical object that validates spiritual support, a little "burning bush," which is God's way of telling me that my dreams are being worked through or giving me new direction. Carriers usually have no idea that God is working through them, and I may not even know who they are. The carrier's gift mysteriously appears when I become discouraged because a desire or dream is taking a long time to manifest or I am undecided about a course of action. The objects have come to me as gifts, as raffle prizes, as objects lying on the ground that catch my eye. Their significance is usually sensed first by my soul and later understood by my intellect.

And some are very special friends, soul friends, whose connection is at a deep, intimate level. With my soul friends, the bond of love between us has been strengthened and deepened through mutual interaction and sharing. These are the special friends who have had the greatest impact on my own personal growth and recovery, the ones that have supported me and cheered me on and helped me find my true self and unique path. These are special friends, assigned to me by God. God has special work that he wants me to do with and for these special friends. Sometimes it is creative, sometimes healing, sometimes challenging, but it always requires at least two of us to get the job done.

Notice what I said here—soul friends, connected at a deep, intimate level. I am no longer afraid to do that, to share myself with others, to draw them close and allow them to draw me close. I can share myself because I know the truth about myself now, and the truth is that I am a lovable, beautiful child of God. Sharing myself with others cannot cause them to leave if they are meant to be a part of my life. And as long as I know my truth and follow it, as long as I stay close to God and trust him to guide and care for me, I cannot lose myself in anyone ever again

Now I no longer look for another's path to follow, because my unique path is much too exciting and meaningful to give up for someone else. Any male soul friend I choose to walk with now will walk beside me, not ahead, on a parallel path. We will walk together, guided by the God of our understanding. We will walk, arm in arm, on a path sourced in love and guided by truth. Two unique paths that have come together for however long they are supposed to be together, simultaneously connected and separate. My soul mate and I will not be alone either. There will still be others with us, performing their various tasks and roles. My self-imposed isolation has truly ended. I do not ever intend to be separated from God, myself, or humanity ever again.

Chapter V

THE MAP

GOD has never intended for us to be separated from him. He has given us many different ways to find and reconnect to him, maps to guide us on our journey, ways as diverse as the world's cultures. Carefully examine all the world's major religions, all the spiritual philosophies, and the basic, underlying, untampered-with message is the same. There is a spiritual something that we all long to reconnect with, a something that will bring us peace and serenity and provide meaning and direction for our lives. Call that something whatever you like. Call it God, a higher power, the universal force, a spirit, the great mystery, Allah, Brahman, the Tao, the Great I-AM, or Buddha consciousness. Whatever it is called, the underlying principle is the same. The principle is infinite, mysterious, and unconditionally loving, and it exists in all of creation. This is a concept both amazingly simple and terribly complex, and most of us will never completely be able to understand it, let alone live it. That's why the maps are there—to help us find our way back to our God, to love, and to universal truth.

The map I was led to and follow was originally given to people suffering from the chronic, progressive, and incurable disease of alcoholism. It was given by God to Bill W. and Dr. Bob, the co-founders of Alcoholics Anonymous. This map proved to be so effective in helping alcoholics stay sober that it has been borrowed (with permission), slightly modified, and used for treatment of almost every addiction known—food, sex, drugs, gambling, relationships, emotions, and on and on. It is also used by those who have been caught up in the effects of addiction. The map is simply referred to as the twelve steps.

The fundamental spiritual gift found in the twelve steps is the invitation to establish a personal relationship with a higher power whose attributes are defined by each individual rather than by a prescribed religious doctrine. Thus, the gift of healing and recovery from addiction is available to anyone, no matter what their religious preference (or non-preference) happens to be. Those who take this invitation seriously are called down a mystical path that can lead to an ever-changing and ever-expanding view and experience of the higher power, or God, of their understanding. This is the path I am walking with my guide. It has developed into the intimate relationship with God that I share with you now. Thus, the twelve steps may lead to a far broader spiritual perspective than originally intended, a perspective that can lead beyond healing from addictive behavior to a true mystical experience.

I have already shared how I was led to the twelve steps, so I won't repeat that here. When I found them, through codependency counseling, I was in so much emotional pain and chaos that I would have done *anything* to relieve it! I found a process called "working the steps," which has become, over time, a way of life. I now live the steps through the expression and experience of the principles that they represent.

Initially, working the steps is a three-part process requiring awareness, acceptance, and action. First, one must become aware, in one's mind, of the need to perform the required actions or intellectually accept their truth. Second, one must accept in one's heart or internalize the underlying principles of the step. Finally, one must take whatever action is required by the step. If any part of the process is incomplete, spiritual healing cannot take place. The spiritual principles connected to the steps will not manifest and become a living part of the person's life.

On my first pass through the steps, partially guided by a counselor, I went rapidly through them, accepting them in my head but not my heart. I skipped the three steps that require interaction with others, did the rest of them superficially, and thought I was done. Needless to say, I was not. My quick fix didn't take, and even though the map had been given to me, I did not use it properly. So I bottomed out again and started over.

My second attempt at working the steps was under the guidance of a program sponsor. A sponsor is a mentor whose task is to guide the sponsored through the various aspects of recovery, the most important of which is working the steps. So this time I attempted to work them thoroughly and completely, and to accept the principles both in mind and heart. And this time I understood, when I was finished, that I would never be done, that working the steps was an ongoing process that had become an integral part of my spiritual life.

The spiritual guidance I have found through working the steps has enabled me to go back into and heal the spiritual wounds created when I rejected Catholicism many years ago. I have made peace, so to speak, with God, Jesus Christ, and Christianity. The Christian community has been a part of my spiritual experience. I have even found a spiritual home within a somewhat unorthodox segment of that community, a Christ-centered philosophical movement simply called Unity. Still, with Christianity, as with all other prescribed doctrines, I have learned how to take what I like and leave the rest.

Since my primary drugs of choice were food and the Piano Player, the steps I follow are those of Overeaters Anonymous and Al-Anon, programs specifically for compulsive overeaters and those persons affected by the disease of alcoholism. And because the steps were designed to emphasize the community, or shared experience, that is so important to recovery in-program, they are written in first person plural, emphasizing the "we" and "our." However, I personally believe that the spiritual principles contained within the steps can be applied positively by any one of us to any situation, person, place, or thing, working alone or with someone, addicted or not, religious or not. I believe the principles of the steps can augment and enhance any religious belief and deeply enrich the life of any nonbeliever. So it is within this context that I share them with you and give my interpretation of their meaning. I emphasize that this is *my* interpretation, not that of any particular twelve-step group or program.

Because the steps work together in groups, I will present them to you that way. Beyond the first step, all the steps are essentially the same. Working the steps thoroughly requires thinking about them, understanding them, and reflecting on their meaning; and for most people, this requires writing to and about them. Guides to working the steps are available in the self-help or addiction section of any bookstore. The ones I'm familiar with are listed in the bibliography.

~ The Surrender Steps

1. "We admitted we were powerless over alcohol (or drugs or food or sex or people, places, or things, or whatever)—that our lives had become unmanageable."

2. "Came to believe that a power greater than ourselves could return us to sanity."

3. "Made a decision to turn our will and our lives over to the care of God *as we understood him.*"

Steps one, two, and three are the steps of surrender and willingness. They are sometimes summarized as: "I can't; God can; I think I'll let him." They teach the principles of honesty, hope, and faith and are the core principles required for recovery from addiction. Steps one, two, and three correspond to the first line of the Serenity Prayer: "God, grant me the serenity to accept the things I cannot change..."

Paradoxically, it is through humbly admitting and accepting my powerlessness and surrendering my will and my life to God that I have become empowered and freed from my compulsive behaviors. Asking him to help *me* do it does not work. Understanding that he can do for me what I cannot do for myself, and allowing him to do that, does.

~ Step One

"We admitted we were powerless over alcohol (or drugs or food or sex or people, places, or things, or whatever)—that our lives had become unmanageable."

Step one is the surrender step. It is the foundation of all of the other steps, and it teaches the principle of honesty. It asks two things of me. First, it asks me to admit and accept that I am truly powerless over whatever it is that I have been unable to control or fix. Second, it asks me for awareness that trying to control or fix this person or thing has altered and disrupted my life, affecting me and those close to me. Taking this step requires me to honestly look at both my life and myself and surrender to its reality.

Applying step one to a substance (such as alcohol, food, or drugs) or a behavior (such as sex, gambling, work, or spending) requires me to honestly admit that I have absolutely no control over my misuse of the substance or behavior. The key is the recognition that whatever I do or use has caused, or is causing, me problems or pain, and that I continue to do or use in spite of the pain it causes. Even if or when I try to change my behavior, I cannot. This is when my life becomes unmanageable and affects the lives of my fellow travelers, particularly those closest to me. That is why Alcoholics Anonymous was followed by Al-Anon. The first program is for those who suffer from the disease of alcoholism, and the second is for those who suffer from the effects of alcoholism on their ability to relate to others. The programs address different aspects of the problem, and I believe that every twelve-step program that deals directly with addiction should have an "anon" program to go with it.

In my case, I am both a recovering addict and one who has been affected by another person's addiction. My addiction is to certain foods, and I was as powerless over these foods as the Piano Player was powerless over alcohol. Whenever I ate them, I had no control over how much I ate, just as he had no control over how much he drank. In fact, it was through being with him that I recognized that I misused certain foods in exactly the same way he misused alcohol and for the same reason—to avoid feeling certain emotions. But I also suffered from living with *his* addiction, and my life was totally unmanageable in both areas. So, for me, when I surrendered to its reality, I was led to both Al-Anon and Overeater's Anonymous almost simultaneously. I knew in my heart that I needed both programs and that one would not work without the other. One of the things that Al-Anon taught me is how to relate to an addict, and although the Piano Player has been gone now for many years, I still live with a recovering addict—me. The principles I have learned through my program are still very applicable to my relationship with myself and also to relationships with anyone else who exhibits and practices addictive behavior.

So that is how step one works for substances and behaviors—but how does it apply to people, places, and things? To show how this works, I'm going to use "other people" as my object of powerlessness. Step one then reads: "We admitted that we were powerless over other people—that our lives had become unmanageable." For most of my life I falsely believed that I could control other people by my own behavior or by telling them what to do. I was what I now call a world-class controller and fixer. I needed to feel in control, at all times, of my own behavior and that of those I loved and emotionally depended on. Of course, I was not in control at all, in either case. Certainly, my eating was out of control most of my life, and my attempts to control others' behaviors were equally as futile. Both resulted in making my own life either repressive or otherwise unmanageable.

When I honestly look at the circumstances of my life, I see that absolute control is an illusion. There is really very little in my life that I have absolute control over. Natural disasters, accidents, unexpected death, terrorism—all of these things and many, many more could change my life in a heartbeat. I used to walk regularly past a fire station that houses an ambulance, and every time I heard a dispatch call for emergency medical treatment this truth hit me once again. My own experience has shown me without a doubt that trying to control an addiction through will power alone is virtually impossible. Trying to control or fix another person's behavior, addictive or not, is insanity. It is also a trap, because the controller ultimately becomes controlled by the person or behavior he or she is trying to control. Think about it. When I live my life focused on what someone else is doing and how to manipulate and control it, I do not have a life. I become controlled by what I have to do to keep that other person in line.

During the times when the Piano Player was not drinking, I altered my behavior to "support" and "help" him stay that way. I stopped using alcohol myself, we stayed away from our bar, I did not leave him alone for any long periods of time, and we did not do things that might tempt him to drink again. Neither of us was free to live our lives as we chose to, and he did not have to accept the responsibility for his own sobriety. And he always had an escape. When things got too stifling, he could always begin to drink again. And he did.

When I admit to powerlessness over other people, I am saying that I cannot control them, change them, fix them, live their lives for them, or live my life through them. For years I not only thought I *could* do these things but that I was *supposed* to do these things. Every time I tried, my life got crazy—it was not mine anymore. It had become totally unmanageable.

I have had to apply step one to many different aspects of my life, and my willingness to admit powerlessness over something or someone always seems to be inversely proportional to the degree of emotional attachment I have to it or them. In other words, the more I am emotionally attached to something or someone, the harder it is to admit I have no control over it. It was easy to admit powerlessness over alcohol. It was *not* easy to admit powerlessness over the Piano Player! Surrendering to powerlessness over my primary addictions, food and sex, was relatively easy once I became willing to reach out for help, but it took me many years to get to that place. Today, my biggest problem is still with people, with trying to control or fix someone I deeply care about. Doing this always makes me crazy, takes me back into what I call the "pit." Doing step one is literally the first step to getting out of the pit and regaining my sanity and serenity. When all else fails, I go back to step one.

~ Step Two

"Came to believe that a power greater than ourselves could restore us to sanity."

Step two is the willingness step. It teaches the principle of hope, and it also asks two things of me. First, it asks me to believe in the existence of a power greater than myself, some force or being or spirit greater, wiser, and stronger than me. Second, it asks me to believe and trust that this higher power can, in fact, bring sanity back into my life And also that it can do for me what I have not been able to do for myself or for others.

What or who is this something or somebody? Step two does not ask me to define my higher power nor does it define a higher power for me. It asks me to go through whatever mental and spiritual process I require to "come to believe" in such an entity and in this entity's ability to restore order in my life. In fact, I am not even required to define my higher power as God—atheists and agnostics may use any higher power that is acceptable to their belief system. Some have used their group, some have used an entity, or force, of nature. Who or what you designate doesn't matter, as long as the essence of step two is honored. I must be willing to depend on "it" to sustain my hope for a sane and happy life.

For me, step two was a logical and necessary corollary to step one. If I have admitted and accepted my powerlessness over certain aspects of my life, and if I have finally understood that I can't control those things I have been unsuccessfully trying to control myself, then there had better be something or somebody out there that *can*. Without step two, I would not have had the courage or the desire to finish step one. I would have just kept on trying to control the uncontrollable.

For me, the "came to believe" part came easily. For those who have been disappointed or feel betrayed or abandoned by God, or who disbelieve totally in any concept of God, coming to believe in a higher power often requires some sort of a dramatic spiritual experience, something that definitively announces and confirms the presence of such a power to the skeptic. I had no such experience before I came to believe, but I have had many since. Perhaps the most bizarre of these is the message of the eight ball.

I walk often for meditation on a route that skirts the perimeters of our local airport. One day, I was feeling very discouraged because things were not working out the way I had hoped they would with the Songteller. I was beginning to feel that the situation was hopeless and that the dream I believed had come from God had been abandoned by him. I began my walk with a sense of doubt and despair. I was walking through a remote area when I happened to glance down and noticed a strange object on the ground. I curiously picked it up, and it was a small plastic replica of an eight ball, probably from some sort of children's game. I turned it over, and there were words written on the back of it. The words were: "Unseen forces are working in your favor." Now, I have no idea how the eight ball physically came to be in that particular place, but I absolutely know that the message was sent by God.

Working step two also required me to redefine my concept of God. As I said before, I have always believed in the existence of a higher power. But God was impersonal and distant, not someone who would care enough about Nadine to restore her to sanity! The God that I believed in had to become a much more personal God, one who was close enough to me, and I to him, to pay attention to and care about the condition of my life. Furthermore, I had to *allow* him to come close. God did not force his way in; I had to invite him. To receive the gift of hope, I had to allow him to be there for me. Working step two meant I had to begin to trust God, which was a new concept for me. And one that would be essential for working step three.

~ Step Three

"Made a decision to turn our will and our lives over to the care of God, *as we understood him.*"

Step three is the turning-it-over-and-letting-go step. It teaches the principle of faith, but also requires trust, willingness, humility, and courage. It was through taking this step that God became my guide, and my path, ultimately, became my own. But it did not happen either easily or quickly, at least not for me. I have been working step three for many years now, committing to it daily, and I am still not completely finished. Close, but not quite. The concept of progress, not perfection, definitely applies to working step three!

Step three asks me do to do one thing and one thing only, but it is a life-changing request. No one is ever the same after taking step three. Step three asks me to *make a decision* to turn my will and my life over to the care of God, *not* to immediately do it. And that is good, because taking step three is a process within a process. I do not know anyone in-program that has ever turned their will and all aspects of their lives over to their God in one clean, permanent, act of surrender. Most of us do what I have done—turn my will and my life over to God in increments, one small piece at a time. I also have spent a great deal of time and effort turning a particularly cherished piece of my life over, then taking it back, then turning it over again, sometimes recycling it many times before final surrender is achieved.

Also implicit in step three is the need to have the God of my understanding defined. What kind of a God would I be willing to turn my will and my life over to? I certainly could not surrender myself to a wrathful, vengeful, punishing God. He would, for me, have to be a God who loves and understands me. Others may have a very different point of view. What is important here is that each of us is free to define our God in whatever way works.

It may be that part of my difficulty with step three has been that my perception of God was not adequately defined when I first attempted to work the step. My understanding of God has evolved over time and is much different today than it was then. Today, God is more loving, more patient, more tolerant, more gentle, and infinitely more trustworthy. Coming to this understanding has also been a process, much as turning my will and my life over has been a process. My experience is that these two processes have been linked and are very dependent on each other.

Making the decision to turn my will and my life over to the care of God seemed to come reasonably easily for me; actually doing it did not. But, I am a person of exceedingly strong will. That may seem to be a contradiction, since I have also spent most of my life following someone else's path, but it's true. I may have lived someone else's life, but I have always done it *my* way, particularly with the Piano Player. His life may have been *our* life, but *we* did it *my* way. At least that is what I tried to do; obviously it did not work out that way most of the time.

I am also a person who did everything myself for many years because I did not trust anyone enough to depend on them to help me. Nor would I allow anyone to come close enough to be there for me. So, surrendering my will to God and allowing him to both guide me and care for me did not come easily. And trusting him to do it *right* (or what I perceived to be right) turned out to be even harder!

Ultimately, I realized that I had missed a very important part of step three. It seems I never really *made a decision* to turn my will and my life over to God. I just *thought* I did. My head said, “Okay, this sounds great, let's do it,” but I never internalized it. The rest of me said, "No way!" Until I made the decision with both mind and heart, God was not free to work with me in releasing the things I was holding onto. Once I finally *made a decision*, I was no longer doing it all alone, and letting go became much easier.

So the lessons of faith and trust have been hard lessons for me to learn. At first, the only aspects of my life that I gave to God to care for were those where I *knew* both in my mind and heart that I was powerless over, first, the Piano Player's alcoholism and, second, my food compulsion. God immediately acted to show me that the principle worked. I was relieved of my food compulsion and have not binged on food since I walked into my first meeting of Overeaters Anonymous. But still I did not trust him with my will and my life in general. I gave him the little things that were not terribly important to me. I kept hanging onto the biggies and trying to control them myself! And absolutely the last things I let go of were relationships with people in my life that I had an emotional investment in. As with step one, the more important the relationship was to me, the tighter I held on!

Eventually, I learned to trust God enough to at least *try* turning over the most cherished aspects of my life. It was sort of like, "Okay, God, I will give you a chance and we will see what happens. But if you do not handle this the way I *want* you to, I am taking it back!" I would let him guide me for a while, and, invariably, when I did, things worked out better for me. The relationship went smoother, progressed and grew, without my trying to force things to happen. God would give me assignments, some footwork to do, I would do them, and then turn the outcome back over to him. At least that's the way it is supposed to work; often I would forget to let go of the outcome. I heard a wonderful one-liner recently that describes what happened then perfectly. It goes something like, "When you turn it over and don't let go, you end up upside down." And that's exactly where I would find myself—upside down and back in an emotional pit created by non-acceptance and expectations. And the only way I could get out again was to let go of what I was hanging on to.

Over time, I have learned to trust God with more and more of my life. I have learned to turn to him for guidance, to ask him what to do instead of telling him how I wanted things done. I have learned to look for his messages, to see and hear them, to understand them, and to follow them. And as I have learned to trust him, I also have learned to trust myself, my inner guidance, my intuition, and the promptings of my heart. And I follow him in that way. I have learned that getting impatient with his time table and taking things back usually makes things worse, not better, and he always has to straighten out the mess I create while doing that. I have learned that when things don't work out according to my plan, it's either because I'm not ready for them to or God has something much better in mind. I have learned how to suit up, show up, wait for marching orders, follow them, release the outcome, and go back to the bench until needed again. And it is only since I have learned these things that life has become a true adventure. I have learned that God's path for me is the one I was intended to walk, and it is much more exciting and rewarding than the course I charted without him. All of this and more has come to me through working step three.

~ The Humility Steps

4. "Made a searching and fearless moral inventory of ourselves."

5. "Admitted to God, to ourselves, and to another human being the exact nature of our wrongs."

6. "Were entirely ready to have God remove all these defects of character."

7. "Humbly asked him to remove our shortcomings."

Steps four, five, six, and seven are the humility steps. They teach the principles of courage, integrity, willingness, and humility and are the key steps required for self-awareness, self-acceptance, and self-actualization through positive change. These steps correspond to the second line of the Serenity Prayer: "...courage to change the things I can..."

Steps four through seven apply the principles of steps one through three (I can't; God can; I think I'll let him) to what I call our road hazards or handicaps—those thoughts, beliefs, attitudes, behaviors, and fears that hinder spiritual growth, separate us from God, and keep us from achieving our highest good. Step four helps us find our road hazards, step five helps us to accept them, step six readies us for change, and step seven humbly asks God to effect these changes.

Step four also helps us to recognize and accept our unique gifts and personal strengths, a prerequisite to sharing them with others. It is through working steps four through seven that I have begun to know, understand, and accept my true self—all aspects of Nadine, both strengths and weaknesses. It is also through working these steps that I have learned how to become entirely ready to humbly ask God for help when I need it.

~ Step Four

"Made a searching and fearless moral inventory of ourselves."

Step four is the step of self-awareness, the first step in the process of change. It teaches me the principle of courage. Step four asks me to honestly and fearlessly take a look at who I am—my attitudes, beliefs, character traits, behaviors, dreams, and fears. It asks me to look at both my strengths and my weaknesses, so that my strengths may be accepted and built upon and my weaknesses may be released or replaced. To do this honestly is truly a courageous step, and also a terribly important one. Until I know and accept who I am, I cannot recognize and walk my own unique path. Nor can I let go of self-defeating beliefs, attitudes, behaviors, or traits that create roadblocks, that make my journey harder and more painful. Working step four leads to true freedom and a peaceful, joyous journey on the road home.

Some people are terrified of step four. They view the fourth step inventory as a list of wrongs, or transgressions, sort of a written confession. I do not see it that way at all. *What* I have done is not as important as *why* I have done it. Although I may begin with actions that have harmed others or myself, it is the root cause of an action that I'm searching for. And it is a search. For me, self-revelation has come in stages. I have completely worked the steps four times now, and each time I have worked step four, I have peeled off another layer of denial and learned something new about Nadine.

Step four is also a lesson in self-awareness without judgment. An inventory is simply a listing of personal qualities and character traits—no more and no less. Judging these qualities and traits, and subsequently judging myself to be good or bad for having certain traits, is not a part of the process. Recognizing that certain traits are self-defeating or no longer serve us (or God) well *is* part of the process, as is recognizing certain traits as gifts that were meant to be developed, used, and shared. One aspect of humility is knowing who we are, which requires an honest appraisal of our strengths and weaknesses. That is what step four is all about.

How does one go about doing a fourth step inventory? There

are probably as many different approaches as there are different twelve-step programs, perhaps more. The *Big Book of Alcoholics Anonymous* begins with a list of people and events that cause emotional discomfort and then moves through and beyond to the underlying causes and associated behaviors. Al-Anon's *Blueprint for Progress* asks questions about love, maturity, attitudes, responsibilities, self-worth, and specific character traits, questions that reveal the presence of an assortment of character assets and liabilities. *The Twelve Steps and Twelve Traditions of Overeaters Anonymous* focuses on false pride, various kinds of fear, anger and resentment, dishonesty, and negative thinking. A very simple approach is to list identified strengths and weaknesses, those aspects of personality that are self-defeating and no longer serve any useful purpose. And all programs emphasize that *how* you do an inventory is not as important as simply *doing* it. I have seen many people get stuck on their fourth step and then wonder why they're still practicing old, outdated, self-defeating behaviors. An imperfect fourth step, at least, gets you started on the road to change. Without that beginning, change simply cannot happen.

Although step four may be done individually, my most effective attempts at the fourth step have been with a trusted mentor, or sponsor. My sponsor always seems to know the right questions to ask to lead me deeper into myself and the underlying causes of my problems. And that is important to me. Before I can allow God to heal my wounded persona, I first have to be aware that the wound exists. Many of us carry around a lot of baggage left over from childhood, and I am no exception to that rule. Step four has helped me ferret out old beliefs, attitudes, and behaviors that are outmoded and no longer fit me. Perfectionism, judgmentalism, grandiosity, false pride, the need to control, the need to be a caretaker, and a grand assortment of fears—all these, and many more, have come to my awareness through working step four. Owning these traits and letting go of them so God can remove them is freeing me to share my unique gifts and strengths in a more positive way, which brings me serenity and peace.

~ Step Five

"Admitted to God, to ourselves, and to another human being the exact nature of our wrongs."

Step five is the step of self-acceptance, the second move through the process of change. It teaches me the principle of integrity but also requires honesty, courage, and trust. Step five asks me to do three things: to honestly accept the findings of my fourth step inventory and then share these findings with both God and another person. Honestly accepting the findings of my fourth step inventory allows me to move ahead in the process of change. I can take action through steps six and seven to allow God to replace negative attitudes with positive ones, false beliefs with truth, and harmful behaviors with beneficial ones. Sharing my fourth step inventory with God tells him that I am aware of and accept what he already is aware of and accepts about me. Again, these are both my strengths and my weaknesses. Sharing my fourth step inventory with another person adds a dimension of reality to it that does not exist otherwise. I can play games of denial with myself and I can play them with God, but once I have admitted something to another person, it is a lot more difficult to deny the truth to myself.

Sharing a fourth step inventory with God is a personal action that may be formal or informal. Sharing a fourth step inventory with another person requires considerably more preparation. If your fourth step was done individually, the person with whom you share it should be carefully chosen. Obviously, your choice should be a person whom you trust, one that will not break a confidence or otherwise misuse your sharing in any way. For those in-program, a common choice is either their sponsor or someone who has completed their own fifth step. For those not in-program, a pastor, priest, or trusted friend may be chosen. It is usually not wise to share a fifth step with a spouse or close family member, or anyone else who may be personally involved.

My own experience has clearly taught me that *all* three parts of step five *must* be completed for the process to work. If I ignore any part of step five (which I did for a long time), God cannot act until I correct my error. The first time I went through the steps, I didn't have the courage to ask anyone to hear my fourth step inventory. I was not close enough to any single person to trust them with the intimate strengths and weaknesses of Nadine, so I just ignored that part of step five. Later, when I redid the steps with my sponsor, that problem disappeared. Sharing step four with her orally meant I was doing that part of step five as we went along, so I did not specifically have to ask anyone to hear my step four inventory. I was done, so I moved on to steps six and seven. But I had left out the other two parts of step five that are crucial to the process. I had not owned my imperfections (or my gifts) by admitting them either to God or myself! To be sure, he already is aware of all of my character traits. I share them with him, not to tell him something he doesn't know, but to tell *me* something I don't know. And, because I did not own, or accept, those traits I wished to have removed, working steps six and seven didn't do a lot for me. Remember, God has to be invited in—he has to be a part of the process from start to finish. He can hardly be faulted for not removing a character trait that he was never told existed! Until I became honest enough with myself to recognize this omission and humble enough to go back and complete the rest of step five, I couldn't move forward.

That revelation came on my fourth pass through the steps with an Overeaters Anonymous sponsor and a different set of questions to write about. As I said earlier, each iteration has peeled away another layer of denial. And with awareness came the courage required to retreat, regroup, and attend to unfinished business. I had already returned to steps six and seven, aware that I hadn't been either willing or humble, so now all of the missing pieces were in place. And amazing changes began to happen! It really does pay to follow directions!

~ Step Six

"Were entirely ready to have God remove all these defects of character."

Step six is the preparation step and is the third move through the process of change. It teaches me the principle of willingness, which is really implicit in all the steps. After all, if I were not a little bit willing, I wouldn't be working them at all! Step six asks me to be entirely ready for change, to be willing to let go of the old, outdated, and harmful beliefs, attitudes, and behaviors identified and owned in steps four and five. Step six seems very simple, but, in fact, it is not. Behaviors that have been ingrained in me for many years are often very hard to let go of, and that is what being entirely ready means. I must be entirely ready to let God have these behaviors, attitudes, or traits. He cannot remove them if I am unwilling to let them go. And I cannot or will not let go until I can face the consequences of letting go.

A good example to use here is resentment. Holding resentment may distance me from someone I have trouble relating to. Letting go of the resentment may force me to have to work through my part in the relationship problems. Being entirely ready to have this resentment removed may be uncomfortable to me. I may be afraid that I cannot handle the work I need to do on the relationship. Until I am willing to do this work, I will not let go of the resentment and I cannot be entirely ready.

A more pertinent personal example is fear. I have, for most of my life, allowed fear to dictate what I did or did not do. If I was afraid to do something (an example I'll use a lot is public speaking), I carefully avoided any activity that might require me to face my fear. If I let go of the fear and God removes it, I no longer have an excuse to avoid those things I didn't do when the fear was present. I am forced to move out of my personal comfort zone. And that thought may be scary enough to keep me hanging on to fear and make it impossible for God to remove it.

I am not really sure exactly how I did it with my alert sponsor, but I managed to sneak past step six (and also seven) twice without really doing anything. (Do you suppose my incomplete step five had something to do with this?!) Somehow, I incorrectly believed that once my errant behaviors, beliefs, attitudes, and fears were identified, they would magically disappear without any further action on my part. Some of them did, or appeared to, but not all. The more stubborn of my fears and flaws either persisted or returned unexpectedly, and I struggled to understand why.

God finally led me gently back to steps six and seven at an Al-Anon international conference. During one session, there were several workshops on the twelve-steps being held concurrently. I had settled down in the workshop that included step eleven, one of my personal favorites, when I was, quite literally, moved out of my chair. Something told me, “No, this is *not* where you're supposed to be.” I was then guided to the workshop on steps six and seven, and there I got the message that I had more work to do. Once again, my self-will was keeping God from doing his part.

Today, I am pleased to share that I am finally willing to let go of these fears and flaws and many of them are disappearing. Willingness is a key that opens many doors to change, and the humility of step seven completes the process.

~ STEP SEVEN

"Humbly asked God to remove our shortcomings."

Step seven is the step of self-actualization through surrender, the final step in the process of change. It teaches me the principle of humility, which is also implicit in all the other steps, but also requires honesty, faith, and trust. Step seven gives God permission to come in and heal my wounds, clear my road hazards, remove my sources of fear, and transform my negative attitudes and traits to positive ones. Step seven teaches me the blessings and rewards of humility, of being able to humbly allow God to do for me what I cannot do without him.

As with the "admitting to God" part of step five, humbly asking God for help may be either a formal or informal process. When I finally did step seven, I went back to my fourth step, made a list of all those aspects of character that are self-defeating, and humbly asked God to transform them into more loving behaviors. The *Big Book of Alcoholics Anonymous* contains a seventh step prayer that can be used as well.

For me, one whose primary road blocks are the perfectionism, judgmentalism, and arrogance that are sourced in false pride, it may be that I had to work through step seven imperfectly to acquire the degree of humility required to go back and do the preceding steps honestly and completely. To be humble requires me to be teachable, and being teachable requires a mind open to seeing and owning both my strengths and my weaknesses. Until I could humbly admit my flaws to God and accept them as part of my humanness, the process could not work for me because I would not allow it to. Humility is, it turns out, the key to spiritual freedom. It is a very important principle indeed.

Step seven taught me another lesson, once I got the hang of it. When I ask God to remove a particular flaw or handicap, but will not let go of it, I am not being humble. Humility requires me to discern between what is mine to deal with and what is not. And if I am still hanging onto something that I cannot control and is harmful to me, I am still arrogantly trying to do his job. I still have not surrendered.

Needless to say, when I finally understood what was holding me back, "entirely ready" and "humbly asked" became my mantra. Steps six and seven are the keys to freedom from the road hazards identified in step four and owned and accepted in step five. All parts of all four steps are required to effect change. None can be omitted. And the results are astounding for anyone willing to do the work.

~ The Forgiveness Steps

8. "Made a list of all persons we had harmed and became willing to make amends to them all."

9. "Made direct amends to such people wherever possible, except when to do so would injure them or others."

Steps eight and nine are the forgiveness steps, and they deal directly with relationships. Together, they teach the principles of self-discipline and love. These steps also lead to positive change through self-awareness and self-acceptance. Steps eight and nine also correlate with the second line of the Serenity Prayer: "...courage to change the things I can..."

Steps eight and nine are a logical extension of step four and are, again, a process within a process. In steps eight and nine, we take the negative or harmful behaviors revealed through working step four and look at how these behaviors have harmed our relationships. We identify those persons we have harmed, admit our behavior to them, forgive ourselves, and personally commit to changing our behavior. In short, we clean up our side of the slate. Steps eight and nine make us both responsible and accountable for our actions and behaviors, past, present, and future. Steps eight and nine also bring relief from some of the most common road hazards: guilt, regret, remorse, and even resentment. Forgiving ourselves often includes forgiving others as well.

It is through working steps eight and nine that I have finally learned how to forgive myself. The person I have harmed the most by my behaviors is me.

~ **STEP EIGHT**

"Made a list of all persons we had harmed and became willing to make amends to them all."

Step eight correlates with steps four and six in that it is a step of self-awareness and willingness. Like step four, working step eight requires both honesty and courage. Whereas step four asked me to identify and own *what* I did, step eight asks me to go beyond that and look at *whom* I did it *to*! Step eight asks me to make a list of all persons I believe I have harmed by my behaviors or actions and, further, to become willing to make amends to them all.

Now, making amends is not simply saying "I apologize." Making amends requires awareness of the harmful action, acceptance through admission to another, and an honest commitment to doing things differently. I do not apologize for lying to you and then turn around and lie to you again. I tell you I lied to you, commit to not lying again, and then apply steps six and seven to lying—or whatever the fault may be. So a willingness to make amends carries with it a willingness to change, not simply to make an apology.

Like step four, making this list requires tremendous honesty and courage. Also like step four, the rewards are well worth the effort. Step eight is the first part of a two-part process designed to make my journey through life happier, lighter, and more serene. It is a process designed to relieve me of the guilt I carry, both earned and unearned. It is a process that leads to forgiveness, both of myself and of others. Becoming willing to make amends to someone for my part in a painful situation usually requires me to release my resentments and forgive them for their part as well. It is very difficult to become willing to make a genuine amend toward someone I am still angry with or resentful of. Unresolved emotions simply get in the way. Self-forgiveness is also difficult when those emotions are present. So often the first step in the process is a prayer for the willingness to become willing, followed by prayers for those we are angry with or resentful of. Even when such prayers are muttered through clenched teeth, change is possible. The miracle of God's love can unclench the tightest jaw and bring the freedom of forgiveness for the seemingly unforgivable.

Working step eight is a process of trial and error and is best done with a trusted mentor, one who can help recognize what was and was not truly hurtful to others. When I made my list for step eight, I limited it to those persons who were close enough to me to be harmed by my errant behaviors. Since I have a small family, no siblings or children, and have few close friends, my list was pretty small. For those with longer lists, I suggest that they concentrate on currently active relationships first and then go back and clean up the dormant ones.

I also placed God and myself at the top of my amends list. After all, I abused myself for years through my addictions and lack of general self-care. All the behaviors that harmed others harmed myself as well. My perfectionism, judgmentalism, and critical nature were more often directed at myself than others and reflected my unowned self-hatred. I may have been passive in my interactions with others, but I was very aggressive in judging and condemning Nadine. God is on my amends list because I willfully and deliberately turned my back on him for so many years. Even though, as my sponsor carefully pointed out to me, I cannot cause God any harm, certainly the intent was there. And, in both cases, my willingness to make amends had to include a willingness to change my behaviors as well.

The behaviors I felt were most harmful to others were personal dishonesty—not sharing my real or unique self with them—and non-acceptance—expecting them to be, or trying to make them be, something other than what they were. I also owed several amends to people I had suddenly and totally cut out of my life when I began following a different path. Most of my biggest individual faults merged together under these behaviors, so becoming willing to make these amends meant being willing to make a lot of changes in my life.

~ Step Nine

"Made direct amends to such people wherever possible, except when to do so would injure them or others."

Step nine is the action step that completes the process. With step eight, it teaches the principles of self-discipline and love. It takes self-discipline to change established behavior patterns, to stop and think of consequences before I speak or act. It takes self-discipline to admit my errors to the persons I have erred against, to own my mistakes, and commit to change. It takes a tremendous amount of love, both of others and of ourselves, to accept and forgive, to let go finally of guilt, shame, resentment, hatred, and fear.

Step nine asks me to make my amends directly but responsibly. When direct amends could do more harm than good, they are best made only by changing behaviors. I will use my own sexual behavior as an example. I went through a time between marriages when I was sexually promiscuous, and many of my partners were married men. In most cases, I did not feel that my behavior had harmed the men, because they were willing participants; but my behavior *could* have harmed their wives. To go to these women and admit to sleeping with their husbands many years earlier would obviously have caused a great deal more harm than good, so my amends came through forgiving myself and changing my behavior. Again, in this example, as with most others, the person I had harmed the most was me.

Working step nine takes a tremendous amount of courage. Steps four, five, eight, and nine could be subtitled the "Facing Your Fear Steps." I also skipped step nine the first time I worked the steps. My false pride would not allow me to make direct amends to anyone, not even to me or to God. I tried, but I could not follow through with changes in behavior.

Working step nine also requires a sense of discretion and the help of a trusted mentor. When I did my second step nine with a sponsor, she had me separate those I was willing to make amends to into three lists. First came those amends I could make directly and immediately. Then came those I could make directly but not immediately because to do so would be harmful, either to them or to me. Last came those that could not be made directly, mostly people who had died or whose whereabouts were unknown to me. Most of my amends were made then, either face to face or through letters, to those not available for direct amends. And, with time, those on the deferred list have also been made.

Also with time, I have become able to forgive myself for my self-destructive actions and behaviors. Again, this has been the hardest for me—applying the process to myself and consistently making the positive changes. My first experience with making amends to myself came through a weekend of experiential emotional processing called Life Training. Part of the processing required me to make amends to myself while looking in a mirror. It was, for me, one of the most powerful emotional healing experiences of my life and also one of the most loving actions I have ever taken for myself. I shed torrents of healing tears, and it was the beginning of true self-forgiveness and positive change. Since then, I have learned that working my program and practicing all of these principles is the best way I know of to make a living amend to myself.

Working step nine does not require me to ask for forgiveness from anyone else, although I may, in some cases, choose to do so. For example, asking myself for forgiveness is a very healing act. So is asking for forgiveness from one I love dearly and am in an intimate relationship with, but only if I can do so without expectation of a specific response. What the other person does with my amend is between them and their higher power, and it's not my concern. Making an amend is not about them; it's about me. It's a way to clear out *my* emotional baggage, and it works.

~ The Growth Steps

10. "Continued to take personal inventory, and when we were wrong promptly admitted it."

11. "Sought through prayer and meditation to improve our conscious contact with God *as we understood him*, praying only for knowledge of his will for us and the power to carry that out."

12. "Having had a spiritual awakening as the result of these steps, we tried to carry this message to others and to practice these principles in all our affairs."

Steps ten, eleven, and twelve are the growth steps, the steps that make the spiritual principles taught in steps one through nine a process and part of daily living. Steps ten, eleven, and twelve teach the principles of perseverance, spiritual awareness, and service. These steps correlate with the last line of the Serenity Prayer: "..and the wisdom to know the difference."

Step ten continues the work done in steps four through nine.

Step eleven gives us tools to keep growing spiritually and deepen our understanding of and connection to God, as defined in steps three and seven. Step twelve tells us that the process is a way of life and that the way we get to keep our spiritual awakening is to share our experience, strength, and hope with someone else.

These three steps have become a natural and accepted part of my life today, the *new* and *true* road home. They continue to bring me understanding of, and closer to, my true self, God, and my fellow travelers. As steps one through nine helped me find my true self and unique path, steps ten through twelve serve to keep me on course.

~ Step Ten

"Continued to take personal inventory, and when we were wrong promptly admitted it."

Step ten takes the principles and actions of steps four through nine and integrates them into my daily life. It adds the principle of perseverance to those already learned in steps four through nine: courage, integrity, willingness, humility, self-discipline, and love.

Step ten asks me to take a daily inventory of my beliefs, attitudes, behaviors, actions, and fears, to become aware of my strengths and weaknesses and how my actions and behaviors reflect them. In steps four through seven, I identified those beliefs, attitudes, and traits that either needed to be enhanced or diminished, and went through a process designed to allow change. In step ten, I am asked to keep a running tally on my progress, to check in with myself and see how I am doing as often as needed.

Step ten also asks me to be constantly aware of how my behaviors are affecting my relationships and to avoid the buildup of resentment and anger by owning my part in disagreements or unpleasant encounters. Steps eight and nine made me responsible and accountable for past actions and behaviors, and step ten keeps me responsible and accountable in the present.

There are many suggested ways of doing step ten, everything from doing a quick mental review to a detailed written inventory. Again, how you do step ten is a matter of personal preference. What is important is to establish some sort of routine as a daily spiritual practice. As such, step ten serves both as an indicator of potential problems and a measure of personal progress. It is often easy for me to concentrate on my failings and forget my improvements. Keeping a current inventory helps me become more aware of both.

Working step ten is a process, one that I have slowly incorporated into my life and fine-tuned as I have grown spiritually. For me, the second part came easier than the first. I can usually tell when I need to make an amends for my own behavior, and experience has taught me how to separate my "stuff" from someone else's and claim responsibility for it. For example, let's say I am talking to a friend on the telephone about some problem she's having. I start trying to fix her by giving unwanted advice, and she gets angry and hangs up on me. Now, I may initially be hurt and angry as well; my feelings and my caretaking behavior are my "stuff." Her reaction, her anger, and her angry behavior are her "stuff." After I have felt and released my anger, step ten teaches me to make amends for my caretaking/controlling behavior. What she chooses to do with her anger and angry behavior is her problem, not mine.

For some time I actively worked the amends part of step ten and ignored the first part. Then I began to notice a behavior pattern I wanted to change. I found myself falling back into old, outdated behaviors, behaviors that no longer fit a belief system centered on love. This happened whenever I encountered life situations that were like those when the behavior patterns had been established and used. When this happened, I invariably went into the old behavior, eventually realized what I was doing, and made a conscious effort to do whatever I had to in order to get spiritually centered and reconnected to God.

Then one day I found myself right in the middle of some old, self-defeating behaviors, and I had gone there *without knowing it*! I did not realize what had happened until long after my emotional "trigger" had gone. I found myself in the pit before I knew I was in it! That is when I realized that the first part of step ten could be used for preventive maintenance and help me recognize the presence of old behaviors *before* they led me into the pit of emotional chaos. As is often the case, it took emotional pain to show me the wisdom of working both parts of step ten.

At first, I tried doing a mental review of my day just before going to sleep, but that did not work well for me. Now, each morning I do a brief written review of the day before, looking not only for problems but also for positive changes in behavior. How were my interactions with others—was I open and loving or closed and fearful? How did I do with kindness and gentleness? Was I humble or arrogant, honest or deceptive? How did I feel—joyous, anxious, happy, sad? Was I judgmental or impatient with others or with myself? How did I do with self-care? Doing this written review helps me to see both my problems *and* my progress and to deal with the problems before they get out of hand. Where there are problems, I humbly release them to God; where there is progress, I gratefully acknowledge the help I have received. Working step ten thus serves to improve my conscious contact with God (step eleven) and strengthen my humility. It also is the best way I know to avoid unknowingly falling into the pit. I may still go there, but at least I am aware of it when I do!

~ STEP ELEVEN

"Sought through prayer and meditation to improve our conscious contact with God *as we understood him*, praying only for knowledge of his will for us and the power to carry that out."

Step eleven takes the decision made in step three and puts it into everyday practice. It teaches me the principle of spiritual awareness, but it also requires humility, self-discipline, and love. Step eleven asks me to use prayer and meditation to strengthen my spiritual connection to God and to deepen my relationship with him. Further, it is the only step that very specifically tells me what to do. I am to pray only for God's will for me and the power to do his will. I don't *tell* God what to do, and I don't beg, plead, or bargain. I humbly ask. I can, and do, tell him what I like, want, or need, but I always place the outcome firmly in his hands.

Step eleven is my favorite step, and one I have been working since I first worked the steps imperfectly and alone. Step eleven is also the step that can take you beyond the steps to a mystical relationship with God. How I work it has evolved over time as my understanding of God has changed and my connection to him has strengthened and deepened. Both prayer and meditation have become a totally ingrained part of my experience, my everyday life, like eating, sleeping, and brushing my teeth. Prayer and meditation are a part of me. I just do it, period.

Prayer and meditation are both forms of communication with God, and the more frequently and openly we communicate, the more intimate we become. Prayer is defined as talking to God, meditation as quieting the mind so that the guidance can be heard and the presence experienced. Although I both talk to and listen to God whenever, however, and wherever I need to during my day, I have set aside a special time for him when I first wake up in the morning.

When I first began this spiritual practice, my morning prayers were quite lengthy and primarily prayers of gratitude. I thanked God for his many gifts, among which are mental, physical, and emotional health, my unique talents, my purpose and mission, love, guidance, and loyalty, and the removal of my food compulsion. I also asked for his help in doing whatever is needed to maintain or share his gifts. My prayers were followed by my spiritual commitments, and it was through my commitments that I took step three every day. These commitments were the "how to's" of my life. They defined *how* I aspired and chose to act and relate—to God, life, myself, and others. I also included specific commitments to God's plan as it has been presented to me through my dreams and desires.

Then, as God and I have become more intimately connected and my outer life has become a continuous expression of prayer, my formal prayers have become much shorter. I still take step three each day, but now I do it by playing and singing God a song whose lyrics say it all very simply and eloquently. The song, written by Claudell Hefner County, is called "My Dedication," and here are the words:

> Here I am, Lord, use me, guide me, fill me, take me, lead me by your will.
> Here I am, Lord, ready to follow, to serve you, to love you, to be you in this world.
> Thy will is done through me this day.
> Thy will is done through me this day.
>
> Lord, you call, I answer, I'm open, I listen, I hear you, I feel you move in me.
> Lord I come closer, humbled, surrendered, lifted, committed to your plan.

Thy will is done through me this day.
Thy will is done through me this day.
Here I am, Lord I come, here I am.

Meditation is also a daily ritual, but, for me, it takes two very different forms. Meditation is usually thought of as a period of sitting quietly and quieting the mind by focusing on something—breath, an object, whatever works. I do this type of meditation for an hour each morning, and I also take mini-breaks where I quiet my mind while waiting for someone, say in a doctor's examination room. Resting with God in the silence is very effective and soothing, but I have only recently disciplined myself to do it both often and long. What I previously did (and still do) both often and long is write. I meditate on paper. I connect with God within through writing, in longhand and with a fountain pen, three pages daily, usually (but not always) in the morning. Morning pages include my step ten review and are used to tap into and work through feelings. Morning pages also include conversations with God and have given me much guidance, insight, and truth. I also meditate when I walk outdoors, usually for about an hour a day. What is important in meditation is to be quiet and listen, to be open to experience God's wisdom and presence. I have a poster on the wall next to my writing table that expresses this very well: "Listening to your heart, finding out who you are, is not simple. It takes time for the chatter to quiet down. In the silence of "not doing," we begin to know what we feel. If we listen and hear what is being offered, then anything in life can be our guide. Listen."

~ Step Twelve

"Having had a spiritual awakening as the result of these steps, we tried to carry this message to others and to practice these principles in all our affairs."

Step twelve is the ending that signals the beginning of a new way of life. It teaches the principle of service, but embodies all of the principles taught by the previous eleven steps. Step twelve includes a promise of spiritual awakening, and asks two things of me. First, it asks me to *share* what I have learned with others. Second, it asks me to *show* what I have learned by *using* it in all aspects of my life. Doing this requires knowing and believing in all of the principles both in my head and my heart. With total acceptance, I become an expression of the spiritual principles of the twelve steps.

Step twelve teaches me that I get back what I give away, understanding that giving is really sharing with others, not evangelizing, preaching, or fixing. We say that ours is a program of attraction, not promotion. In twelve-step groups, step twelve embodies the concept of service through participation in the process—sponsorship, sharing experience, strength, and hope at meetings and one on one; reaching out to others with unconditional love and compassion; doing group tasks, like making coffee and setting out chairs; and taking service positions or positions of leadership within the group. But for anyone embracing twelve-step philosophies as a way of life, step twelve simply says, "Live them." I *carry* the message by *being* the message.

For me, the promise of step twelve has been fulfilled. I am awake spiritually. That part of me that lay unclaimed and ignored for so many years is alive and well today. And as I have grown spiritually, as my connection with God has strengthened and deepened, his presence is guiding me into more challenging spiritual assignments, assignments that take me out of my comfort zone and enhance my capacity for expressing love through forgiveness, compassion, and generosity. These are assignments that require me to continually practice all of the twelve-step principles—honesty, hope, faith, courage, integrity, willingness, humility, self-discipline, love, perseverance, spiritual awareness, and service—plus many more than I will share with you.

The one who gave me the gift of recovery has been gone now for many years, but I will continue receiving his gift for the rest of my life. Step twelve and the principles it represents are a part of me now and will continue to be forever and ever, amen. To be sure, I do not practice them perfectly and never will; my programs ask for spiritual progress, not spiritual perfection. But slowly, integration is occurring and my beliefs and my behaviors are more and more in harmony and balance. Forward progress is guaranteed when life is lived one day and one step at a time.

Chapter VI

THE GIFTS

SINCE I have been traveling the road home with a guide, I have become aware of, and have accepted, the many gifts that God has given me to use on my journey through life. Some of these gifts are uniquely mine; others are universal. These universal gifts were given to me at birth, as they are given to each of us. They were always mine, always available for me to use and share. As a baby, a perfect expression of God, I accepted and used these gifts spontaneously and naturally. Then somehow I lost my spontaneity and naturalness. And as soon as I began to live as others wanted me to, I forgot how to live for me. As I lost parts of myself, I lost many of the gifts as well. Still, part of me remembered how marvelous they were, so I tried to get them back, to reclaim them through others. I tried desperately to take these gifts from someone else, when all the time I had them within myself.

What are these marvelous gifts that I carried with me, unowned and unused, for most of my journey? The gifts are love, faith, intuition, power, community, truth, free will, divine order, strength, judgment, release, sexuality, passion, and creativity. These are the God-given gifts that I lost and have now reclaimed. They are the foundation of my *new* road home, the life I live today. They have helped me find my true self and follow my unique path, and this is how they work together to create the foundation of my life.

God is my guide, and God is love, so my new life is sourced by love, inspired by faith, guided by intuition, motivated by power, and enhanced by community. Truth is who I am, my true self, and knowing and following my truth creates my unique path. Aligning my will with God's will and aligning my life with divine order enable me to follow my unique path, and strength, judgment, and release keep me moving on course. Sexuality, the life force within, inspires me to live my life passionately and creatively.

We not have to *do* anything to earn these gifts. They are freely offered to us simply for *being*. We do, however, have to accept them. And, once accepted, they are enhanced and strengthened by our using and sharing them with others. Giving and receiving are the same; so, in order to keep my gifts, I have to give them away. I enhance love by being loving, truth by being truthful, free will by being willing, power by being powerful. And so it goes, for all the gifts. Certainly sharing our God-given gifts is not a requirement, or they would not be gifts. But I have found that the more I have come to own and appreciate his gifts, the more I desire to honor him by sharing them with others. I personally believe that all of God's gifts to us, both universal and personal, can only be fully experienced through being shared.

~ Love

Love is a gift from God that is God, a gift that each of us carries in our hearts. But what do I mean by love? Love is a word that has many different interpretations. What I understand love to be may be very different than what you understand it to be. The love I speak of here is unconditional. It does not have to be earned. It is the love so eloquently described in this often-quoted biblical text: "Love is patient; love is kind; love is not envious or arrogant or rude. It does not insist on its own way; it is not irritable or resentful; it does not rejoice in wrongdoing, but rejoices in the truth. It bears all things, believes all things, hopes all things, endures all things. Love never ends."

The return address labels I use on my mail contain an excerpt from these lines, and those labels speak my truth. They tell the world that I believe in love.

I have always believed in love, but I have not always understood what love is. My understanding of love has evolved over time much as my understanding of God has evolved over time.

And it is only recently that the two concepts have merged into one universal truth.

I have a soul friend who does numerology charts combined with tarot readings. She began my first reading by showing me my soul card and saying: "This is your soul card. Your soul is the most intimate part of you, and your soul came in thinking that it had to work for love. Nobody would love you just because you were Nadine."

I immediately burst into tears because what she had said was absolutely true. As far back as I could remember, I had believed that love had to be earned. Love was always conditional, depending on what I did, not who I was, because I believed that who I was was unlovable.

I grew up not being able to *feel* love, nor did I have a good model of love to learn from. My parents said they loved me and showed it in the only way they knew how—by doing, not being. I was cared for physically; I never was abused or had to go without food, clothes, books, or toys. Those were provided for me, as were music lessons and a band instrument and transportation to all my school activities. But I was not cared for emotionally. Neither of my parents knew how to express love in an emotionally healthy way. I don't recall them ever hugging or using any other form of healthy, loving touch. So first food, and later sex, became my substitutes for the nurturing I did not receive as a child.

Growing up, I felt that love was not a gift but a trade. If I worked hard enough to please you, you would love me and you would know that I loved you. Love was a game of action and reaction. In my teenage years, my ideas about love changed to the romantic love portrayed in the movies and songs of the 1950s and to the steamy, sexual love I found in the novels I read when nobody was looking! Love was a fantasy, a fairy tale, an "and they lived happily ever after" kind of magical state that existed between a man and a woman who "loved" each other. How this was created in reality I hadn't a clue and did not want to find out. I hid from love behind a wall of fat and masked my loneliness with activities. Still, romantic love plus sex equals marriage, or at least it did in 1954, so my dream was to be married. And so I was—three times, for a total of almost thirty years. The love present in these relationships varied depending on my partner's and my own ability to love, but never did it quite live up to my dream of love. My fantasy loves were never attainable in reality, and my real loves never measured up to my fantasies.

I recreated my childhood model of love in all three relationships. I both earned and showed my love by doing, not being, just as I had been taught to do. I took very good care of my husbands physically, but I shared only as much of myself as I had to. Two of the three let me in, shared themselves with me; but the sharing was never completely returned. My brand of love was a trap for both of us. It was possessive, dishonest, unreal, controlling, caretaking, jealous, and limiting. Their brand of love was, respectively, fragmented, unowned, or diminished by addiction. None of these men was completely emotionally available to me; and I was not emotionally available to them. Working for love never got me what I really needed—love that was genuine, lasting, and real.

None of my spouses, and certainly not I, had any idea of what love is really about or how to build and maintain a lasting and intimate relationship sourced in it. One of them, the Skier/Climber, was honest enough to say that. He told me the night we were married that he did not know what love meant. After that, we never spoke of love, in ten years of marriage. Yet I was not honest enough with myself to admit that I did not know either. I knew infatuation, fantasy, sex, emotional dependence, and desperate need, but I did not know love. I did not know what it was or how to give, receive, or accept it.

As I look back at my life, I am not exactly sure how or when I began to feel and understand love as I know it today. I don't recall any specific event or incident, no "ahas" or burning bushes. All I know is that, somehow, through the process of recovery and renewed contact with God, I rediscovered a tremendous gift. I came to view love in a different way. And as I came out of isolation and felt the sense of connection, first to God and later to those who became my special friends, I began to *feel* love as well. A *flow* of love, of loving energy, from me to God and back, and then from me to my friends and back, sort of a continuous exchange of loving feelings. Now, I am learning how to give love honestly, openly, and unconditionally, and I am learning how to receive and accept love graciously and humbly. I have learned that the cornerstones for the expression of love are forgiveness, compassion, generosity, and humility. I have reclaimed the gift of love that had always been mine as a lovable child of God. And I have also learned to recognize love in its more subtle forms and understand that everyone cannot express love in ways that are easily understood. My parents and my partners did the best they could, just as I did the best I could all those years when I thought I knew how to love and did not.

Here is what I believe love to be now and what I mean when I say I believe in love. First and foremost, I must repeat what I said in the beginning.

LOVE IS UNCONDITIONAL. Love does *not* have to be earned. It is a gift. Love is given freely and without expectation of a payback or return. Love is accepted gratefully and humbly without a sense of obligation. It is not dependent on what you do or whether love is returned. I can love you without liking you or without you liking me. I can love you and not agree with or condone your behavior. I can love you and choose not to have a relationship with you. I can love you and know the beauty that lies within and detest the way you live your life.

The Piano Player never understood this concept. He insisted that if I did not approve of what he did, I did not love him. Our truth was that each of us loved the other as much as we could love anyone at the time.

LOVE IS UNIVERSAL. Love is the ultimate spiritual reality and is present in all of creation. All things and all creatures, both animate and inanimate, have been created in love and are thus deserving of love. Love is the essence of our true self; it is who we are. Each of us is born being able to give and receive love, freely and unconditionally, both to ourselves and to others. Each of us still carries this gift with us in our hearts. Each of us is spiritually connected through love. Fear may mask it; emotional wounds may keep us from risking it; protective walls may make it impossible to feel; but the gift of love is still there, ingrained in our hearts. Like buried gold, if we dig down deep enough, we will find it, a priceless treasure to be dusted off and reclaimed.

LOVE IS UNRESTRICTIVE. Love is neither dominant nor submissive and does not try to control by either tactic. Love treats you as you deserve to be treated—with courtesy, dignity, and respect. Love allows and encourages you to be your true self and walk your unique path. Love allows you to go through whatever struggles are required for you to do that, even when I can see what appears to be a smoother, easier way. Love allows you to find your own way, make your own mistakes, and live your own life. Love allows you to take care of yourself when you are able to do that.

LOVE IS OPEN, HONEST, AND ACCEPTING. Love attracts love by sharing my truth, who I am, openly and honestly, with you. Love allows, accepts, and encourages you to share your truth, who you are, openly and honestly, with me. Love accepts all parts of both of us, strengths and weaknesses, positives and negatives. Love knows and accepts that the dark side exists, but believes in the light.

LOVE IS SUPPORTIVE. Love encourages you to grow mentally, physically, emotionally, spiritually, and creatively. Love encourages you to be and do the best you can be and do, to walk the path that leads to your highest good. But love is also realistic. It does not demand perfection. Love allows you to make mistakes and hopes that you will learn from them. Love knows the difference between supporting you and carrying you.

LOVE IS LOYAL AND COMMITTED. Love remains a constant; it does not flit from flower to flower like a butterfly. Once love is felt, accepted, and acknowledged, it remains. Love does not fade or disappear; it remains even in the face of loss or separation. Relationships may end, but love does not.

LOVE IS PATIENT. Love allows life to flow and events to unfold as they are meant to unfold, as a flower unfolds. Love never tries to hurry things along. Love understands and respects the perfection of God's timing and divine order. Love lives in the present and is not concerned with either the past or the future.

LOVE IS GENEROUS. Love does not ask what you can give to me, but rather asks what I can give to you. Love is fully present and attentive, not mentally, emotionally, physically, or spiritually unavailable. Love gives from the heart and acts in response to the heart's guidance. Love gives without expectation, at the same time knowing that when love is given, love will return. Love gives generously, because the source of love is unlimited. Love is not a finite resource. There is plenty of love to go around for everyone.

LOVE IS FORGIVING. Love sees the innocence within and forgives without judgment. Love does not hold on to anger, resentment, or regret. Love does not turn anger around and create depression, apathy, and indifference. Love understands that the ever-present source of divine love within each of us is filtered through our human imperfections. Love does not expect perfection in love from human sources; only divine love is perfect. Love understands that each of us gives and shows love the very best way we know how to at the time. Love accepts love from another in the various and diverse forms that it may take.

LOVE IS COMPASSIONATE. Love is able to recognize, understand, and empathize with your emotional pain, but love does not try to carry it for you. Love allows you to feel and express your emotions and to experience the natural consequences of your actions. Love knows when to treat or medicate pain and when to allow it to be felt and released. Love does not intentionally cause pain and suffering to any of God's creations. Love knows and accepts pain as a part of the human condition, but also knows that prolonged suffering is a choice.

LOVE IS HUMBLE. Love is an equal; it is neither greater than nor less than. Love observes and discerns but does not judge; love neither compares nor competes. Love does not arrogantly try to impose certain beliefs, preferences, views, moral standards, or life styles on others. Love is open to and respects your beliefs, opinions, and perceptions even when they differ from mine. Love sees and listens from the heart. Love sets aside all that it thinks it knows in order to be open to truth. Love accepts your humanness as well as its own humanness.

LOVE IS GENTLE AND KIND. Love instructs, but does not criticize. Love guides, but does not tell you what to do. Love suggests, but does not insist. Love nurtures through both words and actions but does not smother. Love cares for you when you are unable to care for yourself. Love is attentive, but not overbearing or possessive. Love is not abusive, but love sets boundaries in the face of abuse. Love knows when to hold you and when to leave you alone. Love knows when to come close and when to move away.

LOVE HAS A SENSE OF HUMOR. Love laughs with you,

not at you, and encourages you not to take your human imperfections *too* seriously. Love knows that laughter heals and laughs often, joyously, and heartily. Love is light and airy, not dark and melodramatic. Love smiles a lot and encourages you to smile back.

LOVE IS HEALING. All wounds, whether physical, mental, emotional, or spiritual, can be healed by massive doses of love. All pain can be lessened through a generous application of love. Love casts out fear; love and fear cannot exist simultaneously in time or space. To truly love is to be unafraid. To love flying is to be unafraid to soar. To love yourself is to be unafraid of pain. To love life is to be unafraid of death.

LOVE IS DIVINE. All that I have said about love can be said about God as well. God and love are at once both separate and the same. God is the source of all love; that source is infinite and boundless and can be tapped into at any time by any one of us. When I turn my life over to God, I turn it over to love. And when I say I believe in love, I am also saying that I believe in God.

~ Faith

Faith is the gift that is the foundation for all spiritual growth. Faith sees the unseen, hears the unspoken, feels that which cannot be felt. Faith allows me to see and hear and feel my guide, to know that he is there for me. Faith allows me to define my relationship with him in ways that work for me, that make it easier for me to find my true self and walk my unique path. Faith gives me hope when I temporarily lose my way. Faith is the beacon that illuminates my path and leads me back to God.

Faith is also a principle that I use in my physical world, which makes faith difficult for me to define. As with love, there are many meanings and uses of the word faith, and no one definition seems to fit my personal experience completely. Faith can apply to physical phenomena that are not sensually verifiable. I have faith that when I flip a switch, unseen electrons will create light. I have faith that when I turn on my radio or stereo, unseen waves will create sound. I have faith that air molecules support birds, kites, and airplanes. Faith can also apply to the myriad of body functions that keep us alive without conscious effort. I have faith that one breath will be followed by another, that my heart will continue to beat, that all the bodily functions required for life will continue to function smoothly. I have faith that when I go to sleep at night I will wake up the next morning, alive and well.

Faith, from this view, is clearly a gift from God, one we have had since birth and one we use continually and often unconsciously. But, since I am speaking of spiritual matters here, I will use a spiritual definition. Faith is defined as a knowing of and belief in the existence of a higher power, a supreme being, a God of my understanding, whose existence cannot be proven in the physical world. In other words, as with some of the examples given above, I cannot use my five physical senses to prove the existence of God. I also cannot prove his existence through logic and reasoning. Philosophers have been pondering this question for centuries. For those who know that God exists, there is proof all around us. For those who do *not* know, there is no proof. But neither is there proof that he does *not* exist.

By this definition, I have had faith ever since I was old enough to experience and, ultimately, believe in God. As I shared earlier, I have never doubted the existence of a master creator, if you will, an entity who fashioned the perfection and intricacy of our physical world. Even as a child, it seemed pretty obvious to me that somebody a lot smarter than I (or anyone else, for that matter) has masterfully planned the universe and all it contains. What I did not have was a *living* faith, an active faith, one that I could use in my daily life. To have a faith that is practical and applicable to living, God had to be defined in a personal way, and he was not. He was "out there" somewhere, a disinterested observer. At least that is where I perceived him to be for me. He might love you and be there for you, but he was not there for me. I never defined a personal God. If there was any definition at all, it was defined for me through religious doctrine. And although I believed in his existence, I did not believe that those wonderful qualities attributed to him by Christianity were there for me. Love, forgiveness, grace—none of that had any meaning. My heart was closed to love, both human and divine. And without being able to feel love, my belief in God was a head trip. My mind accepted him, but my heart did not truly believe.

Also, I have already shared with you that, for most of my adult life, I turned my back on this God that I knew existed "out there." During those years, my faith was misplaced and misdirected. I deified both myself and others by believing we had powers we did not have. Certainly, my own power to control, fix, and manipulate was grossly distorted. I also did a third step on the Skier/Climber. In other words, I turned my will and my life over to his care. That was, in some ways, literally true. All the years I climbed mountains with him, I naively believed that if I fell while on belay (roped for protection), he would somehow magically pull me back on the mountain to safety. It was not until I actually *did* fall that I found out the sobering truth. All he could do was hold me and keep me from falling further. It was up to *me* to reestablish handholds and footholds and to get back on the mountain as quickly as possible.

When I invited God back into my life, my first task was to define a living faith, the faith required to deal with addictions and addictive behavior. I had to expand my faith to include my heart and redefine God in a more personal way. To make faith a true part of my life, the God of my understanding had to be there for *me*. He had to care about me, love me, protect me, and watch over me. He had to want me to evolve and grow spiritually, to reach only for my highest good, to remember who I am, to find my true self, to walk my unique path, and to serve him as best I could. But most of all, he had to be a God who could do for me what I could not do for myself. He had to be a God in whom I had enough faith to surrender my will and my life into his care.

Thus my living faith in God evolved as my understanding of God evolved—one day at a time and one step at a time. It has not come quickly and it has not come easily. A living faith requires more than just believing in my head. A living faith requires that I know without question, both in my mind and heart, that I can depend on God to be there for me. A living faith requires that I know without question, both in my mind and heart, that whatever happens in my life, it will always turn out to be the best for me, even when it is not the outcome I desire. In fact, a living faith requires me to relinquish all attachment to outcomes, period.

This is where I have struggled the most with faith, and this is where I have been the most severely tested. God has brought me a number of "what ifs," life experiences that have caused me to consider some potentially serious outcomes that were not at all desirable. A questionable spot on my liver caused me to consider my own mortality and something other than the long life I desire to live. A potential lawsuit caused me to ponder the loss of my financial security. A flood threat caused me to think about the loss of my most valued personal possessions. A couple of near-accidents while driving my car caused me to consider losing both it *and* my life. In all cases, I was able to face the potential of loss and accept it even if I did not like it very much. It was sort of like, "OK, God, this does not make very much sense to me and it is certainly not at all what I would choose, but I know that you're with me no matter what happens." And, in all cases, once I accepted the possibility of loss, the threat vanished.

The one area of my life where I have had the most trouble accepting potential losses and unexpected outcomes is in relationships. These are the outcomes I hang on to, the dreams that I forgot to turn back over to God. It is easy to have faith when prayers and desires are immediately and clearly answered in ways that positively affect my life. It is easy to have faith when my path and timing perfectly coincide with God's. As I often say, I can work a marvelous twelve-step program when I have no stressors in my life! It is easy to stay detached from outcomes when I have no emotional investment in the actions that create them or the people involved in them. It is *not* easy to stay detached from outcomes when I *do*!

Doubt comes easily to me in matters of the heart. It is much easier for me to have faith in his guidance in my life than it is to have faith in his guidance in the life of one I love deeply. Doubt comes easily to me when expected outcomes are not apparent. Doubt comes easily to me when my heart's desires do not manifest in reality as quickly as I think they should, when God's time table and mine do not agree, or when the miracles required to create the desires of my heart are not obviously happening. Doubt comes easily to me when I see a person I care about take what appears to be a wrong turn onto a painful path that, for me, was a dead end.

To be sure, doubt is a corollary of fear, fear of outcomes that are unwanted, unpleasant, or unexpected. And fear and faith cannot coexist any more than fear and love can coexist. So when I doubt, I lose my faith, not in my heart, but in my mind. My heart still knows God's truth, but my mind does not. Fear has closed my mind to both God and his truth and tried to close my heart as well, bringing me the pain of separation from him. Fear is faith's greatest enemy, and the only antidote to fear is a return to love and to God. When the pain of separation gets too great to bear, my mind will open through surrender, acceptance, and forgiveness and the place in my heart that has closed will open again to love. When my heart opens fully again to love, faith returns.

This faith, when it returns, is a truer faith, a stronger faith, because it is born again out of the pain of separation from God. This is a faith that allows me to surrender the dreams, given to me by God, back to him and to accept and embrace his agenda, timing, and outcomes. This faith allows me to commit to my dreams even when they appear to be impossible or implausible. "Leap and the net shall appear" is a directive built upon a living faith in a higher power who loves, cares, protects, and supports my being the best I can be. This faith brings me total acceptance of God's plan for my life, even when his plan is different than mine. This faith allows my soul to dare to go farther than it can see. This faith allows me to be compassionate and kind toward those who have temporarily lost their way. This faith allows my heart to be free and open to God, to love, and to others.

~ INTUITION

Intuition is my connection to the divinity within myself. It is knowledge based on spiritual perception, not mental reasoning. It is God talk or heart talk, not mind talk. Some refer to intuition as understanding, as intuition and understanding are one and the same. Intuition is knowing, simply knowing, that a feeling, an event, a perception, or an action is right, is correct, is for the highest good for all concerned. My guide sends me messages in any form I am receptive to, both external and internal. But external messages, those that come through people, events, activities, places, or dreams, are filtered through my mind and thus can be misinterpreted. Intuition is a direct line to the God within, to universal wisdom and truth. Internal messages are *not* filtered, they simply are. Intuition is a recognition and acceptance of divine guidance. Acting on intuition, following my heart, is acting on faith alone. Allowing myself to be guided by intuition is allowing myself to be guided by God.

Intuition is also a gift we are given at birth that is often lost as we adapt to the physical world. Intuition cannot be sensually validated. You cannot see, hear, taste, smell, or touch it. Intuition can only be felt. Intuition very often contradicts and defies logic and reasoning, and certainly cannot be explained. Analyzing or questioning intuition weakens it and may render it useless. So those of us who learn to be logical, mental, and analytical also learn to ignore or disbelieve intuition. Those of us who learn that God is an external force do not look for the God within, nor do we understand that intuition links us to that very important part of ourselves. Many eastern religions teach us to go within to find spiritual peace, wisdom, and truth. Intuition is the gift I rediscover when I do that.

When I began to write this piece, I debated about whether to call it intuition or insight. Insight also comes from the God within, but to me, insight is understanding or clarification of a spiritual truth. Intuition *is* a spiritual truth, a knowing, that may relate to past, present, or future. Intuition may guide me away from danger or toward a vision of God's plan for my life. Intuition gives me the meaning behind the words others speak and tells me what is in their hearts. Intuition is the link between hearts.

I knew little about intuition or insight for most of my life, since I had no use for spiritual guidance, either external or internal. Still, there were certain things along the way that I simply knew. I knew that the Piano Player loved me as much as he could love anyone. I knew when we met that we were going to be together. I knew when a casual sexual encounter wasn't casual, when there was some sort of an inner connection that became activated through close physical contact. None of these knowings were based on mental evaluation—they just were. What I did not know was where these knowings came from. It was not until I allowed God back into my life that I began to be consciously aware of my knowings, my intuition. It was not until I reclaimed my spiritual self that I came to understand their source, to know that they were messages from

God. It was not until I began to trust God that I began to trust my inner guidance enough to accept it and act upon it.

In the months before the Piano Player's final relapse, I knew he was going to drink again. In the months before his illness and death, I knew I was being prepared for a loss. Both of these knowings were part intuition and part mental observation, but I took no action in either case, either for him or for me. I neither accepted nor acted upon my intuition, my knowings. As I put it then, I knew but did not know.

I did not heed my guide when he spoke to me directly because I did not trust my sense of knowing. So at first he guided me, spoke to me, through other people. Through program people at meetings, through the books he guided me to read, and through the chosen ones, my soul friends. He spoke to me through psychics, through tarot readings and medicine cards, through the messages of a Christian pastor. He has spoken to me through movies, television, and the creative arts. He still speaks to me through these media and many more, but his most important guidance comes to me directly in one of two ways. He touches my soul, connects me to others, and heals me through music. And he guides me from within through writing.

Exactly one year after the Piano Player died, I began to write every day, three pages in longhand, usually in the morning. The purpose of this exercise was to de-clutter my mind and open a creative channel; what it did was open a channel, a direct line, to my inner spirit, the God within. First came insight, then came the knowings. Eventually, I was brave enough to talk directly to God, to ask him questions and receive his answers. Sometimes the answers were direct, sometimes philosophical, sometimes in the form of questions that forced me to look deeper within for my own answers. Oftentimes my messages got confused with mind talk, and I received my own wishful and incorrect thinking. But, in time, I was given the gift of discernment; and more and more truth came to me through my writing. And as my heart has become more open, it has become easier and easier to feel and follow its guidance.

Now when I ask for wisdom or direction from my guide, the primary medium he uses to affect this is my intuition. My knowledge based on spiritual perception comes to me directly and effortlessly. Writing is still a powerful transmittal medium. Often when I write, it feels more like transcribing than originating. Often when I write, the words bring me clarity where clarity did not previously exist. Much of what I am writing here falls into this category. But, as I become stronger in my personal truth, as I know myself better and trust my perceptions, my path is guided simply by a sense of knowing, sometimes consciously, sometimes unconsciously. I may write to this knowing to clarify it, or I may not. My knowing may be validated by supporting events, or it may not. But my sense of knowing always leads me down a path I need to follow to grow, to heal, or to honor my spiritual commitments. My intuition always brings me closer to home.

Not long ago, I committed to opening my heart to love and intimacy in a relationship. To do this required a tremendous amount of healing. I had many emotional wounds left from previous relationships that needed to be opened, purged, and healed. That summer, God took me on what I called a pilgrimage, a healing journey, by myself, to western Canada. I have strong emotional ties to that area, so spending four weeks revisiting the old and exploring the new was very appealing to me. I did not realize until midway through my pilgrimage that the places I was revisiting touched every major, real relationship I have had with a man in the past thirty-five years. I had visited some part of my route with each of these men, and the places I was led to where the places were I needed to feel and release my buried feelings. Intuition took me to all of these places, sometimes more than once, so I could feel what I had to in order to clear out the refuse from my heart. When I got home, intuition led me downstairs to my basement, where more ghosts of relationships past remained. Clearing out and reclaiming my basement correlated with clearing out and reclaiming the recesses of my heart.

A similar experience came more recently through another pilgrimage to Canada. On this journey, I had planned to return from Vancouver Island to the British Columbia mainland via a particular ferry route. A few days before the scheduled sailing, I was guided to take a different route to avoid Vancouver traffic. This change in plan created emotional resistance that I really didn't understand until I boarded the ferry. Then I knew the reason for my resistance.

This was the ferry route I had taken when I scattered the Piano Player's ashes, less than a year after his death. At that time, I was unable to fully feel the attendant pain—it was simply too soon. So I was led back to feel and release it four years later.

The gifts of intuition and insight are strong within me today, and they serve me well as long as my faith and trust in God remain strong. Still, sometimes the direct line gets temporarily blocked by fear, and he has to use other means to reach me. Sometimes a knowing that I feel, but do not quite believe, requires external validation, some sort of a sign that it is real and attainable. But most of the time I simply know, and follow, the direction of my guide. And when I do, the process works very well. I know what my part in the grand scheme of things is supposed to be, and I follow the path prescribed by my knowing. Certainly, there are times when my reaction is, "You want me to do *what*?" But I have learned through experience that it is best not to question whatever it is and just do it, to follow my heart, always leaving the outcome firmly planted in the hands of God.

~ POWER

Power is the gift that manifests thoughts into words, ideas into accomplishments, beliefs into actions. Power is the great activator; power gets things done, makes things work, turns things on, and keeps them going. Power is the driving force behind great speeches, books, music, art, theater, athletes, dancers, statesmen, or just about anything expressed through action. Power is a doer, not a be-er or a passive observer. Power is the great creator that turns ideas into thoughts and thoughts into physical reality.

There are many sources of power in my physical world—generators, dynamos, engines, motors, wind, water, batteries, money, fame, weapons, anything that propels things or people into action. In my spiritual world, however, there is only one source, and that is God. Connecting to that source is how I activate the power that he has given me.

We are born connected to the source of power, for we are born as a perfect expression of God. Infants are connected to the source and use that power to get their needs met. However, life in this world requires us to develop our sense of individuality, or self, and with that comes our sense of personal power. Personal power fueled by a connection to divine power is awesome indeed, but most of us do not maintain that connection. We lose that sense of connection to divine power and rely on our own sense of personal power to get us through life, inspire us to action, and for some of us this works very well. For others (including myself), personal power comes up woefully short of what is needed to become a master of life.

For much of my life, I didn't believe I had any personal power or, if I did, I certainly didn't use it. Most of the time I gave it away to anyone who would take it! Any time I let the actions of another person determine either my mood or the course of my life, I was giving away my personal power. As a child and young adult, I did that continually. I was very sensitive, took everything personally, and was pretty much convinced that I was the center of the universe. People who devalue themselves, as I did, are always self-centered, and I was (in my eyes) flawed, unlovable, and powerless.

As an adult, any sense of personal power I had came through career accomplishments. There, what I did was reasonably self-motivated, although I still worked very hard to excel and please my supervisors, as I had done previously in school. Certainly, I was a doer, particularly in my outdoor life, but the power source was the Skier/Climber, not me. I was, in those days, a power parasite, using other people to motivate me into action—with one exception. When I created through the medium of black-and-white photography, I believe I was connected to the source. As I look at my photographs today, they are very symbolically spiritual. My specialty was mountain scenes with red-filtered clouds. However, if I was connected to the source, I certainly wasn't aware of it at the time, nor would I have acknowledged it if I were aware. Since I had turned my back on God, I was hardly in a position to purposely connect to him as the source of power. Even if I had known that his power was available to me, I probably would have insisted on going it alone, too filled with false pride to ask for a power boost.

This illustrates an interesting phenomenon. Oftentimes, creative artists are connected to the source directly when they use their creative gifts, but they are not necessarily aware of that connection and are not connected otherwise. The Songteller is directly connected to God when he sings and plays the guitar. He calls it playing and singing from the heart, and he's been doing it for as long as I've known him. That is the primary spiritual reason that his music (and his guitars) are so important to him and why I am so touched by his music. But I'm not sure that he really understands that the same source of infinite power is available to him in other areas of his life. Certainly, the Piano Player, too, was connected to his source whenever he played, but he didn't understand it. If he had, he would have allowed that power to help him cope with his alcoholism.

I was also unknowingly connected to the source when the Piano Player and I performed on stage, and that was undoubtedly one of the reasons I had such a difficult time letting go of our music when he died. To be sure, I was talking to God again by then, but he was still very distant. It would be many years before I developed the close relationship I have today with my guide, and even more years before I would allow him to be my power source and express through me in my actions and activities.

It happened first with my music. Part of my recovery was the reclaiming of my own personal musical gifts, and that process began with my relearning how to play classical music. Understand that I was, for most of my life, *not* connected to the source when I played my music, even though I played it very well. It came from me, not through me. Fear and false pride would not allow a creative connection with my source, and surrendering fear and false pride was a gradual process within a process.

One of the first instances when I absolutely *know* I was plugged into the source happened when I was doing a solo one Sunday in church. It was Mother's Day, and I decided to play "Clair de Lune," which was one of my mother's favorite pieces, in her honor. At the time, my fear of solo performing was so severe that I would often physically shake while playing the piano. I had been working with this fear, owning it, and turning it over to God, but for some reason that day it didn't do any good. My hands started to shake when I began playing, and by the time I got to the end of the first page, they were shaking so badly that I couldn't turn the page, let alone play. So I stopped, announced to the surprised congregation that I was going to start over, and did. Only the second time, I didn't do it, God did. I had totally surrendered and allowed him to guide my fingers from that point on. Granted, since I was still very fearful, it was anything but a perfect performance, but we got through it. After that incident, I realized that all I had to do was show up prepared, surrender, and he would do the rest through me.

Later, I was also able to surrender another long-time fear, the fear of speaking in public. Then, I allowed him to speak through me, but only on very specific occasions when it was very clear that without him as my source of power, I would be incapable of doing what was required of me. Certainly, I have been plugged into the source while writing this book; much of what has been written was not formulated in my mind before it came out on paper. In fact, that's one of the ways I know that God is expressing through me, particularly when I speak. If, after I've finished talking, I don't remember what I said, I know the words came through me, not from me.

These are specific instances of situations where I *knew* I needed help and specifically asked God to express through me. It would be a very long time before I realized that this power source is available to me at all times. And it is a gift we all have, only most of us are either unaware or afraid to tap into the source. Ironically, we usually strive for more personal power, which is limited, but are afraid to surrender to the power of God within us, which is limitless.

The one area where I *am* continually connected to God as my power source is in my addictions. When I admit my powerlessness over food and people (step one) and turn my obsession for these drugs of choice over to God, I become empowered to abstain from their use. In that one aspect of my life, I am plugged into the source--the power to abstain comes directly from God. The power to do anything I choose within the limits of my physical capabilities also comes from God, and I can connect to that power any time I connect to my source. I can recharge my batteries, so to speak, during meditation by going into the quiet with God. And, during the rest of my day, I allow his presence to express through me any time I surrender to the experience.

~ COMMUNITY

Community is my connection to the divine within all of creation, and it is a bond of love. Community may exist among human beings or between human beings and other forms of God's creation. Native Americans and other aboriginal groups have a tremendous sense of community with all aspects of their environment—earth, sky, moon, sun, plants, animals, rocks, and trees—and show love and respect and reverence to them all. Some humans form this communal bond with their pets or certain species of wildlife. I have a particularly strong communal bond with California redwoods and the trees on Quadra Island in British Columbia. I am literally a tree hugger, receiving love and spiritual energy from the trees. I also, however, receive love and spiritual energy from hugging people.

True community between or among people is a spiritual connection, a God connection, a love connection. It is a connection that transcends time, space, and physicality. When I am connected to you spiritually, the connection may be strongly felt even when we are physically separated. We are spiritually close even though we are physically distant. I do not have to be physically close to you to feel close to you, although it is generally much nicer when I am!

True community between or among people is a connection that, once felt and accepted, cannot be broken. Mental, physical, and emotional connections can be severed and often are. A spiritual connection, one sourced in love, endures. Fear may create circumstances and behaviors that make it appear as if the connection has been broken, but the break is an illusion. Prolonged physical separation or a lack of physical interaction may weaken the connection, may seem to diminish it, but it still remains and is easily rekindled. A communal relationship may remain dormant for weeks, months, or even years, then pick up right where it left off when reactivated. I have a soul friend I call my first sister friend; our friendship has gone unattended off and on for long periods of time over a time span of over forty-five years. When we get together, we may be in a different place because our lives have changed, but the connection remains solid and strong. Ours is a true communal bond, even though for most of our forty-five years I did not know it as such.

Once a person who has lived in isolation rediscovers community, connects spiritually to even one person, it is very difficult, if not impossible, to return to isolation. It is also impossible to deliberately disconnect, to distance oneself from a loved one in this way. It is simply too painful to do this without completely shutting down emotionally. Some of the most severe pain that I have created for myself since I rediscovered community has come when I tried to deny the reality of a spiritual connection, tried to pretend that love for another did not exist, tried to distance myself or separate from someone I deeply cared about because of fear caused by anger, betrayal, or indifference. To separate myself from one with whom I am spiritually connected is to separate myself from God, and I simply cannot do it anymore. It hurts too much.

Each of us is born with a need for community, for a sense of spiritual belonging, and this need is a gift. It is God's way of helping us connect to him through our connections with others. Usually, this need is first satisfied through our parents. Later it may be satisfied through brothers and sisters, grandparents, aunts, uncles, and cousins. Still later, it may come through a church family, through being part of a team effort, through uniting with others in a common cause, through belonging to communal groups such as lodges, fraternities, or support groups. For most of us, however, our sense of community is limited and has definite boundaries. I am comfortable within my communal group but not outside of it. Nor am I always comfortable when an outsider first comes into my communal group. As the Songteller put it in one of his songs, "You're out if you ain't in." How wonderful life in our world would be if our communal boundaries were dissolved by the healing power of love.

For some of us, the circumstances of our lives somehow short-circuited our need for spiritual connection, and the gift of community became lost. For too many of us, physical, sexual, or emotional abuse destroyed our ability to trust other people and made us afraid or suspicious of community. We learned to trust no one, not even ourselves or God. We refuse to connect spiritually or to allow ourselves to feel or accept a spiritual connection, even when it is offered to us unconditionally. We reject love from others, and we reject love from ourselves, and in the process we reject love from God.

I have already shared that I came into this world thinking I had to earn love. Along with this misperception came a lack of trust.

Obviously, if I had to earn love, I could not trust my parents (or anyone else) to provide it for me or meet my needs. Without trust, and sourced in fear, I could not feel love nor would I allow myself to feel a sense of connection to anyone. My parents and I bonded emotionally; in fact, we were very emotionally enmeshed. And it may be that the emotional dependency masked our true spiritual connection, because I believe now that it was always there. But I never felt it. I never felt truly connected to anyone—not family, friends, coworkers, or even spouses. The only true sense of community I felt was with animals—the dogs that were my childhood pets and the cats that were part of my life with the Piano Player. The animals loved unconditionally and were always there for me. People loved conditionally and were not there for me emotionally. So I bonded communally with animals, but never with people.

This sense of separation from other people continued through most of my adult life. I had many acquaintances but few close friends, and I lived my life simultaneously independently and dependently. Because I was able to accept support from so few people, I was very dependent on those I did accept support from. I was mentally, physically, and emotionally connected to my husbands, but I was not aware of being connected spiritually except with one and in one area only. The Piano Player and I were connected spiritually through our music. That was the bond that I could not force myself to break.

The first time I can recall recognizing true community in others was the bond I saw among the newly recovering alcoholics who went through in-patient treatment with the Piano Player. I could feel the special bond they had and envied it. I remember wishing that there was an in-patient program for codependents so that I could experience that special connection. Still, I had no understanding of what this communal bond was, or that I was carrying that gift within me, ready to use whenever I was ready to reclaim it. It was another four years before I chose to place myself in a communal setting with Al-Anon and Overeaters Anonymous. There, part of the bond was created through sharing of common problems. But the bond that was formed was a spiritual connection, true community, because they are spiritual programs. Part of the Al-Anon closing at the end of meetings is "...you may not like us all, but you will come to love us, the same way that we already love you."

Even in this safe setting, it would be a long time before I allowed myself to feel the community that was there for me, the sense of connection to other human beings. Many times, in meetings, I have shared that my recovery brought me the gift of reconnecting with the human race! Once I took a risk and opened up to both giving and receiving love, an amazing thing happened. I understood that the spiritual connections to my family of origin, friends, and spouses, had always been there, and I had blocked their presence with my own fear and mistrust. My separation had been self-created, and it had always been in my power to release it. The gift of community had always been there for me to use.

Still, my reconnection to others has been a process, and I, too, had rigid boundaries. But these boundaries have gradually grown and expanded as I have grown and expanded spiritually. I first connected to select, trusted individuals. Then to those in my twelve-step programs, and then to those in other twelve-step programs, and then to anyone in any twelve-step program. Eventually, my sense of being connected spiritually to others extended beyond my family of origin and program families. My sense of love, of community, became more universal. And with that sense of agape love, of spiritual connection, I have been freed from many of my old fears. I no longer have to cling to one person physically, mentally, and emotionally because I am now spiritually connected, in community, with many people. I am now free to travel by myself comfortably because I am never alone. All I have to do is be out among people, and I become spiritually recharged. That doesn't mean that I take extraordinary risks—I do not. What it does mean is that I am no longer shackled to a need for someone else being with me. When I am with someone, it is because I desire to be with someone, not because I need to have someone with me.

I wish I could say that my sense of community has become truly global, encompassing all of creation, but it has not. Not yet, anyway. I believe that we are all connected in love, which is God, but I have not totally integrated this belief into my personal experience. Nor do I affirm it through action. I tend to be disinterested in national and international affairs and am in no sense an activist in any cause. Still, I am much more compassionate and open to the suffering of the world and all of its creations, animate and inanimate, both individually and collectively, and I pray and grieve for anyone or anything anywhere that is victimized by the forces of fear, hatred, and ignorance. Their pain becomes my pain because we are all spiritually connected, and any pain I inflict on anyone or anything is pain I inflict on myself as well. My prayers are prayers for spiritual healing for both the victims and the perpetrators, for thoughts, words, and actions sourced in fear, hatred, and ignorance to be transformed into thoughts, words, and actions sourced in love. And it matters not if the victims and perpetrators are World Trade Center employees and fanatical terrorists, old growth forests and logging companies, endangered species and poachers, or ghetto children and slum lords. I have become a spiritual activist with a global sense of community, and that is a form of activism that anyone can embrace.

~ TRUTH

Each of us is born with the gift of truth, both individual and universal. Our universal truth is that each of us is a lovable child of God. Our essence is love. And, as such, God is a part of us all. We are as one with him, and he is as one with us. Because of this, he wants only the best for us and will lead us to our highest good if we ask him to and allow him to do that. That is our birthright, and it is constant and unchanging. It is the same for every one of us.

Our individual truths vary, as each individual varies. What is true for you may not be true for me. My individual truth is who I am, what I am, what is right for me. It includes those personal gifts that are uniquely mine, gifts given to me by God to use in creating the life he intends me to create in his name. It includes those aspects of self that assure that the role I play in life is uniquely mine, a starring role that can be claimed by no other person. Knowing my individual, or personal, truth and following it assures me that I am walking my unique path. Following my truth is following God.

For most of my life, I neither knew my truth nor followed it. For most of my life, I did not want to know my truth, for I falsely believed myself to be unlovable and flawed. Separated from God and unaware of my true identity as his beloved child, I was afraid to know my personal truth, afraid to know who I was, so I hid from it and hid it from others as well. Instead of a human being, I became a human doing and defined my truth by what I did rather than who I was. I was Nadine the pianist, Nadine the secretary, Nadine the college student, Nadine the backpacker, climber, and skier, Nadine the bass player, Nadine the bar owner, Nadine the tech writer. I was never Nadine the bright, loving, caring person. My various and sundry roles defined who I was and masked the emptiness within.

All of these different personas contained aspects of me, but none of these things were me because they only partially reflected my own personal truth. Who I was was determined by what I did, and what I did shifted depending on whose path I was following at the time. And how I did what I did, what aspects of my being I used to do them, also shifted depending on whose path I was following. I was a chameleon who changed attributes and lives seemingly at will.

I used to marvel at the diversity of the different stages of my life, so different that I still refer to them as lives one, two, and three. Life one went through childhood and my marriage to the Rescuer and was closer to being *my* life than any of the others. Life two, my hiking, skiing, backpacking, trekking, climbing life, began shortly thereafter and included marriage to the Skier/Climber. Life three, my musician, bar owner, and addicted life, encompassed my marriage to the Piano Player. I used to chuckle to myself and somewhat proudly say that I was the only person I had ever known who had climbed the Grand Teton and had her name in lights on the Las Vegas Strip all in the same lifetime. I laughed about it, that is, until one day I realized the sad truth. The diversity came because these were not my lives at all. They were someone else's lives, and the two someone's whose paths I followed just happened to be very, very different.

Still, there were certain aspects of my being that refused to be stifled and remained relatively constant throughout all my various and sundry lives. My intelligence, my responsible nature, my organizational skills, my tenacity and perseverance, my optimism and hope—these were personal qualities that were useful to me in all my doings, so I retained them. All of these are inherently me, gifts I was given to use in my life. They are all part of my personal truth.

Other parts of my personal truth were not constant. They shifted as I shifted. My loving, caring nature was tarnished by my need to please others, to hold their love by doing for them rather than by sharing myself with them. My passion for life was sometimes expressed through my doings, but as often as not was buried beneath a multitude of fears. My independence, my free spirit, was shackled by a need to be with someone else who could lead the way. My creative gifts were used, discarded, or molded to fit the person whose path I was following. With a writer, I could be a writer. With a musician, I could be a musician. With a climber, backpacker, and skier, I could be a climber, backpacker, and skier. With a photographer, I could be a photographer. With someone who was loved and admired by others, I could be loved and admired. Yet I always believed in these qualities and greatly admired them in others. I believed in them, knew they were a part of me, but did not know how to live them or show them. What I believed in and how I lived my life were two very different things.

Then there were the other parts of my personal truth that I neither recognized in myself nor admired in others. These were the parts of me that, when I saw them in others, made me uncomfortable or afraid because I did not want to see them in myself. My spiritual self was one such part, my need for and my connection to God, that part of me that knew my universal truth, who I really was. A corollary to this that I also feared was my need for and connection to other people on a spiritual plane. Oddly, these were the parts of my personal truth that had to be rediscovered and reclaimed first. Once I found my "lost" spirituality, I found the courage to go back and look for the other missing parts.

Today, I know my truth. I know who I am. I am, first and foremost, a human being, and it is my being that creates my doing, not the other way around. Although the details of my personality, my likes and dislikes, my strengths and weaknesses, are in a continual process of refinement, I am basically defined. I know what fits my persona and what does not. I know what clothes fit, what experiences fit, what activities fit, what environments fit, what people fit. And I no longer shift and bow and bend myself to fit anyone else. I am me, and I am becoming more and more comfortable with and accepting of who I am.

Today, I know who I am, but I still do not always share all of who I am with you. Old behaviors sometimes die hard. It has taken me a long time to begin to soften, to let my loving nature shine through so you can see it, to allow myself to be vulnerable by owning and expressing my feelings. It has taken me a long time to begin to own and love those less desirable aspects of my personality that mask or hinder my truth. It has taken me a long time to let my free spirit soar with God as the wind beneath my wings. It has taken me a long time to begin to trust in my knowings, my intuition, and follow them, to follow my heart, to live my life with passion for what is right for me. It has taken me a long time to understand and know that I am a writer, a musician, an outdoor person, a photographer, and a lovable person, with or without someone else to validate my gifts. I am all of these things. They are a part of my personal truth.

It has also taken me a long time to correctly value the many parts of my personal truth and give credit to the source for my gifts. It has taken me a long time to understand that to undervalue my gifts, to discount their worth, is to discount the worth of God. Discounting my worth is discounting the creative work of God, the great creator, who created my truth, my true self. To know my truth, value my truth, and follow my truth is an affirmation of my love and respect for my creator. To know, love, and honor myself, who I am, my personal truth, is to know, love, and honor God.

Today, as always, my truth is that I am, first and foremost, a lovable child of God. I am also loving, peaceful, gentle, caring, intelligent, passionate, responsible, independent, organized, tenacious, persevering, optimistic, hopeful, and gifted artistically and musically. I am many other things in the physical world, but these are the gifts I was given and brought in here to create the rest. Discovering my personal truth is a continuous process, so I will undoubtedly find more gifts as my spiritual journey continues and my self-awareness deepens. All that I find are the tools I was given to create my life, to walk my unique path, the path that will take me home.

~ WILL

Will, or free will, is the gift that allows me to choose the course of my life. It is the one God-given gift that defines my humanness and is what sets humans apart from all of God's other creations. Everything else in God's world follows the natural order of its existence automatically without the ability to do otherwise. Free will allows me the option of saying yes or no to almost every aspect of my life, including life itself. Free will allows me to choose to honor life or to abuse life, to honor or abuse my body, to honor or abuse others, to live a life based on love or to live a life based on fear. Free will allows me to choose to follow God, ignore God, or even reject God, and free will assures me that my choices are honored by God. This is a very important aspect of free will; God will not force me to do anything against my will, no matter how self-damaging or self-defeating my choices may be. However, free will also assures me that I will be allowed to experience the consequences of my choices, and the consequences of choosing not to follow God are often painful enough to bring me back to him. At least that's how it has worked with me, and I don't believe I'm the only person who has ever had this experience.

Free will thus allows me to choose my perceptions, my attitudes, my beliefs, my behaviors, my actions, my friends, my partners in life, my occupation, my education, life style, my status in life, and a million other things, both large and small, that make up the details of my life. Free will also allows me to choose to dye my hair, pierce my body, lift my face, change my sexual orientation, or otherwise alter that which was given to me originally by God to use in this life. And, depending on how it is used, free will creates either freedom or bondage. Paradoxically, freedom comes from freely choosing to humbly surrender my will and my life to God and align my will with his, thus allowing divine love to guide my life. Bondage results from freely choosing to reject God's wisdom and guidance and make my life choices a do-it-yourself project, a head trip, one that allows fear the opportunity to guide the way. Free will thus determines whether or not I am truly free or chained to the fear-based road hazards that are always present and waiting to take over my life. And when I choose incorrectly or am displeased with the consequences of my choices, free will gives me the opportunity to choose again.

Since free will defines us as human beings, it is obviously with us from birth. True, the choices made by me as an infant were based primarily on getting my needs met and were totally irrational, but I still had the gift of choice. Later, when I discovered that I had this gift of choice, I chose to give it away and let others make my choices for me. I surrendered my right to choose to my parents. This was a choice, and I could have chosen differently. Doing this as an adult, surrendering my right to choose, was also a choice and I could have chosen differently. Free will is a gift that can never be lost, only misused. Even when I surrender my will to God, I can always choose to take it back. And I have many times!

Recovering alcoholics in Alcoholics Anonymous refer to their use and abuse of alcohol as an example of self-will run riot, which is really just another name for free will misused. And with alcoholics, as with all addicts, no matter the drug of choice, the consequences of misusing free will are very severe. Lost jobs, jail sentences, destroyed marriages, spouse and child abuse, sexual promiscuity, and the potential for life-threatening disease, all of these and more are, for the alcoholic and drug addict, the potential consequences of misusing free will. For the compulsive eater, bulimic, or anorexic, the consequences of misusing free will are chronic health problems, diabetes, heart disease, and all sorts of other severe health problems. For those who use sex, gambling, work, spending, or other drugs of choice, misusing free will has other severe consequences. However, for anyone dealing with any addiction, there is always hope and that hope lies with the gift of free will. No matter how desperate the situation may be, free will is always with me and gives me the opportunity to choose again. And for the addict, there is but one choice—to use or not to use. Free will guarantees that that choice is there for everyone.

Throughout my life, when I thought I had surrendered my will to others, it really was with me all the time, waiting to be rediscovered and redirected toward a more positive experience. It waited a long time. For most of my life, my choices were determined either by my drugs of choice or by what I believed I needed to do or be in order to please others. It was only when the consequences of my choices became very painful that I became open to doing things differently. Obviously, it was not until I opened my mind and heart again to God that I began to use my gift of free will wisely.

It is easy to tell whether or not free will is being used with or without wisdom. All I have to do is look at the consequences of my choices. During the years when I chose to live with the Piano Player and the disease of alcoholism, my gift of free will was very misused. In fact, I thought I had given away my power of choice to the man and his disease. Of course, I hadn't; it was always there with me, as God was with me, waiting patiently for the time when I would rediscover and reconnect with both of them. But, until that happened, the choices I made (or didn't make) led to some very unpleasant consequences, most of which I blamed on alcohol.

During those years of non-choice, I chose to give up a duplex (traded in as part of the down payment on our bar) and a car and piano (both sold to get cash to live on). These were prized possessions of mine before I chose to love an alcoholic. In all cases, the choices were made based on my evaluation of the circumstances of our lives at that time. There were my choices and I freely made them, but with no directive other than my own. True, I exercised my free will; but without the wisdom and guidance of God, the consequences were not at all pleasant or desirable. And eventually, the consequences of my misguided choices were severe enough to bring me to back to the God I had rejected years earlier. Unfortunately, the consequences of the Piano Player's self-directed choices were even more severe. They took his life.

Now I choose to walk a different path, my unique path, as guided by God. Now my free will is no longer free but has been surrendered to my guide, and the consequences of my choices are much more desirable. Every aspect of my life is improving as a result of my choice to walk with him, partly due to changed circumstances and partly due to changed perceptions (miracles). And, as a result of using my free will wisely and under God's direction, I was able to replace everything that I had lost—house, car, and piano—with something better and more appropriate to my new path. God-directed choices result in God-directed consequences, and God-directed consequences are always for our highest good.

Allowing God to guide me and direct my choices has continued to greatly improve the consequences of my choices over time. Certainly, this is a process, as all spiritual growth is a process, but one that continues to improve with me as I strengthen my relationship with my guide. The more I am able to consistently and continuously surrender my will and my choices to God, the more my life just seems to flow. And the consequences of God-directed choices are usually infinitely better than anything I could have chosen for myself.

~ DIVINE ORDER

Divine order is a gift that has been given by God to all of his creations, living and nonliving. Nonliving creations are made through an orderly process defined by their creator. Living creations come into being, live, reproduce, and die according to an orderly process defined by their creator. All of God's creations except human beings follow the laws of divine order automatically. Plants, birds, fish, and animals do not question the process that defines their lives—they simply follow it. Neither do they wish to be something they are not. That is a peculiarly human perturbation of divine order.

For us, then, divine order is a gift that, like all the rest of God's gifts, we must relearn how to use and then learn how to use wisely. There is an orderly divine plan in place for each of us, but free will gives us the option of deviating from the plan, of veering off our unique path. Free will allows us to change course, and our society encourages us to change course. We are trained from birth in those skills that prepare us to make our way in the physical world, but have little or no formal training in the practices that support spiritual development. Life thus becomes *our* plan, not God's. I have thought, since I began purposely walking a spiritual path with God, that Spirituality 101 should be a part of every child's required school curriculum. Obviously, it is not. So we forge ahead in life, trying to make it what we think it should be rather than simply letting it unfold in accordance with divine order. And then we weep and wonder why life is treating us so unfairly.

Divine order sets priorities, and the first priority of divine order is God. After all, I can hardly follow a divine plan if I do not first acknowledge that God is the guide who will unfold that plan in my life. God must come first, and his will must be the guiding force in my life. Then, and only then, will all other aspects of life follow in their proper order and in accordance with divine order. Then life will unfold naturally and provide me with the experiences I need to rediscover my true self, find and walk my unique path, and fulfill my mission as God created me to do. Then I will know my calling and I will follow it. That is how life is meant to be lived.

And, like most of us, divine order is not a gift I have used wisely. I have shared with you that, for most of my life, I didn't even consider God, so obviously, he didn't come first. I certainly wasn't consciously following a divine plan or allowing God to order my life. And, although it is true that God works with whatever choices we make and that we will eventually get where we are supposed to go, my unguided and unwise choices made the trip a lot longer and more painful for me than it should have been.

As I see it, my life path contains three major detours. The first detour occurred when I used food, sex, and relationships as substitutes for divine love. This detour went from soon after I was born until I began my spiritual journey through my twelve-step programs. Obviously, since I was using these substances as substitutes for God, they were my guiding factors, not him. The other two detours occurred when I chose to follow my spouses' paths instead of my own. However, since I was not yet, at the time, either capable of letting or willing to let God guide me, those detours were not as counterproductive as they might have been otherwise. Besides, during the time I was on these detours (which was most of my life), God was continuously working to give me the opportunities required to bring me back into alignment with divine order.

Also during my detours, I was, I believe, being divinely protected until such time as I was ready to begin to follow the divine plan for my life. Certainly, this was true in my outdoor life when I participated in potentially life-threatening activities beyond the level of my physical ability. But perhaps the most bizarre example of divine protection happened not once, but twice. The first incident occurred as I was resting quietly in the coach car of a train taking me from Illinois to Idaho many years ago. It was already dark out, and I was sitting on the inside seat with my face pressed against the window, just sort of staring out into the darkness. Suddenly, I heard the sound of shattering glass. I looked up and saw that the window just ahead of mine had been shattered by a stray bullet! The train conductor told me this happened quite often during hunting season; however, only a split second earlier and the bullet would have hit *my* window and I would have had, at the very least, a face full of glass.

The second incident happened years later. The Piano Player and I were traveling through Utah en route to Idaho in Fred, our Ford van. I was riding in the passenger seat, as usual, when we heard something hit the side of the van right behind me. That something, too, was a stray bullet, and the dent in the side of the van was the same height as my head. Again, a split second earlier and I would have either been shot or, again, showered with glass. I remember, after both incidents, being scared thinking about what could have happened and didn't, but that's as far as I went with it then. The idea of divine protection never even occurred to me. Now, I see that God may have been trying to get my attention in a rather bizarre way. Certainly I was being protected

As my relationship with my guide has deepened, as I have learned more consistently to surrender to his will, divine order has become more and more visible in my life. Now, at least *most* of the time, I allow my guide to show me his orderly way and I attempt to follow it. And when I do, life becomes a glorious and meaningful experience. When I am living in synchronicity with the divine plan, my life simply flows. It is like I am free-floating down a smooth river, and I have a sense that everything that happens, all of my life experiences, are happening exactly when, how, and where they are supposed to. Nothing feels awkward or forced. Further, when the river becomes rough, when rapids appear or when routes divide, I am automatically given the guidance to navigate rough waters and stay on course. It's an amazing feeling, and I can tell right away when I lose it. When my life feels somehow out of balance, when I am trying too hard to make things happen or not happen, to speed up or slow down life, I have lost my connection to divine order. These are the times when I am either racing ahead of my guide or dawdling behind. When we walk arm in arm, all is in divine order and all is right in my world.

Still, even for those of us like me who have spent most of their lives doing it their way instead of God's, there is no reason for regret, for even the detours seem to end up being a part of the plan. Now, as I scan back over my life using twenty-twenty hindsight, I can see how it has unfolded according to divine plan, even as I consciously resisted it. In the chapter entitled, "The Fellow Travelers," I shared how my life had been guided through my relationships, and how the right people always appeared at the right time, giving me the opportunity to move to the next stage of my spiritual journey. To be sure, I had to make the correct choices, and I am sure that, oftentimes, I did not make choices that would have carried me over God's preferred route. But still, in spite of my attempts to foil it, God's plan ultimately prevailed, over a very circuitous route that required the aid of numerous fellow travelers to move me along. But, even while I was on my detours, I was preparing to follow my unique path and its spiritual calling. No experience was ever wasted, and no skill was developed without an ultimate spiritual purpose. Now that I am following my unique path, I am being given the opportunity to use these skills in the way that God intended me to use them. All of my experience and skills are being, or will be, used as I walk my unique path and fulfill God's divinely ordered plan for my life. And one personal gift I am using the most is music.

In the essay on creativity, I tell the story of how I came to rediscover and value my musical gift for playing soft, gentle piano music. Once my gift had been reclaimed and regenerated, God planted another dream in my mind, a way I could share my gift with others and honor its return. This dream was to create a tape of high sound quality that I could have professionally reproduced and give to people who enjoy my quiet brand of classical music. However, my desire was to create this tape in my home, playing my wonderful baby grand piano, Kawai. Now, the manifestation of this dream is a perfect example of divine order at its finest, because it absolutely required him to handle the timing and logistics. The Songteller had the digital recording equipment and technical expertise to do the recording, but he lived 643 miles from me. He would have to be willing to use vacation time from his job, drive up to Idaho, spend several days doing the recording, and many more hours doing the sound mix and locating the studio that would do the reproduction for me. Beyond these obvious logistical details, creating the recording would require (of both of us) patience, gentleness, openness, letting go of fear, tolerance, cooperation, and space-sharing. So there were a number of hurdles to be overcome and had I tried to force it to happen, it probably wouldn't have. But I didn't. I presented the idea to my friend and then released the outcome to God.

Manifesting this dream in reality took eight months from its inception to the finished product, and many things could have happened along the way to abort it. Nothing did; everything just flowed. The Songteller came to Idaho, recorded me, did the sound mix, found the studio, and much, much more, all in perfect order. The tape we co-created is wonderful and definitely sourced in divine love and co-created in divine order. It is an important symbol of my spiritual and emotional healing—a thank you to God. The title he gave me for the tape is *A Gift of Love*, and so it has been. I have celebrated the return of my neglected gift of love with many people, and that is, after all, what it is all about. Sharing my gifts with others is how I give back to God what he has given me and is definitely a part of the divine plan.

~ STRENGTH

Strength is the gift from God that sustains, stabilizes, and endures. Strength is the gift that brings me staying power, the ability to keep on going when the going gets tough, and to be willing to wait for God's plan for my life to unfold. Strength is the gift that can be used with the other God-given gifts to sustain them over time. In fact, strength most often couples with other gifts in order to attain long-term goals and desires.

Strength coupled with power manifests as endurance. Power initiates action, and strength keeps the action going. Power is the sprinter, whereas power plus strength is the marathon runner. Strength coupled with power also manifests as tenacity and perseverance. It was my personal strength plus the Skier/Climber's power that got me to the summits of all the mountains I climbed in my outdoor life. It was my personal strength and the Piano Player's power that kept me doing whatever it took to keep us playing music together. It is God's strength and power working through me that keeps me persevering and dedicated to walking with him on my unique path while being my true self.

Strength coupled with faith manifests as abiding or steadfast faith, the kind of faith that endures in the face of life's blessings and challenges. A literal interpretation of the trials of Job is an example of steadfast faith. Strength coupled with faith, power, and will manifests as courage, the ability to feel our fears and choose to move through them, knowing that God is there with us all the way. Strength coupled with faith and will allows me to choose to surrender and continue to allow God's will to be the guiding force for my life, thus opening the door for all of my gifts to manifest through me.

Strength coupled with judgment or wisdom manifests as integrity, the ability to know my truth and live it, to be my true self and walk my unique path. Wisdom defines my truth, and strength enables me to continuously express it. Strength coupled with order manifests as patience, the willingness to allow God's perfect plan to unfold according to God's time table, not mine. Strength coupled with order doesn't look for a quick and easy solution to all of life's problems, but is willing to wait for the blessings that God has in store for me. Strength coupled with order allows things to happen rather than my trying to force them to happen.

Strength coupled with love manifests as what some refer to as "tough" love, the ability to detach emotionally and allow others the freedom to experience the consequences of their actions. Strength coupled with love is the force behind interventions performed to inspire alcoholics or drug users to choose to seek treatment for their addictions. Strength coupled with love also manifests as loyalty, particularly as expressed in long-term, committed relationships. If love is the blossoming rose of romantic relationships, strength is the stem that supports and sustains them.

Strength coupled with release manifests as the ability not to take back what has been let go of, whether it be a drug of choice, an emotional attachment to another person, or negative thoughts or feelings. Release may get me clean and sober, but strength coupled with release keeps me there. Understand that this is God's strength, which is unlimited, not personal strength, which is limited. Personal strength kept the Piano Player clean and sober and ultimately failed him. God's strength, when accepted, is unlimited and does not fail.

Strength coupled with passion sustains it, allowing the flame of passion to burn not only brightly but steadily. Strength coupled with sexuality, the life force, sustains the desire for life itself. My personal desire to live to 120 in this incarnation will, over time, require a great deal of strength. And, as any mother will confirm, so does giving birth to a child.

As noted above, strength, like power, can be either personal or spiritual, that which comes when I allow myself to be connected to my source, the God of my understanding. Strength also applies to all aspects of my being—physical, mental, emotional, spiritual, and creative. Physical strength is stamina, not simply muscle development. I do not have to look like Charles Atlas to have physical strength. Giving birth requires a great deal of physical strength, or stamina, as does tending the child after it is born. Mental strength is also more than brain development. Standing firm in my beliefs requires mental strength, and so does being open to changing them. Emotional strength does not mean hiding my feelings, but rather having the courage to embrace and share them. Creative strength is believing in my dreams and pursuing them. Spiritual strength is what I have already described as abiding or steadfast faith, the kind of faith that never wavers, no matter how difficult life's challenges become. Jesus personified the ultimate in spiritual strength, and his strength came directly from the source.

Again, as perfect expressions of God, we are all born with the gift of strength. And, as with power, personal strength is developed as our sense of our original connection with the source diminishes or disappears. Interestingly, although personal power was not developed as I grew up, personal strength was. As a dependent child, I conformed to my parents' desires in order to get my needs met, all the time thinking that as soon as I could, I was going to learn how to take care of myself and become independent. I became what I call a do-it-myself person who was quite able to take care of myself, certainly mentally, physically, financially, and in most other ways, except emotionally. As a do-it-myself-er, I refused to ask for help from anyone except in areas where I clearly was unable to do something or was unwilling to learn. Most of what I call "guy" stuff fell into this category. I would happily request help from a plumber, carpenter, roofer, or mechanic, but I would *never* ask for help for anything that I believed I should be able to do for myself. That's why surrendering to my need to have help with my food compulsion and dealing with alcoholism was such a *huge* step for me. My false pride simply wouldn't let me do it.

Even as a follower, when I got my personal power from my spouses, I was a do-it-myself follower, and personal strength was always present. The Skier/Climber may have provided the motivating power for me to climb mountains and ski, but I provided the personal strength that kept me doing it. The Piano Player was the power source for all of our musical endeavors, but it was my personal strength that kept us going. In that situation, because of his disease, my personal strength oftentimes carried us both and therefore became dangerously depleted.

Unfortunately (or fortunately), there usually comes a time for most do-it-myself-ers when personal strength just isn't enough to cope with life's challenges. When my father died suddenly of a heart attack, my personal strength was directed toward providing support for my mother. At the time of Dad's death, the Piano Player was serving a thirty-day sentence for a driving under the influence conviction, and I had to get a court order to get him out of jail so he could attend the funeral. He did, and he provided as much support for me as he was able to, but it wasn't enough. Soft music was played before the service, and when I heard “Clair de Lune,” one of my parents' favorites, I burst into tears. Embarrassed, I left the room and started wandering through the funeral home, sobbing uncontrollably. One of the employees saw me, comforted me, gave me some coffee, and I calmed down a bit; then I walked outside to calm down some more. I remember feeling totally alone and saying to myself, “Why do I always have to be the strong one? Why isn't there someone I can lean on and turn to for strength?” My personal strength, which is always limited, was totally depleted, and I hadn't yet rediscovered my truth. The source of unlimited strength was right there with me all the time, just waiting for me to allow him to help me.

Now that I have reconnected with that source of strength and allowed him to guide me as I walk my unique path, my personal strength has been gradually replaced by spiritual strength. I am still independent, but I no longer pridefully resist allowing other people and God to help me when help is required or desirable. Both God and other people were there to provide love and support when the Piano Player died, and all of their love and support was gratefully received and appreciated. And, although the outer manifestation of strength is the same, the source of the strength is very different. As with power, I had to surrender my personal strength in order to tap into the source and let God work through me. Now I am no longer alone, and the source of my strength is unlimited and always with me. Now I no longer have a need to depend upon others for power or strength, and that truth has brought me the independence I always desired, but never quite achieved. Paradoxically, freedom is one of the rewards for surrendering my will and my life to the care of God, and independence is one aspect of freedom. As with power, it is only through surrendering my limited personal strength that I have been reconnected to the source of unlimited strength that was always mine.

~ JUDGMENT

Judgment is the gift from God that allows me to discern and evaluate different courses of action or thought patterns prior to making choices. Judgment also allows me to establish preferences and choose that which is the most pleasing, useful, or suitable to my needs and desires. Without judgment, I would be unable to discern which man to marry, house to buy, job to take, food to cook for dinner, belief system to follow, and so on. Without judgment, I would be unable to make any kind of choice based on discernment. My choices, when made, would be random and made according to the whim of the moment, and thus subject to change without notice. Unpredictable behavior is usually a sign of a lack of judgment in making life choices.

Judgment thus helps me to identify those activities, experiences, and behaviors that are representative of my true self—who I am and what I believe—and make choices based on that knowledge. Judgment is what helps me determine what fits and what doesn't, whether it be a material possession, profession, creative pursuit, or spiritual belief. Judgment also helps me to identify those actions required to keep me on my unique path and make choices based on that knowledge. Judgment can keep me from taking unnecessary detours that make my spiritual journey longer and more difficult. When my will and my life have been turned over to the care of my guide, judgment becomes wise judgment, or wisdom, and my wise judgments lead to choices that are always toward my highest good. The wisdom to know the difference, as stated in the last line of the Serenity Prayer, is wisdom that comes through allowing God to direct my judgment.

Judgment is impartial and impersonal and is based on observation, not condemnation. Judgment does not put a greater than or less than label on its evaluations, but rather discerns what is the best thing for me at this time and in this situation. Judgment also does not impose right or wrong, guilt or innocence, on its choices. Judgment leads to an informed or guided choice without any implication of judgmentalism. Judgmentalism assumes that if I am right, you are wrong, than when you do not live up to my standards, your behavior is unacceptable. Judgment merely defines my standards and has nothing at all to say about yours. Judgment is, in fact, only about me, not about you, and allows me to choose according to my personal preferences. Preferences are neither right nor wrong; they are preferences, and whether or not you agree with or follow them is not important. Judgment is always self-directed, never other-directed. An observation is made of someone or something relative to my desires and needs, and a choice is made based on that observation.

Judgment also allows me to envision the probable consequences of my choices and factor that vision into my decisions. The disease of alcoholism clouded the Piano Player's judgment, and he almost never considered the consequences of his choices. Certainly, when he chose to drive drunk, he was neither exercising wise judgment nor considering the potential consequences of his actions. Certainly, when I chose to binge on desserts with a family history of diabetes, I was not exercising wise judgment or considering the potential consequences of my actions. Addictions nullify the gift of judgment. Addicts seldom exercise wise judgment, for their choices are self-directed, not God-directed. However, when I, as an addict, make the choice *not* to use my drugs of choice, that choice represents wise judgment from a spiritual perspective, since it is a choice directed toward my highest good. It may be self-directed or God-directed, but, in either case, the gift of judgment has been restored.

Judgment is also variable. I can be God-directed in some aspects of my life and totally self-directed in others. One of my soul sisters is very God-directed in her work as a counselor, and thus capable of exercising wise judgment, but very self-directed in her relationships, where her judgments are not always wise. In fact, most of us, I believe, use wise or God-directed judgment in some areas of our lives and use extremely misdirected judgment in others. This seems to be a contradiction, but it's not. When I turn my will and my life over to God one piece at a time, there are aspects of my life that I am still attached to, an area where my judgment is still self-directed, and the choices I make may not always be in my best interests.

As an infant, my judgments were always God-directed and enabled me to make the choices that resulted in getting my needs met. Later, as with the other gifts, my newly discovered self took over and my connection to the God within was forgotten. And, since I did not rediscover my connection with God until very late in life, for most of my life, the gift of judgment was self-directed. However, judgment is a gift I have always used. Making decisions has never been a problem for me, and I usually am aware of the potential consequences of whatever decision I make. But, as with most addicts, my judgment was extremely distorted whenever my drugs of choice were involved.

Sometimes my self-directed judgments were in my best interests; sometimes they were not. Certainly, refusing to admit I need help when help is needed is an example of self-directed judgment that doesn't lead me to my highest good. Accepting the Skier/Climber's invitation to go to college was certainly in my best worldly interests, as were the decisions to travel and expand my horizons. However, my desire to be and do what he was and did was self-directed judgment based on illusion. I never even considered the possibility that I could be injured or killed while climbing mountains or skiing, nor did I recognize the extent of my own physical limitations. The fact that I wasn't injured or killed doesn't change the truth that my self-directed judgment was faulty.

Obviously, my self-directed judgment relative to running off with the Piano Player was distorted. What adult, using wise judgment, would choose to marry a practicing, late-stage alcoholic? The answer is no one. But, remember, I always followed my heart with my relationships, which means that my judgment was also God-directed, even though, from a worldly point of view, my choice was very unwise, which brings up a peculiar truth about God-directed judgment: what is ultimately for my highest good, spiritually, may sometimes look to be the exact opposite in the eyes of the physical world. Following my heart and running off with the Piano Player may have appeared to be very unwise judgment, but it ultimately led to my reconciliation with God. From a spiritual perspective, that makes it a choice based on very wise judgment indeed.

As I have deepened my relationship with God and have become more and more willing to call on him to guide me, my judgment, in more and more aspects of my life, has become wise, or God-directed. There are still people, places, or things to which I am attached and where self-directed judgment prevails, but these are becoming fewer and fewer. Perhaps the one aspect of my life where self-directed judgment still reigns is in my dreams. I tend to attach to my dreams and become unwilling to release them when they no longer fit who I am or where I am on my unique path.

During my last years with the Piano Player, when he was sober and we were tied down to our bar and I to my job as a technical writer/editor, my dream for us was that, after the bar was paid for, we would sell it and retire to a life of travel, moving from RV park to RV park and playing music and golf at each stop along the way. My dream, of course, required a sober Piano Player; if he was drinking, it was not possible. As part of the manifestation of that dream, I bought (for us) a three-quarter-ton pickup and a thirty-one-foot travel trailer. There was only one problem with the dream.It was *my* dream for *us* and, had God been directing my judgment, I might not have been so eager to spend the money for the truck and trailer. Of course, he wasn't. Ultimately, the dream was shattered when the Piano Player went into his final and fatal relapse. Still, I refused to let go of either the dream *or* the pickup and trailer.

After the Piano Player died, I still clung to this dream. However, I knew I couldn't handle hitching and unhitching a trailer by myself, so I decided to sell the pickup and trade the trailer for a twenty-seven-foot motor home, at considerable financial loss. Again, my judgment was self-directed, not God-directed, for God would have suggested that I wait a bit to see if *my* dream for *us* fit *me*. Of course, it didn't. I went on one long Canadian trip with the motor home, and soon discovered that the dream did *not* fit me at all. What fit me as a sixty-year-old single woman was a sporty little car and motel rooms or cabins with showers and cooking facilities, not RV parks and campgrounds. So I sold the motor home, too, at considerable financial loss. Because my judgment was distorted by my attachment to the dream, my self-directed choices were not in my best interests.

A similar situation developed later involving the Songteller and a dream I created around us being together. The substance of the dream came from God, and I still believe in it today. What I attached myself to was a very specific form of the dream, which distorted my judgment relative to whose job it was to make the dream happen. Obviously, if it's a dream authored by God, it's his job, not mine, to create its manifestation in reality. I take my instructions, or marching orders, from God, *not* the other way around! But that's not what I did. I created this neat little picture of *how* and *when* this was going to happen and tried to make it happen, not just once, but many times. It wasn't until I released the form of the dream that my judgment became God-directed and my choices became directed toward our highest good. Now, the form of our relationship is no longer important; what matters is that we are still friends today. That truth is in the best interests of us both.

~ Release

Release is the gift that allows me to let go of unhealthy emotional attachments—to people, places, things, thoughts, feelings, and behaviors. Most of us form emotional attachments in life—to parents, siblings, spouses, children, pets, friends, home towns, or favorite places or activities. There are as many people, places, and things to become attached to as there are people, places, and things! A healthy emotional attachment is sourced in love, and, although the loss of that which we are attached to would be painful, it would be bearable and ultimately could be accepted. For me, an emotional attachment becomes unhealthy when I am so fearful of losing the object that I no longer enjoy having it. An emotional attachment to something or someone becomes unhealthy when using, doing, or being with the object causes me pain, yet I continue to do, use, or be with this thing or person. Any thing, any place, or any person that I can't live without is a thing, place, or person that I am attached to in an unhealthy way. Any and all addictive substances or activities are unhealthy emotional attachments, and release is the gift from God that allows me to turn over the control of addictions to God, as required by steps one, two, and three of the twelve steps.

Release is, in fact, a requirement for working the steps. Without release, I would not be able to surrender to God (step three), become entirely ready to have him remove my character defects (step six), or attain the forgiveness of self and others required to make amends (step nine). Release is a key requirement for just about any process designed to replace self-defeating behaviors with more positive ones. Release is an absolute necessity on my road home, for before I can follow my guide, I must release my false pride and allow God to replace it with humility. This illustrates the magic of release when that which is let go of is turned over to God. Anything I release to God will always be replaced by something much better, designed to lead me to my highest good. Note that I said *always*—that is an unquestionable spiritual truth. That which is released, though it may not be replaced immediately, will be replaced by something of greater spiritual worth.

Unhealthy emotional attachment is a phenomenon I know very well. My unhealthy emotional attachment to excessive quantities of certain foods was with me most of my life, and it wasn't until I began recovery in twelve-step programs that I was able to use the gift of release to turn over my obsessions to God. I was also emotionally attached to my parents in an unhealthy way, as they were to each other and to me. Ours was a very enmeshed trio, and my dad, especially, was very afraid I would hurt myself or that he would somehow lose me. As a result, I became very emotionally dependent upon them, even as I consciously exercised independence by moving to Idaho. Even 1,500 miles away, I was still dependent. I wrote them a letter every week and called them every holiday for twenty-five years, not because I wanted to, but because I felt that I should. Final release did not come until many years after their deaths, and at least one event was not released until I wrote about it ("Forgiveness").

Release can be immediate or it can be a process. It can also be deceptive. Oftentimes, I can believe I have released my unhealthy attachment to a person when I really haven't. I then immediately move it to another person. I refer to this as my emotional hook, and I planted the hook still attached to my father into every male in my life that was willing to receive it. Of course, all of my spouses were, or they wouldn't have been spouses. The Skier/Climber allowed me to become emotionally dependent on him and, as with my parents, physical and legal independence did not bring emotional release. In many ways, I became more dependent on him *after* our divorce than I had before. I tried planting the hook in the Marlboro man (see "Fear") but he refused to keep it. Final release from the Skier/Climber only came when I moved the hook to the Piano Player. He, being an addict, gratefully accepted it and then planted one of his own, which I also accepted. Of all of my spouses, he was the closest in personality to my dad, so release from him became literally impossible.

Even with his death, the hook remained until I found myself another potential recipient in the Songteller. Fortunately for us both, he also refused to accept it and the double-pronged hook that attached me both to the Piano Player and my dad was eventually released to God. This assures me that, when I'm ready, I will have the opportunity to co-create a healthy relationship, a spiritual partnership, with a man chosen by God to help me heal and lead me to my highest good. Could it be the Songteller? Possibly, but not today.

Today, I am still in what some call the void and I call the in-between place. The in-between place is sort of a spiritual purgatory without the aspect of punishment. It's the place in between where I was when I released my attachment and where God ultimately wants me to be. While in the in-between place, I prepare myself for the good that is coming but not yet here, the replacement of that which has been released. Sometimes my stay in the in-between place is short-lived or nonexistent. When I finally released my attachment to certain foods, I was immediately gifted with the relief from the compulsion to eat them. Sometimes my stay in the in-between place lasts for many years. My transition from the release of my life as it was at the time of the Piano Player's death to the acceptance of my present God-centered life has been more than seven years, and my in-between place for intimate relationship is ongoing as I write.

This, of course, is only one example of how release can free me from enslavement to unhealthy attachments. I can have an unhealthy attachment to negative and self-defeating thoughts and feelings. Release allows me to turn such thoughts and feelings over to God and replace them with affirmations, or positive self-talk. I personally believe that release of self-defeating thoughts and feelings must be followed by a positive replacement or the void created by the release may easily be taken over again by the same thoughts and feelings. Conversely, affirming positive change without first releasing the negative also seems a little futile. I know, from personal experience, that God can't take away what I refuse to let go of, nor will he bring me something better before I let go of what I am attached to now. This is a perfect lead-in to a story often told by a minister friend of mine to demonstrate this point.

Once there was a little girl whose most prized possession was a necklace of plastic pearls. She valued this necklace above all of her other possessions, even wore the pearls while she slept. One night, while tucking her into bed, her father asked her to give him the pearls. "No, Daddy, I can't do that. I can't bear not to have them and won't give them up to you or anyone else."

Time passed. Several more times, the father asked his daughter to give him the pearls, and each time the girl refused. Then, one night, when he came to tuck her in bed, he found his daughter in tears, clutching in her hands what was left of the strand of plastic pearls. A playmate had accidentally grabbed them and destroyed the necklace. "Will you give me the pearls now?" her father asked. Tearfully, she handed him the remains of the plastic pearl necklace, at which point he reached into his pocket and handed his daughter a long, slim jewelry case. "Open it, my child," he said. Inside the box was a beautiful necklace of real pearls. "I've been waiting to give these to you for a long time," the father said. "But before I could give them to you, you had to be willing to let go of what you had."

That story perfectly illustrates how using the gift of release works. God cannot give us the good we are entitled to as his children until we release to him what we're holding on to that is blocking the way. Sometimes, when we wait too long or hold on too hard, the matter is taken out of our hands, as it was for me and the Piano Player. When it's time to move, I will be moved, but release is still a choice. I can hang on to what was, or I can let go and allow God to move me forward on my unique path. My choice now is to use the gift of release and move forward, with my guide always beside me, directing my forward progress.

~ SEXUALITY

Sexuality is the life force, the ultimate source of all creation. Sexuality fuels and fires passion and inspires all creative actions and events. Sexuality is as much a part of creating a great symphony, a stirring novel, or a priceless painting as it is a part of creating a human life. Sexuality is vital to creating a vibrant, healthy, productive, meaningful, and God-guided life.

Sex is an expression of sexuality, but sexuality is not sex. There are many ways to express sexuality, and sex is simply one of them. The life force is exactly that—the force that creates life and keeps it going. It is present from the time of inception, long before one develops sexually. And it is present until the day one leaves, which may be long after the body has stopped functioning sexually. Babies exude sexuality, as expressed through their passion for and involvement in life. So do the eighty-, ninety-, or 100-something folks who are alert, charismatic, vibrant, and still very much involved in the process of being alive.

I once attended the memorial service for a woman I had only met a couple of times. I knew of her through mutual friends, but I barely knew her personally at all. Yet, the two times I had been with her made such a profound and positive impression on me that I felt like I had known her forever. Sexuality burst forth from her sparkling blue eyes and evidenced itself in her passion for living her life as fully as her aging body would allow. Her sexuality, the life force within, burned brightly in her until the day she left this life.

So I repeat, sexuality is *not* only the force behind sexual desire. I repeat this truth because too many of us falsely believe sexuality and sex are one and the same. As spirituality and religion are different, so are sexuality and sex. Religion and sex are but practices that express spirituality and sexuality, respectively, in our daily lives. One has been created to propagate spiritual life and the other to propagate human life. Unfortunately, the same unhappy result may be true for both. Just as religion can lose sight of its roots, can lose the connection to true spirituality, so can sex lose its connection to sexuality. Both spirituality and sexuality are gifts from God that are God. God is love, life, and creativity, and spirituality and sexuality are love, life, and creativity as well. Losing the God connection reduces both religion and sex to physical practices. Both may become highly ritualistic and lose their depth and meaning. They may still be physically and emotionally pleasant but are spiritually bereft. And the reason is very simple. Without a connection to God, to the great creator and giver of life, I am no longer alive. I am dead. I may be breathing, walking, and talking, but that is all I am doing. When the fire that fuels life is gone, I am gone. And sexuality is the fire that fuels life.

Again, babies exude sexuality, which is a very natural state. As we grow and develop sexually, we are taught to control or repress our natural desires. The natural curiosity of young children about the differences between their bodies may be distorted and repressed. Natural urges, too, are repressed and, eventually, sex goes underground. Sex is something we learn about from our peers, not our parents. It becomes a source of ridicule, something dirty and sinful instead of what God intended it to be—a supremely beautiful act of creation. And, as sex is repressed, so is sexuality. The life force is subverted and submerged.

Please do not misinterpret what I am saying here. I am not advocating promiscuity or that people run around naked and fornicate on street corners. Too many teenage pregnancies and the world's overgrowing population evidence the consequences of immature and irresponsible sexual behavior. What I am saying is that it is sex, not sexuality, that requires self-discipline and restraint, which is very different from repression and control. The sexual revolution in our society created exactly the opposite result. The sexual revolution liberated sex but not sexuality, without self-discipline or restraint, and the result was sexual and emotional chaos. Without sexuality, without the God connection, sex is reduced to a series of physical sensations—very pleasant but not very spiritually meaningful. And the emotional havoc created by physical coupling without a spiritual foundation for true intimacy has been nothing short of devastating for many of us.

Our society seems to have become obsessed with technique, performance, and orgasms (both faked and real). If you doubt this, pick up any issue of any magazine directed towards men, women, or families, and you will find a byline telling you how to have "great sex." Even *Modern Maturity*, the magazine for those of us over fifty, has had "great sex" as its theme. Which is fine, if one recognizes that there is more to great sex than just great technique and knowing where the hot spots are. Without sexuality, sex is, as one author described it, aerobic exercise. Without sexuality, sex can be used to control, manipulate, terrorize, or tempt and can bring out or create every emotional demon and wound present in humanity. With sexuality, with the God connection, sex can be the most beautiful, wonderful, ecstatic, glorious, and creative experience possible for a man and a woman, with or without great technique.

I have already shared with you that I threw out God with the religion whose dogma I could not live perfectly. So it should come as no surprise that my sexual experience was not connected to my sexuality. I am not exactly sure when that disconnect occurred, possibly the same time I disconnected from my spirituality. Or maybe it happened earlier, I don't know. The false equation, sex equals love, was a belief I had when I met the Rescuer, and it was a belief I carried with me through all my marriages. Sex was in and sexuality was out, which means the life force did not fuel my other creative acts either. No life force, no passion, no inspired creativity, as you will find out when you read on.

Since sex equaled love, lots of sex meant lots of love. Right? Not exactly. The Skier/Climber is the man who said he didn't know what love was—but we had lots of sex. My outdoor life was a very physical life in all ways, and I continued that precedent after my divorce. Only then, it was with multiple partners, most of whom I perceived as "safe." "Safe" meant only physical sex, nothing more; nothing emotional or spiritual. But, the one thing that has apparently always been able to reach my soul, to stir my repressed sexuality, is music. The life force definitely moves through me when I sing or dance, and music that touches my soul awakens my sexuality as well. Those sexual partners with whom I connected through music were definitely *not* safe, nor was I safe for them. The Piano Player was one of these, and there were others as well. And, for a time, with him, sexuality and sex were reunited, but that's as far as it went. In most other areas of my life, I was still disconnected and dead.

It was not until I began walking with my guide that I gradually reclaimed my sexuality, and my life, and found the only equation that is truth. God equals love, and sexuality, the God force within, fuels a lot more than just sexual desire. Whereas before I may have only experienced my sexuality through sex, now I feel it, recognize it as the life force, and express it in many different ways, none of which is explicitly sexual. I express my sexuality through my music, my writing, my photography, and any other creative aspect of my life. I can express my sexuality through hiking, running, skiing, cooking, any activity to which creativity can be applied. I can also certainly express it in bed, and I enjoy doing that very much, under the proper circumstances. But that is not my sole outlet, and neither is sex without sexuality and love a desirable pastime anymore. I can be sexual, I can feel my sexuality, but I choose not to act on it without the God connection firmly in place.

I can be greatly attracted to a man, care deeply about him, become sexually aroused by being near him, share a bed with him, and *not* come on to him when doing so would cause him (or me) the pain of guilt. That is a choice I am able to make because I do care about him, because I am choosing to practice sexual restraint, and because I practice sexual self-care. Again, sex is what needs to be treated wisely and responsibly, not sexuality. The life force created us and creates our humanness, and it was intended to inspire us to live passionately and creatively. The purpose of God's creations is to create in whatever ways we are gifted to create. Children, books, poems, songs, inventions, new medical treatments, recipes, art, paintings, architecture, woodworking, handcrafts, sewing—all of these plus a million more are works of creation. And sexuality is the God force that brings life into them all, and into those of us who create them.

~ Passion

Passion is the gift of feelings, emotions, and presence. With passion, I live; without passion, I only exist or survive. I read or heard somewhere that too many of us go through life as if we were rehearsing for the real thing. A life lived with passion is not a rehearsal. It is a ten-curtain-call performance!

How do I define passion? Passion is both wildly exuberant and quietly dedicated. Passion is spontaneous, flexible, self-disciplined, and orderly. Passion is sensual, sexual, and always grounded in the spiritual. To live my life passionately means that I am fully present, fully aware, fully centered in the moment. I am fully present physically, mentally, emotionally, spiritually, and creatively. I am present both with myself and with you. I am not physically close, but emotionally distant. I am not mentally alert, but spiritually bereft; life is not a head trip. I am not creating a future based on a projection of fear. My mind is not 1,000 miles away or even twenty feet away. I am here, and I am awake. I am not lost in a recreation of past events, nor am I fantasizing about the future. These are places I may need to visit from time to time, to learn from or to create my dreams, but I do not dwell in those places. As the Songteller says in one of his songs, "It's good to seek old times again and visit with the past/But don't try and stay too long, your welcome may not last." He is singing of the past, but the words apply equally as well to the future.

When I have passion, all of my senses are fine-tuned and my mind is alert. I do not simply listen, I hear. And if I'm really spiritually present, I listen with my heart and hear beyond the words to what is really being said. I do not simply observe, I see, not only the events of the moment but the big picture as well. I do not simply taste, I savor. I do not simply touch, I caress. I do not simply smell,

I delight in fragrance and aroma. When I am with you, you are the focus of my attention and gaze. When I am creating, I lose myself in the act of creating. Time stands still. I am not easily distracted or sidetracked. I am totally and completely present, experiencing life as it happens.

Babies personify passion in its purest form. They know neither past nor future. They are totally absorbed in the immediacy of the present, and they are highly sensual. Then, as we grow, we are taught to curb or deny our passion, to learn self-control. Some of us are taught to always be in control of our passion, of our emotions. Most of us, including me, were taught self-control and not self-discipline. Self-control stifles passion. Self-discipline allows passion free reign but within appropriate boundaries. Self-control stifles anger and creates rage or depression. Self-discipline feels anger and releases it in a way that does no physical or emotional harm to anyone.

I have always had a passion for life, but I have not always lived my life with passion. By that I mean that life is very precious to me and I have always aspired to live a long time. But what I called living was really existing or surviving; in fact, I viewed myself as a survivor. I was rarely present, usually lost in fantasy or magical thinking. I allowed my fears to dictate what I did or did not do. I was never fully present emotionally with anyone, not even myself, and I had no spiritual foundation, no source to fire me with passion. I lived by doing, not being, but what I did was done without true passion. Passion creates a depth and intensity and level of commitment that I never had for anything I did. It simply wasn't there. It couldn't be, because I did not allow myself to feel my feelings, to be fully present for all the sensations of life. Because I did not learn how to cope with emotional pain, I medicated myself to dull the pain. I did this primarily with food, but also with sex, nicotine, caffeine, and alcohol. And in deadening my senses to feeling pain, I deadened them to feeling anything else.

They say that emotional growth stops at the age we begin using our drug of choice. If that is true, I stopped growing emotionally in infancy. I do know that emotional recovery has been the hardest process for me. It has taken me the longest time and has required the most arduous work. To learn how to live and not merely survive, I had to learn how to feel my feelings. To learn how to feel my feelings, I had to allow myself to feel them—all of them. Love, fear, joy, peace, pain, anger, hate, sadness—all of them. That meant no more medicating, no more use of my drugs of choice in a compulsive way. One by one, they have been eliminated—sugar and other binge foods, nicotine, caffeine, alcohol, and soulless sex. Little by little, I am learning how to feel my feelings, own them, and allow them to pass through me. And with time I have learned how to go back into the painful and fearful events of my past, open the wounds where feelings were buried alive, own and feel the buried feelings, and release them so the wounds can heal properly. Feelings buried alive never die; it doesn't matter what the feeling is. Buried love can be as damaging as buried anger or pain. To be able to live with passion, all must be purged and healed. To be able to love with passion, all wounds must be opened and released for healing by God's love and forgiveness.

I have struggled to live my life with passion, even after I began daily committing to live my life fully, passionately, lovingly, compassionately, forgivingly, generously, humbly, with an open mind and heart, and always in the service of my guide. I also committed to have the courage to take risks and to accept life's challenges and to moving away from my past and into my future by living as much as possible with God in the present. This is, of course, the key to living a life filled with passion. The closer I walk with God, who is found only in the present, the more passionate my life experiences have become.

These are my commitments, but I do not yet follow them as I hope to one day. To do so requires both mental self-discipline and emotional courage, and I sometimes lack either or both. When I am with others, I am very aware when I begin to leave, to shut down, or otherwise not be present. But when I am alone, it is not always so clear. My mind flits back and forth among past, present, and future, and sometimes I get stuck too long in the past or future.

I am also not always willing and eager to feel uncomfortable feelings like fear and sadness when they come to me and will try to avoid them, pretend they are not there. This almost always creates tension, and eventually they come out anyway, with a burst of emotional release. Resistance only postpones the inevitable.

A few years after his death, I was guided to go back into time and watch a video that was taken at a family reunion the Piano Player and I attended and played music for. The reunion was held about four months before he died, and one could see in the video how very, very sick he was. But I was called back to see how very, very sick *I* was. The Nadine I saw in that video looked and sounded like me, but beyond that, there was little resemblance to the Nadine I see when I look in a mirror today. The Nadine in the video is a zombie, a walking, talking, singing dead person. My resurrection from death is one of the miracles of my life and recovery, one I thank God for every day. I still aspire to live a long life, but not as a survivor or a passive observer. I am reclaiming the gift of passion, and it is truly a precious gift.

One of the greatest lessons in this process has come through my music. My musical training was in the classics, and that is the music I have used to share my gift since reclaiming it. Then I found a new passion—modern romantic music, songs that speak of love and require the passionate expression of love and the feeling of love, songs that absolutely must be played from the heart. When I first began learning this music, I sent a tape to the Songteller and asked him for his opinion. Well, he gave it to me, and his response was not at all what I expected. He told me, candidly and courageously, that he didn't feel anything—that there was no heart in my playing. He could not feel love and was "not impressed."

I was shattered by his candor, but I also knew it was absolutely true. I had, for years, been hiding behind a mask—the "I think I know how to do this" mask sourced in false pride that kept my mind closed to the messages from my heart. And after the pain subsided, I realized that what had been shattered was not me, but the mask. That I had been freed to be open to a new way of both playing and loving and that I had much to relearn in both areas. Now I understand that passion requires me to strip away all the "I think I knows" that keep me from being open to experiencing life as it happens. And this, of course, is just another lesson in replacing false pride with humility.

~ Creativity

Each of us carries within us the ability to create our own lives through thoughts, words, and actions. This is the universal gift of creativity, given to us by the great creator. All of us have this gift, but most of us either do not know that we have it or do not consciously use it. Instead of committing to and following our dreams, we just let life happen and wonder why our dreams do not come true. Instead of consciously striving to create a life sourced in love and filled with joy and serenity, we allow fear to chart our course and live instead with anger, hatred, negativity, cynicism, doubt, despair, boredom, apathy, jealousy, rage, and chaos. Instead of working with God and co-creating a true and meaningful life, one that follows our unique path, we work against him and wonder why we get lost, why there is an emptiness within that never quite gets filled. It is one thing to have the gift of creativity; it is quite another to own it and be able to use it wisely.

I believe that what I see or expect out of life is what I will get from life. If I view the world negatively and cynically, that is the kind of world I will create for myself. If I believe everyone is out to get me, cheat me, or rob me, my life will continually confirm this. If I believe myself to be vulnerable to sickness and poor health, or if I would rather deal with physical pain than emotional pain, my life will probably reflect this as well. So I strive to create positives, not negatives. I do not believe that people will take advantage of me, and, mostly, they do not. I view life as an adventure, not a tragedy, and I have had few tragic losses. I dislike being physically ill, view myself as being in good health, and almost always am. And when I am not, when a tooth abscesses or my gall bladder attacks me, I look for the lesson in the experience, take corrective action, and move through it as quickly as possible.

But these are only aspects of life. What about our dreams, hopes, and aspirations? And how does self-creation merge with my acceptance of God's guidance? At first glance, that seems like a contradiction, but it is not. In fact, it is the only way it works. Without the source, something very important is missing.

For me, this is how the process works. I believe that my dreams are offered to me by God—all of them, even those that bring me unexpected results, a lesson I had not planned to learn. God also offers me relationship assignments, very special people to love and to work with and learn through and from, sometimes as teacher and sometimes as student, usually as both simultaneously. I also believe that a dream or an assignment is not offered to me unless that which is offered is possible or attainable. This separates dreams from fantasies, because fantasy is never attainable. Seeing something as fantasy, by definition, makes it unattainable in reality. My desire to co-create a healthy relationship with a male soul friend is a dream; however, choosing Harrison Ford as my partner would, most likely, turn my dream into a fantasy!

So first, God offers me a dream or a relationship assignment. Since I have free will, I can either choose to accept or reject it. If I am really connected to my source, if I am following my heart and truly allowing God to guide me, if it feels right to my inner spirit, I will accept the dream or assignment immediately. If I am *not* connected to my source, if I do not yet trust my inner guidance, or if I am afraid to follow my heart, I may resist it. It may be that I have to clear out some emotional baggage before I can accept it, particularly if the dream involves a relationship. It may also be that I become so enthralled by the dream that I push God aside and try to force it to happen.

So I may move back and forth from acceptance to rejection—yes, I can do this, no, I can't. I call this indecision waffling. As long as I waffle, as long as I hesitate for any reason, God and I are both stalled. The universe cannot move until I first *accept* and then *commit* to the dream or assignment. Do you see the difference? Acceptance says yes, I will do this. Thy will be done. Commitment says not only do I *agree* to do it, but it is my *intention* to do it. I really do desire this dream or want this relationship in my life. My will and God's will are then in tune, in concert. God and I have come to a meeting of minds and hearts.

Now comes the tricky part. In order for the dream or assignment to be created, I must now give it back to God. If I do not do that, if I try to do it alone, I will either not succeed or the result will be without spirit or soul. Surrendering the dream back to God allows him to orchestrate its creation because he is the only one that can. He sees the big picture, how it all has to fit together. I only see my part in whatever my dream entails. Surrendering the dream or relationship assignment back to God allows him to sequence events in proper order, to perfect the timing of events, to give me the tools and experiences I need to clear the way so that I am ready for events as they unfold, to show me what I can do to prepare, and to perform the miracles required to manifest the dream in reality. For any dream requires both preparation and miracles—the "lucky break" that gets me where I need to be when I need to be there, or the shift in perception that opens a door or a heart. Humility has taught me that the preparation is my job and the miracles are God's.

For most of my life, I did not use my creative power wisely. Since I was a strong-willed, do-it-myself person, I tried to make things happen in my life and sometimes did. But without a guide, without a connection to the source, the things I made happen usually did not turn out as I had hoped or dreamed. To be sure, I learned much from these experiences, but some of the lessons were very painful. And the one thing I did not learn was how to create my own life, how to be me. For many years, I did not want to, but even when I wanted to, I no longer knew how.

It has only been recently that I have begun to use my creative power to create my own life experiences under the guidance of God. Thus, I do not have a lot of experience to share in creating life experiences. There are many such dreams in various stages of the process, but none that have fully and tangibly manifested in reality. I do know that in each instance the process is working. I am being guided and led to the footwork required to manifest the dreams in reality.

The desire to open my heart is one dream that is very near completion. When I committed to opening my heart and allowed God to guide me, I was led to places I needed to go to open, purge, and heal old emotional wounds. These places are as diverse as a Christian church, certain mountains in the Canadian Rockies, the west coast beaches of Vancouver Island, a fiftieth anniversary celebration, and my basement. Opening my heart and keeping it open is a process in itself, one that is never fully complete. I believe my heart is open now to most people most of the time, but my new position has not been thoroughly tested by someone I deeply love. Also, as I wrote earlier, an open heart is not terribly effective when paired with a closed mind. So my mind has to be open as well for my dreams to be fulfilled.

So far I have been speaking about creating life experiences, our universal creative gift. But the same process applies to our personal creative gifts, those unique talents that are part of who I am, my true self. The process is perfectly designed for fulfilling personal creative dreams as well. After all, if our creative talents are God-given gifts, it only makes sense that he would want us to use them and inspire us to do so! The problem, of course, is that we do not always understand what the source is and use the process to create it. For sure, I did not, not for most of my life. But I do now, and I do have some experience to share that shows how the process works.

Personal creativity comes in many forms. My hair stylist is a genius with cut and color—those are two of her personal creative gifts. I have known creative cooks, a creative artist and bookmaker, creative mentors, creative engineers, creative woodworkers, a creative piano player, a creative songwriter and guitarist, creative pastors, a creative organist, a creative realtor, even a creative bartender. In each case, their creations are sourced in love. In most cases, they recognize and give credit to the source as God. Many of us do neither. Our creative gifts are not credited to God and get lost somewhere along the way. Or we own them but believe we are the source and try to do it all ourselves. Neither follows the plan; neither allows me to be my true self and follow my unique path.

My personal creative gifts are artistic. I can draw and paint, play the piano, sing, I have natural rhythm, and I can write. And for most of my life, these gifts were discounted and devalued to match my opinion of my true self. All but writing were unused for many years, and the source was certainly never acknowledged or called upon. As a young adult, I'm not sure I even knew who the source was. I just knew I was gifted in these areas and was expected to do these things and do them well. So as soon as I was no longer required to do this, I quit. Besides, there were too many gifts, and I wasn't interested enough in any one talent to pursue it exclusively. I was a jack of all creative trades and master of none. I always envied those people who were clearly called to do one certain thing and did it. The Piano Player was born to play barroom piano—period. That was what Julia Cameron would call his "vein of gold." The

Songteller is a fine singer, guitarist, and songwriter, but his vein of gold is singing ballads, for that is where his heart can be felt most readily. Musically, my vein of gold is playing quiet romantic music that requires artistry in touch rather than expert technique. This is the creative gift that was devalued, cast aside, disowned, and went essentially unused for nearly forty years.

With the Piano Player, I played and sang, but it was his music we performed together, not mine. A year after he died, I was copying a tape of my music that I had made seventeen years earlier for a friend who told me she liked quiet, classical music. Suddenly, possibly for the first time in my life, I listened with my heart and realized how valuable a gift I had thrown away. I remember I stood in my kitchen and wept, ashamed and afraid that it was too late to reclaim my gift, that my finger strength and touch were gone. My dream was that I could resurrect this gift well enough to share with others, and I began to play again. My dream came from God, I accepted it and committed to it, turned it back over to him, and my gift was restored. I play publicly again and have created tapes for others. That I was able to reclaim this gift and share it after so long is truly a miracle and proof enough for me that the process works.

Chapter VII

THE REWARDS

NOW that I have some experience walking the road home under the direction of my guide, I have come to realize that there are certain rewards that come from practicing these principles in all my affairs, as required by step twelve. At first, I considered these rewards to be gifts from God, but I later realized that they really aren't gifts because I have to *do* something to receive them. These rewards are the direct result of accepting the invitation inherent in the steps to initiate and sustain an ever-deepening personal relationship with God and turning my will and my life over to his care. The rewards are never truly attainable or sustainable without having taken that action.

The rewards are freedom, serenity, joy, hope, and miracles. I may have fleeting periods of freedom, joy, serenity, hope, and miracles in my life without having God's presence in my life, but these periods will be short-lived and never totally satisfying. True and long-lasting freedom, joy, serenity, hope, and the many miracles of my life only come when God is in complete charge and I no longer resist his direction. Practicing the principles and minimizing the road hazards thus ensure that my God-given gifts are fully utilized and my God-given rewards are ever present.

~ FREEDOM

Freedom is the state of being unrestrained, unhampered, unafraid, at ease with myself, my life, and the world. Freedom is a spiritually grounded state of mind. I may be physically restrained and still be mentally, emotionally, or spiritually free. Such is the case with many who survive horrible physical experiences, prisoners of war or concentration camp survivors. Or I may be physically free and in mental, emotional, or spiritual bondage. Such is the case with one who depends upon external sources, people, places, events, or things, to fill the well, to provide the things that must come from within. Such was the case with me for most of my life.

Freedom requires an open mind and open heart. A closed mind is not free to explore, to challenge, to innovate, to expand, to create beyond prescribed boundaries. A closed heart is not free to feel love, compassion, forgiveness, or a true sense of community, of spiritual connection to the divine within any or all of creation. Any time there is any kind of self-imposed restriction on mind or heart, freedom has been lessened.

Freedom is a manifestation of faith in action. Freedom is loving unconditionally without expectation of love in return. Freedom is being, doing, or creating anything without expectation and attachment to a specific outcome. Freedom is absolutely knowing that no matter what happens in my life, to me or to those I love, God is there with me to help meet the challenge, and the outcome will ultimately bring me closer to my highest good. Freedom is owning my power and not allowing other people, events, or circumstances to determine my state of mind or feelings. Freedom is not being chained to the past by regret or guilt or to the future by worry or fear. Freedom is not being chained to others through resentment, anger, jealousy, or hatred. Freedom is knowing and accepting myself, all parts of me, and knowing that who I am is lovable and deserving of the best I can attain. Freedom is not having to have my sense of self worth validated through the acceptance and praise of others. Freedom is knowing my truth and following my heart. Freedom is the acceptance of reality and the power to change my life. Freedom is knowing that I have the power to create my life by choosing how I perceive it—by choosing my thoughts, words, attitudes, beliefs, behaviors, actions, path, and fellow travelers. True freedom is allowing my guide to direct me in making the choices that lead to my highest good.

Free will is the basis for freedom, and free will is a gift from God. Free will allows me to choose my perceptions, my attitudes, my behaviors, my actions. Free will determines whether or not I am truly free or chained to the handicaps, the road hazards, that are ever present on the road home. The greatest challenge to freedom is fear and all of its corollaries—hate, anger, shame, false pride, guilt, doubt, remorse, regret, resentment, despair, and devastation. Freedom comes from being sourced in love, from being spiritually guided, from following my heart. Paradoxically, true freedom only comes through humbly surrendering my will and my life to God and aligning my will with his. Surrendering my will to God then empowers me, gives me the freedom to make the correct choices, choices sourced in love. Choices sourced in love are always for my highest good, and that is God's will for us all.

As a corollary to the gift of free will, freedom, too, is evident at birth. Certainly, babies are not physically and emotionally free—they are totally dependant on their parents for physical care and emotional nurturing—but they are free to choose their responses, as any frustrated parent of an unhappy, inconsolable, crying infant knows. And they are free to be who they are and act accordingly until this freedom is eroded by parental restraints. To be sure, freedom has to be tempered by discipline, but too many times discipline is not discipline but control. Discipline allows me to be free within certain prescribed boundaries. Discipline says, "Yes, you can do that, but under these guidelines." Discipline tells me, "Yes, you can safely cross the street, but only after carefully looking both ways for cars." Control shackles me with set behaviors, inhibition, and fear. Control tells me *never* to cross the street without looking both ways, or I could be killed. Discipline says, "Do, but do it safely." Control says, "Do *not,*" and introduces the idea of fear. I have often wondered how different our world would be if children were taught to respect potential hazards instead of to fear them. But that is not the way it works. We all learn fear, and we all teach fear. And the fears I embrace as a child stay with me until I choose to view things differently as an adult. Free will brings me free choice, and I can freely choose to replace fear with love.

For most of my life, my freedom was impaired by a collection of fears that kept me from living the kind of life I believed in. Fear of abandonment, fear of not being loved, fear of not meeting your expectations, fear of falling, fear of physical harm and death, fear of water, fear of public speaking, fear of performing, fear of intimacy, fear of sharing myself with you, fear of failure, fear of success—all of these fears, and many more, stole my freedom from me for as long as I allowed them to. Some of these fears were passed on to me by my parents; others I learned myself through life experiences. But it matters not where they came from. Until I consciously decided to own, face, and release my fears, the freedom and independence I so admired in others would never be mine. Until I reclaimed the gift of freedom by surrendering my will and my life to God, I could not fully embrace and share my true self, nor could I freely walk my unique path. Freedom then allows me to be me and to do God's will and his service without the restraints created by fear.

It has taken me a very long time to reclaim my freedom and to understand what true freedom is all about. Even with God as my guide, even with my commitment to follow his direction, I am still hampered, held back, by refusing to let go of old fears so that he can remove them. Fear still strikes me when I play my soul music publicly as a soloist. Fear still haunts me when I get up to speak before a group of people. And even though I know that who and what I am is lovable and others will not leave me if I reveal myself to them, even though I know and believe all those things, fear still grips my heart when I choose to expose my deepest thoughts and vulnerabilities to one who is physically and emotionally close to me. Still, the fears are lessening, diminishing, and my sense of freedom is, at the same time, growing as my spiritual world expands and my relationship with God deepens and strengthens. The more I turn over to him, including my fears, the freer I have become. Every time I choose to embrace love, not fear, my sense of freedom grows and deepens.

One of the spiritual tools I use for divine guidance is medicine cards, which are a Native American spiritual practice. Native Americans believe in the power and medicine of animal guides. They further believe that each of us has animals that are our primary guides, animals that we strongly identify with. The Songteller identifies strongly with the coyote; he used the coyote as a logo and in the name of his bands when he was performing.

My personal animal guides are the deer and the eagle. I have often attributed my pacifist nature and my dislike for hunting and killing to the fact that I saw the Walt Disney movie *Bambi* as a young child. The deer represents gentleness and personifies unconditional love. The deer encourages me to show my loving nature to others through gentleness and caring and keeps me centered and grounded. The eagle represents spirit, my connection to the divine. The eagle personifies freedom and encourages me to soar, to reach out, to fly as far and as high as I can, to be the very best that I can be, to chase my dreams and follow my heart.

It is through the eagle that I have found my free spirit, the freedom to soar—but not without the deer. The deer's unconditional love and the eagle's free spirit complement each other. The deer's love supports the eagle in her flight and allows her to fly high and free but also to land gently and smoothly back on earth. Without the deer's love and support, the eagle may fly too high, too fast and end up crashing. I know because I've done it many times in my life. Carly Simon sings a song that includes the line "...makin' me just a little too free..." and that is what I think of when the eagle tries to fly alone. My freedom to soar high and land gently has come only with God as the wind beneath my wings.

~ Serenity

Serenity is inner peace that radiates outward. It is a calm knowing, an acceptance that who I am is wonderful and all is right in my world. Serenity is God's reward to me for accepting him as my guide, for allowing him to chart the course of my life. Serenity is my reward to me for doing the work required to clear away the beliefs, attitudes, and behaviors that destroy it.

Serenity, too, is natural to an infant. There is nothing as serene as a newborn babe lying peacefully in his mother's arms. But serenity, too, is quickly lost. Serenity is lost to competition, when we are taught that outcomes are more important than actions, that winning is more important than how we play the game. Serenity is lost to false pride when being better than or richer than or brighter than requires us to mask our true selves with a persona of external accomplishment. Serenity is lost to the fear of inadequacy and shame that is the foundation of this behavior. Serenity is lost to perfectionism, to having to be the best, the brightest, the prettiest, or the sexiest. Serenity is lost to judgmentalism, to being less than or greater than someone else, to superimposing our values, beliefs, and attitudes on others and expecting them to measure up. Serenity is lost to addiction, to trying to fill an internal spiritual need with external stimulants. Serenity is lost to the chaos that surrounds addicts and the insanity of their lives. Serenity is lost to denial, to stifling anger, pain, guilt, fear, regret, and resentment, instead of feeling these feelings and releasing them. Serenity is lost when my outer world becomes more important to me than my inner one. Serenity is lost to arrogance when my will, not God's, tries to run not only my show but everyone else's. Serenity is lost when who I am is lost, subverted to acquire love, fame, money, or a sense of belonging. Serenity is lost when I refuse to follow my heart or to listen to and talk to God.

I have lost my serenity through nearly all of these examples plus many more that I have not thought to mention here. Yet my life, for the most part, has been externally calm. I am basically a peace-loving person. My parents and I were quietly dysfunctional, unhappy but stable. I do not thrive on chaos and confusion as some people do who grew up in chaotic home environments. For me, an outer calm masked my inner turmoil, for inside I was anything but serene. Numb, yes; serene, no. My numbness cushioned me from the pain and fear that had closed my heart to love and God. The Marlboro Man, who gave me the gift of self-examination, described us both very well when he said: "I may look whole, but I'm not." On the outside, I may have looked pretty good. But on the inside I was a mess.

The keys to reacquiring and maintaining serenity are found in the words of the Serenity Prayer:

> "God, grant me the serenity to accept the things I
> cannot change, Courage to change the things I can,
> And the wisdom to know the difference."

The recipe calls for the humility to surrender my will and my life to a kind and loving God, plus generous amounts of acceptance, courage, and wisdom.

For me, having the courage to change the things I can and doing the spiritual work required to effect change was essential to acquiring and maintaining serenity. The changes I needed to make were many—opening my mind and heart, feeling and releasing buried pain and guilt, owning, feeling, and letting go of my fears, transforming false pride into true pride sourced in humility, transforming narcissism into compassion and generosity, and clearing out all the junk and allowing love and forgiveness of myself and others to take its place. All this had to be done to achieve self-acceptance—to know myself, know my truth, and know that I am okay. So that was the work God and I had to do in order for me to begin to acquire serenity.

Maintaining my outer serenity requires acceptance as well. Most of my externally created frustrations are based on non-acceptance, either of other people's behaviors or my own. Judgmentalism and perfectionism are byproducts of false pride, and they run strong in my personality. All of these inherently embrace non-acceptance. Anger is always preceded by a judgment call—a judgment of "right" versus "wrong," an evaluation of others' behavior against my standards. Keeping my serenity requires me to judge less and observe more. It also requires me to accept the truth that I cannot, and should not, attempt to fix, change, save, or otherwise live others' lives for them, with or without their permission. Accepting the things I cannot change includes every person, place, or thing that is not me.

Serenity can be addictive, and it is possibly the only positive addiction that I can name. As I have grown spiritually, as my serenity has been established and nurtured, I have grown to treasure and to guard and protect it fiercely from either inner or outer stressors. That is one of the big reasons that I choose to work through and clear negative feelings as quickly as possible by making appropriate amends. Negative feelings, such as fear, anger, guilt, jealousy, envy, and self-hatred—any of the road hazards—are anything but serene. Emotional pits are never serene and peaceful places. That's also the reason why the Al-Anon slogan "How important is it?" is so important in my life today. Is it (whatever "it" is) important enough to destroy my serenity? More and more the answer has become no. I choose to allow fewer and fewer external stressors to push internal buttons and erode my serenity. Little things that used to infuriate me don't. Inconsiderate or inept or inattentive driving, slow checkout clerks in grocery stores, line jumpers—all these used to really irritate me. Not anymore. Big things that used to infuriate me usually don't either. When I married the Piano Player, I tried to save him from his own self-destructive behavior, and that really destroyed my serenity. Now I concentrate on saving myself from my own self-destructive behavior. It was never about saving him, it was always about saving me.

Now the greatest challenges of my life and the greatest opportunities to heal and grow spiritually are always ushered in with a loss of serenity. That is when I make conscious contact with God and allow him to help me meet the challenge. Emotional pain is always a sign of non-acceptance or lack of forgiveness, of my trying one more time to close my heart to one I dearly love. And sometimes the pain is excruciating, requiring a major miracle for its relief. Such an event happened when the Songteller rejected something I believed to be God's plan for us both. I was absolutely devastated, furious with God for giving me the plan in the first place, and spent most of the night in tears. The next morning, I was still angry, did not want to either see or talk to my friend. Then he called, and I found myself saying things to him I hadn't planned to say—loving, lucid, and caring things that put our friendship back on track. When I hung up the phone, I said to myself, "Where did *that* come from?" I suddenly had a totally different view of the event. My heart had opened again and my serenity had been miraculously restored.

Many summers ago, while traveling on Vancouver Island in British Columbia, my soul found an island, a place it has been before in another life, and told me that it wanted to come home to this place, to create and ultimately to leave from it. So I returned the following February, to experience winter there. In summer, the waters that separate Vancouver Island from Quadra Island are calm and serene, and a ferry makes hourly trips back and forth over those serene waters. In winter, things can be very different. Wind and rain come screaming in, the ocean roars and shudders as the waves crash into shore, and sometimes the ferry cannot sail at all. That February, the waters were choppy and turbulent and hardly could be described as serene. But I was strangely content. My soul had come home for a visit, and the serenity I felt came from following my heart's direction, through accepting the path my guide had given me to walk. That sense of serenity continued, even as the storm raged and the seas churned. I trusted my guide to lead me safely home. Tomorrow, or the next day, the seas would calm again. And serenity would return to the these waters to match the serenity found in my heart.

~ JOY

Joy is inner happiness that radiates outward. Joy is created by adding my desire to my acceptance of God's will for my life, by perfectly aligning my will with his, by enthusiastically agreeing to the divine plan. To accept and not resist the suggestions of my guide brings me serenity; to go beyond acceptance and wholeheartedly desire his will for me brings me joy.

Recovering members of Alcoholics Anonymous describe themselves as happy, joyous, and free; their definition of joy fits mine. For an alcoholic to get sober, he has to turn his life and his will over to the care of a higher power. This is surrender, or acceptance. But, for an alcoholic to *stay* sober, he has to add desire to acceptance. That is what brings him joy and freedom.

Joy has also been defined as absence of fear, and this also fits my definition. When my will and God's are perfectly aligned, I am perfectly sourced in love because that's what his will for me is. And when I am perfectly sourced in love, there is no room for fear in my mind or heart. Love and fear cannot coexist under those circumstances.

As perfect expressions of God, infants are naturally joyous because they have not yet learned either to fear or to exercise their free will. There is nothing more wondrous than a happy, joyous baby. But true joy, like serenity, is easily lost. Serenity and joy are very closely linked. All that causes me to lose serenity causes me to lose joy as well. All that causes me to lose love, truth, community, and passion causes me to lose joy.

All the years I turned my back on God and love, I turned away from joy as well. To be sure, there were times when my will and his aligned by accident, sort of like the astrological effects of planetary alignment, and this accidental alignment produced a feeling of joy. Using my creative gifts—playing music, singing, writing letters, taking photographs, or dancing—was often joyous. Using our creative gifts is part of God's plan for everyone, so my choosing to use them, with or without this awareness, brought me joy. Understand, however, that it was the act of using them that brought me unexpected joy. Being attached to the outcome introduced fear, and at that point joy vanished.

Although parts of my life were joyous by default, the whole of my life was not. Joy and happiness came, if they came at all, from the outside in, not from the inside out. My well of internal happiness had to be continually filled through external sources and stimulants. As with most of us, I had to be entertained and stimulated, and I attempted to fill the well through the compulsive use of various substances and behaviors. As with too many of us, I tried to take from others something that could only be given to me by myself. Happiness is an inside job; it cannot be begged, borrowed, or stolen from anyone else. To depend upon other people, places, things, or circumstances for my joy and happiness is to give these people, places, things, or circumstances total control over the quality of my life. It is doing a step three on persons, places, or things—turning my will and my life over to the care of someone or something other than God. Doing this may create the illusion of happiness for as long as the people, places, things, or circumstances are willing and able to provide what I need to maintain the illusion. But it is still an illusion that can vanish as quickly as it came, and emotionally depending on non-spiritual externals is risky business indeed. Doing this can easily create a victim, a martyr, or anger, hate, resentment, and any number of other negative emotions, but it definitely will not create joy.

By my definition, joy can only come into my life to stay when God comes into my life to stay. Still, it requires more than his mere presence. It requires my turning my will and my life over to his care, not reluctantly but enthusiastically. Joy is saying, "Wow, I'm really glad you want me to do this because it's so much fun and it feels *so* good!" Joy is driving my little sporty car, which I consider to be a gift from God. Joy is both traveling to and spending time at my second home on Quadra Island and returning to Saraswati, my home in Idaho, because God has led me to both. Joy is riding the ferries, gazing at the islands, and walking the path on Rebecca Spit, feeling perfectly at one with my surroundings, because those, too, are places God has led me to. Joy is playing love songs on my wonderful piano, Kawai, a piano that responds to my touch like no other piano ever has. Joy is lying next to and being with someone I dearly love and knowing that I am where God wants me to be. Joy is smiling at and chatting with people I don't know, being totally present for and connected to people I do know, the warmth and comfort of a good hug, and opening my heart to express love so that I may experience love because expressing and experiencing love is the ultimate high and unquestionably God's will for my life.

Joy is still harder for me to attain than serenity, although it is becoming more and more a part of my life as I continue to walk with my guide. Surrendering my will to God has not come easily to me, let alone learning to do it gladly and eagerly! Joy requires active participation, not merely passive acceptance or nonresistance. Joy says, "Yes, I know that what you want for me is a great idea, and I really desire it for my life." Joy happens when I embrace God's dreams and desires for me as my own. Joy comes to visit me and stays when I maintain my faith in his ability to manifest these dreams and desires into my life. Joy stays as long as I remain in a state of love because joy, like love, cannot coexist with fear. That is why acceptance or nonresistance does not automatically bring joy. With acceptance or nonresistance, fear will remain until I choose to let it go.

One of my major lifelong fears has been a fear of public speaking. For years, this fear has controlled and limited my life in that I avoided doing anything that could conceivably require me to stand up and speak to a group of people. However, once I began to walk my unique path, my guide led me to situations that required me to face this fear and move through it. Through my twelve-step programs, he asked me to chair meetings, share my story at speaker meetings, read the steps or traditions to large groups, and lead workshops. And, because I am committed to follow his guidance, I am also committed to facing my fear and moving through it by accepting all of these challenges in public speaking. Acceptance means I will do whatever is asked of me, not turn any opportunity to speak publicly down. But it does not mean that I am comfortable doing it. Acceptance has not brought me joy because my fears have still been present in many cases. Although I accepted God's will, I still clung to my old fears. With time and experience, I found myself hanging on more loosely to them, but my fears were still not completely gone. Again, old habits die hard. God cannot remove what I refuse to release to him, no matter how often I ask him to. It was only in situations where I truly had something I wanted to share with others, where I really wanted to do what God wants me to do, that I felt joy and the fears have disappeared.

When I was finally ready to surrender my fear, God brought me three opportunities to do so. First, I was asked to be a panelist at an Alcoholics Anonymous/Al-Anon workshop on spirituality. Each presentation was to be fifteen minutes long on a pre-selected topic. Next, I volunteered for my third time as an Al-Anon brunch speaker. Finally, I was asked to speak at a retreat for all twelve-step women and became the spiritual speaker and leader of the sessions on steps eleven and twelve. Each event was progressively more demanding, and thus potentially more terrifying. To make things even scarier, I made the decision to speak without written notes of any kind, to trust God to give me the words I was supposed to share. For the workshop, I made a mental outline of the thoughts I would share. For the brunch, I simply told my Al-Anon story for the first time. (Previously, I had given prepared speeches.) For the retreat, I shared my spiritual story and added a labyrinth walk and a time for sharing. In all cases, I was anything but joyous right before I began to speak, but then something very strange happened. I became calm and centered and filled with a quiet sense of joy. Partnered with God, the words just flowed, and I have tape recordings of the brunch and retreat sharings to prove to myself that I can do this if and when I am asked to speak again. Ultimately, I believe that I will *want* to speak, to share God's message with others at all times. Then joy will be automatic and fear will no longer be an option.

The same process has been obvious to me with my other predominant life-controlling fears—my fear of solo performing on the piano and my fear of intimacy. All of these fears involve my reluctance to reveal my true self to others, to show them who I am, to allow myself to truly reflect the magnitude of my personal gifts from God. In all cases, I will only feel joy when I truly appreciate the value of my gift, desire to share myself and my gift with others, and surrender my fear to God.

~ Hope

Hope is the spiritual principle that motivates me to keep on going when the going gets tough. Hope knows that all things shall pass and believes in the promise of a brighter future and a better tomorrow. Hope is thus an optimist, not a pessimist. Hope walks along side of faith, trust, and mindfulness and is very much a part of living in the moment. There is always hope in the eternal moment, for hope is an eternal principle. Hope knows that as long as God is with me, guiding my life, and I am following his direction, everything that happens to me in my life is ultimately leading me to my highest good.

Hope was given to me by my parents when I was born, although I am sure they did not know it. My name, Nadine, means hope. So I have always had hope, even when I have chosen not to consciously claim it. Hope has kept me from suffering extended bouts of depression and despair, and I cannot recall ever feeling a sense of hopelessness about life or any part of life. To be sure, I have been in an emotional pit many times, but never with a sense that I was doomed to stay there. I always have known at some level of consciousness that life would shift and things would get better. I always have had hope.

Hope is firmly grounded in spiritual truth. Hope comes with believing in a higher power, or God, and sustained hope comes from having the faith and trust to surrender to and follow the direction of God. Hope without spiritual basis becomes false hope, or wishful thinking, and can be very destructive. Wishful thinking does not let go of the situation it wants to change, hope does. Hope turns it over to God, with whom true hope rests. It is wishful thinking to put my life on hold and cling to the notion that a severed relationship will someday be put back together. Hope comes through acceptance of what has occurred, letting go of the relationship, turning it over to God, and moving on with my life.

When the Rescuer and I separated and eventually divorced, he did not let our relationship go. He clung to the belief that I would someday come back to him, and that was his wishful thinking. After I remarried, he drove from Illinois to Idaho to see me and verify that I was happy. Without his false hope, he apparently had no hope at all, no faith in life or desire to move on with his life. I say that because he died a little over a year later at the age of forty-four from simply choosing not to seek medical attention soon enough. False hope can be a very dangerous condition.

Hope believes in the miracle of physical healing but knows that miracles only happen when God and the person requiring the healing are open to them. For me to hope that a loved one dying of cancer will be miraculously healed is not really hope but false hope, because I simply do not know and am not qualified to decide whether or not it is time for this person to die. To pray for a miracle and then turn the outcome over to God is an action based on hope—hope for the best outcome for my loved one, even if it results in a loss for me. Hope is sourced in unconditional love. False hope is what I want and is usually based upon fear of loss. Miracles of physical healing can happen, and often do, but not because I want them to. They happen because both God and the person afflicted want them to.

A young woman that I knew through church, the mother of two small children, was diagnosed with a recurrence of leukemia. While being prepared for a bone marrow transplant, which required that her immune system be deactivated, she developed a severe intestinal infection. Surgeons performed a colostomy to remove infected tissue but gave her little chance for survival. She called for her pastor and his wife. They went to her and basically gave up any false hope they had and turned it over to God. But, Laurel was not ready to leave. Apparently, she and God both knew that her husband and children were not prepared for it. So she miraculously recovered, not from the cancer but from the infection, and spent six more months with her family. She was able to return home to her family and to the church family that had prayed so hard for her. Then she got sick again, and this time there was no miraculous recovery. Her work with her family was finished, and Laurel, God, and all of us who had prayed for her knew that it was time for her to leave. So she did. Hope understands that death is a part of life and trusts in the wisdom of God's plan.

Hope grieves its losses, but does not despair.

And, since hope is grounded in faith in God, hope recognizes and believes that we are spiritual beings with bodies, not bodies endowed with spiritual qualities. Hope understands that the body dies, not the spirit, which is eternal. What my particular belief system is does not matter. It can be in heaven and hell, reincarnation, or free choice of either. Hope is eternal and believes in the eternal as well.

As I said earlier, hope is a personal gift and one I have learned to value greatly since I have been walking with my guide. Actually, as I look back at my life, what I labeled as hope was probably more often false hope, or wishful thinking. But the real thing was still there. Even though I was not talking to God, I never quit believing that he was there. And as long as I believed, there was always hope. I know there are many of us who believe in God, but still lose hope. I could lose hope if I believed that God had abandoned me. But he did not abandon me, I abandoned him. Fortunately for me, God does not hold grudges. He was very happy to welcome me back, and from his perspective, I never left.

As I have come to know and understand God better, I treasure my hopeful nature. It is only when I begin to lose faith and trust in the wisdom of his plan and schedule that I begin to lose hope as well, hope for a specific outcome, which is really false hope. Hope grounded in faith knows that my highest good can come from any outcome if I look for the lessons contained therein and learn and grow from them.

Hope is a prerequisite to beginning to work the twelve steps, my road map for spiritual growth. Hope is inherent in twelve-step programs—the hope of relief from the compulsion to use my drug of choice. Even when I struggle with my abstinence from whatever I am addicted to, I still know that hope can be found in the steps, specifically the "came to believe" step, step two. Many of us know and understand that working the steps is our *only* hope.

When the Piano Player went through an alcohol-dependency treatment program the first time, my hope was that he would be fixed or miraculously cured—that was false hope. By the time he went through treatment the second time, I knew there was no quick fix. Then, my hope was that he would practice the principles he learned there and come to enjoy his sobriety. That too was false hope, based on his behavior. When he relapsed, I knew that his only hope for long-term freedom from his compulsion was total commitment to working the program of Alcoholics Anonymous. I also knew that my only hope for sanity was total commitment to working the programs of Al-Anon and Overeaters Anonymous. I was right, of course. But I was also too new in the program to fully understand that the only hope for our relationship was for me to fully and completely turn every aspect of it over to God, and I never did. Even when we were physically separated, I still hung on. I still hoped, falsely, that somehow I could make a difference in his life, that I had to be there for him to make it. I was there, and I did not make a difference in the end.

When he quit drinking, I falsely hoped that his health would get better. It did not; it got worse. When he stabilized after hospitalization, I still had the hope that he would live. Again, this was false hope because I had not turned his life over to God. When it became clear that he would not live, that his body was shutting down, my hope was that he would die quickly and not linger on comatose. That hope was true. I took it to God and he responded. My prayer was the Piano Player's prayer as well. We both let go and he left shortly thereafter.

Then my hope was for me—that I would somehow work through my grief and come out of it a whole person. If someone had told me then about the miracles that would happen to me, if they had said that a few short years from then I would be the Nadine I am today, I would have laughed and said, "That's ridiculous!" Never, in my wildest dreams, could I have imagined or visualized the transformation I have experienced. I hoped for sanity and peace, not resurrection from the dead because I did not know I was dead. My hopes were small indeed, compared to the changes that have occurred because of faith and trust in my guide and his ability to create miracles. My life today is a testimonial to hope grounded in spiritual truth.

~ Miracles

A miracle is a shift in perception that aligns my will more perfectly with God's will for my life. Each of us can choose to be a miracle worker, but not without help. Miraculous shifts in perception are not self-created. Hearts hardened or deadened to love do not soften voluntarily. Oftentimes, the shift must be precluded and precipitated by a tremendous amount of pain. Only then is God invited in and allowed to co-create the miraculous shift, for this is how miracles occur. Major miracles may require massive doses of love and a tremendous amount of faith, particularly when the miracle is requested for another. Intimate relationships require many such miracles, intertwined and interwoven so intricately that only God can guide us through the perfection of timing required for success. A holy relationship, sourced in love, is a miracle in progress.

Babies enter a miraculous world—that is their perception as perfect expressions of God. Life viewed through passionate, loving, and joyous eyes is a miracle; but, again, too often this perception is lost. Getting it back, reclaiming my God-given gifts, remembering and rediscovering who I really am, finding and following my unique path—these events that bring me home to God and to myself are all miracles. All involve a shift in perception, replacing falsity with truth. All require me to see myself, my life, my beliefs, my attitudes, and my behaviors from a different point of view. Any shift, great or small, that brings me closer to alignment with God's plan is a miracle. All miracles are sourced in love and thus co-created by God.

For years there were no miracles in my life, simply because I refused to allow them to be. Miracles come through God, and he was not a part of my life that I either owned or acknowledged. My mind and my heart were closed to love, to God, and to miracles. Fear, not love, guided my life, and my self-directed will was the only will I knew. It led me down many false paths, paths that were either very hard or very painful to follow. The greatest miracles of my life, the miracles that brought me back to life, were birthed in pain. Living with the pain caused by the disease of alcoholism created the shift in perception that brought God back into my life. Working through the pain of the Piano Player's death created the shift in perception that brought me back my life.

I believe in miracles as I believe in God, love, and life. I believe in miracles because my life today has been created by a whole series of miracles, some great, some small, but all bringing me closer to God's plan for my life. They all occurred after I made the decision to turn my will and my life over to my guide. All of my miracles have brought me closer to being my true self and walking my unique path. Some have been solely mine. Some have involved, or are involving, others. I have already shared many of them with you, but there are many, many more. Reclaiming my musical gift, opening my mind and my heart to giving and receiving love, allowing people to come close to me, surrendering my will and my life to God, acquiring compassion and humility—these are all major miracles composed of a myriad of lesser ones. Acquiring and maintaining serenity and joy through shifting my perception of others, changing my behaviors toward them—every behavior shift is a miracle. To convert caretaking into caregiving and respect, need for control into freely allowing and trusting, judging into impartially observing, perfectionism into realism and permission to learn through trial and error—these are all miracles. To convert false, ego-centered pride into true, God-centered pride sourced in humility is truly a miracle. To let go, sit back, and get out of the way so that God can work miracles in other people's lives—this too is a miracle. Having the courage to look at myself, to love myself in my divine perfection and human imperfection, and to accept myself as I am today—this is a true miracle. Following my heart, listening to the promptings of my soul, feeling my feelings, living in the moment, acting on the guidance of God—these are manifestations of a miracle in progress, the miracle that is my life today.

I could cite many more examples of miracles, and every example, every miraculous component, has a common thread. In every case, the shift in perception required to create the miracle has been a shift in vision from fear to love. In every miracle of my miraculous life, I had to change my view from a position of fear to that of love, which is the shift required to effect a miracle. That is how God works through and with us to create them. Under his direction, I can be used to affect miracles in others, but only under his direction. Without his guidance, my efforts are usually misdirected and ineffective. My primary role under his guidance is as a conveyor of love. To be a miracle worker, for myself or others, I have to come from a position of love.

Miracles happen in the present because that is where God does his work, not in yesterday or tomorrow. Miracles are a process as life is a process, and forward progress is made one arduous step at a time. That was how I climbed mountains—one slow, determined step at a time. Looking back shows how far I have come during times when it was hard to discern forward progress. I have already shared my video story, my miraculous resurrection from a near-life experience (see "Passion"). There is another, somewhat related story that also illustrates the miracle of my life. It is the story of the Saratoga Inn.

When the Piano Player and I were working as a road musician duo, our best gig was at a resort motel in Wyoming, the Saratoga Inn. We worked there often and were well-liked. It was a special place for us and held many special memories for us, for our music, and even for my parents (both gone), who visited us there several times. True, the memories were both pleasant and unpleasant, but very important in all cases.

Our last visit to Saratoga together was in 1994 on our way back home from the family reunion I described in "Passion." The Piano Player's brother was traveling with us. We stayed two nights so we could play golf one more time on the course where we had played so many times when we worked there. When the Piano Player died four months later, I knew that at some point in time I would have to go back and put closure on my memories at Saratoga.

I made the trip back to Saratoga, finally, nearly four years after the Piano Player's death. I had spent most of my summer being led to places where I could heal past emotional wounds, as part of the process required to open my heart fully to love. So I knew it was time to return to Saratoga. I did not know what I would find or feel there, but I knew it was time to go back.

When we were there in 1994, the Piano Player was dying, his brother was dying (he left the next year), I was dying, and the inn was dying, so we all fit. The grand resort motel of the 1980s had been mismanaged, neglected, and was in need of major repairs. The roof leaked, the paint was peeling, concrete walks and steps were cracked and broken. Only the golf course was being maintained. The inn had been up for sale for some months and was very close to being shut down. So, four years later, when I called for a reservation, all I knew was that it was still open and the room rates had gone up drastically. The reservations person asked how I knew about the inn, and I told him that I had entertained there in the 1980s and had last been there in August of 1994. He said, "Oh, we've made a few changes since then." That turned out to be the understatement of the century!

At Saratoga, the expected turned into the unexpected, as is often the case. What I expected was a minor upgrade; what I found was a total makeover. The Saratoga Inn presented me with a mirror reflection of my life. The inn had been totally refurbished, from the inside out, in a wonderful western decor. The rooms were filled with handmade log furniture, and the beds had feather mattresses and Pendleton blankets. The only things remaining from the old rooms were the casement windows and the plumbing. The main lodge and rooms had a new metal roof, there were new cobblestone walks and wooden steps, a new pool area with cabanas, and miniature mineral spas dot the lawn. The restaurant specialized in vintage wines, the lounge where we played was now a microbrewery, bar, and short-order cafe, and the lobby and reception area had been totally redesigned and redecorated, all in a decor I describe as comfortable class.

What had been was gone, replaced by something as far removed from its past as my life is from *its* past. That is what hit me there, the realization that both of us, both me and the Saratoga Inn, had been made over from the inside out. We both have been revitalized and brought back to life, better than ever. The Piano Player and his disease would not fit there now, but I do fit there. We both changed, a miraculous change, a resurrection from near death. Old memories remained only on the golf course, and those were felt and released on the ninth tee. Nothing else of the past remained. God and I had come a very long way in four years. Together we had co-created many miracles. Proof of this was waiting for me at the new Saratoga Inn Resort and Spa.

Chapter VIII

THE PRINCIPLES

AS I walk the road home now, following the direction of my guide and bearing his gifts, he has shown me certain spiritual principles that, when learned and practiced, make my journey much smoother and more pleasant. All of these principles enhance my God-given gifts and make it easier and simpler to develop and use them to their fullest potential. All of the principles help to ensure that my God-given rewards are sustained and not temporarily lost. All of the principles are teaching me things I need to know or giving me skills I need to have in order to find my true self and follow my unique path. Some of the principles apply specifically to my relationship with God. Some of the principles apply specifically to my relationships with other people. Some of the principles apply specifically to my relationship with myself. Most of the principles apply universally to all three types of relationships, and all are interrelated.

I have presented them in no particular order, although the first ones—willingness, gratitude, trust, surrender, awareness, acceptance, humility, forgiveness, compassion, generosity, patience, commitment, and courage—possibly have been my most difficult but important lessons. They are principles that are basic and fundamental to my journey, and they have not come easily to me. Until I began to learn and use these principles regularly and routinely, I could not walk with my guide consistently. Like an uncooperative dance partner, I kept wanting to lead, lag behind, set my own tempo, or even dance a different dance. Until I began to learn and use these principles in all my affairs, I could not stay sourced in love nor did I know how to express love. Fear would return, and I would get lost again.

Willingness is the key that opens the doorway to all aspects of spiritual growth, and gratitude keeps the doorway open. Trust, surrender, awareness, and acceptance connect me with my guide, his plan for my life, and his perfect time table for creating it. Forgiveness, compassion, generosity, and humility are the principles that allow me to freely express love. Forgiveness and humility, plus patience, help me find my way back to my guide when my human imperfections cause me to lose my way. Commitment aligns my will with his and is the part I play in co-creating my life. Courage allows me to rediscover and reclaim my true self and to follow my unique path even when it is unfamiliar and uncomfortable. Practicing these principles enhances and strengthens all of my gifts and my ability to use them as I follow my unique path. Optimism, tenacity, and perseverance, principles that are part of my personal truth, also enhance all of my gifts and go arm in arm with hope. Through optimistic eyes, all of my perceptions are positive and affirming. With tenacity and perseverance, I am able to continue learning and practicing these principles even when the going gets tough and progress is slow. Tenacity keeps me committed and loyal. Perseverance keeps me on task and on my path.

Other principles are somewhat less universal, although most of them can be applied to more than one of the gifts or rewards. Honesty and staying in reality help me find my truth, and integrity keeps me following it. Trust and compassion are essential for community, but willingness to experience intimacy and loyalty enhance, strengthen, and deepen relationships. Besides surrender, forgiveness, and acceptance, true freedom requires detachment. Serenity and joy are enhanced by these principles, as well as flexibility, tolerance, gratitude, simplicity, order, balance, humor, and maturity. Sexuality, passion, and creativity are manifested through commitment and synchronicity, the right sequence of events occurring at exactly the right time. And when all the principles are practiced, miracles become an everyday occurrence.

Some of these principles come easily to me, but most do not.

Some are gifts, part of my personal truth, but most are acquired skills. All of the principles can be learned through application and practice. Practicing these principles while traveling the road home continues to make my journey meaningful, rewarding, exciting, challenging, and infinitely more joyous, serene, and free. God has never intended the journey to be otherwise. Everything I need for the trip has been provided for me by my guide. All I have to provide is the willingness to become aware of the principles, accept them, and practice them in all my affairs.

~ WILLINGNESS

Willingness is the principle that unlocks the potential for spiritual growth. Willingness is the underlying principle that must be present before I can believe in and walk with my guide, use his road map for recovery, connect with my fellow travelers, accept my God-given gifts, receive my God-given rewards, find my true self, and walk my unique path. Willingness is the principle that allows me to reclaim all my gifts and practice all the other principles as they apply to my life. I have to be willing to have faith, to trust, to be patient, to commit, to be courageous, to be humble, and to surrender. I have to be willing to do whatever it takes to keep me free of my compulsive behaviors. And when I lose my willingness and my way, I have to be willing to humble myself before God and begin again.

To be willing requires first an open mind and ultimately an open heart. To be unwilling is to be closed in both mind and heart. I have known many people who have closed their minds to what is in their hearts and thus are unwilling to feel, accept, or express love. I recognize this in others because it has been a part of my own experience. In fact, I have had a lot of experience with being unwilling. The members of Alcoholics Anonymous have a term for this; they call it self-will run riot. My story is filled with examples of unwillingness. For years I was unwilling to allow an infinitely patient God to come back into my life because I was unwilling to acknowledge my own spiritual self and needs. For years I was unwilling to trust and kept my fellow travelers both physically and emotionally distant. For years I was unwilling to love unselfishly and unwilling to feel or accept love from others. For years I was unwilling to surrender to the reality and insanity of my own compulsive behaviors.

For years I was unwilling to look at my true self, who I was, because I was afraid of what I might see. During those years, I avoided looking into mirrors and had no clear mental image of what I looked like. For years I was unwilling to take an emotional risk, unwilling to share any part of myself with others, unwilling to feel emotional pain. For years I was unwilling to see or hear truth; I preferred to live in fantasy and denial. In fantasy, I received the perfect love I could not accept in reality. In denial, I lived with and accepted unacceptable behavior from the Piano Player and was unwilling to see the ravages of his disease in my face, body, and life style.

For years I was willing to do anything I could to please others, but I was unwilling to do anything simply to please myself. I worked hard and played hard, but always in ways that were important to others, such as my spouse or friend. I fragmented myself and deluded myself into thinking it was all right by saying, well, it does not matter. I have so many things that I like to do that I will just concentrate on the ones we can do together.

For years I was both unwilling to hold on and unwilling to let go. When I divorced my first two husbands, I was unwilling to stay and try and work things out. When I could not leave the Piano Player, when leaving would have been the best thing for both of us, I was unwilling to accept that truth and let him go. For years I was unwilling to admit to myself that I was unwilling in any area of my life.

For years I was unwilling to own and accept my dark side, my vulnerabilities, my needs, my fears, my guilt, my pain, my resentments, my anger, my prejudices, my character defects. I would neither own nor accept my dark side, nor would I let others get close enough to see it. I projected an image to you of self-sufficiency and independence. Because of that, for years, I was unable to ask for help or support from anyone. I was unwilling to ask for or accept the help of others, except in those areas where I either did not have the skills or interest to act. I could ask for someone else's help in mowing the lawn or changing a tire, but I couldn't ask them for a hug or for help in changing a behavior. Those were things I either did not need or was supposed to take care of myself.

Desperation is a great cure for self-will run riot. Recovering addicts refer to that desperation as bottoming out, of reaching the point where it is more painful to use than to surrender to our powerlessness over our drug of choice, whatever it may be. Bottoming out brings with it the gift of willingness to do whatever it takes to get clean and sober, to quit abusing whatever it is we have been abusing. But when the desperation is no longer felt, when not using becomes routine, delusion and denial can replace willingness, and relapse almost always follows. Then, again, willingness is required to go back to step one, to surrender, to humbly reconnect with our God, and begin again.

It seems I had a lot of willingness for others but not very much for myself. I was very willing for the Piano Player to go to AA meetings during those times when he did not drink, but I was not very willing to go to Al-Anon or any other supportive twelve-step program. It took ten years of living with him, a falling-down-drunk, late-stage alcoholic, for me to bottom out and become willing to, first, learn about the disease and how it had affected him and, second, learn about how it had affected me and get help for myself. It took me another four years to become willing to do whatever it took to recover from the destructive effects of living with his disease. In this case, "whatever it took" included attending Al-Anon meetings, getting a sponsor, working the steps, and a tremendous amount of reading, writing, and soul-searching. It took me fifty-six years of compulsive overeating, of gaining weight and losing weight, of dieting and bingeing, of regaining control and, more often, having no control at all, to bottom out and become willing to do whatever it took to become and stay abstinent from my compulsion. In this case, "whatever it took" included not eating sweets and desserts and any other primary binge food, eating nutritionally and moderately, attending Overeaters Anonymous meetings, working the steps, and more reading, writing, and soul-searching. With my food compulsion, the willingness has stayed with me. Since I have been in program, I have had minor slips but never a full-blown relapse. Unfortunately, I cannot say the same about my recovery from the effects of alcoholism. My codependent behaviors and fears have routinely come back to haunt me, and my willingness to do "whatever it takes" has come slowly and painfully and is still far from perfect. Here, in most cases, the key is to pray for the willingness to become willing.

Being willing to do whatever it takes *most of the time* has led me down the spiritual path I walk today with God. Walking a spiritual path that is uniquely mine requires continuous and ever-expanding willingness, as I have already shared with you. It requires the willingness to walk with my guide and follow his direction wherever he may choose to lead me. It requires the willingness to have faith and trust and to continually strengthen and deepen my relationship with God. It requires the willingness to work my programs as best I can, to follow the road map, to stay close to my guide. It requires the willingness to pick myself up when I fall or falter, find my way back when I get lost, allow God to help me and ask my fellow travelers for help when I need it.

To be my true self and walk my unique path requires me to be willing to love and be loved, both by others and myself, to open my heart to both divine and human love, to love fully and take the risks that come with loving openly and honestly. I must also be willing to open my mind, to become teachable, to set aside all that I think I already know so that the understanding that comes from my heart may be allowed to enter my mind and direct my actions. I must be willing to look honestly and impartially at my strengths and weaknesses so that I may accept the things I cannot change and allow God to change the things I can. I must be willing to surrender, to let go and let God. I must be willing to allow myself to feel and release pain, anger, resentment, guilt, and regret, so that old emotional wounds can be cleansed and healed. I must be willing to allow myself to feel love, serenity, joy, gratitude, and all other emotions sourced in love, not fear. I must also allow myself to feel and release all my other emotions, the ones sourced in fear, so that new unhealed emotional wounds are not created. I must be willing to release the past, forgive myself and others for perceived errors, and see the loving and innocent essence of God that lies beneath these errors. And, after I have allowed myself to feel and heal from my own pain, I must be willing to acknowledge and honor the pain of others through compassion and forgiveness.

To enjoy the community of God, myself, and my fellow travelers, I must be willing to allow others to be there for me. I must also be willing to allow myself to be there for others and for myself. I must be willing to perform selfless, joyous service, to give and receive, to teach and to learn, to let go of those aspects of my being that no longer fit my true self or my unique path. I must be willing to release fear and be the very best I can be, let my God-given gifts shine for all to enjoy and share. I must be willing to believe that I deserve the very best from God and from life. I must be willing to connect and stay connected to God, to myself, and to others. I must be willing to be present for others, to honor them, and to treat them with courtesy and respect. I must also be willing to treat myself with the same courtesy and respect that I extend to others.

~ GRATITUDE

Gratitude is the principle of appreciation and transformation. Gratitude lives in the present, with my guide, and appreciates what is rather than yearning for what was or what will be. Gratitude appreciates all of life's blessings and God's gifts, from the tiniest flower to the grandeur of the universe. Gratitude recognizes the source of all my gifts and gives God credit where credit is due. Gratitude also recognizes the gifts that come disguised as loss, rejection, indifference, failure, hostility, and physical and emotional discomfort. Gratitude says thank you sincerely and often, even in those times when most would see little to be grateful for. Gratitude sees life itself as a gift, no matter how difficult the path may be or how challenging the journey.

Gratitude transforms through a shift in perception. Gratitude transforms pessimism into optimism, dark into light, fear into love, scarcity into abundance. Gratitude transforms ugliness into beauty, survival into living, boredom and apathy into enthusiasm, despair into hope, sickness into health. There is absolutely nothing in my life—no experience, no event, no relationship, no possession, no circumstance—that cannot be transformed by the attitude of gratitude. The closing read at the end of Al-Anon meetings contains these words: "You will come to realize that there is no situation too difficult to be bettered and no unhappiness too great to be lessened" These words are based, to a great extent, on practicing the principle of gratitude.

Complacency and self-pity are the road hazards that are removed through the miracle of gratitude. When I am complacent, I take things for granted. I may acknowledge the gifts but I neither appreciate nor show appreciation for them. Self-pity sees no gifts at all, recognizing only lack, hardship, and pain. Gratitude instills the complacent with appreciation and opens the eyes of the self-pitying to a different view. A miracle is defined as a shift in perception, and gratitude is the miracle that effects the shift in both cases.

One winter, my wonderful car, Mitsu, was damaged through no fault of mine. We were stopped in a line of traffic waiting for a light to change and got rear-ended by an inattentive driver. The self-pitying view of this event would have seen only the damage to Mitsu, the incompetence and irresponsibility of the other driver, the time required to talk to the police and file an accident report, the inconvenience of dealing with the insurance company, locating a body shop and getting Mitsu repaired, and the slight neck discomfort experienced that evening. My view, through grateful eyes, was a bit different. First, I was very grateful that I was not seriously hurt and my car was not seriously damaged. I was also grateful that I knew the woman who hit me and had no problems with either her or her insurance adjuster. Because I knew her, I took her recommendation of a body shop that was both reliable and efficient. The repair was completed while I was out of town with a minimum of disruption, and Mitsu came out of it looking as good as new.

Had this accident occurred some years earlier, my view would probably have been quite different. And, again, maybe not. My personal road hazard has been complacency, not self-pity. Being an optimist, I usually took a positive view, and I knew the gifts were there. But I did not appreciate them, nor did I acknowledge or give thanks to their source. Remember, I discounted my personal gifts for many years.. I also took a lot of things for granted—things like food and clothing, a house to live in, money to spend, the beauty of nature, a car to drive, a good job, all the gifts that determine or enhance the quality of my physical life. And I also discounted their source by refusing to allow God to be a part of my life.

During the first years when the Piano Player did not drink, I took his sobriety for granted, until he relapsed. When the relapse ended and another nondrinking period began, I was very grateful and swore to myself that I would not become complacent again. I had, by this time, reconciled with God but did not really understand that the gift of sobriety had come from him. It was during the Piano Player's final and fatal relapse, when the gift of alcoholic abstinence was given to him freely and without an apparent reason, that I finally understood and acknowledged God as the source of all gifts. Four months later, the Piano Player died a sober man. That was God's gift to him, and to me, and I am eternally grateful.

Gratitude is a principle I have only discovered and begun to use effectively since I began walking with my guide. I have already shared the story of how I came to appreciate my creative gifts (see "Creativity"). And, with time and recovery, I have learned to be grateful for the more commonplace as well. My daily prayers are prayers of gratitude for those aspects of my life that are the most important to me. I also keep a gratitude journal and write down five things each day that I am grateful for. Sometimes they are very simple gifts, like a glorious, warm, sunny, fall day. Sometimes they are profound, like the gift of surrender to love given to me at the center of the labyrinth (see "Surrender"). Always they are gifts that are important and pertinent for that day, to remind me that my gifts are found only in the present. Yesterday's gifts belong to yesterday, and tomorrow's gifts may or may not ever be. The gifts are given, as life is given, one day at a time.

Still, as is true with most of us, my lessons in gratitude also come through life's challenges, not life's obvious blessings. It is much harder for me to be grateful for the opportunities for growth found in painful experiences than it is to be grateful for the pleasures of life. Gifts of love often come in very odd packages indeed. For me, that form of gratitude usually comes after the pain has subsided, not while the pain is being felt and experienced. I saw little reason to be grateful for the pain of loss in the months immediately following the Piano Player's death. Only with time and healing could I see and be grateful for the many spiritual gifts that have come to me through the experience. All things are cyclic, and life and death are no exception to that rule. All endings are beginnings as well, and death is followed by life. But sometimes it takes awhile to see and understand that truth.

In 1988, wildfires ravaged Yellowstone National Park. Developed areas were saved, but huge areas of forest, particularly around the west, south, and northeast entrances, were destroyed. This was a horrendous loss for me, because I knew that what had been would not be restored in my current lifetime. For several years, when rebirth was barely noticeable, I could hardly bear to drive through these areas. And when I did, I closed my heart to avoid feeling the pain. Then, over time, the forests began to heal and so did I. I became aware that my heart was closed and opened it, cutting loose the floodgate that held back the tears. I remember I cried and cried as I drove through the burns, even though the new forests were beginning to emerge. Although I had relieved my pain and accepted the loss, I still could not see the promise of new life and be grateful.

More time passed, and I was called to Yellowstone for a spiritual retreat, a journey to the center of a labyrinth much closer to my home. My quest was for clarity and vision, and my destination was the geyser basins and other thermal areas. I did not even think about the burned forests until I saw them, and what I saw was a miracle. Finally, after eleven years, the cycle of healing and rebirth was apparent. The new forests of lodge pole pines, tiny trees some three to four feet high, have formed a green carpet of life beneath the stark skeletons of those that were destroyed. I was absolutely thrilled. Even though I will not see these trees grow to maturity, I know that restoration is in progress.

I also saw and understood the parallel between the rebirth of the forests and my own spiritual recovery, the path I have found and traveled with God since the Piano Player's death. In both cases, healing began immediately following the loss, but was imperceptible for what seemed like a very long time. In both cases, the miracle of healing and rebirth was not assured, at least not in my eyes, until it began to visibly manifest itself, until it could be seen and felt. That finally happened to me, more than seven years after my loss. I see the visible changes in me and in my relationships that have come through walking with and following the direction of my guide, opening my mind and my heart, and surrendering to love. I also see the changes in others who are walking a similar path of healing and recovery and understand that the miracle of healing is in progress and has been all along. The cycle of beginnings and endings, of life and death, in God's world has been confirmed, and I am very grateful.

~ Trust

Trust is the principle that enhances and expands the gift of faith. Trust is faith's sidekick, a partner who works with faith, side by side and hand in hand. Together, they create a living faith, a faith that works with me and for me as an integral part of my life. In fact, faith and trust are so interrelated that I puzzled over how to write about them separately. Then the subtle difference came to me. If faith is my belief in a God to whom I can turn my will and my life over to, trust is what allows me to do that. A faith without trust is not a living faith because it cannot be used. God cannot be there for me unless I let him be. And I will not let him be if I do not trust him to take care of me and my life. To accept him as my guide requires absolute trust in his ability and desire to guide me.

For most of my life, I falsely believed myself to be a very trusting person when, in fact, I was very distrustful. To be sure, I trusted *in* people and things. I trusted the words and actions of others unless or until they were proven to be lies. Being an optimist, I assumed that what others said was truth and that they would keep their word, their promises, and their commitments. But I did not trust them enough to ask for their help unless I had no other choice. I did not trust others enough to let them come close to me or to come close to them. I did not trust others enough to share my vulnerabilities with them—my pain, my needs, my loneliness. I did not trust others enough to share my true self with them. I certainly did not trust myself to be able to take care of myself while with another person. That is why I did not share my vulnerabilities. Someone else might use them to take advantage of me and I would not be able to defend myself, to protect myself from pain.

If I did not trust others and I did not trust me, for sure I was not going to trust God! After all, he did not come racing in on a white horse, brandishing his sword, to attack those who unjustly and unmercifully caused me so much pain as a child. No one did, including me, so I trusted no one. At a distance, yes, but never up close.

My self-imposed isolation was based on a lack of trust. My emotional unavailability was created by a lack of trust. Not trusting in people is what kept me away from twelve-step programs and meetings when everything I heard or read told me that was where I needed to be. Not trusting God is what made my third step so difficult, why I turned my will and my life over to him in small, select increments. It wasn't that I lacked faith in his ability to care for me. I knew he could, and would, do this if I allowed him to. But, would he do it right? Would he do it the way I wanted and needed it to be done? What I had not learned was that his way is always the best for me, even when it appears not to be. What I hadn't learned to do was trust in his wisdom and plan for my life.

My struggles with practicing faith, with putting a living faith to work in my life, have really been created by my lack of trust. At first I only trusted him with those things I clearly could not manage—the Piano Player's alcoholism, my own food compulsion. When he showed me he could, and would, help me with these, I started turning over small, relatively unimportant aspects of my life. Gradually, I moved into more important things, and finally I trusted him enough to turn over those people, places, and things that I had a strong emotional investment in. Those were the hardest to trust him with, because I knew what outcome I wanted and needed, particularly in relationships. I still wanted to both write the script for my life and direct the play. But, with time and experience, I understood that his scripts and direction were much better than mine for all concerned. Certainly I would not have scripted the Piano Player's death, but it was the best for both him and for me. So I have gradually learned to let God write the script for my life. I give him input, certainly, but the final edit is his.

Slowly, over time, I have become more trusting—of myself, of others, and of God. After all, if I trust God to guide me and follow his guidance, I can then trust myself in my interactions with others. I can let others come close and know that I can take care of myself in all situations. This also means that I will not trust in the behavior of someone else if it has been shown to be untrustworthy, and will take measures to protect myself, if necessary. I will not trust the promises of a practicing addict because the addiction is always stronger than their best and most sincere intention. In the presence of physical, sexual, mental, or emotional abuse, trusting in God and in myself means trusting in whatever action is best for me and taking it.

Trust has come to me slowly and sometimes painfully when lack of trust causes me to lose faith. Now, after many years of recovery, I have learned to trust in most aspects of my life. I certainly trust God's guidance and follow it, almost instinctively. I just sort of know what to do, where to go, and when to do it by listening to the God within, by following my heart-guided intuition. I trust in my guide's wisdom, plan, and timing *most* of the time. I allow myself to share my true self and all its vulnerabilities with others when it is appropriate to do so because I know now that they do not have the power to hurt me emotionally unless I give it to them. I trust myself to choose not to give others that power *most* of the time. And if others do have the power to affect my life in physical ways, I trust my judgment as to what and how much to share with them. I trust the inner truth of others and trust in them to follow it unless it is clear that they cannot because of their own fears or addictions. I trust in God to bring me the dreams and desires that will keep me on my unique path, as well as the relationships I need to learn, heal, and discover my true self. I trust my guide to co-create the dreams he and I agree to follow *most* of the time. Notice that I have qualified these statements. I have to, because I do not do this perfectly, by any means. My old fears return, and I revert back to old behaviors. I want it my way, and when God moves too slowly or change cannot be seen, I stop trusting him to do his job and begin to script and direct again. And every time I do this, I get a new version of a very old lesson.

Shortly after the Piano Player died, God offered me a relationship assignment with a man I had known for many years, the man I refer to as the Songteller. This man, too, was gravely wounded by the loss of a love, and God knew that we were possibly the only ones who could bring healing to each other because we were spiritually connected. I soon realized that I was greatly attracted to this man and had buried my feelings for him years before. So I eagerly accepted the assignment and proceeded to take the scripting and direction of this relationship out of God's hands. I wrote a happy ending to the story before it had even begun, and nearly ruined the relationship by trying to force it to happen.

At that point, I surrendered our relationship back to God, and somehow it managed to survive this awful beginning. Over several years, this relationship has evolved into a very special friendship between two soul friends. We have shared ourselves with each other openly and honestly, but safely, from a distance. Over time, we have come to care for each other in a very special way and have brought much emotional healing to each other. Because of him, I have opened my heart again to love and my mind to relearning how to express love. I have learned much through and because of loving this man and have for some time trusted God to provide the miracles required for us to open our minds and our hearts to each other. I also have trusted him to both write and direct the script, but with one condition. He had to keep the "happy ending" I scripted when our relationship first began, the ending that creates a new beginning by bringing us together in a committed love relationship. I refused to let go of this ending and accept any other possible outcome.

What I could not see or understand was that my love for the Songteller requires that I trust God to give us both the outcome that will lead to our highest good, no matter what that outcome turns out to be. As long as I insist on my ending, God cannot freely create any ending, either his or mine. As long as I cling to my desired outcome, I am an easy target for doubt and fear, fears of my own creation. Nothing, absolutely nothing, has happened to indicate that my desires and God's are not the same. In fact, I have had several signs that indicate we are in agreement on this. But until the miracle happens, until the Songteller and I are healed enough to open both our minds and our hearts to love and to each other and become willing to act on it, there can be no "happy ending." Until I let go of the ending I desire and trust God to do his thing, there can be no miracles for either of us.

Possibly, I do have my miracle because I have healed enough now to let my happy ending go. I have taken it and planted it firmly in God's hands, and said, "Here. You know what my desires are, and I trust you to write and direct this in any way you choose." As I write this, the Songteller and I are going through a relationship adjustment, still safely from a distance, and God is still working on both the miracles and the script. But I trust, finally, that God's script, however it is written, will be the very best for us both. God's will is love, and it will be done. Love, as always.

~ Surrender

Surrender is a principle that is often misunderstood. Surrender is not simply giving up. Surrender is choosing to give up based on an awareness and acceptance of reality. Surrender is an admission of powerlessness where powerlessness truly exists, an admission that it is not possible for me to be or do whatever it is I have been trying, over and over, to be or do. Surrender says I have tried my best and it has not worked, so I admit that it is insane for me to try again. Surrender does not say, "Well, I cannot do it now, but later may be different"; that is submission. Surrender knows and accepts that I cannot do it *ever*.

Surrender goes against the old adage: "If at first you don't succeed, try, try again." But, doing something the same way over and over and expecting different results is the definition of insanity. Surrender restores sanity and leads to peace and serenity. Surrender is an aspect of humility that replaces the frustration of futile resistance with the calm freedom of acceptance. Still, for many people, surrender has a shameful connotation. Throughout the history of war, men have been glorified and exalted for fighting and dying rather than surrendering. (Remember the Alamo!) Yet, in many areas of life, surrender is not how I lose; often it is a way I can ultimately win. In the world of addictions and spiritual truth, surrender is the *only* way I can win.

Surrender is the principle that works with faith and trust to make walking with my guide a glorious, happy, joyous, and free journey. If faith gives me a belief in a God who can and will care for me, and trust creates the willingness for me to allow him to do that, surrender then is the action that allows it to happen. Surrender is essential to working the twelve steps, my personal road map for spiritual growth. When I surrender by admitting my powerlessness over my addictive behaviors (step one), I allow God to remove my compulsion to use. When I surrender my character defects, or road blocks (step six), and humbly ask God to remove them (step seven), I allow him to graciously oblige. When I surrender my will and my life to God's care (implicit in step three), I allow God to come in and guide me as we walk together down my unique path, the road home. All of his gifts are restored, and my journey becomes a wondrous experience no matter where my path takes me. Without total surrender, or when surrender is not sustainable, the path gets a little less happy, joyous, and free, less well-defined. I get lost when I try, once more, to find my own way or tell God which path we are to take. Backseat driving or trying to take the wheel will always teach me something, and the lesson learned usually is a refresher course in humility and surrender.

When surrender is complete and sustainable, many of the principles I have written about just fall into place. When surrender is incomplete or unsustainable, then these principles serve to get me back on track beside my guide. That is when humility, courage, patience, forgiveness, honesty, acceptance, and many other principles become absolutely essential to my spiritual well-being. And these are in place because few of us have mastered the principle of surrender perfectly. In fact, I doubt that anyone has. To surrender completely to God is to be open to allowing God to express love through me at all times. To surrender completely to God is to see every aspect of every experience of my life through God's eyes, the eyes of love. To see through the eyes of love means that I see beyond fear, anger, hostility, cruelty, abuse, and all other forms of unloving and destructive human behavior to the loving, innocent, and perfect God-self within and respond not with fear, anger, hostility, and so on, but with love and forgiveness. To see through the eyes of love means that I view all fear-based and unloving human behavior as errors that are a call for love. To see through the eyes of love means that I understand that to open my heart and love you is to open my heart and love God because human and divine love are one and the same. Divine love filtered through human imperfections is still divine. To see through the eyes of love is to know that to love one another is God's will, the path each of us is to follow in our own unique way. It also means that when I allow fear to come in and close my heart to you, I am also closing my heart to God. We are all connected; it is all the same love.

My personal surrender to God and love has been a slow, painful process. It has taken me a very long time to even begin to understand what it means and how it feels. Several times I've thought I was there, then the freedom and joy vanished as I allowed fear to close my heart or false pride to cause me to take back aspects of my life that I had given to God. I will say one thing, however. Without exception, that which I have totally surrendered has been removed and has not returned. That which I have taken back was probably never surrendered in the first place!

I have surrendered many things to God, turned over my addictions and addictive behaviors, my relationships, my life path, and, to a great degree, my will. But there is one very important part of me that I had not surrendered, the part of me that rightfully belongs to love. I had not surrendered my heart. To surrender my heart to God, to love, is to open my heart wide and let love in, to allow love to flow freely into my heart so that I may then share it with others, to let love work both in me and through me. I thought I had done that, but I had not, not completely. Every day I asked God to channel me in love, but still I was not letting love come in and take over. I had not surrendered my heart completely to love in any form, either human or divine. And because I had not surrendered, had not opened my heart completely to receiving love in either form, my attempts to share love with others were not being sustained. I gave more love than I was willing to accept, and, after awhile, I would feel depleted, spent, and even put upon because what was going out was not being replenished. So I would have to withdraw from those I loved for awhile until I regained my balance. I knew something was wrong, that what I believed about love didn't seem to be working for me, that I didn't seem to be able to feel the love that I knew was there for me from God and from those who loved me.

I have a very dear soul friend who has created a gift of love in her backyard, a labyrinth whose circular path is marked by river rocks. For those who do not know, a labyrinth is a kind of circular path with no dead ends, a path that winds back and forth and around, and ultimately leads to a center, like the bull's-eye of a dart board. Walking a labyrinth is a spiritual journey, a form of meditation. On the way in, I prepare myself to receive spiritual gifts by emptying myself, quieting my mind, removing thoughts of negativity and pain. By the time I reach the center of the labyrinth, I am open to receiving the gifts God has for me there. I may ask for certain gifts or simply let God choose. Then, as I walk the path in reverse, I take the gifts with me and ready myself to recognize and use them in my life.

I have been told that surrender to love is a gift, and I now know that to be true. Not too long after my friend created her labyrinth, I took a four-week trip, alone, back to Quadra Island, the place my soul has chosen for my final home in this life. I soon realized that this was a spiritual journey, that I was supposed to go alone, and that I would learn something very important on the journey. My desire was to be able to speak from the heart to the Songteller, as I had asked him to speak to me, and I knew that surrender was somehow a part of this. What I did not know, until I found myself there, was that my journey symbolized walking a labyrinth and that Quadra was its center. It was there, in my beach house on the quiet side of the island, with a backdrop of calm waters, lush islands, and the majestic coastal mountains of the British Columbia mainland, that I would receive my spiritual gifts. I had been led to design my journey such that the places I visited on the way to Quadra readied me to receive them, and the places I visited after I left Quadra gently transitioned me back to my present home, the place where I would be able to recognize and use the gifts I had been given.

At first I did not know what the gifts were; then I began to feel the changes within me. The gift I had been given was an open heart—surrender to love, both human and divine. I can feel the difference, the flow of love from God through me to all his creations, the flow of love to and from the special people in my life, the loving presence of those who are with me spiritually but not physically. I can feel the difference in the words I share—they seem to come from a different place, a centered, honest place. Although my mind forms them and my lips speak them, they originate in my heart. I can feel the difference when I interact with my soul friends in a more loving, gentle, patient, and compassionate way. I can feel when my heart is open to love and when it begins to close to love, when I allow fear or other emotions based on projection to come into my mind. And because I can feel it, I can call on God to help me open my heart again. I can move back into the present where God and love are found, where time is eternal, and where all is well and on schedule. To be sure, I am not saying my surrender to love is complete and sustainable, that I now see all things at all times through the eyes of love. Fear still returns and clouds my vision. But at least now I know what surrender to love feels like and how to allow those feelings to be. I know finally how it feels to have an open, receptive, humble, and compassionate heart. And the key to freedom and joy is surrender to love—that is what turning my will and my life over to God is all about.

~ AWARENESS

Awareness is simply the state of being aware, of clearly seeing, knowing, and understanding a particular truth or reality. Awareness is the principle that begins to convert self-deception into honesty and thus is a key to finding and knowing my true self and recognizing my personal truths. Awareness is also a cornerstone for spiritual growth, the principle that must be present before change is possible. In twelve-step programs, we often speak of the three A's—awareness, acceptance, and action. The concepts expressed in the Serenity Prayer are based on awareness—awareness of what cannot be changed and of what can and needs to be changed. The wisdom to know the difference also is grounded in awareness.

Awareness comes when the protective blankets of denial and self-deception no longer serve a useful purpose. As such, awareness is, I believe, a gift from God. Awareness is often born through a great deal of emotional pain and will absolutely not be given to me until I am ready to receive it. Awareness will not come until I am ready to see, know, or understand whatever it is that denial or self-deception has kept me from seeing, knowing, or understanding. My truth or a certain reality in my life may be very obvious to someone else and not at all obvious to me. You may tell me what you see as my truth quietly, loudly, or often, but until I am ready to become aware I will not hear anything you say. Life may send me harsh, painful, or loving experiences designed to show me my truth, but until I am ready to become aware, I simply will not get the message. Not from you, not from life, and not from God.

All of the twelve steps, my road map for the spiritual journey home, are grounded in the awareness of certain truths. But it is the self-awareness gained through taking several fourth step inventories that has given me a clearer picture of who I am, my true self. I have already shared many of the traits I became aware of through working the fourth step. False pride, arrogance, grandiosity, self-centeredness, and a grand assortment of fears—all these and many more were brought to my awareness. I also became aware of the true worth of the many wonderful gifts God has given me—those aspects of my personal truth that I now gratefully own and joyously share. My artistic and musical gifts, the words I am writing here, the divine love in my heart, its humble expression through compassion, forgiveness, and generosity, and many other positive qualities have been brought out of hiding and incorporated into who I perceive myself to be through awareness.

I have also discovered other aspects of who I am, simple things that fill in the essence of my personality, through the gift of awareness. Nadine loves yellow flowers and hot showers and loose-cut, long dresses that flow. She loves to listen to the sound of the ocean and watch the endless parade of waves breaking on shore. She loves to place both hands on the massive trunk of a giant redwood and feel the strength and energy present in that magnificent tree. She loves the colors of the sea and forest, aqua's and deep greens and browns, colors that reflect the island to which she is being called home. She loves loose-fitting jeans and sweatshirts with a soft, feminine touch and casual western living. She loves to walk outdoors and meditate, drive her sporty little car over curvy mountain roads, hike through fields of wild flowers, photograph mountains and streams and all natural vistas, play her magnificent piano, fly in small planes, and listen to and play romantic piano music. She loves to give and receive hugs and share herself and her life with her soul friends. Through experience and a newfound awareness of my feelings about my experiences, I have learned these and many more things about myself. A few years ago, my likes and dislikes were often the likes and dislikes of my fellow travelers. Awareness has allowed me to discern between what is mine and what is not.

Awareness must be present before change can be effected, but awareness does not guarantee change. Often change through acceptance and action comes much later, or may not come at all. Through numerous arrests for driving under the influence and two sessions in treatment for chemical dependency, the Piano Player became *aware* that he was an alcoholic and verbally admitted to being an alcoholic. But I do not believe he ever *accepted* his disease in his heart, and he certainly did not do what was needed to arrest his disease. I was *aware* that I used and abused certain foods the same way he used and abused alcohol long before I accepted my disease and was willing to do whatever it took to become and remain abstinent from my food compulsion.

Awareness too may be a long time coming. Two of my female soul friends were married more than twenty years to addicts before they became aware that their marriages were over. It was several more years in both cases before they were able to accept and act on their knowings. The same pattern is true with my reaction to the Piano Player's alcoholism. I was not aware, for over five years, of the uncontrollable nature of his drinking, even though I was immersed in the insanity of living and working with a man who drank continuously from the time he got up until he passed out. When awareness finally did come to me, I expected his first treatment session to fix the problem (which, incidentally, was the only problem I was aware of in our marriage!). My acceptance did not come for another three years and had to be triggered by his relapse into drinking again. Only then did I begin to act—to read and learn about the disease of alcoholism and ultimately to get help for myself in dealing with it.

The same process applies to what the sixth step calls "defects of character" and that I prefer to call “road hazards.” These are the thoughts, beliefs, behaviors, and attitudes that limit me, keep me from being and doing that which God would have me be and do, and make it more difficult for me to be my true self and walk my unique path. For me, awareness happened only as I became willing to become aware, and acceptance and action (as required by steps five through seven) came much later. This was a case where I was willing to become aware, but not ready to go beyond that. I thought I was ready and believed that I had taken those steps to have my road hazards removed, but I became aware much later that I had deluded myself into believing that I had done them. Here again, awareness only came to me when I was finally ready to complete the process and release them to God.

I could go on and on with examples from my life where awareness of a problem came to me much later than it would have to any casual observer of my life. It took me twenty-one years, two divorces, and innumerable relationship breakups before I became aware that my own behaviors played a part in these breakups. (Before that, I just believed I picked the wrong men!) It took me eleven years of changing jobs and/or bosses every couple of years to become aware that I was mentally under-challenged in my chosen profession as a secretary. It took me almost thirty years to become aware of my need for a spiritual guide and another five years to become aware of how to follow his direction. And it has taken me many more years to manifest the principles I understood in my mind and felt in my heart into my behaviors, to truly practice these principles in all my affairs.

The greatest gift of all has been the awareness that God is not only with me, but a part of me, a presence I can experience during meditation and feel whenever I am an open channel for him to express through me. This awareness has just come to me in my sixties, together with the awareness that all those wonderful gifts I expected other people, things, activities, and experiences to provide for me are gifts my guide had already given to me. Everything I could ever need is already within me or within my ability to give to myself. Love, joy, truth, passion, approval, acceptance, validation, nurturing, serenity, creativity—all these things are internal, not external. Anything you and life and my experiences give me is a bonus, an additional wondrous gift from God.

Awareness comes sooner to me now that I am following the direction of my guide, but there are new, exciting, and enlightening discoveries yet to be made. I will never, in this lifetime, be fully aware of who my true self is, nor will I be fully free of denial and self-deception. Awareness and the change that awareness may lead to is a process that moves with me as I walk with God down my unique path and travel the road home.

~ ACCEPTANCE

Acceptance is the principle that both restores serenity and precedes change. Before my serenity can be restored, I must accept the reality of whatever is disturbing it. Before change can happen, I must accept the reality of my current position. Thus, acceptance is a close relative to surrender and a prerequisite to forgiveness, which is a change of perception. Whereas surrender deals with the big picture, the principle of acceptance can, and should be, applied to every minute aspect of my life. As the Serenity Prayer indicates, acceptance applies to those things I can change *and* those I cannot change. Accepting the things I cannot change replaces frustration and despair with serenity and peace. Accepting the things I can change empowers me to go ahead and change them.

Acceptance neither approves nor disapproves. It does not carry with it a judgment call; it merely observes what is. Thus, to accept is not to condone or tolerate. When the protective cloak of denial was lifted and I accepted the reality of the Piano Player's alcoholism, that acceptance did not carry with it the implicit approval of the bizarre behavior that results from the disease. When I accepted the reality of my own addictive behaviors, I was then given the freedom to choose recovery from those addictive behaviors. Before acceptance of my reality, I had no choice. I cannot choose to treat and recover from something before I accept the truth that I am ill.

Since acceptance and surrender are so closely linked, acceptance is crucial to following my road map for spiritual growth, the twelve steps. I have already said that working each step requires that the three A's—awareness, acceptance, and action—be applied to the spiritual truth represented by the step. Beyond this, certain steps are themselves steps of acceptance. Step two, the "came to believe" step, requires me to accept the concept of a higher power, a God of my understanding. Step five requires me to accept the reality of my road hazards by acknowledging their presence to God, myself, and another person. The second part of step eight, "became willing to make amends," requires acceptance of my part in harmful behavior. Step ten, the first growth step, requires me to continue to accept the reality of my own behaviors by keeping a running inventory and promptly making amends.

Aside from its value and need in working the steps, acceptance is one of the most useful principles I have learned since I began walking with my guide. Acceptance can be applied to absolutely every problem, challenge, and aspect of my life. Acceptance allows me to receive others' gifts of love, to open the flow of loving energy between others, me, and God. Acceptance of what is and is not my truth and reality allows me to make life choices based on my truth and reality. Acceptance of people, actions, and events, as they are, silences judgmentalism, perfectionism, false pride, and self-righteousness. My acceptance of me, my actions, and my behaviors, as they are, replaces arrogance and grandiosity with humility. Acceptance of the humanness of others, and mine, replaces regret, guilt, anger, resentment, and fear with love, forgiveness, and compassion. Acceptance of actions and events as they are today, not as they were in the past or might be in the future, relieves the pain that accompanies unmet expectations. Acceptance of loss, failure, rejection, indifference, hostility, and physical discomfort as life challenges instead of life tragedies helps me to move through them more painlessly. Serenity and freedom are the gifts of acceptance, whereas non-acceptance creates discomfort and chaos. To love others unconditionally is to accept them as they are. To love myself unconditionally is to accept myself as I am. These are simple concepts, but are very difficult to apply. Still, if I had to choose the one principle that relates to all the others, that one principle would be acceptance.

Oddly, acceptance has come much more easily to me than its big brother, surrender. I have valued my serenity for some time now and have learned that acceptance is the key to maintaining it. This was, of course, not true back in the insane days before I allowed God to come back into my life as my guide. I certainly did not accept or love unconditionally those people in my life that I was determined to fix or save. I certainly did not accept the Piano Player's behavior for what it was—the bizarre symptoms of a crippling disease of body, mind, and spirit. True, I tolerated it, but I did not accept it. I certainly did not accept political or religious views I disagreed with, nor those who held them. And, most definitely, I did not accept myself, the essence of Nadine. Otherwise I would not have spent so much time and energy trying to be like someone else!

As I gradually began to practice acceptance in my life, it was much easier to apply to those persons, events, and actions that did not directly affect me. The closer a person was to me, the more judgmental and less accepting I would be. So it stands to reason that the one I was the most un-accepting of the longest was me. As with forgiveness, acceptance came first with others and last with myself. Self-acceptance has been much harder to achieve and consistently maintain. Even though I commit to loving and accepting myself daily, I still tend to beat myself up when an unwanted fear or outdated behavior from my past creeps back into my present. Often I attempt to ignore these fears and behaviors instead of accepting and surrendering them, and that is when they rise up and grab me unexpectedly. When I compassionately accept my fears and unwanted behaviors and love the part of me that is afraid or acting out old life scenes, the fears and behaviors mysteriously become less formidable and more manageable. Eventually, though I haven't quite reached this stage yet, I believe I will release them to God and they will dissipate completely. .

One of the most difficult applications of acceptance for me has been acceptance of the loss of one I love. There are many stages of grief—denial, anger, bargaining, pain, and so on—but the final, healing step in the grief process is acceptance. Acceptance allows me to move on with my life after death, divorce, or any other life challenge perceived as a traumatic loss. Until acceptance is achieved, a broken heart cannot be completely healed and made free to love again. To be sure, love applied in massive doses can, and does, heal any wound. But only if I am open to accepting love and allow myself to be healed. Often, attaining acceptance requires my being willing to accept the love required to achieve it. The gifts of love that came to me at the center of the labyrinth were gifts both of surrender and acceptance—final acceptance and healing of the wounds created by the death of the Piano Player and the loss of the music we shared.

The Songteller has also been walking a healing path that leads to acceptance. He was, for many years, a bandleader and stage performer. He is a fine guitar player and an exceptional balladeer and has for some time been creating and recording his music in a home studio. Not too long ago, he sent me a song he had just finished recording, together with a challenge. Affixed to the tape was a yellow Post-it bearing the message, "Analyze this, ol' Swami!" My friend grieves and heals through the music he creates, and the losses he has been grieving for many years are similar to mine—his musical career and the very special lady who was his wife during that time. I had recognized the message in a previous song to be a very important part of his healing and had told him so, which prompted the challenge.

The first time I listened to the song, called "Defying Gravity," by Jesse Winchester, I felt this wonderful sense of peace and calm, but I didn't have a clue as to what the song meant. Here are the enigmatic, obscure, and profound words:

> I live on a big blue ball. I never did dream I would fall.
> But even the day that I do I'll jump off and smile back at you.
>
> We don't even know where we are. They say that we're circling a star.
> But I'll take their word for I don't know. I'm dizzy, so maybe it's so.
>
> I'm riding a big blue ball and never did dream I would fall.
> But even the highest must lay low. When I do fall, I'll be glad to go.

It took Swami several reads to get it, but the message I finally heard and gave to my friend was this: The song speaks to his life, both as a stage musician and with the lady he loved. In both cases, he lived on a self-created pedestal and tried to maintain an image that was not quite real, an image without human vulnerabilities. In both cases, his humanness led to the fall and the subsequent loss. In a sense, this brought relief because he no longer had to pretend to be what he was not. Still, the true meaning, the most important message, and one that I did not understand for a long time, was that he has finally come to terms with what happened, how it happened, and why it happened. This is projected not in the notes or the lyrics, but in the soulful way he plays and sings them. The wonderful sense of peace and calm that I feel when I listen to the song is the peace and calm of acceptance.

~ HUMILITY

Humility is a principle that is often misunderstood. Humility is not subservience, and it has nothing at all to do with humiliation. Humility does not ask me to be less than anyone or anything. Humility asks me to be open and teachable, to consider different options and views, to be willing to learn and grow. Humility asks me to be my true self and walk my unique path, to honestly look at who and what I am and how I relate to God. Humility honestly appraises and accepts who and what I am, but never flaunts it. Humility is neither greater than nor less then, comparative nor competitive. In the eyes of humility, and of God, we are all equal and unique. Each of us has a unique and important role to play in God's grand scheme of things. Humility is the key to playing that role, of starring in my own life, of not being afraid to share the unique gifts that are mine to share. Humility keeps me open to my director's cues, willing to follow them, and allows me to be the very best I can be. Humility is the principle that takes my faith and puts it to work in my life.

Humility teaches me whose job is whose, and which tasks and responsibilities belong to me and which ones belong to God. Humility teaches me to allow my guide to show me the way when I become lost or confused, to accept help from him when I need it. Humility brings me the wisdom to know what things I can change and what things I cannot change. Humility allows me to accept God's guidance in all areas of my life. Humility requires me to let go of arrogance, false pride, self-centeredness, self-righteousness, grandiosity, perfectionism, and judgmentalism. Humility requires me to let go of any ego-driven personal trait that deifies me, or is based on the illusion that I am as wise, or wiser, than God.

Humility allows me to openly, honestly, and willingly express the love I feel in my heart through forgiveness, compassion, and generosity. Humility works with faith, trust, and surrender to make it easier to accept the direction of my guide, to walk with him, not behind or ahead. When I succumb to fear and lose either a part of my true self or my unique path, humility allows me to admit I am lost and accept help in finding my way back. When I take back what I have previously surrendered to God or otherwise try to do his work for him, humility allows me to forgive myself and start over again. With humility, I can lose my way temporarily, but never permanently. With humility, I can always find my way back to God.

Humility was not a principle I had ever thought very much about before I was given my road map back to God, the twelve steps. And humility certainly wasn't a principle I had used in my life. After all, God and I didn't have a relationship, so how could I know what my place was, relative to him? Still, it took me a very long time in recovery and several fourth steps for me to recognize my lack of humility—my arrogance, grandiosity, self-centeredness, self-righteousness, perfectionism, judgmentalism, intolerance, and closed-mindedness. And it took even longer for me to recognize and release the false pride that is the root cause of these traits. In fact, false pride is what did not allow me to see that I had any of these traits. Mine was a passive personality. I was neither aggressive nor abrasive, so my lack of humility was not flaunted openly. But it certainly was present, unacknowledged and unaccepted.

In fact, I really disliked these traits when I saw them openly displayed by other people. My father, in particular, openly displayed them to a great degree, and I certainly wasn't like him! Or was I? Dad was Archie Bunker in the flesh, at least with his family. He was a wonderful, loving man disguised as a domineering, opinionated, intolerant, prejudiced, prideful, judgmental, perfectionistic, and fearful person. I could never discuss anything we disagreed on with him because he was always right! I had trouble getting along with my dad all my life, and as I write this I can see quite clearly why. He mirrored all the things in me that I didn't want to see, could not admit were there. We didn't get along because we were too much alike! The only difference was that he let his personal defects show, whereas I kept mine carefully hidden, if not from others, certainly from myself.

I was a do-it-myself-er. I didn't need help or advice from anyone in charting the course of *my* life—not from you and certainly not from God! That is grandiosity. I also knew better than you did how you should chart the course of *your* life. Under the guise of friendship, I would cheerfully tell you, asked or unasked, how to live your life and deal with your problems. That is arrogance. My need to please you, to be only what I believed you wanted me to be or do what you wanted me to do was based on self-centeredness, judgmentalism, and perfectionism. So were my feelings of inferiority when doing something I did not excel in. Low self-esteem is self-centeredness, by definition. So is seeing the world as composed of greater-thans and less-thans, always comparing others against myself. Those whom I and my peers admired were greater-thans; those who differed from us in lifestyle, politics, religion, or most anything else were the less-thans. We did not consider their views to be worth very much and we hardly even listened to them. My views (although they were subject to change, depending on who happened to be greater than at the time) were *always* the right views. That is self-righteousness, intolerance, and closed-mindedness. And when I refused to share myself with others, to let them come close, to see my vulnerabilities, to admit my imperfections and my needs, to allow others to be there for me when I needed them to be—that is an example of false pride. In fact, all of these traits are corollaries to false pride, the need to compensate for feeling "less than" by being "better than." All of these traits kept me separate and isolated from people, from God, and from myself. Inherent in all of these traits is Nadine acting as King Baby, frightened and alone, trying to do things that are best left in God's capable hands. I do not know what is best for me, let alone for others; only God does. I certainly do not know what path either of us should walk; only God does. I do not know what is right or what is wrong, for others or for the world in general, and it's not my place to pass judgment on views that are different from mine. My job is to love and accept. Humility teaches me how to do that.

Life has brought me many lessons in humility, some life-changing and some simply designed to gently remind me who is the guide and who is the one receiving the guidance. Notice that all of my lessons in humility have a common theme. They all involve false pride and/or its corollaries, and they all result in a painful experience. My lessons in humility have all been born in pain. To be sure, some are more painful than others, and some are more life-changing. But it is all the same lesson with the same result . Once more I end up, first flat on the ground and then back on my knees before my guide. And once more, God gently picks me up, dusts me off, gives me a hug, shakes his head lovingly, and says, "Are you ready to try again?" So once more I forgive myself, vow to stay close to my guide and accept help when I need it, and try once more to keep my rightful place with God, all of which requires me to practice humility, to exercise it in my daily life. Identifying and letting go of the "I think I knows" and opening my mind to new ideas and experiences is an exercise in humility, as is consciously and continuously allowing God to express love and compassion through me. Any time I consciously open my mind and heart, I am exercising humility and expressing love—to myself, to others, and to God.

~ Forgiveness

Forgiveness is the principle that relieves the burden of anger, resentment, guilt, and hatred. Forgiveness is one of the cornerstones of freedom from the emotional chains that bind me to the past and to my fellow travelers. Forgiveness is the principle that releases me to enjoy the present and co-create my future unhampered by the burdens and blessings of my past. Forgiveness allows me to keep the memories and let go of the pain—or the joy. Hanging on to past joys can be as damaging as hanging on to past pain or grievances. Both keep me from living today and anticipating tomorrow with an open mind and heart.

Forgiveness is also a cornerstone for the expression of unconditional love, a prerequisite for fully opening my heart, surrendering it to love. To be sure, the act of forgiveness, as most of us understand and practice it, requires that a judgment has been made, either of me or of someone else, and a sentence of guilty pronounced. In a perfect world filled with perfect love, forgiveness means seeing only the innocence within and holding each other blameless, without judgment. Sins are not sins but errors to be corrected, not punished or condemned. But, ours is not a perfect world and I am far from being a perfectly loving person. I still judge, as do most of us. The need for forgiveness is in me—forgiveness of others and forgiveness of myself. And sometimes even forgiveness of God.

Without forgiveness, I am spiritually separated from the one who is not forgiven. Who it is does not matter—it could be you or it could be me. The result is the same, since we are all connected. When I separate from you, or myself, I separate from God. The part of my heart that remains closed and wounded is also closed to God, and to love, causing a tremendous amount of pain.

Without forgiveness, I am also doomed to carry my past with me into my future. How many of us carry the leftover baggage from old relationships into new ones? Instead of greeting each new person and experience as a new beginning, we judge it against our past experience. An unforgiving heart closed to love will never fully open to a new love until it is healed. And the great healers are love and forgiveness.

Forgiveness is a two-part process, involving the opening of both my mind and my heart, and the magic key that opens both is acceptance. If my heart opens, my mind usually follows, but the reverse is not necessarily true. Since I am an optimist, my mind does not believe in negative emotions such as resentment, guilt, and regret. So I became an expert at intellectualizing these emotions away, of forgiving others and myself only with my mind, and burying the feelings that are tied to them. Thus, my mind was open, but my heart was still closed. Feelings buried alive do not die, and often come out at unexpected times and in unexpected ways. Buried anger and resentment create passive-aggressive behavior that subtly sabotages intimacy and relationship. Buried guilt and regret creates unseen and unowned emotional hooks, ties that emotionally bind me to the past and to others if they are part of my past. In all instances, until I clear and release the buried feelings and open my heart, I will not be freed from the chains of past relationships, past events, and past behaviors.

The residue of being unforgiving comes in several forms, creating many of what I call the road hazards. The road hazards are baggage I carry with me as I walk my path, the baggage that makes the journey much more difficult than it need be and often keeps me from being my true self and walking my unique path. The residue of not forgiving others is resentment and anger. The residue of not forgiving myself can also be resentment and anger, plus guilt, shame, regret, and depression. Many of us who carry this baggage with us do it willingly as a form of self-punishment or martyrdom. This is *our* stuff, not God's. He has never intended for us to have to learn through pain. His will would have us travel the road easily, lightly, happily, joyously, and freely.

There is a movie called *The Mission* that most vividly and graphically illustrates how reluctant we are to surrender the baggage of unforgiveness. In the movie, Robert De Niro returns to his village and is told by his brother that he and De Niro's girlfriend have fallen in love. In a fit of rage, De Niro kills his brother. In confinement, he sentences himself to a living death. A priest takes custody of him, and they begin the arduous journey through the jungle to the priest's native mission. De Niro insists on carrying a huge bag of rocks, making his trek through the jungle formidable. When he collapses, the rocks are taken from him. When he recovers enough to continue, he insists on picking them up again. Climbing a steep and dangerous cliff, he nearly falls to his death and still won't surrender his bag of rocks. Finally, after much pain and suffering, he surrenders his will in service to the priest and puts down the bag of rocks.

Forgiveness is something I thought I was very good at and really was not. Head, yes; heart, no. And, since being judgmental is one of my personal challenges, that meant I had a lot of opportunities to forgive. With the Piano Player, I perfected the art. I was always judging his behavior, always criticizing, always being hurt or angry, and always forgiving. With him, forgiveness came first from the heart and thus it truly did come. With others, the path was longer and rockier. Actually, there were few others who evoked these feelings, since I let few people come close enough. My major resentments were directed toward my parents, and most were first intellectualized away. Later, after I began walking with my guide, I was able to go back and forgive most of these resentments with my heart.

Still, there was only one person in my life for whom forgiveness was impossible, and that, of course, was me. I have read that until I have forgiven myself for making a judgment, I cannot fully forgive the one I have judged. I have also read that any time there is emotional pain, there is unforgiveness, that the pain I feel when my heart begins to close can only be relieved through acceptance and forgiveness. But, what about buried pain? Shame is the one that really got me—who I was was not okay. I remember reading John Bradshaw's book, *Healing the Shame that Binds You*, many years ago, when I was just beginning recovery. At the time, I did not understand shame or recognize it operating in my life (see "Shame"). Now I know what it is, and that, of course, is the key to forgiveness. Before I can release old pain and forgive myself, I have to become aware and accept that it is there.

For some time now, and under the loving direction of my guide, I have been working on self-forgiveness. To be sure, making the amends required by steps eight and nine cleared away the earned guilt and most of my resentments. But with those feelings, both earned and unearned, that are buried deep in my soul, I found that following the direction of my guide has helped me the most in processing what I call buried emotional land mines, pockets of pain, guilt, anger, and fear that I did not even know were there. The events of my life, the places I am led to visit, often point me to their location. For example, an attack of severe neck pain led me to one such land mine, only it took me awhile to find it. My original attack of neck pain occurred a few months before the Piano Player and I were married, so this recent attack pointed me back to that time. Still, I did not find the land mine for several weeks—until one morning when I realized that it would have been our twentieth wedding anniversary. That was where the land mine of grief was buried—at the beginning, when all the dreams, both personal and musical, were fresh, new, and alive. I had gone back and cleared other pain pockets of our relationship, but this very important one had not been touched. After it was released and healed, my neck pains diminished and eventually disappeared. Forgiveness allows me to keep the memories and release the emotions.

Still, the toughest emotional land mines for me to find are the ones that have been buried the deepest because the pain caused was the greatest and most long-lasting. I have just found one of these, attached to an event I believed I had long ago forgiven and released. When I was eleven or twelve, I was sexually molested by my father. Not raped—molested. Sensually kissed, held, and vaginally fondled. As soon as my dad felt my resistance, he stopped and said to me, "Don't tell your mother." I never did. But this one event terrified me. I was afraid to be alone with my dad for many years afterwards, afraid that he would try it again. Of course, he never did. But the wall of fear this one event created separated me from him for the rest of his life. It was still there the day he died and for many years after. Long after I understood that he was sexually addicted and never intended to hurt me in any way. Long after I understood that this was a minor trauma compared to incest and rape. I opened my mind, but kept my heart closed, shutting out the one source of love I always knew was there for me. Long after I had forgiven him, or so I thought, I withheld love from him. Long after I forgave him for his part, I could not forgive myself for my part, and my heart remained closed.

I discovered this deeply buried land mine while I was thinking about what personal experience to share on forgiveness. I discovered it, and it exploded with pain—all I could say was "I love you," over and over. I know his soul heard me, wherever it is, and, with God's help, I have finally released this part of my past. One more hook gone, one more wound healed.

~ Compassion

Compassion is the principle that feels and cares about my fellow traveler and me. Compassion recognizes pain, honors it, and administers to it when appropriate. Compassion, too, is a cornerstone for the expression of unconditional love, and compassion toward myself manifests as self-care. Compassion sees beyond the outer facade of fear-based emotion, the wall erected to keep me away from you, feels your pain, hears your disguised call for love, and responds to it. Compassion cares for the ill, comforts the dying, educates the illiterate, and retrains the mentally and physically challenged. Compassion counsels, mediates, prays, observes, and discerns. Compassion gives selflessly without attachment to outcomes. People gifted with compassion are drawn to be the caregivers of the world—doctors, nurses, ministers, social workers. Not everyone is called to be a professional caregiver, but everyone can be compassionate.

A compassionate heart feels the spiritual connection among all hearts and knows that what affects any one of us affects us all. A compassionate heart honors, accepts, and has compassion for its own pain and, thus, is able to honor, accept, and have compassion for the hearts of others. A compassionate heart loves for the joy of loving, shares for the joy of sharing, gives for the joy of giving, without any attachment to a specific outcome. A compassionate heart is not attached, period. Even though a compassionate heart honors your pain and problems, it does not get pulled into them emotionally or carry them for you. A compassionate heart understands and knows how to practice the Al-Anon principle of detachment with love.

Having a compassionate heart may lead me to be a caregiver, but never a caretaker. Caretakers do exactly that—they do not give, they take. The actions may appear to be the same, but the motives behind them are very different. Compassionate caregiving is sourced in love. Caretaking is sourced in fear and false pride, since caretaking often is used to bolster low self-esteem. If the primary reason I care for you is to make me feel good or to control you, I am caretaking. If I care for you because I care *about* you, without consideration of my own rewards, then I am being a compassionate caregiver. There will be rewards, to be sure, but that is not why I give. What I give selflessly to someone else, I will also receive. A compassionate and generous gift of love will return to me many times over, but that is spiritual law, not an expectation. If it is an expectation, then the gift becomes a trade and caregiving becomes caretaking. And the recipient can usually tell the difference.

The hospice workers that administered to the Piano Player before his death and to me after his death all have compassionate hearts. To be sure, they are paid for what they do, but that is not why they do it. Compassionate caregiving touches the hearts that are open to being touched, and mine certainly was.

I have already shared with you that I am gifted with a loving nature, but one I did not share with anyone until I had reconnected with my guide and had begun to rediscover and reclaim my true self. Before that time, I was self-centered and narcissistic, not selfless. Anything I did had a hook attached to it, usually some hidden expectation based on emotional need. Fear had closed my loving heart, and compassion was totally unknown to me—pity, perhaps, but not compassion. Compassion requires an open, loving heart and a sense of connection to others, and I had neither. Compassion requires sensitivity and awareness of those actions and behaviors that can cause pain in others and a conscious decision not to intentionally act or behave in a hurtful way. As long as I was absorbed in my own pain, I could hardly be genuinely sensitive to someone else's pain.

Compassion also inspires a desire to serve others, and I definitely did not have any such desires. I remember, as a teenager, thinking that I could never be a doctor, a nurse, a teacher, or any one of a number of other caregiving professions. It just could not happen and did not happen. My professions were service-oriented, but not caregiving in any sense. My skills were in working with numbers and words, not people. And I have no children, the one calling where a compassionate heart might have surfaced.

Compassion is a skill I must relearn, one that requires an open and strong mind-heart connection, one I am working to manifest into my life even as I write these words. If mine is a loving, gentle heart, guided by the deer, surely it must be a compassionate heart as well. Or is it? For a long time, I have wondered. Only now, many years after reconnecting with God and following his guidance in earnest, am I beginning to feel the stirrings of my compassionate heart and the desire to act upon it. To be sure, I have done service work ever since I began following my twelve-step road map. But my service work has been doing things *for* people, not working directly *with* people on a one-on-one basis. I wrote checks, kept books, and sold raffle tickets, but I did not sponsor, mostly because nobody asked me to be their sponsor. I turned down the first person who did ask me to be her sponsor because I "wasn't ready." A fundamental requirement for a sponsor is a compassionate heart, plus the desire to act as a program guide and spiritual mentor, and I had neither gift. Being a sponsor takes time, dedication, detachment, love, patience, experience in working the steps, and a willingness to allow God to orchestrate the whole process. Without compassion and humility, sponsorship can turn into caretaking, advice-giving, and a source of resentment.

Now, after three false starts, I am finally working with sponsor-ees in Overeaters Anonymous, and the relationships are very rewarding. In fact, one of my sponsor-ees paid me a wonderful compliment one evening. She said, "Thank you for what you *don't* say." Another sponsor-ee has gifted me in many ways, but her greatest gift was telling me that I was the most unconditionally loving person she knew. I have also been guided to service work in Al-Anon that requires me to work with people, not for them, in a loving, caring, and compassionate way. Maybe there is hope for me after all.

Another area of service requiring a compassionate heart is being a hospice volunteer. Hospice volunteers are assigned to the families of terminally ill patients and go into their homes to provide relief for the family caregivers. It is rather like being a babysitter, except that the babies are older people in various stages of physical decline. I went through hospice volunteer training the spring after the Piano Player died, primarily as a part of my own grief process. But my volunteer work has been strictly clerical. I have not had any desire to work with patients.

Recently, I was guided to let go of the clerical tasks and to dissociate from hospice. When I did, I realized that I was not really dissociating from hospice, but rather preparing to enter a new phase. My sense now is that I will eventually go through the volunteer training again and then begin to work with patients. This has not happened yet, but it's still "out there." Again, this seems to be the sign of a budding compassionate heart, and there are other hopeful signs as well. I seem to be in a place of transition now; something is shifting inside me. And that shift hopefully is the manifestation of a compassionate heart into my life.

I say “hopefully” because the place where compassion is most needed is in intimate relationships, and that is where God seems to be guiding me now. It is there that seeing and hearing with eyes and ears connected to a compassionate and loving heart is the most desirable and necessary. It is in intimate relationships that sensitivity to and awareness of the intimate partner's pain and fear is most critical. Intimacy demands compassionate commitment, not to either intentionally or unintentionally cause emotional wounds. To love unconditionally, as required by true intimacy, is to love selflessly and compassionately. To create a holy relationship, sourced in love and dedicated to the service of God, demands a compassionate, humble, forgiving, and generous heart. And any intimate relationship, whether it be with a soul friend, a family member, or a spouse, requires the willingness to care for when caring for is required.

Intimate relationships also require the willingness to let go when letting go is required, which is an act of compassion. Letting go of loved ones when it is time for them to leave, letting go of loved ones when they choose different and diverging paths, letting go of a relationship when it has served its purpose and it is time for both parties to move on—these are all acts of compassion. I have done some of these things, but not all and not always willingly. However, I am reasonably sure that God will keep on bringing me opportunities to hone my skills and practice the art of compassionate living. At least I hope so, because I am committed to walking with my guide and doing his work for the rest of my journey down the road home. And this commitment requires a compassionate heart.

~ Generosity

Generosity is the art of selfless giving and is the third cornerstone for the expression of unconditional love. Generosity, compassion, and forgiveness are all interrelated and work together in harmony. A forgiving heart is generous in spirit. A compassionate heart is generous in service. A generous heart is both forgiving and compassionate. All three principles work to manifest love through loving actions.

Generosity selflessly gives those things which it is aware it has to give. The key is the desire to give, not to withhold, that which is known to be available for giving. I can hardly be generous with something I do not know I have to share. I must be aware that I have whatever it is and freely choose to share it with others. Generosity is often thought of with reference to money, but that is only one of many avenues for generosity. A person without wealth may be loving, forgiving, compassionate, and, thus, generous of spirit. A person with wealth may be generous with money but not at all generous with time, praise, or other loving attributes. Generosity, like forgiveness, requires both an open mind and an open heart. An open heart is naturally generous, compassionate, forgiving, and loving, but it matters not what my heart is saying if my mind refuses to listen.

A truly generous heart is generous in all areas of self—physical, mental, emotional, spiritual, and creative. Physical generosity is the selfless giving of those goods and services that meet physical needs—food, shelter, money, medical care, and so on. Mental generosity is selfless giving of my knowledge and experience. Educators, mentors, guides, anyone who selflessly shares their experience, strength, and hope at a twelve-step meeting—all these demonstrate mental generosity. Emotional generosity is the selfless giving of my emotions and their expression through caring and concern. Emotionally generous people are open, warm, enthusiastic, and passionate. They do not repress or medicate feelings. Spiritual generosity is the selfless giving of spiritual truths by allowing God to express them through me, by practicing these principles in all their affairs, as required by step twelve. Creative generosity is selflessly giving my creative gifts—sharing them with others. My tape of classical music, *A Gift of Love*, is an example of creative generosity (see "Divine Order"). Sharing my total presence, my true self, with another is an action made by a truly generous heart.

A truly generous heart also understands that selfless giving must be included as a part of self-care. Persons who are not generous (and forgiving and compassionate) to themselves are not expressing love to themselves and, thus, will find it difficult to be truly generous with others. The words "Love thy neighbor as thyself" mean exactly that.

A generous heart believes in abundance, not scarcity, and trusts that its needs will always be met. Thus, a generous heart must be grounded in faith, must trust in a source who can and will meet those needs, and have the humility necessary to allow and accept help from that source. A generous heart believes in and is connected to a loving, caring God and knows that the one thing that can always be generously shared is love. A generous heart is open to giving love and receiving love and knows that the source of love is limitless. As long as my heart is open and I am allowing God's love to be expressed through me, I can give it generously and without hesitation. The supply will never run out. Expressing and experiencing are the same.

It should be quite clear from my story so far that my generous heart was stifled and ignored for most of my life. My natural gifts were discounted and neither owned nor shared, and selfless giving was unknown to me. I "gave" as I learned to "give" from my family—with a hook or an expectation firmly attached to the "gift." And yet, with this, as with many other principles, I thought I knew how to give, and thus was closed to really knowing anything. Like my mother, I have been relatively generous with money and material things, but I have *never* been generous with myself. I deliberately withheld myself from others because I had lost sight of my gifts in all aspects of my being.

Since generosity is an expression of love, to find my generous heart I first had to find my loving heart, the part of me connected to God, who is love. I had to reconnect with God, to know him as love, and come to know that he was a part of me. Then I had to become willing to let God guide me and open my mind and heart to both expressing and experiencing his love in all forms. I also had to recognize and accept my gifts so that I could choose to share them, acquire the humility to share them selflessly, and open my mind to relearning how to do that. This is, of course, a description of finding my true self and unique path through following the direction of my guide and the prerequisite for a curriculum I refer to as learning to love (see “Integrity”).

The course work for learning to love has led me back to my generous heart, and now it is becoming increasingly easier to selflessly give the two things I can always give no matter what my life circumstances are. The first is my presence and my attention. Presence is essential to intimacy, and it is the gift of a generous heart. Presence is the selfless giving of self—being fully and completely available to another person, emotionally, physically, mentally, spiritually, and creatively. As those of us raised by parents who were, in some aspect, unavailable will quickly testify, presence is one of the most treasured gifts one human can give another. The only gift more precious than presence is the second and most important gift that we each have to give generously: love itself. As I said before, each of us has love to give because each of us *is* love—it is our essence through our connection with the God within. Who we are is love, and sharing who we are is, in a sense, sharing love. But, again, to do that requires both an open mind and an open heart.

I now allow God to help me keep my mind and heart open to both expressing and experiencing love, and he is very graciously responding to that request. Giving and receiving truly are the same. The more love I give, the more I receive, and vice versa. One Christmas, I went "home" to Quadra Island and spent Christmas eve at the center of the labyrinth, by myself, but not alone. My generous heart was filled with the love of my soul friends, many of whom I called to wish a Merry Christmas Eve. One of the contacts was a God shot—the sister friend I called who wasn't home just happened to be at the other sister friend's house, so I got to talk to them both. The love I gave with the flowers I sent to my aunt in Illinois returned to me in the form of flowers from a friend in Idaho; the bouquets were delivered both on Quadra Island and in Illinois on the same day. The Songteller was there with me through the music he sent me for Christmas and copies of the music I sent him.

The gift that I asked for from the center of the labyrinth was humility, and what my generous God gave me was the insight and clarity required for me to accept and keep this gift. This insight and clarity came through another gift, a book, given to me by a Methodist pastor, on the basic tenets of Christianity. The book, *Mere Christianity*, by C. S. Lewis, contains an absolutely wonderful (and thoroughly pertinent) chapter entitled, “The Great Sin.” It was through reading this chapter that I recognized false pride as the root of my decidedly anti-humble behaviors, and this awareness had to come before I could accept the gift of humility and be able to share it with others.

But there was yet another gift from God hidden in the pastor’s gift to me. The book has also given me the understanding I needed to reconcile my personal belief system with that of traditional Christianity, and that is a truly generous gift of love and healing.

Throughout all this, the gift I am most obviously receiving and giving is love. To travel the road home generously requires a generous portion of both humility and love.

~ Patience

Patience is the willing acceptance of God's perfect timing as it applies to every aspect of my life. It is a principle that brings serenity to my life, that makes traveling the road home calmer and more pleasant, not frantic or chaotic. Patience is a byproduct of humility and a manifestation of strength. Practicing patience helps me to follow the direction of my guide, to stay on course and in rhythm with his plan. Patience allows me to keep a steady pace, to walk with him, not ahead or behind. Patience allows me to wait for his cues for action, my time of active participation in the divine plan. Patience allows me to keep my serenity when life becomes frustrating or chaotic. Patience allows me to share what I have learned with others without any requirement for immediate results, or any results at all, for that matter. Patience allows both of us to learn at our own pace, to make mistakes, to fall down, and pick ourselves up again. Patience allows me to keep my faith and trust when the desires of my heart take a long time to get here. Patience creates a natural wonder like the Grand Canyon over millions of years; patience creates the blessings of my life over the span of time I have to receive them.

My guide has proven to me time after time that he is infinitely patient. Unfortunately, I cannot claim to have been very patient with him at all. Patience is definitely not one of my personal gifts; it is a principle that has taken me forever (or so it seems) to learn and apply in my life. The one thing that I have learned, without a doubt, is that God's time table and mine are never the same. His schedule is almost always longer than mine, which has forced me to learn how to be patient. I have been forced to learn patience because every time I have superimposed my time table over his and forced things to happen prematurely, the result has not been successful. God has shown me, over and over, that his timing is perfect and mine is not. He has also shown me, over and over, that when I have to wait for something or someone to come into my life, it is always because I am not ready to accept that something or someone into my life. It is never about them not being ready; it is always about me not being ready. That is why moving too fast or forcing the issue (whatever the issue may be) does not work. Neither does moving too slow, or lagging behind my guide. Walking with God, in perfect step, does work for the highest good of all concerned.

Even my music has brought me a lesson in patience. When I began learning and listening to tapes of my playing the romantic music I love to play now, the first message I got was, "Don't force it. Slow down and let it flow." My heart is in tune with God, and when my heart directs my fingers or my life, the tempo is much slower and gentler.

It has taken me a long time to understand the value of patience and even longer to incorporate patience into my life. I had, after all, been willfully managing my life, unaided and unguided, right or wrong, for a very long time. And when it was my turn to act, to perform some task, I did it all by myself. I did not have the patience to stop and teach others how to do it so they could help me. (It was easier just to do it myself.) Nor did I have any patience when forced to slow down because of others for any reason. I wanted coworkers to be as fast and as efficient as I was, drivers to drive as fast as I wanted to drive, checkout clerks not to waste time in chitchat with customers. Perceived inefficiency or incompetence or just plain inattentiveness drove me absolutely nuts! Of course, I hardly ever let others see how impatient I was with them. What I did do was a lot of muttering under my breath and swearing behind the wheel of my car!

Still, my impatience with others was exceeded only by my impatience with myself. I was continually giving myself unreasonable deadlines or unrealistic goals, forcing the course of relationships instead of just letting them unfold, trying to make things happen instead of letting them happen. In short, I did not simply go with the flow. And, since I was impatient with myself, I could not understand people who were patient with me. The Skier/Climber is a very patient man. He patiently nursed me down ski hills when I was too scared to ski, patiently waited for me to slowly descend mountains he could have bounded down in a quarter of the time required for me to do it, patiently allowed three days for climbs that usually took two. Now I understand that his patience was a gift of love. But I became impatient with his patience! I threw tantrums, trying to ruffle his unruffle-able persona. I wanted him to be as impatient with me as I was with myself.

With the Piano Player, it was even worse. I had no patience with his drinking and even less patience with me for staying with him. My mantra in those days was, "Why do I put up with this shit?!!!" I used to set myself deadlines like, "I'll wait until June, and if he's still drinking, I'll leave." June came and went, but I did not, and my impatience turned to anger, both at him and at me. It was my wise Al-Anon sponsor who suggested that I stop agonizing over my indecision. She said, "When it's time to do something, you'll know and you'll be able to do it." And she was, of course, right because that is the way it works when I allow God to set the schedule. When it is time to move, I am moved, either voluntarily or involuntarily. And I was, only certainly not in a way I had expected.

After the Piano Player died, I gave myself a year to grieve my losses. God was with me; I had been in twelve-step programs for nearly two years. My guide had provided all kinds of emotional support for me, not the least of which was the hospice team that cared for the Piano Player during his final days. They provided counseling, grief support groups, a lending library of books on death, dying, and grieving, and volunteer training, all of which I participated in. The top layers of grief were peeled away in that first year, when the most obvious attachments and dreams were grieved and released. But my healing hardly began until the second year and has continued ever since. Still, I was very impatient with myself for taking so long to get on with my life!

Even though I was walking with my guide, even though I was gradually turning my will and my life over to him, even though I was discovering my true self and accepting his plan, my unique path, I still was not accepting his time table for that plan. My impatience with others, and, to a great degree, myself, was relieved when I discovered my judgmentalism and chose to replace it with attitudes that enhanced my serenity. But my impatience with God, my lack of complete trust in his intentions, stayed with me. I got impatient if things did not happen as quickly as I wanted them to or if there were no visible signs of a miracle in progress. I got impatient and began to lose faith, to doubt. So I would try to speed things up—my recovery, my healing, and my relationships. And every time I did that I got another lesson in patience and humility.

Every time I get impatient and race ahead of my guide, I start wandering around again and lose my way. Every time I wait for him, adjust my pace to match his, the timing is perfect. Events unfold in perfect order to bring me the healing I need to be ready for the next phase, the next encounter, or the next test. Miracles begin to happen, but in God's time, not mine. Slowly, finally, I began to understand what worked and what did not work. Slowly, I began to believe and know that, even when change is imperceptible, it doesn't mean that change is not happening. Slowly, I began to believe and know that miracles most often require time and patience. Slowly, ever so slowly, I began to learn how to wait for the miracles of my life, to let life flow, to get out of the way and let events happen, to let God set the agenda and its timing. When I practice the principle of patience, I marvel at how well my life is managed and am in total awe of the perfection of God's timing. When I do *not* do that, the result is always the same. I lose my serenity, I lose my faith, I stop trusting, I begin to separate from my source and his guidance, and I begin to feel pain. And, when the pain gets bad enough, humility brings me back to God and we begin again.

I have gone through this many times because of impatience. When God offers me a dream or a vision and I accept it, I still have a tendency to take off and run with it rather than let him set the pace. When my free spirit, the eagle, flies, often he will fly too high, too fast, too far. Then, when I realize that I have left my guide behind, I get scared, which separates me even more. Working back through the fear is painful, but it is the only way I can reconnect with my guide and get back on course. I call this process, going into the pink cloud, going into the dark side of the pink cloud, and working my way back through it, back to center. Center is where my guide is. Center is where God and I co-create my unique path. Center is the road home.

~ Commitment

Commitment is a stated intention and is the principle that gives my life direction. Commitment tells my guide and my fellow travelers who I choose to be, what I choose to do, where I choose to go, and whom I choose to go there with. Commitment thus allows me to co-create the dreams and visions God has offered to me and to fashion the content of my life. Commitment based on awareness of my true self leads me down my unique path. Commitment says, "Yes, this is my desire, my choice." When commitment aligns my will with God's will for me, miracles happen.

In relationships with fellow travelers or myself, commitment says, "This is what I will do or be for you." There is absolutely no area of my life that does not require some sort of commitment. When I am employed, I commit to performing a stated task in exchange for compensation. When I marry, I commit to sharing my love and my life with another person. When I shop, I commit to paying for the things I purchase. When I have children, I commit to caring for them, providing for their needs, until they are able to care for themselves. The very act of living is a commitment, or should be, to love, feed, clothe, nurture, and care for my body, mind, and soul.

Commitment applies to all aspects of my being. I can be committed physically, mentally, emotionally, spiritually, or creatively. Many commitments involve more than one aspect of self—a true, or total, commitment embraces them all. In fact, total commitment must include my total being. By definition, it requires me to commit with my body, mind, emotions, creative spirit, and soul. Anything less is incomplete. Thus, a commitment to marriage or a special friendship certainly should involve all aspects of self. Any commitment that involves service to others should as well. Any commitment entered into from a position of love will, by its very nature, involve all aspects of my being.

Total commitment also has to be a choice. I commit not because I need to, but because I *desire* to. Nor do I commit because others want me to; the desire, the choice, has to be totally mine. This applies to all commitments, whether to myself, another human, or God. Commitments made because of need or a desire to please cannot be total commitments, because part of me will resist the commitment and attempt to sabotage it. Commitments of this nature are designed to fail.

Inherent in commitment is a pledge to put forth my very best effort to fulfill my part of the plan and to accept the responsibilities that come with the commitment. All commitments, great or small, come with responsibilities. When I commit to chairing a meeting, I assume the responsibility of showing up, on time and prepared with a topic for the group. When I committed to write this book, I assumed the responsibilities of focusing on my task, setting aside time and space to do this, and actually doing it. When I commit to living a long life, I assume the responsibility of self-care required to honor that commitment. When I commit to being your friend, I assume the responsibility of friendship as mutually agreed on by each of us. When I commit my will and my life to God, I assume the responsibilities of spiritual practice that allow and encourage me to do that.

To make a commitment without accepting the responsibilities that go with it is to make a commitment to fail, as I did in my marriages. I semi-committed to the person but not to the responsibility of maintaining the relationship. I did this in several professional assignments. I committed to the tasks, accepted the assignments, but did not accept the responsibility of acquiring the knowledge or skills required to do the work. In both situations, when things got too tough, I did not keep my commitment. I left. Leaving is one way to avoid either success or failure. Break the commitment and leave.

As you may have already guessed, commitment is not something I knew how to do very well for most of my life. I have two soul friends who are in stable, loving, long-term, and committed relationships. One has been married for over fifty years, the other more than thirty years. Both of these women have told me the same thing. When they married, they knew they were choosing life partners. (So, fortunately, did their spouses!) These couples committed to both the person *and* the relationship with all parts of themselves, and they accepted the responsibilities inherent in their commitments. I, on the other hand, have not, as of this writing, ever made that kind of a commitment to a spouse. I am committed in this way now to my special friends, but certainly was not to my husbands. I neither committed with my total being nor accepted the responsibilities of maintaining a marital relationship.

When I married the Rescuer, I remember thinking to myself,

"Well, if this doesn't work, I can always get a divorce." I loved this man, or so I believed, so I was committed emotionally, but certainly not mentally. Nor was I committed either spiritually or physically, since I betrayed him sexually before we separated. I also did exactly what I said I would do. When I perceived the relationship as "not working" for me, I got a divorce. I didn't honor the commitment, I simply left.

With the Skier/Climber, the commitment was mental and physical, but not emotional or spiritual. True, we were emotionally dependent, but dependence is based on need, not choice. And there, too, when I perceived the relationship was "not working" for me, I left. I basically told him, "Sorry. I don't think I want to be married anymore. 'Bye." End of commitment.

Ironically, I came closer to true commitment with the Piano Player than I did with either of his predecessors. We both had two prior marriages, so we said, "The third time's the charm." I committed to him with head, heart, body, and creative soul through our musical bond. But I did not commit to the relationship or to the actions required to maintain it. I did not view it as a life commitment because of his alcoholism. When we married, I remember thinking we'd probably only have about ten years together, unless he chose to stop drinking. Certainly, there was no spiritual commitment, since I had turned my back on God. Still, there was enough of a commitment to keep me there. As I have shared before, things got very tough and I did not leave. God absolutely knew what he was doing when he gave me the Piano Player as an assignment. He knew I was attached to our music and that I would have to stay long enough to find him. He knew the pain of addictive behavior would lead me home to him, and it did. When I threatened to leave (which I often did), the Piano Player always said, "What ever happened to 'Until death do us part?'" And that is, of course, what it took, in the end, to break the bond.

Still, that commitment was not really based on choice. It is through my spiritual commitments to my guide that I am finally learning the true meaning of commitment—to God, to myself, and to others. My first real commitment was to my recovery—to working the steps and doing whatever it takes to maintain abstinence and serenity. It was through working the steps, especially step three, that I began to understand that commitment fashioned the course of my life. I also committed to finding my true self and my unique path. Over time, I developed a number of spiritual commitments that I recommitted to daily for many years. These commitments defined my mission and purpose and the way I desired to live my life. They are my commitments to God, to life, to myself, and to others, and some are commitments to specific desires or dreams. Here is an abbreviated version of what I said to God each morning: "Now, dear God, I wish to recommit to the commitments I have made in your name. For the next twenty-four hours, I surrender to love and I recommit to you. I surrender and recommit my will, my life, my heart, and my body to your care and your service. I surrender and recommit to your plan for my life and to your time table for that plan. I surrender and recommit to my purpose in life as you have shown it to be, and that is to serve as your channel and share your love and wisdom with others through sharing my true self and my creative gifts with them.

"I recommit to life itself. To living my life fully, passionately, lovingly, compassionately, generously forgivingly, humbly, with an open mind and heart, and always in your service, having the courage to take risks and to accept life's challenges, including loss, rejection, failure, indifference, hostility, and physical discomfort.

"I recommit to myself and to others, knowing that, spiritually, we are one and what I do to me I also do to you. I recommit to loving, accepting, and forgiving each of us unconditionally.

"I recommit to the self-care required to fulfill these commitments in a positive way and the responsibilities inherent in making them. I recommit to all these things, Lord, in your name. Amen."

Then, as God and I developed a closer and more constant relationship, I found a song called, “My Dedication,” which very simply says what I took many words to say (see “Step Eleven” for the words). Singing it is now a regular part of my daily prayer practice.

Since I began making spiritual commitments daily, I have noticed a strange phenomenon in my life. Once a commitment is made, I am always given the tools for healing that I need in order to fulfill it. I have also been given life experiences to test how well I'm doing and show me where more work needs to be done. I have also noticed that committing myself to God each day has led to my taking my personal commitments, both to others and to myself, much more seriously. I am totally committed to life, to my spiritual path, to expressing and experiencing divine love with all creation, to loving service, and to sharing my creative gifts. And should God choose to bring me the desires of my heart, I will choose to be totally committed to both the man and the relationship. With commitment, my self and my path are clearly defined. Without it, my self and my path become obscure and hard to follow. Today, I choose to commit and allow my guide to direct my life.

~ Courage

Courage, too, is a principle that is often misunderstood. Courage is not acting without fear; courage is acting *in spite of* fear. Courage is the principle that frees me from the shackles of fear, that puts fear in its proper place. Courage faces fear and keeps on going or goes back and does it again. Courage does not allow fear to determine what is done or not done, what is believed or not believed, what is learned or not learned, what is attempted or not attempted. Courage allows me to be me, to express my true self and walk my unique path, even when doing so exposes me to fears that have not yet been surrendered to God. Courage allows me to allow God and divine order to define the details of my life.

I am committed to sharing myself with my fellow travelers through public speaking, through playing the piano and singing, and through opening my heart and sharing myself with them. In all of these areas, fear still haunts me and can come out of nowhere, seemingly at will. I was singing a duet in church one Sunday, and an old fear from years past descended on me halfway through the song. I relived that old scene, and my body began to shake with fear, just as it had some forty-six years earlier. Courage kept my voice steady and allowed me to sing through my fear. Courage will allow me to sing again, under similar circumstances, and move beyond the fear.

Courage allows me to work through my fears and eventually release them completely. Courage allows me to take risks when the risks involve facing my fears. When I began writing this book, I was afraid to share my writing with my soul friends. I was not afraid to share it with you, my writing audience, because you do not know me personally. I was afraid to share my writing because I was still afraid to share myself with those who are close to me. My old, outdated fear had returned. If others knew who I was, how I think, what I believe, and they did not agree with it or thought it was weird or scary, then they would stop loving me and leave. Courage allowed me to risk sharing my writing with my soul friends, and guess what. They may or may not think I have weird beliefs, but they are all still with me. Nobody has been frightened away.

Courage has also been defined as fear that has said its prayers. To be sure, true courage does require faith and trust in God, others, and myself. Being courageous without faith in something or somebody is a very difficult feat. As I look back on my life, one of the most courageous things I have ever done was in an area of my life where I had little faith in anything—none in God, some in others, and very little in myself. One of the fears that I committed to facing in the past was my fear of water. Now, I love being on water, but I do not love being *in* it. I have taken three formal swimming courses and know enough to keep from drowning, if I don't panic. And of course, I do panic. As soon as the water gets deep enough to approach my nose and mouth, I become very afraid.

During the last swimming course I took, years ago in college, the instructor insisted that I jump, feet first, into the deep end of the pool. I was terrified, completely immobilized by fear. I simply could not bring myself to step off the edge of the pool, even though she was right there, ready to rescue me if I got into trouble. I don't remember exactly how long she patiently waited, gently coaxing me to face my fear, trying to give me the faith in myself—and her—to do it. Eventually, after what seemed like hours, I did it. I jumped into the deep end of the pool and miraculously survived. I was absolutely thrilled that I had done it, but I never did it again. Courage without faith and trust usually happens only once. Courage *with* faith and trust keeps going back until the fear finally disappears.

I have never thought of myself as being a particularly courageous person, since I have allowed fear to chart my course far too often in my life. To avoid facing my fear of intimacy, of letting others come close enough to see me, I stayed emotionally distant and isolated from love and from them for most of my life. I also hid or downplayed my personal gifts, my intelligence, and my creative talents, for fear that their full expression would intimidate others or frighten them away. To avoid facing my fear of feeling emotional pain, I dulled or stuffed it, medicated it, buried it, did absolutely anything but feel it and release it. To avoid facing my fear of public speaking, I said "no" to any profession or life experience that could conceivably require me to make any kind of talk or presentation to others. Not having the courage to face this fear kept me from going to graduate school or assuming any kind of a leadership position. It drastically limited me both in my professional and personal life.

To avoid facing my fear of physical injury and being less than the best, I avoided participation in any kind of team sports or competition. To avoid facing my fear of failure, I never took any risks, physical, emotional, or mental. To avoid facing my fear of rejection, I never allowed others to see my vulnerabilities. To avoid facing my fear of hostility, I always tried to please others. To avoid facing my fear of confrontation, I used the inertia technique. I ignored the problem, whatever it was, hoping it would go away. Some problems did; others did not. Some were eventually confronted when they got too big to ignore; most were not.

Still, I have had my courageous moments. Childhood injuries coupled with parental paranoia left me with a fear of falling and injuring myself again, and I learned how to ski with this fear ever present. I skied for over ten years, and I always said it took me the first five years to get over being scared enough to learn how! Moving from Illinois to Idaho took the courage to face my fear of the unknown. So did being married to the Piano Player, in many ways, since the unknown catastrophe always lurked on the horizon.

Before I could truly practice the principle of courage, I had to have faith and trust in something besides myself. The most courageous actions I have ever undertaken have occurred since I began walking with my guide. In fact, inviting God back into my life before I had faith and trust in him was my first courageous act. I was very afraid, but I was also desperate, and courage is often born through desperation. One of my Al-Anon friends lived in terror for many years with a physically abusive spouse. When she tried to leave, he threatened to kill her. The desperation of knowing that living with him in terror was worse than taking the risk of being killed gave her the courage to leave and end the marriage.

Going to my first Al-Anon and Overeaters Anonymous meetings were also acts of courage born out of desperation, a "when all else fails" act of surrender. So was working the twelve steps the first time. But without faith and trust, I did them superficially. Going deeper into myself, facing my imperfections, admitting my mistakes, asking for help, and making amends—all of these things required courage based on faith and trust. Breaking my isolation, connecting with my guide and my fellow travelers, sharing myself with them, learning to take emotional risks—these, too, required courage based on faith and trust. Facing my primary fears, moving anywhere outside of my comfort zone, allowing God to speak through me, allowing myself to be vulnerable and share my feelings with others, all these, too, required courage based on faith and trust. Hanging in there and facing life's challenges, staying when leaving would be the easier, softer way, required courage based on faith and trust. But possibly the most courageous act I have done so far is having the courage to open my heart to love, to God, and to others.

Opening my heart to love, both human and divine, requires me to be healed enough to take the risk. Healing requires me to love myself enough to open old emotional wounds, feel and release the buried fear, anger, pain, and guilt, and cleanse the wounds with tears so they may heal properly. Courage based on faith and trust in God has allowed me to do this, to face my fear of emotional pain, the pain I had buried, stuffed, medicated, and otherwise attempted to avoid or dull for most of my life. Courage was required to open my heart to love, and courage helps me keep it open. Courage takes me into and through my fear, and that is the key to an open heart. Fear closes my heart; courage takes me out of fear and back into love. Courage keeps me walking with my guide when our path takes me through a mine field of unresolved fears and improperly healed wounds. Courage allows me to work through my human imperfections and remain connected to the divine.

~ Optimism

Optimism is the principle that springs naturally from faith and trust, nurtures and enhances serenity and joy, and fires passion. Optimism sees the bright side, not the dark side, positives instead of negatives. Optimism sees the love within even when it is masked by fear. Optimism sees the glass as half-full, not half-empty. Optimism knows that God wants only the best, the highest good for me and is eager to help him create it. Optimism sees the silver linings inherent in the dark clouds of my life. Optimism in its extreme personifies unconditional love. Optimism lives in the present, where it is busy creating an optimistic future. Optimism believes things will get better, not worse, and that pain is a temporary condition. Optimism knows that love can change the world, both individually and collectively. Optimism knows that loss, grief, and pain are a part of life and looks for the lessons they teach us or the strengths they inspire. Optimism knows that human tragedy often inspires greatness, both human and spiritual, and can bring spiritual healing in the midst of physical catastrophe. Optimism believes in miracles, and, thus, helps create them.

Optimism is one of my personal gifts. I cannot ever remember being pessimistic, even though I was raised by very pessimistic parents. My dad seemed to see only the negative side of everything. No politician ever did anything right—either they did not support the farmer or they only supported the wealthy ones. In fact, hardly anybody ever did anything right in his eyes (except possibly me). And things could only get worse, from his view. I can still hear him proclaiming, in a deep, doom's day voice, "This world has seen its best days!" And my mother wasn't much better, except that her pessimism was of a more personal nature. She obsessed over the things she lacked in her life—Mother's glass was always half empty. She didn't have enough money or a nice enough house or expensive clothes or a happy life, and it was all her fault because, "I married your father and he had those kids to support." "Those kids" were his three children from a previous marriage, children I did not know existed until I was a teenager. That marriage and *those* kids were our family secret. They were carefully hidden for many years from friends and family alike. Ironically, as a child, I always yearned for a brother or sister. And all the time I had three that I never knew about.

But, back to optimism. Again, I believe my optimism was a gift I brought in with me, a characteristic that I was born with. No matter how painful or unpleasant my life became, I never expected or anticipated the worst. I always assumed the best until life gave me something else. And therein lies the inherent danger in optimism. I have heard that optimists are less realistic than pessimists, and that has certainly been true for me. Because I usually expect the best to happen, I am not always prepared for the worst, nor do I always recognize and accept real hazards and concerns. I tend to minimize potential threats to my well-being, whether they be physical, mental, emotional, or spiritual. I also tend to replace reality with a fantasy that better fits my optimistic views.

When I was skiing and climbing and backpacking, I optimistically believed that I would not be injured in these activities, and that was not at all realistic. I habitually did things beyond my physical abilities, which increased the likelihood of injury. The fact that I was not injured during those years was, I suspect, more of a God thing than a Nadine thing, even though I certainly did not give him any credit for his protection at the time.

Still, pessimists are not always realistic either. The summer after the Piano Player died, a friend from my outdoor life proposed that we go on a wilderness trip together and hire a packer to carry our gear in for us. This was something that really appealed to me. I was in no physical shape to backpack and had pretty much given up any thoughts of revisiting wilderness areas that are only accessible by foot or horseback. So I said, "Yes, I'd like to do this," but I suggested a different area. My area was one that I have strong emotional ties to, a very special part of the Wyoming Wind River Range. There was only one problem. Going into this area required a fourteen-mile hike versus a seven-mile hike in the areas my friend suggested. I optimistically believed I could hike that far without a pack, even though I had not been on those trails in over twenty years. My friend pessimistically came back with all the things that could possibly go wrong (rain, wind, snow, injuries, obscured trails, physical collapse, bear attacks, and so on), said she would not accept the responsibility of going in there with me, and cancelled the trip. Certainly, I was not being realistic, but neither was she. Reality was somewhere in the middle of both views.

Optimism, for me, tends to favor the denial of reality, even as it creates a more positive experience. I optimistically believed that my love and support could help the Piano Player deal with his drinking problem, when, in reality, my love and support could no more do that than it could cure him of cancer. To be sure, love is healing. But the love has to be unconditional, and the recipient has to love himself or herself as well and be open to healing. I optimistically believed the words, "I'm ready to get help for my drinking," even when his actions did not match his words. I optimistically believed that my mother was able to care for herself and continue to live alone even though she kept trying to tell me indirectly that she was failing mentally. It took a cry for help in the form of undiagnosable physical problems to break through my denial and establish her reality. I optimistically believed in "happily ever after" and was then unprepared and unwilling to deal with the challenges of love and intimacy.

Still, even with its pitfalls, I consider my optimism to be a tremendous gift, a real blessing. My inherent optimism makes it much easier to accept my new life, the new road home, sourced in love and based on universal truth. My optimism makes it much easier to follow the direction of my guide, to know that he only wants the best for me. My optimism makes it much easier to learn the principles I have struggled with and to release my crippling fears and self-defeating behaviors. My optimism, even when I do not consciously use it, helps me to create a storehouse of positive experiences in many areas of my life. When I expect the worst, my perception shows me the worst and I unknowingly work to create the worst. When I expect the best, or look for something positive in all of life's experiences, my perception sees the best and I unknowingly work to create the best. To be sure, it may not always seem to be the best thing at the time, but, often, the most painful and tragic experiences are laced with love and compassion and bring us some very unexpected spiritual gifts.

So I repeat, I consider my inherent optimism a wondrous gift from God. Especially when I observe the difficulties of those not blessed with this gift. My soul friends whose life experiences have caused them to look for the worst almost always seem to find it. And when they do not find it, they seem to have a need to create it. One of my soul sisters lived through childhood experiences that taught her that people could not be trusted to be there for her. So she, like me, does not trust. Still, even though I do not trust others enough to show them my true self or to depend on them for help, I optimistically trust *in* them. If a person becomes my friend and shows that friendship through their actions, I trust in them and expect them to behave like a friend. My soul sister, on the other hand, still looks warily at the best and anticipates the worst.

About two years into our friendship, I overstepped my bounds and made some unkind and unsolicited remarks about her behavior. I betrayed her trust and wounded her, and she struck back, angrily and viciously. I call it her sword attack. During her attack, one of the things she said was, "If this is the kind of a friend you are, I don't need you as a friend!" I remember thinking, "Wait a minute. So I screwed up once—what about all the times I *have* been there for you?!" Later, I understood what had happened and saw it as a pattern she used in other relationships as well. Because she looks for and expects the worst, that one event negated all of the positive ones. This one negative incident proved what she had believed all along—that I was not to be trusted as a friend. For me, because I optimistically did not expect to be viciously attacked by a friend, I suffered emotional wounds that took a long time to heal. Today, we are still soul sisters and friends, but with a difference. I still do not expect her to attack, but I understand that she is capable of doing that. My optimism has been tempered with reality. As for my soul sister, she still is wary but does understand that I am her friend, that I am there for her. Her pessimism has been tempered with reality as well.

~ TENACITY

Tenacity is the ability or desire to hold on—to a dream, to a belief, to a knowing, to a relationship. Tenacity is the principle that gives me staying power, that allows me to hang in there when my path gets rocky or the journey takes me into unfamiliar and uncharted territory. Tenacity keeps me holding on tightly to the spiritual lifeline that connects me to my guide. Tenacity keeps me holding on tightly to my true self when my identity is challenged, ridiculed, or invalidated by others. In the program, there's a saying: "Don't give up before the miracle happens." The principle that keeps me holding on until it does is tenacity.

Tenacity is an expression of strength and the heart of commitment. Commitment, as I have said, requires me to put forth my very best effort to fulfill my role, to keep my end of the bargain. Tenacity, coupled with its sidekick, perseverance, helps me do that. Tenacity keeps me connected, and perseverance keeps me moving. If my commitment is to climbing a mountain, tenacity keeps me committed to reaching the summit, and perseverance keeps me moving, slowly but steadily, toward that goal.

Commitment to a relationship is strengthened by tenacity. The traditional wedding vows are fashioned from tenacity. To be there for someone "for better or worse, richer or poorer, through sickness and in health, until death do us part" requires a tremendous amount of tenacity. To honor any commitment wholeheartedly requires tenacity. To make and keep a commitment to anyone or anything under all circumstances requires a massive dose of tenacity.

When used wisely, tenacity is the adhesive that cements our relationships—to our guide, to ourselves, to our fellow travelers. When used unwisely, tenacity can choke and strangle, can hamper spiritual growth, can lead to stagnation and repression of myself and others. Tenacity is one of the trickier principles to put into practice. To use tenacity wisely, I have to know when to hold on and when to let go. I have to be able to recognize when holding on to an attitude, a dream, a behavior, a fear, or a commitment is no longer appropriate. I have to be able to recognize when holding on is harmful, is no longer to the highest good of anyone concerned. And once I have reached this place of recognition, I have to be willing to release my hold and let go.

Tenacity is, I believe, one of my personal gifts, and it is one that I am only now beginning to learn how to use wisely. I have, historically, either let go too soon or hung on too long. In the words of the country song called “The Gambler,” "You've got to know when to hold, know when to fold." My tarot reader/numerologist put it another way. She told me, "You don't know when to cut your losses." And I did not. Tenaciously holding on to fantasy relationships kept me from establishing real ones. Tenaciously holding on to both the Piano Player and our music cost me dearly, both financially and emotionally. However, that same tenacity, when applied to rebuilding my life after his death, has brought me rewards beyond anything I could have ever imagined.

I have also not known when my tenacity was used wisely and when it was not. It is never wise to tenaciously cling to another person or to a specific outcome. It is never wise to tenaciously cling to outdated or addictive behaviors, self-defeating beliefs and attitudes, negative thoughts, guilt, resentment, and regret, dreams that no longer fit, or fears that stifle growth. It is never wise to tenaciously cling to something or someone that is a part of my past and cannot be a part of my future. It is always wise to tenaciously cling to the strength, hope, wisdom, courage, and love that are the gifts received through faith and trust in my guide. In fact, the wisdom to properly use my gift of tenacity has only come since I began to trust in my guide to signal me, to let me know when to hold and when to fold.

The criterion he uses to determine this is really very simple. When holding on no longer serves any useful purpose either to me or the object of my tenacity, he suggests that it is time to let go. When holding on is not serving or creating the highest good for anyone or anything, when holding on becomes painful or stifling for all concerned, he suggests that it is time to let go, to release my commitment. He suggests this by first gently nudging me in that direction and waiting for my response. If I do not respond and continue to tenaciously hold on to whatever it is I am holding on to, he may use more forceful means to make his point. Doors will slam shut on outdated dreams. Relationships may end, jobs may vanish, health problems may force me to reevaluate my lifestyle and my life. The secret is to sense and respond to the first nudge and not wait for a terminal blow!

I have tenaciously clung to addictions, people, fears, very specific outcomes, and all sorts of self-destructive behavior. But possibly the one area that has been the hardest for me has been to know when to let go of my dreams, when to recognize that they no longer fit or that God is refashioning them in a way I had not anticipated. Clinging tenaciously to dreams that no longer fit, hanging on to form instead of substance, can keep me from accepting and creating new ones that do fit. The best example I can think of to illustrate this is not about me but about my mother.

Genetically, my musical gifts came to me through my mother. Her musical gift, her vein of gold, her absolute first love was playing the organ. As a young girl, her dream was to be a theater organist. Theater organists were common in the days of silent movies, and she pursued her dream seriously. She went to Chicago and studied theater organ for several years, practicing in darkened theaters and working toward the realization of her dream. Then, something happened that changed everything. Talkies came in, and theater pianists and organists went out. And while a door had slammed shut on her very specific dream, she tenaciously clung to it and refused to consider any other options. So she quit playing the organ. All the time I was playing the piano as a child, and for many years after I left home, she did not play. It wasn't until she had reached her late sixties that my dad insisted she get an organ to play in their home. So she did. She bought a three-manual Wurlitzer with Leslie speakers and began to take organ lessons. In her seventies, she was competing in music contests against teenaged kids, and winning. (I still have the best of her trophies.) In her late years, her dream was resurrected, only it had shifted somewhat. Instead of playing in theaters, she dreamed of mimicking her organ teacher, who played nightly in a quiet restaurant lounge in a nearby city. Her teacher had been doing this for years and knew how to entertain as well as play; mother only knew how to play. And she did that, for a short time, in a restaurant/bar in the small town near their farm. For about six months, she was able to recreate her dream as she envisioned it.

Then my parents moved to Idaho to be closer to their only child. There, her dream was to play in the tavern that the Piano Player and I played our music in and were struggling to buy. Except that what had been accepted in Illinois was not accepted in our blue-collar bar. Our customers simply would not accept her music in their tavern. Once again, my mother tenaciously held on to her dream and would not consider any other options. She could have shared her gift with senior citizens and they would have loved her, but she refused. So her gift was lost again, except to the friends and family who heard her play in her home. Hers was a wonderful gift, but it was never fully shared because she tenaciously clung to her particular version of the dream.

When the Piano Player died and the music we had been creating together for over fifteen years died with him, I started to follow in my mother's footsteps. Even though I knew our music was gone, I clung tenaciously to our dream and refused to consider any other ways of using my musical gifts. Letting go of our music was much harder than letting go of the man who co-created it, and it took over a year for me to rediscover, revalue, and begin to use my own special musical gifts. It was then that I finally understood that when a door closes to one specific version of a dream, it means that God wants me to consider something different. And I did. Now, instead of singing in a smoky bar, I sing wherever the opportunity presents itself—sometimes in church or chorale, sometimes simply for the sheer joy of singing. Now, instead of playing electronic keyboards on stage with a band (which was great fun), I share my classical and romantic piano music at anniversary parties, receptions, memorial services, in church, and with family and friends through my tapes. What matters, I have discovered, is not how I share my gifts but *that* I share my gifts. And God will show me how to do that when I allow him to. All I have to do is loosen my tenacious hold on the old dreams that no longer fit, open my mind and my heart, and wait for him to bring me new ones.

~ PERSEVERANCE

Perseverance is the desire to continue, to keep moving steadily toward reaching a goal or attaining a dream, and is another expression of strength. Perseverance is the principle that ensures continuing spiritual growth. Coupled with tenacity, perseverance keeps me walking with my guide no matter where he might lead me or how difficult or uncomfortable the journey may be. Coupled with patience, perseverance keeps me walking with him in perfect rhythm and harmony. Perseverance in my twelve-step programs kept me coming back until the miracle happened. Perseverance in life keeps me moving and growing and always reaching for my highest good.

Perseverance moves through life one day at a time and toward goals one step at a time. Perseverance is a marathon runner, not a sprinter. Perseverance paces itself and is prepared for the long haul. Perseverance may not win the race, but it will always finish. Perseverance may lag behind, but it will always come out ahead in the end.

I used to believe that I learned perseverance through backpacking and mountain climbing. Now I believe that perseverance, too, is one of my personal gifts, one I brought with me into this life. In fact, it took perseverance to get here at all, because my mother aborted several pregnancies before she chose to give me life. Threads of perseverance (coupled with tenacity) run through most of my life.

When I was learning how to play the piano, perseverance got me through scales, chords, and the finger exercises of Czerny and Hanon, none of which I liked doing, but all of which honed my natural abilities. Perseverance kept me studying and achieving even when the rewards and awards I received seemed empty and meaningless. Perseverance kept me moving through my lost child years in spite of the pain and my teens in spite of my lack of peer acceptance. Perseverance kept me going in the face of ridicule and rejection. To be sure, I was persevering for others, not for myself. But I did persevere.

Perseverance took me from Illinois to Idaho in pursuit of a dream I ultimately rejected. Perseverance kept me successfully employed and financially stable. Perseverance got me a bachelor's degree in mathematics as an adult student. Perseverance kept me skiing when I was terrified of falling, and perseverance kept me moving down trails when I was too physically exhausted to move at all. Perseverance got me through portage trails ankle-deep in mud, carrying one end of a too-heavy kayak. Perseverance got me up and over a 19,100-foot Himalayan mountain pass, over many miles of wilderness trails carrying a heavy pack, and up to and down from the summits of more than thirty-four mountain peaks.

One of these summits was Mt. Moran in Grand Teton National Park. Moran was the last of the major Teton peaks that I climbed and unquestionably the most challenging. The ascent of Moran involves a seven to eight mile hike around two lakes, a 3,000-foot, very steep, trail-less, vertical ascent to an overnight camp (all with pack), and another 2,500 vertical feet of technically challenging (for me) rock climbing to the summit. The descent follows the same route in reverse, and for me, with my creaky knees, coming down always took longer than going up. So we always scheduled three days for a climb of this difficulty—two for the approach and return and one for the actual climb.

Even under these conditions, it took three tries to reach the summit of Mt. Moran. On both of the first two tries, I was too physically exhausted from the long and arduous approach to safely attempt the climb. On the third try, we took a two-man kayak and paddled across the lakes, mooring the kayak at the base of Moran. Eliminating the long hike around the lakes gave me the physical break that I needed, and the Moran summit was finally reached. Reaching that summit required three three-day weekends and a huge investment in physical stamina and mental ingenuity. That, my friends, is perseverance.

With the Piano Player, perseverance kept us playing music together when our jobs and money ran out. Perseverance put me to work to support us so we could make the payments on the tavern we were buying. Perseverance ultimately got it paid for, and perseverance has subsequently gotten it sold. Perseverance kept me going through arrests, confinement, treatment, sobriety, relapse, physical decline, hospitalization, and death.

Perseverance is a survival trait, and I have always been a survivor. Now that I am walking with my guide, I live instead of merely surviving; and perseverance is playing an important role in the transition from survival to life. Perseverance keeps me moving, slowly and steadily, in my quest for spiritual, mental, emotional, physical, and creative maturity. Perseverance keeps me searching for all aspects of my true self, even when the search reveals traits I would just as soon were not there. Perseverance keeps me reaching out to others, performing service work, living the twelve steps. Perseverance keeps me reading, writing, sharing with others, learning, and growing. Perseverance kept on gently chipping away at the wall of separation that I had built around my heart until one day it fell away and revealed the love that had always been there for me and for others. Perseverance keeps a constant vigil against the fear and doubt that tempt me to shut down and rebuild the wall of separation.

Perseverance coupled with patience and humility allows me to wait for my dreams to manifest in reality, to release my agendas and scripts and let God handle the timing and the schedule. Perseverance brought back my musical gifts and inspires me to share them. Perseverance is helping me write this spiritual autobiography and will ensure that it is finished and shared.

Perseverance is persistent and does not give up easily. Thus, like tenacity, perseverance can be used inappropriately or unwisely. As tenacity has to know when to let go, perseverance has to know when to quit. To persevere when doing so is obviously not to anyone's highest good is not using perseverance wisely. In fact, God uses the same criterion for perseverance as he uses for tenacity. When persevering is not serving or creating the highest good for anyone or anything, when persevering becomes painful, stifling, or possibly even dangerous, he suggests that it is time to quit and do something different.

To be used wisely, perseverance must not only know when to quit—it must also be flexible. Perseverance used wisely stops when it comes to a dead end and searches for another path. Perseverance used wisely does not try to force open a closed door; instead, it seeks out another way. Perseverance used wisely knows that its most effective weapon for opening doors and dissolving walls is love. And, again, the wisdom to use perseverance wisely comes from listening to my guide, watching for his clues, and being open to whatever path he reveals to me. Sometimes, his path is not the one I would choose, but always his path is uniquely mine and ultimately leads to my highest good. Often I struggle for some time before heeding and acting on his suggestion, and my struggles become part of the lesson.

When I first came to Al-Anon, the home group I chose resonated with love, hope, and recovery. It was a very strong group with a large core of members solidly committed both to the program and to their own personal spiritual growth. The strength, hope, and love I found there literally supported me until I began to find these things within myself and God. Then, one by one, for reasons as varied as the members themselves, core members began to leave the group and were not replaced. Others seemed to lose their commitment to attend meetings regularly and hold service positions within the group. Meeting attendance dropped drastically, and I began to feel that my commitment, strength, hope, and love were all that was holding the group together. Still, this was my home group, and I had a strong emotional investment in it. Even though it was not the same group and hadn't been for some time, even though the group was no longer meeting my own spiritual needs, I found it painful to consider change. My tenacity and perseverance were working against me now. I did not want to let go and certainly could not quit. But it was not my job to "fix" the group, and God was nudging me pretty hard to get out of the way so he could work on it. Still, I struggled, for well over a year before I became open to other options, even after I knew he wanted me to be somewhere else.

The "somewhere else" I ultimately chose led me to where he wants me to be to move ahead on my spiritual path. I was guided to help start a new group that meets at the same time and location as an Alcoholics Anonymous group. The Al-Anon's with AA spouses who attend this meeting have given me their unique perspective on the challenges of intimacy. One of these women has also come into my life to show me what humility looks like in action, a wonderful guide I could not have connected with otherwise. My old group? It stayed alive, but struggled for another two years before it finally disbanded.

~ HONESTY

Honesty is choosing to accept, speak, and live the truth as I understand it to be. Honesty is the principle that allows me to find my truth, to identify, recognize, and accept who I am, what I think and believe, and how I feel. Honesty is freedom from deception, either of others or of myself. Honesty does not deliberately lie, cheat, steal, mislead, trick, connive, or misrepresent the truth. Honesty may, however, do all of these things when its foundation rests on self-deception or denial. You see, honesty is also relative. No matter how hard I try to be honest or how much I pride myself on being an honest person, I can only be as honest with others as I am with myself.

Honesty searches for, locates, accepts, and shares who I am. Honesty shares my true self with you and does not attempt to hide imperfections and vulnerabilities. Honesty does not play games but asks for what it needs directly and clearly. Honesty does, however, use discretion and is gentle and kind. Honesty does not go around ripping off your blanket of denial in the name of showing you your truth. Honesty reveals your truth to you only when asked.

The *Big Book of Alcoholics Anonymous* describes their program of recovery as "...a manner of living which demands rigorous honesty" and defines how it works—*honest*, open, and willing. Indeed, the first step of the twelve steps of spiritual growth, the foundation of recovery from compulsive behaviors, introduces the principle of honesty. That first step requires me to honestly look at my relationship to my drug of choice and how using that drug has impacted my life. All of the steps require me to be honest, first with myself and God, and then with others. Taking my inventory and sharing it (steps four and five), making my amends (steps eight and nine), and continuing the process (step ten) all require rigorous honesty.

The Songteller wrote a song that includes this line: "I'll be honest—as honest with you as you are with me." Obviously, his view of honesty at the time was somewhat conditional. So was mine for most of my life, only the condition was a bit different. For me, the line should have been changed to read: "I'll be honest—as honest with you as I am with me." I have, for most of my life, thought of myself as a very honest person. I did not deliberately lie to others or take something from them that was not rightfully mine to take. I would never consider cheating on an examination or shoplifting from a store. If you asked me a question about my thoughts, beliefs, attitudes, or behaviors, I would give you *what I believed to be* an honest answer. Because what I believed to be my truth and what was actually my truth were often very, very different.

One night at an Al-Anon meeting, the leader chose the topic of self-deception. I thought, "I'm not exactly sure what that is." Then, after listening to several readings and sharings, I suddenly realized and understood what self-deception is. I have practiced it all of my life, a practice I had perfected to an art form! As an avowedly honest person, when I become aware of a truth about myself or my life, I become obligated to honestly face that truth and follow it. By that I mean that I have to accept the truth and ultimately make whatever changes to my life that accepting that particular truth requires. So when I am not ready or willing to follow the path prescribed by a particular truth, as an honest person I simply refuse to become aware of it. I choose not to see it until I am ready and willing to follow it. I deceive myself into believing that truth is not truth at all for me, and I honestly believe in this self-deception.

As a practicing food addict, when I vowed to quit bingeing, or to cut down, or whatever, I was honestly speaking my view of the truth. But that view was distorted by self-deception. The truth was that the strength of the addiction negated my most honestly stated intentions. So I would vow in the morning not to binge, then break that vow by getting up in the middle of the night several times to eat. Or I would stuff myself with cookies and ice cream and vow to begin dieting "tomorrow." When I made these vows, I honestly believed that I would and could keep them. But, again, my honest intentions were based on self-deception, not on my truth. My truth is that I am powerless over my compulsion to misuse certain foods, and the way I lived my life confirmed that truth over and over. Others could see my truth evidenced in excess weight, but I could not. And I would not see it, would not honestly look at this truth, until I was ready and willing to do something about it.

But self-deception was not the only way that dishonesty manifested in my life. In fact, my most dishonest behaviors were acts of omission. I lied to you not directly, but indirectly, by being only who I thought you wanted me to be rather than being my true self. Every time I hid a part of who I am because it did not fit my perception of who you wanted me to be, I was being dishonest. Every time I did something I did not want to do in order to please you, I was being dishonest. Every time I hid my personal beliefs about politics, religion, world affairs, or whatever, because they did not agree with yours, I was being dishonest. Every time I chose to reveal these same beliefs only because they did agree with yours, I was being dishonest.

The Skier/Climber smoked cigars when we first met, so I did too, some twenty-plus years before it became fashionable for women to smoke cigars. He also had a Honda motorcycle, which I rode on and even tried to drive. I am not comfortable around motorcycles—the Rescuer and I were involved in an accident in which two motorcycle riders were killed. To pretend to like cigars and riding motorcycles was grossly dishonest, and both practices stopped (surprise!) as soon as we were married.

Walking with my guide and following his road map for recovery has helped me replace both self-deception and deception of others with honesty and is gradually leading me to my personal truth. Still, it should come as no surprise to you that the one area of my life where I still am not totally honest is in relationships. Again, my dishonesty is more covert than overt. I am getting much better at knowing and being myself, and I no longer do, or don't do, things simply to impress you. So what you see is usually the real me, my true self. But what you do *not* see is me as well, and therein lies my dishonesty. I do not always show others my fear, my anger, my doubt, my anguish, my pain, my impatience, my hurting, vulnerable, needy side. I have not always shown others my loving, kind, gentle, caring, compassionate side either. I still have a difficult time showing others what I call my dark side, my human imperfections. I have a difficult time showing them to you, to myself, and to God.

When the Piano Player died, I wept publicly during his funeral, but after that, for the most part, I grieved privately and alone. I have opened many old emotional wounds, felt the pain, and wept the healing tears privately and alone. I have gone into the pit of emotional insanity, felt fear, terror, rage, despair, anxiety, and desolation privately and alone. I will share these feelings with others when I can talk about them, but I will not share them directly as I am experiencing them. I will tell others about my fear and pain, but I will not let them experience my fear and pain. And the closer we are, the less likely I am to share these vulnerable feelings. I can cry in church when the pastor's words touch my heart, and often do. I can cry at AA/Al-Anon assemblies, when several hundred people join hands and say the Lord's Prayer, and often do. But I do not cry in my home group meetings, nor do I often cry with my soul friends. I have shared feelings of pain and anger with my spouses and parents, but not with my soul friends.

Still, I am making some progress in being honest with others.

As my heart has opened to love, to life, and to others, I have become more open and honest in sharing my vulnerable side with them as well. I used to send the Songteller carefully scripted letters, very eloquent but also very controlled and grounded more in fantasy than reality. Then I began to send him talk tapes with background music, unscripted and unedited. What came out of my mind and my heart was what he got, and what he got was grounded in my truth. The first time my truth took me into my fears and pain, my dark side, I was terrified that he would move away from me. He did not. If anything, he moved closer, as I have moved closer to him when he has shared his humanness with me. In Al-Anon and Overeaters Anonymous, we say that ours is a program of attraction, not promotion. And the underlying principle of attraction is honesty.

~ Reality

Reality is simply what is—the observable aspects of my life in a physical world. Reality is who I am, what I look like, where I live, what I do, whom I do it with, how I do it, how I feel, and what I think and believe. If another person shares my life in any way, reality is all these things plus how we use them to relate to each other. Living in reality is the principle that allows me to be aware and accept the realities of my life and act accordingly. Living in reality allows me to make rational choices based on the realities of my life that affect those choices. Living in reality allows me to follow my unique path as it is defined by the truth of who I am in the physical world. Living in reality allows me to both connect to and separate from my fellow travelers in an honest, loving, and healthy way.

Reality is constant; how I perceive my reality is not. Anorexics perceive themselves as fat even when their weight, clothes size, and mirrors define them as dangerously thin. Their disease distorts their perception of reality. Fantasy also distorts reality, and fantasy comes when my perception of reality is not what I desire it to be. Fantasy comes when reality is painful and I perceive that I am powerless to change it. Children with abusive parents may use fantasy as an escape from the inescapable. As a child, I often used fantasy to escape loneliness and isolation. As a teenager, I fantasized great romances with movie stars and upper classmen to compensate for the lack of dates and real male relationships in my life. But this is where fantasy can become harmful, a road hazard. Fantasy becomes a road hazard when it supports denial and self-deception. Fantasy becomes a road hazard when the choices I make in my life are based on fantasy, not reality. Fantasy becomes a road hazard when it keeps me from attaining my dreams and desires in reality. As I have said before, fantasy is, by definition, unattainable and unsustainable. Those dreams and desires that are attainable, the ones that come from God, are firmly grounded in reality.

As I write this, part of my reality is that I am over sixty-five years old, slightly overweight, with knees damaged through the overexertion of skiing and climbing. For me to dream of becoming a great ballet dancer is unrealistic based on my age and physical condition. Such a dream would most likely be based on the fantasy that I am still young and in good physical condition, which is as much a distortion of reality as the anorexic's distorted body image. For me to desire to become more physically fit and begin an exercise program appropriate for my age and condition is a desire grounded in reality. It is both attainable and sustainable.

As you might suspect, fantasy has been a road hazard for me for much of my life. Fantasy has blurred my perception of reality in many areas of my life, but nowhere has it done more harm than in relationships with my male fellow travelers. Going back to those high school years, living in fantasy kept me from honestly looking at myself, accepting my strengths and weaknesses, and making the changes needed to attract real relationships with young men. Without that self-awareness, when my real relationships with men finally came, they were anything but successful! And when they failed, I went back into fantasy mode again. Fantasies were unattainable. Even as I craved them, I was unavailable to them. Fantasies were safe. Still, I spent a great portion of my younger life and put a great deal of energy into pursuing fantasy relationships. A fantasy relationship based on sex moved me 1,500 miles across the country to Idaho. Yet I was so caught up in the fantasy, and ultimately disillusioned by it, that when the chance came to have a real relationship with this man, I turned it down. And that illustrates another danger of fantasy. If I live in it too long, I may not know what to do if it suddenly becomes real. Sort of like the old adage: "Be careful what you pray for, you may get it." I can think of several fantasy lovers who would have been impossible for me to relate to in a real relationship.

Then there were the ones where the relationship existed in reality, but my perception of it was based on fantasy. One such fantasy relationship was built around a goodnight kiss—that man remains a bachelor to this day. Another was created out of a very real work relationship that I chose to fantasize as something more, even though the man was (and still is) very committed to his wife and his marriage.

My most painful lesson in fantasy versus reality was the lesson that led me finally to the awareness of my part in the failure of my relationships. This relationship was with the Marlboro Man, and it was very real, very comfortable, very enjoyable, and very sexual. But we were both wounded, and our real relationship was built on a fantasy—the fantasy that we could continue this relationship indefinitely in its depth and intensity without love and commitment. He was terrified of love and commitment, so when things got too intense, he ended it, shattering my heart. I spent the next two years trying to piece together my wounded heart, repair my confused psyche, and create a new relationship with him that was grounded in reality, a friendship without the sex that took it to a place neither of us could handle. I tried, and he tried, but we never made it. The fantasy kept coming back, as did the sex, and got in the way of the genuine love that could have come through a friendship. Finally, we both got tired of trying. I met the Piano Player and he met someone he eventually married and later divorced.

Fantasy distorted my view of my relationship with the Piano Player as well. I likened us to Sonny and Cher and fantasized a glorious future for us as a musical duo. Never mind that he often got too drunk to play when he was still working with a band—that would change as soon as we put our show on the road. That was the fantasy. Reality was getting fired from our first two jobs and many more over the three years we traveled on the road. Reality was too many nights when he was too drunk to finish the last set. Fantasy was a geographical cure. We packed up and moved to Las Vegas, where we'd get our "big break." In Vegas, reality was working at a sleazy casino on the strip for a percentage of zero, not working at all, gambling our savings, and selling my car to get the money to go back on the road. Fantasy was all the great bookings the new agency promised us. Reality was driving from Idaho to Louisiana, only to get fired after the first week of a two-week contract. Reality was driving from Indiana to Montana in two days, ending up back in Vegas in a third-rate motel, selling my piano to keep us going, and going back to Idaho, broke, living off credit cards, without a home to go to.

You would think that our reality would have destroyed all of my fantasies, right? Wrong! Fantasy was a sit-down gig, so I traded my duplex and borrowed money from my parents for the down payment on an overpriced tavern, noted for its fights and a live band on Sunday night. When we bought the tavern, I fantasized that we could hire someone else to run it and just play music six nights a week. Reality was, first, firing our manager after six months and my taking over, then later my managing it and working full-time as a technical writer to support us, so we could make the payments. Reality was first six nights of music, then four, then three, and finally only one—Sunday night, when all the other bars in town had to close. Reality either came slowly or with a loud crash, but it eventually came and I could see it, at least in our professional life. In our personal life, it was more elusive. Fantasy was "happily ever after," and I put a great deal of energy into trying to create it, particularly during the years when the Piano Player was not drinking. Without alcohol, my life with him was perfect, or so I deluded myself into believing. I have often thought since that if I had put all the energy I spent maintaining the fantasy into maintaining the real relationship, we might have actually had one! But I didn't. I probably held on to fantasy until the last days of his life, when reality hit finally with its heartbreaking truth.

Since then, over time, and with the help of my guide, I am learning to discern between fantasy and reality and between fantasy and dreams. I view myself, my life, and my relationships through mostly realistic eyes and make the choices of my life based both on divine guidance and my realistic assessment of my gifts and abilities. To be sure, some dreams are harder to achieve than others, but they are still dreams, not fantasies. Also with time, and the help of my guide, I have learned finally how to move a relationship with a man from fantasy into reality. That is what has happened with the Songteller, who shares himself with me (and I with him) safely from a distance ("Trust"). When our relationship began after the Piano Player's death, it was very much a fantasy for us both, sort of unfinished business from years before. So we tried to play out the fantasy and discovered it to be impossible in reality. Out of the ashes of that fantasy has grown the caring and healing friendship we share today, which provides a solid foundation for whatever God has in store for us in the future. And whatever that future may be, it will be lived in reality, not fantasy. Now that I am learning to know and be my true self, walking with God down my unique path, I no longer want or need fantasy to alter the truth of my life. I accept and embrace its gifts and challenges. I may use a little bit of fantasy to enhance it, but not to change its course.

~ Integrity

Integrity is living my perception of my truth. It is an authentic integration of my inner self and my outer persona. Integrity is not being afraid to let you see who I am or what I think and believe. Integrity is living my life according to my values, standards, beliefs, and ideals. Integrity is being who I am and knowing and following the guidance of my heart. Following my heart is following the direction of my guide.

Integrity, like honesty, is relative. If my perception of who I am is distorted or hidden behind a false mask and if my beliefs are based on that false persona, then integrity will reflect and reinforce those false perceptions and beliefs. When integrity is applied to my true self, it is the principle that leads me to and keeps me on my unique path. Integrity ensures that my actions and behaviors match my personal truth and the promptings of my heart.

Living in integrity is a two-part process that first requires me to know my truth and then accurately and honestly express it and/or courageously and authentically act on it. To do this requires that my connection between mind and heart be continuously and consciously open. To maintain integrity accurately, express who I am and what I believe, I must be fully aware of those things and diligently look for those aspects of my life where there are inconsistencies and incongruities between my authentic self and outer persona. Then, once an incongruity is noticed, the next step is to identify the reason for the discrepancy, to notice what fear-based road hazard or character defect is causing it, and to take the steps required for change.

This is, of course, easier said than done. When God and I co-created the first draft of this spiritual autobiography, we pretty well defined Nadine and her personal belief system, which is based on twelve-step philosophy, a core belief that God is everywhere present in the essence of all creation and that to walk with him is to live a life sourced in love, not fear. Once completed, I was guided to put the draft aside and let it "rest" while my beliefs slowly integrated into my behaviors. Of course, I thought they already had, but I turned out to be very wrong. In order for this to happen, I had to go through the process required to have God replace my false pride and those defects rooted in false pride with humility. Only then was I able to begin to recognize the "I think I knows," those actions or skills that I thought I already knew how to do. As long as I clung to the "I think I knows," my mind was closed to any new direction coming from my heart. I was stuck in my fear-based past, and my behaviors could not change.

I shared with you earlier (“Passion”) that the Songteller jolted me when he told me he couldn't feel love when I played love songs, that I was not playing from my heart. This revelation led me to the one "I think I know" that had to be released before I could honor and act on any of my beliefs. It wasn't just that I thought I knew how to play love songs—it was that I thought I knew how to express love, and I didn't. And until I became aware of that, nothing could change. My old fear-based behaviors could not be released until I opened my mind to the promptings of my heart.

Since then, I have been pursuing a new curriculum that I call learning to love. The course work couples love with humility to express love through the principles of forgiveness, compassion, and generosity, augmented by patience, humor, gentleness, courtesy, awe, gratitude, and delight. Many of my struggles in following the direction of my guide have come from my deficiencies in this area, and this is a curriculum I will be pursuing for a very long time, probably the rest of my life and beyond. Integrity not only requires me to listen to and follow my heart, it also requires me to love by being loving as I walk the path my heart directs me to walk. Integrity is not just what I do, but *how* I do it.

Integrity stands firm in the face of obstacles and opposition. When the Rescuer and I set a wedding date after a two-year engagement, my parents became very upset. Shortly before the scheduled date, I received a letter from them, telling me that I would be disinherited if I married him. My perception of my truth at that time was that I loved this man and my desire was to marry him, so I followed my truth as I perceived it. Integrity is following my heart, and I did. The Rescuer and I were married, and shortly after, my parents reversed their decision and accepted us both into the family. Ironically, they were the ones who lost the most. They refused to attend our wedding and missed the only chance they would have to see their only daughter married to anyone.

That is an example of integrity in a life that was certainly not based on my personal truth, who and what I am. Certainly, all those years when I was following the paths of others and being what I thought they wanted me to be I was not being true to myself. But I did practice integrity to my truth as I perceived it, to the degree that was required to do and be what I thought others wanted me to do and be. I was always true to those aspects of myself required to succeed in my professional life—intelligence, responsibility, organizational skills, writing, and cooperativeness. I was hardly ever true to those aspects of myself required to succeed in my personal life—unconditional love, gentleness, compassion, honesty, humility, and acceptance. All of these characteristics have always been a part of me, but were not owned, understood, or shared with you. And I certainly did not practice integrity with my creative gifts, which were sometimes shared, often discarded, and never expressed fully and passionately to anyone. In those areas of my life, I neither stood firm in my truth nor followed my heart.

Still, there was one area of my life where I did stand firm in my truth and follow my heart, and that was in my love relationships with men. I called these men the shapers, the ones who moved me along a path that would eventually reunite me with my guide. God was very wise and patient with me then. He knew I would follow my heart in my love relationships and worked through these men to lead me back to him. And when I closed my mind and my heart to one path, as I did when I chose not to marry the Catholic man I followed to Idaho, he gently led me down a longer, more circuitous route. He knew that I would eventually find my way home to him as long as I kept following my heart, and thus following his guidance, via the men whose paths I followed. He counted on my integrity to move me along, and it did. To be sure, mine was a fickle heart; that's what made the path so erratic. But when my heart spoke to me, I both listened and acted, often after being severely tested. My parents' attempts to stop my marriage to the Rescuer was not the only challenge to my integrity I met and overcame. Following my heart with the Catholic man required a divorce, a religious conversion, a papal dispensation and dissolution of my marriage so I could be baptized and married in the Catholic faith, and a job transfer from Illinois to Idaho. In 1959, moving from Illinois to Idaho was akin to being transported to another planet! Integrity helped me follow my heart despite these challenges, and the obstacles fell one by one. The path was cleared, but only after I had chosen another one.

Following my head, not my heart, took me into my marriage to the Skier/Climber, but integrity to my perception of my truth was still present. Following my heart took me out of that marriage when it was time to leave my mental/physical life and move on into emotional and spiritual healing. Following my heart into my marriage to the Piano Player involved both the man and his music, and that, too, was a path filled with obstacles. Following my heart with the Piano Player involved teaching myself how to play electric bass guitar, leaving a solid, responsible, well-paying job, living and cooking in crowded motel rooms, and eventually accepting his drinking and pot smoking as a part of our life together. Following my heart with him brought many more obstacles, but I still followed it. I still stood firm in my truth as I perceived it. I may not have been true to myself, but I was true to our playing music together. Following my heart with our music kept me around long enough to rediscover my need to follow my heart in all things. And to understand finally that following my heart was following the direction of God.

Today, I am learning how to practice integrity in all aspects of my life, and it is a process of continuous transformation. Now that I have come to know and accept who I am and what my gifts are, integrity assures that I do my best to be who I am, live according to my values and beliefs, and do what God would have me do to share my gifts with others. Integrity strengthens my commitment to move through my fear of honestly sharing myself. Of course, I still follow my heart, but now there is a difference. Now I understand that following my heart, following the path of love, is following the direction of God. When I finally hear the promptings of my heart, I know where the marching orders are coming from. So, in a sense, integrity helps to keep my will aligned with God's will for me. Integrity assures that I am on my unique path, the one that will take me home. Integrity keeps me following my heart and doing that in a loving, compassionate way.

Following my heart leads me to the fellow travelers I have been assigned to learn from and teach, to give love to and receive love from. Following my heart inspires me to share my creative gifts with others and receive their gifts in return. Following my heart leads me to the places I am to go to do the work God has planned for me to do in this life. Following my heart brings me all my soul friends, shares my music, inspires my words, and heals my emotional wounds. Following my heart brings me an authentic, passionate life, love, creativity, joy, serenity, freedom, and community.

Following my heart also brings me surprises—the expected turns into the unexpected. I hardly expected to be guided to leave my home and my friends at this stage of my life, but that is what my heart is telling me to do (see "Resistance"). I hardly expected to be assigned a man to love that is only available to me safely from a distance. Here, following my heart requires me to prepare and wait until the time is right for us to be together, and mastering the challenges of the learning to love curriculum is a huge part of that process. Many of my fellow travelers believe me to be foolish to pursue either dream. But, I know where my dreams and desires originate. So I will continue to pursue them unless or until my heart gives me new instructions. "To thine own self be true." That is integrity.

~ Intimacy

Intimacy is a reciprocal sharing of personal truths in relationships. It is a principle that strengthens, deepens, and expands the spiritual connection that exists among me, God, and my fellow travelers. Intimacy shares my true self with you and listens to, accepts, and encourages your sharing of your true self with me. Intimacy brings us close to each other, allows us to both merge as one and retain our individuality. Intimacy is heart to heart, mind to mind, body to body, and soul to soul.

Intimacy operates under the principle of attraction, not promotion. Intimacy does not force closeness; it encourages closeness by being open and vulnerable. Openly, honestly, and willingly sharing my thoughts, beliefs, and feelings with you will draw you closer to me unless you consciously resist it due to a lack of trust or fear of manipulation. Openly, honestly, and willingly sharing your thoughts, beliefs, and feelings with me will draw me closer to you unless I consciously resist. Thus, the formula for intimacy is the same as the formula for recovery, given in the *Big Book of Alcoholics Anonymous*. There, how it works is defined as becoming honest, open, and willing. True intimacy between two people requires honesty, openness, willingness, and trust—in God, in ourselves, and in each other.

True intimacy also requires large quantities of love, humility, acceptance, forgiveness, compassion, generosity, patience, humor, respect, courtesy, integrity, commitment, and courage. In fact, all of these gifts and principles apply to relationships and, thus, enhance intimacy, which is the heart of relationships. Without intimacy, relationships are superficial, unfulfilling, incomplete, and spiritually unsatisfying. With intimacy, relationships are meaningful, fulfilling, complete, and spiritually rewarding. Without intimacy, you and I may be simultaneously physically close and very far apart. With intimacy, you and I may be physically distant and very close to each other. If I feel alone in a relationship, I am in a relationship without intimacy. If I do not feel alone, with or without another person being physically present, I have achieved intimacy both with myself and with others.

Intimacy requires total presence as well as honesty, trust, and forgiveness. Intimacy requires me to be there for others, not only physically, but mentally, emotionally, creatively, and spiritually, to the degree that I am able to be. To deliberately withhold any aspect of my being from others makes intimacy impossible. Conversely, to expect or demand something of others that they are incapable of giving me also makes intimacy impossible. What is important here is honesty with and acceptance of each other. Intimacy does not create unrealistic expectations, but trusts in the process of personal growth in relationships. Without intimacy, personal growth, ultimately, is stifled and the relationship gradually withers and dies. With intimacy, personal growth flourishes and the relationship deepens, strengthens, and is very much alive.

Intimacy requires honesty and trust, but intimacy also requires discretion. That is where love, respect, and courtesy take their place as part of intimacy. Intimacy does not require me to perform a brain dump of every thought that goes through my mind, nor does it ask me to vent all my emotions on others. Intimacy is not brutal, harsh, or critical; it is sourced in gentleness and love. If it is not, then it is not true intimacy.

Intimacy may be present in all relationships and, in fact, should be. It is as important to my sense of community to have intimate friendships as it is to achieve intimacy with a soul mate. And, without question, the most important intimate relationships I will ever create are those with myself and God. Yet intimacy is usually connected with love relationships or couplings and with committed relationships, such as marriage. It is in that context that misconceptions create confusion for some of us.

Intimacy is not sex, although sex can be a wondrously intimate experience. But only when sex is transformed and expanded beyond the physical to include the emotional and spiritual aspects of self. Intimacy is, as I said earlier, not physical closeness. In fact, true intimacy often requires less physical closeness, not more, because the spiritual, mental, and emotional connections are all present. Those who require constant physical interaction and reassurance are usual not in an intimate relationship, but rather in a relationship based on need, not love. Intimacy and need do not coexist well, since intimacy is sourced in love and need is sourced in fear. True intimacy is always sourced in unconditional love and sharing.

An enchanted love, a holy relationship, one where both partners have surrendered to love and have humbly asked God to guide their partnership as the ever-present mystical third, is based on a willingness to be intimate, to strengthen the spiritual connection between themselves, their God, and each other. Intimacy, particularly in a love relationship, is a process that does not occur either immediately or easily. Again, trust, honesty, and forgiveness are the keys to intimacy, and these grow as I grow more honest with and trusting of my guide and forgiving of myself and others. My dream is to co-create a holy relationship in this lifetime, but as I write this it is still a dream.

Certainly, I have not either experienced intimacy or created a holy relationship in my marriages, since most of the qualities of intimacy were not present either in me or my partners. I have already shared my unwillingness to share myself with these men and that I was not present spiritually for them. And, as long as I was using either food or sex to medicate feelings, I was not present emotionally either. With the Skier/Climber, I was fully present mentally, but with the Rescuer and the Piano Player, I was not. With the Piano Player, I was creatively present, which substituted for spiritual presence. With none of these men was I completely honest or trusting. The Piano Player used to tell me that I was mysterious, that there was a part of me that I refused to share with anyone, and he was absolutely right. None of these relationships were intimate, and none could be holy because they did not have an acknowledged spiritual source. To be sure, I followed my heart in two of the three marriages, but I was not knowingly following the direction of God. Even after I invited God back into my life, I did not invite God into my relationships. Nor did I turn our path over to him. Had I chosen to do that, our stories would have been written in a different way.

So it has only been since I have been walking with my guide that intimacy in relationships has been possible for me to strive for. And "strive for" is the proper term to use because I am not there completely yet with anyone—not God, not myself, not with any of my soul friends. Almost, but not quite, with myself and God; again, it's called progress, not perfection. The principles that get me into trouble are lack of trust, lack of humility, and self-deception. With my wonderful female friends, I am intimate, but in varying degrees of closeness. There, the blocks are sharing vulnerabilities and openness, which are also related to trust. With them, and with others who are more peripheral in my life, my desire is to be present for them, keep my mind and my heart open to them, and share myself to the degree that is appropriate for the relationship. The principles of intimacy do not vary, but the depth of intimacy does.

Of all the special people in my life today, the one I have achieved the greatest depth of intimacy with is the one who is not physically present. And that, of course, is the Songteller. Sharing safely from a distance has allowed us to become very close, much closer than either of us would have allowed had we been physically present in each other's lives before I was either capable of being or willing to be intimate with anyone. The ultimate challenge for me is to achieve this level of intimacy with a soul mate that *is* physically close. This requires me to have learned my lessons of love well enough to be capable of co-creating a spiritual partnership, a holy relationship with him. I believe it will happen, but not until both of us are capable of creating it and willing for it to happen. That is why I leave the how and when to my guide. Only he is qualified to determine the how and when, for only he knows what is in both of our minds and our hearts.

~ Loyalty

Loyalty is the act of being faithful—to my beliefs, to my values and personal standards, to my fellow travelers, to myself, and to my guide. Loyalty is the principle that demonstrates, through behavior, my desire to keep my side of the bargain, whatever that may be. Loyalty is a cornerstone of commitment and is very closely related to integrity. Integrity requires me to follow my heart and be true to my self. Loyalty requires me to be true to whatever my heart leads me to.

Loyalty is subjective, as are our beliefs, values, and standards. Loyalties based on fear will be very different than those based on love. A member of a street gang may show his loyalty by stealing, raping, and killing. These are certainly not my values, nor those of my guide, so I will define loyalty as he would, through the eyes of love. These are some of the places to which my heart may lead me, and this is how I would demonstrate loyalty.

Loyalty to a country, group, or cause places principles above personalities and works for the highest good of all concerned in the face of conflict, personal agendas, and other causes of dissension. Loyalty to my beliefs, values, and personal standards means that my words are validated through my actions. Loyalty to my profession or place of employment requires me to perform my tasks ethically, responsibly, and honestly. Loyalty to my fellow travelers and the world we live in requires me to treat them with dignity, respect, and love. Loyalty to family and my soul friends means that I am there for them, no matter what, with love, support, and encouragement. Loyalty in an intimate relationship implies loyalty to the values and standards agreed to for that relationship. It does not matter who the intimate relationship is with—a soul friend, a spouse, myself, or God. In the case of my relationship with God and with myself, the values and standards are God's and mine. When two or more people are concerned, the values and standards are those agreed to for the relationship or the group.

Inherent in all of these definitions of loyalty is support for the group, for the cause, for the person, or for the relationship. It is impossible to be loyal and unsupportive. Loyal sports fans support their teams by going to the games and cheering them on. Those of us loyal to twelve-step groups support them through service and contributions. If I am loyal to any cause, I will support it in whatever way I can, through service and/or financial contributions. If I am a loyal friend or lover, I will be there for you and support you with love and acceptance—support, not carry. Being there for you does not mean that I will enable you, deprive you of the right to learn from your own mistakes and live your own life. Nor does it mean that I will support your choices and actions if I disagree with them. If I disagree with your choices and actions, I do not have to support *them*, but I will still support and love *you*. The same applies to me. Loyalty requires me to be there for me, to love and support myself unconditionally. Loyalty to God requires me to be there for him, to be faithful to his guidance and his plan. To be loyal to God requires me to be loyal to love, create my life according to the dictates of love, to follow my heart in all things. To be loyal to God requires me to love my fellow travelers as I do myself.

Also inherent in loyalty is the desire to behaviorally demonstrate that I am worthy of your trust by being faithful, supportive, and by keeping my side of the bargain. Thus, the antithesis of loyalty is betrayal, and betrayal is something that I know how to do all too well. Betrayal is a breach of faith, a violation of values or standards. In my marriages, as in most marriages, sexual infidelity was betrayal. I thus betrayed two of three spouses and was a willing participant in betrayal with the married men I slept with as a single woman. I have betrayed my spouses and friends by talking about them behind their backs or by criticizing and analyzing their behaviors or choices. I have betrayed them as well by trying to fix them, by offering unsolicited advice, or by pushing my perception of their reality down their throats. I continuously did this with the Piano Player and have done it with my soul friends as well. Developing intimacy in relationships requires mutual trust and openness. If I take something you share with me and turn it against you or use it to try to force you to see what you are unwilling to see, that is betrayal.

When one of my soul sisters began a relationship with a new man, I recognized the path she was walking as one I had walked unsuccessfully years ago. So every time she shared something with me about this man's behavior that fit my experience, I took her words and used them to warn her of the dangers and pitfalls I had experienced. I was trying to protect her, to keep her from making the same mistakes I had made in relationships. But I was betraying her trust and forcing my perception of her relationship on her. Whether my perception was right or wrong was immaterial. It was her path to walk any way she chose. Needless to say, she stayed in the relationship, but no longer shared the details of it with me. The degree of intimacy we shared was lessened because of my betrayal of her trust. It would be nearly three years before she shared honestly with me about her relationship with this man, and I feel very fortunate to have finally regained her trust.

A variation on this theme is even more brutal. I call it "ripping off the security blanket" or, alternately, "kicking out the crutches." This is an unsolicited attempt to break through another person's self-deception and denial. I used this once on the Songteller, who I perceived to be stagnating in a mediocre job and an obviously (to me) unhealthy relationship. So I took his openly shared words about both and wrote him a letter, telling him exactly what was wrong with his life and what he had to do to straighten it out. This was a huge betrayal of his trust in me, and I did not hear from him for seven months. Had I not owned my error and made amends to him for my behavior, I probably would have never heard from him again! Miraculously, the relationship survived, but trust in certain areas still has not been fully regained. He shares his true feelings with me about his work and has just barely begun to share his true feelings about his relationships. Once again, intimacy has been damaged by betrayal.

Still, without question, the person I have harmed the most through betrayal has been me. I betrayed myself every time I chose to pretend to be who I was not or consciously hid parts of who I am. I betrayed myself every time I accepted the beliefs, values, and standards of others without bothering to question them. I betrayed myself every time I judged, criticized, or condemned any aspect of myself or my behaviors. I betrayed myself every time I turned to someone else to meet my emotional needs instead of taking care of them myself. I betrayed myself every time I turned to food or sex or any other addiction for love instead of turning to God. I betrayed myself every time I followed my head and not my heart. True, I also betrayed God by doing these things, but the harm always came back to me. I cannot harm an unconditionally loving God by my behavior, but I certainly could, and did, do a tremendous amount of harm to Nadine.

Loyalty to myself and to others comes easier to me now that I am following the direction of my guide, since loyalty to him is a prerequisite to being my true self and following my unique path. Most of my acts of self-betrayal have been corrected, but not all. I still betray myself every time I lose faith and take back part of my life from God. And I do still have a problem with dissecting and analyzing other people's behavior. In twelve-step programs, we call it taking their inventory for them. Thankfully, God is gentle, loving, and loyal. He does not rip off my security blankets or kick out the crutches. He waits patiently for me to figure these things out for myself.

~ DETACHMENT

Detachment can be defined very simply as minding my own business. Detachment is letting go of what was never mine to begin with—other people's problems, emotions, responsibilities, actions, and lives. Detachment may be physical, mental, emotional, or all of the above. Detachment untangles emotional enmeshment, the joined-at-the-hip syndrome. Detachment removes mental and emotional hooks between people and frees each of us to find our true selves and walk our unique paths. Detachment is a principle that is a cornerstone of freedom; in fact, true freedom is impossible without detachment. Like acceptance, detachment can and should be applied to every aspect of my life. The concept that I am in this physical world, but not *of* it is the ultimate in detachment.

Detachment, however, is often misused and misapplied. Notice that I defined detachment as being emotional, mental, and/or physical, but *not* spiritual. Spiritual detachment is, I believe, an impossible illusion, even though most of us will, at one time or another, attempt to do it. Spiritual detachment, cutting off love to and from another person, requires me to close my heart to that person, to block the spiritual connection. Again, notice that I said block, not sever, because I do not believe that a true spiritual, or love, connection, once established and owned, can ever be severed. To detach spiritually, or detach without love, is an illusion destined to cause me much pain and create many road hazards in my spiritual path. Detaching with love is healthy and desirable. Detaching without love is never healthy and only desirable when it is the only way I can leave an abusive or potentially life-threatening relationship.

Detaching with love means that I can care about others, be compassionately concerned, but stay emotionally uninvolved. I am a caring observer of, not a participant in, others' emotional dramas. Detaching with love means that I allow others to accept the consequences of their behaviors and assume the responsibility for the quality of their lives. Detaching with love means that I allow them to live their own lives, walk their own paths, and make their own mistakes. Detachment is a principle taught to those of us who love addicts and have to cope with addictive behavior and the effects of loving an addict, but it can be used effectively by anyone in any life situation. It can be applied to any area of my life where I have an unhealthy mental, physical, or emotional investment. I can detach with love from people, possessions, activities, events, places, anything that I have become so attached to that losing it will cause me great distress. Whenever I have become so attached to someone or something that the fear of losing it is greater than the joy of having it, then it is definitely time to detach.

Detachment is a principle that is unknown to fixers and controllers, and thus was unknown to me for most of my life. My unacknowledged and unmet need for true intimacy led me into emotional dependence on those who were physically close to me. Thus, even when I chose to leave a relationship or distance myself from a relationship, the hooks remained. I was emotionally hooked to my parents for years, even though we were 1,500 miles apart (see "Release"). Even after I chose to leave my first two marriages, the emotional hooks were not severed. I remained mentally, physically, and emotionally involved with my ex-spouses until the hook could be transferred to a new relationship. Thus, I carried the same emotional hook with me for more than forty years, until I learned to recognize and own my emotional needs, stopped expecting someone else to fulfill them, and began taking care of them myself. Detachment requires self-care. As long as I believe that you and you alone can fulfill certain needs for me (whoever or whatever "you" happens to be), it is impossible to detach.

It was, of course, through and because of the Piano Player that I was introduced to the principle of detachment. Since we both lived and worked together, my emotional dependence and involvement with him were extreme. It is unfortunately true that when you both live and work with an addict, the consequences of his disease affect you both. When the Piano Player started to drink heavily again after three and a half years of not using, my first reaction was, "How can he do this to me?" But what he did or did not do had absolutely nothing to do with me personally. It was my unhealthy attachment that created that illusion. It would be many years before I could face the truth that neither alcohol nor his alcoholic behaviors were to blame for the losses I suffered—car, house, piano, self-esteem. Losing these personal possessions and losing myself was my choice because I chose to remain with him, the end result of my not being able to detach with love.

Even after I had learned about detachment, it was difficult for me to practice it. I detached first from the Piano Player, physically and mentally. The emotional attachment was still intact when he died, and the hook remained, waiting to be implanted in someone new. Breaking my isolation, letting others come close to me, allowing their and God's love to touch and heal me, learning to love, accept, forgive, having compassion for my whole self, and recognizing my needs and learning that I could satisfy them—these are the changes that eventually replaced the hook with the gift of being able to give and receive unconditional love. Unconditional love by its very nature demands detachment. I cannot love you unconditionally and allow you to be free if I am emotionally dependent on you, if I perceive that I need you and only you to be whole and happy. I cannot love God unconditionally if I have other Gods to which I am attached.

Emotional attachment is the root of all compulsive behavior. Be wary of anything or anyone that you cannot live without. To be sure, with chemical addictions, there is a physical attachment as well. But with many, the emotional and mental attachment is equally as strong, if not stronger. I smoked cigarettes for twenty-seven years of my adult life, and while I was doing that I could not imagine myself without a cigarette in my hand. I can also recall questioning a friend who was dating a non-drinking Mormon girl if he was willing to "give up" social drinking. Certainly, I was not, nor was I willing to give up my primary drug of choice—sugar. Following my road map and walking with my guide has given me the gift of detachment with love from all of my primary compulsions. Mental, physical, and emotional attachment to people and things is being replaced with a healthy attachment to spiritual truth. Dependence on people and substances has been replaced by dependence on God. The false equations that ruled my life have been replaced by the one true one. Food does not equal love. Sex does not equal love. God equals love.

The one area of my life where I still struggle is in detaching from outcomes. Again, this goes along with my tendency to want to do God's job for him, to orchestrate the events and experiences of my life. Detachment from outcomes is one of the most important uses of the principle because that aspect alone frees me to create, to teach, to be, and to do without fear and anxiety. Fear and anxiety haunt me when I become too emotionally attached to a specific result, whether it be having a certain person in my life, having my children behave as I would have them behave, winning a sports competition, being successful in my chosen profession, or giving a flawless performance. It is the creating, the act of being and doing, that is important, not the result.

Certainly, it is healthy to strive to do my best, but attachment to the outcome often keeps me from doing my best. If I were not still attached to others' responses and opinions of my piano playing, I would not be struck by fear when I solo perform. Playing because I love to play, as I do for myself at home, generates no fear. Add an audience, and the fear returns. I have become attached to an outcome, an attachment that is baggage left over from my past. The same applies to my fear of public speaking. Again, I have become dissociated from the doing, which is an act of love, and have become overly attached to the outcome. To be sure, praise and compliments on my sharing are nice, but they are not the reason I create and share my gifts. And it sometimes happens that when I become too attached to the outcome and too dissociated from the act of doing and sharing, the opportunity to share and sometimes even the gift may be lost.

Michael Ballam is an opera star who has performed on all the great operatic stages of the world. He is also a spiritual man who does much service work for his church and hospice organizations. He tells the story on one of his tapes about losing his magnificent voice for over two years. For many months, he could not speak, let alone sing. He readily admits to having become much too attached to the outcome—his career—and too detached from the sheer love of singing and sharing his gift with others. The miraculous restoration of his voice, and ultimately his career, was a lesson in humility, faith, prayer, perseverance, reconnection to his creative source, and detachment from outcomes.

~ FLEXIBILITY

Flexibility is the principle that allows me to go with the flow of life even when the flow is erratic and constantly changing course. My unique path is not always straight and smooth and is, thus, never boring. My guide likes to give me twists, turns, and challenges to keep me growing spiritually. Just as flexibility allows a skier to adjust to the bumps and shifts in the terrain of the ski run, flexibility allows me to adjust to the bumps and shifts of the road home. Without flexibility, I will soon wear down trying to adjust to the shifts, shocks, and quirks of life. Without flexibility, I will soon find myself out of rhythm with either my true self or my unique path, scrambling to keep up with my guide or stubbornly trying to resist his direction. With flexibility, following my unique path can be simple, relaxed, free, and a lot of fun. Rigidity and resistance make walking with my guide more difficult and work against the principles of trust, surrender, and acceptance.

One day, not too long ago, the area where I live experienced several days of very high winds, and watching the way the trees were affected by the force of the winds was a study in flexibility. The weeping birches, ashes, and evergreens were, for the most part, unharmed. The willows and other deciduous trees did not fare as well. Huge branches were ripped away from them and the debris of smaller branches littered many yards. The trees that were damaged the most were more fragile and rigid. Those that were not harmed as much were pliable and flexible and able to bend with the wind without breaking. The same analogy applies to me and my life. Flexibility allows me to weather the high winds and storms of life with less potential for harm, to bend with the winds and not break. Those of us who love life, readily adapt to life's challenges, and show it by our actions are usually flexible. Survivors also adapt, but they are not necessarily flexible and their adaptation may be painful, not pleasant.

Flexibility does not only apply to the events of my life. Flexibility also enhances my relationships with my fellow travelers and is a manifestation of unconditional love and caring. But, flexibility is not submission. Flexibility is bending, not bowing or breaking. Flexibility works with boundaries to create relationship parameters. Boundaries are, by definition, flexible; they pliably mold and adapt themselves to specific situations, but they do not break under pressure. Flexibility allows me to adapt in acceptable ways to personal differences and views, but flexibility never asks me to deviate either from being my true self or walking my unique path. Flexibility applies to my doing and not my being. Flexibility without boundaries can lead to loss of self.

Flexibility, too, applies to all aspects of my being—mental, physical, emotional, spiritual, and creative. Mental flexibility is also known as open-mindedness, the willingness to consider, allow, and, perhaps, even accept another person's differing opinion or view. Mental flexibility allows me to be teachable, to be open to receiving and accepting new and different ideas, beliefs, and attitudes. Mental flexibility also lets me discard old ideas, beliefs, and attitudes that no longer fit me or are no longer serving a useful purpose in my life. Mental flexibility is an aspect of humility, allows me to see and consider my choices, and is thus a prerequisite for change. A rigid, closed mind does not see choices, and change becomes very difficult, if not impossible. Mental flexibility is an absolute necessity for accepting the principles of spiritual recovery offered through the twelve steps. With mental flexibility, I can move from despair to hope, pessimism to optimism, negativity to positive thinking, fear to love, egocentrism to God-centrism. Mental flexibility allows me to recreate and restructure my life.

Physical flexibility applies not just to the condition of my physical body, but to every aspect of my life in a physical world. Physical flexibility enhances both body motion and mind motion and may also be described as adaptability. Physical flexibility allows me to adapt and adjust to my ever-changing physical world—disturbed routines, rescheduled appointments, cancelled flights, unexpected visitors, illness and death, emergencies and natural disasters, all those times in life when the expected turns into the unexpected. Physical flexibility enhances the quality of my life by replacing anxiety, panic, and chaos with serenity, calm, and acceptance.

Emotional flexibility allows me to stay current with my feelings, allowing them to emerge and subsequently dissipate. Emotional flexibility allows me to feel and release buried fear, pain, sadness, anger, and any other emotion I have stuffed, knowing that the discomfort of the healing process is necessary and temporary. With emotional flexibility, I do not cling to ecstasy, nor do I wallow in despair. I once told a friend that an open heart can love you for a night, or for a lifetime, and then let you go when it is time.

Spiritual flexibility allows me to remain loving, calm, centered, and with an open heart in the presence of chaos, fear, negativity, attack, rejection, and other unloving and unpleasant challenges of life. Thus, for spirituality, flexibility is paradoxically both a constant and a variable. Even though I flow with and accept the spiritual challenges of life, my response to the spiritual challenges of life is constant. I do not react to fear with fear, anger with anger, hatred with hatred, or abuse with abuse. I see all of these behaviors as a call for love, and I respond accordingly. Spiritual flexibility is unquestionably the most difficult to achieve, at least it has been for me. It is also the most rewarding, once it is attained.

Creative flexibility is sourced in imagination and is the heart of all creation. Creative flexibility is the reason that no two snowflakes, or people, are exactly alike. Creative flexibility allows me to view life, and all aspects of it, from a new and different perspective, a perspective that is uniquely mine and one that will lead to a unique solution or creation. Creative flexibility may be applied to science, art, music, drama, writing, poetry, business, politics, parenting, teaching, and almost every problem of everyday life.

As you may have guessed, flexibility is not a principle that I have always practiced. I am responsible and organized by nature, and those traits do not always yield graciously to unexpected change or spontaneity. As I have learned to relax and walk with my guide, I have also learned how to be more flexible. Still, I tend to insert a fair amount of structure into my relatively unstructured life, and I also tend to resist altering my routine. God, with wisdom and humor, provides me with challenges to show me how flexible or rigid I really am. And, while I was writing this piece, he guided me to an event that challenged my flexibility in all aspects of my life.

This event was a spiritual two-day retreat sponsored through one of my twelve-step programs. There were three other female soul friends from my home group going. The distance required us to stay overnight, and the usual procedure under these circumstances is to share both a ride and a room. I had done this once before several years earlier with different women, and the experience was so unpleasant for me that I swore I would never do it again. Still, these were women I knew well and this was only one night. So I chose to share a room with them.

Attending the retreat and sharing a room with my friends challenged my physical flexibility because it totally changed my daily spiritual routine. There would be no time or opportunity to do morning pages, so they were done the night before I left and again after I returned. My morning prayers became night-before prayers, and my daily reading and journaling were done for both days after I got home. I didn't even take my books with me! Still, there was another problem to be solved. I require more alone time than my married friends, and this was my challenge in creative flexibility. I met the challenge by choosing to drive myself, which gave me more freedom to create my alone time. I could play my soul music both going and coming and come and go according to my desires and needs, not theirs. All of this worked very well for all of us, and the experience was both pleasant and fun.

The events of the retreat itself provided some pretty severe challenges to my mental, spiritual, and emotional flexibility. The retreat leaders chose to deviate from program tradition and used a lot of non-program meditations and exercises, some of which were uncomfortable and even threatening to me. I found myself closing my mind to these experiences (mental) and closing my heart (spiritual) because of fear, which disconnected me spiritually from the group. Through contact with my guide, I was able to re-center, reconnect spiritually, and get back into a position of love, but my loving feelings were less intense because of these experiences. And I never did express my opinions about the retreat to the group leaders in a kind and loving way.

It was one of these non-program exercises that challenged my emotional flexibility in a way that was both frightening and potentially healing. This was an exercise in nonverbal communication that required each of us to "talk" to a partner with eyes closed using only hand and finger contact, to a background of soulful music. It was an experience designed to demonstrate the connection that could be created through the touching of hands and fingers, and for me it was an intensely intimate and deeply moving experience. We were asked to communicate love, joy, anger, peace, playfulness, and, at the end, say goodbye. It was then that I began to weep uncontrollably. The exercise in intimate touch had unearthed a land mine buried so deeply in my psyche that I still do not know exactly what it represents. All I know is that part of me was, at one time in my life, so deprived of intimate touch that once I felt it, I could not bear to have it end, to have my partner say goodbye. And that part of me must be found, nurtured, loved, and healed if I am to lead an emotionally healthy life with an intimate partner. I have asked God for help with this, and I know he will respond with healing love. All I have to do is feel it, accept it, and follow his guidance.

~ TOLERANCE

Tolerance is the acceptance of differences, even though I may not understand or agree with these differences. Tolerance allows me to accept different languages, customs, behaviors, sexual preferences, political views, religious views, social levels, dress, speech, tastes in music, art, literature, and so on. Remember, acceptance is *not* condoning or approving—it is merely an observation of reality. Acceptance does not include a judgment call, and neither does tolerance. Intolerance does. In fact, intolerance demands a judgment call. Intolerance says, "I do not accept your differences. I do not honor your right to your differences, and I have judged these differences to be wrong or inferior." Tolerance is sourced in love. Intolerance is sourced in fear.

One of my soul sisters, while working her fourth step with me, had a real problem with tolerance. She believed that being tolerant required her to endure unacceptable behavior, which is what most of us who have lived with alcoholics did. Oddly enough, in such situations, many of us were very intolerant of unacceptable behavior—but still endured it. Tolerance only asks me to accept your differences and your right to be different. What my boundaries are relative to those differences is strictly up to me. Being tolerant of your behaviors when I find them personally objectionable does not require me to allow myself to be subjected to them. Being tolerant of your views when they differ from mine does not require me to agree with them or even listen to them. What it does require me to do is not ridicule them, berate them, or persecute you because of them. That is intolerance.

Like courtesy, tolerance is also a cornerstone of relationships that can and should be applied to anyone and everyone. The greater and more expansive my sense of community is, the broader my range of tolerance will be. When community, or spiritual connection, is extended to all of mankind, when the God within is recognized in us all, tolerance becomes a principle that can be easily applied to all of mankind. If my sense of community is limited to family, church affiliation, or a twelve-step program, then tolerance, too, may be limited. When there is no sense of community and I perceive myself as separated and isolated from my fellow man or certain groups of people, then tolerance may be easily replaced by intolerance. In fact, intolerance demands separation as well as judgment—me or us against you or them. Intolerance often also involves dehumanization. It is much easier to be intolerant of nameless, faceless beings than someone you know personally. This is particularly true when intolerance manifests itself as persecution.

Tolerance, too, is an expression and manifestation of unconditional love. When I view you as God views you, through the eyes of love, intolerance becomes impossible. The most difficult challenges to tolerance are those who are intolerant and whose behaviors and beliefs disagree with or violate my personal beliefs and moral code. Patriots are intolerant of flag burners. Ultraliberals are intolerant of ultraconservatives. Feminists are intolerant of male chauvinists. Straights are intolerant of gays and lesbians. The unprejudiced are intolerant of all forms of racial prejudice and discrimination. Doves are intolerant of hawks, and hawks are intolerant of doves. Those who obey the laws of society are intolerant of those who do not. Christians are intolerant of non-Christians and atheists. Again, let me repeat that tolerance does not keep me from making laws or setting boundaries where laws and boundaries are appropriate. Tolerance accepts, but does not judge or condone, and acts accordingly. Intolerance judges, condemns, and also acts accordingly.

Tolerance is another principle that I thought I practiced correctly and really did not. To be sure, I am not and was not openly racially or culturally prejudiced. Traveling to Third World countries gave me a much broader view of different cultures, customs, and races than I had before I experienced them firsthand. I seemed to instinctively disagree with my dad's bigotry and derogatory names for blacks, Jews, Italians, and others he singled out for ridicule. I do not agree with sexual discrimination against women (or men), nor am I intolerant of homosexuals and lesbians, since I personally believe that sexual orientation is genetic and not a matter of choice. I am and have been tolerant of what people *are*. What I was not tolerant of before I began walking with my guide was what others thought, believed, or did when those thoughts, beliefs, attitudes, or behaviors did not agree with mine or meet my own personal standards. Back then, everything was either black or white, right or wrong, and I was always right. You were always wrong if you had differing views. Conservatives were wrong. Fundamentalists were wrong. Male chauvinists were wrong. Violent radicals were wrong. Religions that teach that theirs is the only path to God were wrong. Warmongers were wrong. Racists and bigots were wrong. Negative thinkers were wrong. People who wore tattoos, listened to rap music, and drove motorcycles were wrong. Abusers of all kinds were wrong. Addictive behavior was wrong. Spiked hair, sloppy dress, and constantly using street language were wrong. Not just different—wrong! I judged, condemned, and ridiculed, and that is intolerance.

Since God and I reconciled, I have learned how to be more tolerant, accepting, and less judgmental. Seeing people through God's eyes, the eyes of unconditional love, offers a different view. Knowing and feeling the God connection among all of his creations makes intolerant views much more difficult to maintain. Knowing and believing that I get back what I give, that loving and being tolerant of others is loving and being tolerant of me, makes intolerance a foolish and self-defeating practice. Just as courtesy recognizes our intrinsic value and worth, tolerance recognizes our intrinsic right to be our true selves and walk our unique path, no matter how odd that self and path may look to me. I do not have to like others' personas or agree with their chosen paths, but neither do I have a right to judge and condemn them for their choices.

Now, those with whom I disagree are no longer wrong; they are merely different. I can accept others' positions—and other people—even when I disagree with them. And in the process of learning how to be tolerant of others, I have learned how to be tolerant of myself, my humanness, my fears and odd quirks, the traces of intolerance that have not as yet been released and removed by God. And, since God is well aware of the traces of intolerance I still carry, he brings me lessons in tolerance that show me where the wounds remain.

In one of my programs, I have been the spiritual mentor, or sponsor, of a very intelligent, articulate, attractive, and open young woman, in many ways like the Nadine of twenty years ago. This girl also happens to be a devout and practicing member of the predominant religion in my area. My biased views of those who practice this religion are, shall I say, less than flattering, and my sponsor-ee exhibits none of these unflattering characteristics. Years ago, I would not have worked with her because of her religious beliefs. Now, I am delighted to work with her and her religion has no bearing on that. This is a lesson in tolerance. However, since I first wrote these words, this sponsor/sponsor-ee relationship ended, so, guess what? I now have three other sponsor-ees with the same religious background, two of whom actively practice their religious preference.

Then there was the disruptive child lesson. Normally, twelve-step program meetings are meetings for adults only. Members do not bring their children with them. Recently, both of my groups experienced the same phenomenon: two mothers came to meetings with their toddler. In both cases, the babies, by simply doing what babies do, were very disruptive. One mother took her child and left the meeting, but the other did not. Years earlier, when a similar situation occurred at an Al-Anon speaker luncheon, I was furious and formed an instant and immediate dislike for the thoughtless woman who irresponsibly allowed her grandchild to wander about, distract the speaker, and annoy a large number of people. Obviously, her view on this was different than mine, and I was completely intolerant of it. Now, when faced with a similar experience, my reaction was somewhat different. I was tolerant of the mothers even though I disagreed with their behaviors. I also understood that whether or not to allow children in meetings is a group decision, not mine. If the group agrees that it is okay (one group did), I can choose to stay or leave. This, too, is a lesson in tolerance.

But the ultimate lesson in tolerance (and many other things) will come through an intimate relationship. The Songteller and I are very much alike in many important ways—and very different in others. As long as we continue to share safely from a distance, these differences do not affect our relationship. But should God choose to bring us together, I will be face to face with several views and attitudes that I had previously and intolerantly categorized as wrong, not different. And, knowing how God chooses to work with me, this is his way to challenge me to finally get it right. I loved my dad, but I was intolerant of his intolerance. I loved my mother, but I was intolerant of her negativity and submissiveness. I loved the Piano Player, but I was intolerant of his alcoholic behaviors. I love the Songteller—can I now be tolerant of our different views? I believe I can, but the challenge is yet to come.

~ SIMPLICITY

Simplicity is the principle that uncomplicates the complicated. Simplicity makes being my true self and walking my unique path more joyous, happy, and free. The more complicated I make my life, the more difficult it becomes to live. The more complex I make the events of my life, the more difficult it becomes to enjoy them. Quite simply, simple is fun. Complicated is not fun. Unless, perhaps, you are playing chess—and even then I suspect that the most dramatic moves are the simplest.

In Al-Anon, one of the slogans is "Keep It Simple." Another well-known variation is KISS—"Keep It Simple, Stupid!" Those of us who have lived with active alcoholism understand the value of this principle as few others can. Most of us have made an already complicated situation more complex through our attempts to control the uncontrollable and our worrisome thoughts. One of the best ways I found to complicate my alcoholic situation was to play the game of what if. *What if* he freezes to death while he is passed out in the car? *What if* he drives drunk, gets into an accident, kills someone, and we are sued and destroyed financially? *What if* he has an affair and brings home AIDS or some other awful sexually transmitted disease? To be sure, any or all of these things can happen, but they probably will not. And even if they do, worrying about them ahead of time will not make the situation any better. Taking whatever precautions are possible to protect myself against these possible events is a much better course of action and a much simpler one. What-ifs take me into the future, into fear, and away from love. Simplicity keeps me here in the present with God.

As with most of the principles, simplicity can be effectively applied to all aspects of my life. Simplicity in my physical world requires restraint, especially for those of us who are gatherers, or collectors, of stuff. The more stuff I have, the more complicated my life is. That is a simple truth. The more cars, houses, boats, clothes, furniture, knick-knacks, treasures, junk, motorcycles, snowmachines, guns, etc. I have, the more I have to maintain, organize, arrange, house, and move, should the need arise. I have a soul friend whose spouse could not face moving to the house of her dreams because they had so much stuff. (They did move.) The Skier/Climber once said that we should be able to fit all of our prized possessions into the glove box of a Volkswagen, but we did not live that philosophy. We had multiple pairs of skis, multiple packs, multiple tents, multiples of everything that supported our outdoor lifestyle. Most of us do have multiples of the things we place importance on. One of my soul sisters was shoe-deprived while married to an alcoholic; now she has enough shoes to last her a lifetime! My personal collection of stuff includes the treasures that represent very special places and very special people, so each time I travel or receive a gift from a soul friend, my collection of treasures expands. My home, which I have consciously tried to simplify, is now filled with such treasures, and it is becoming increasingly more difficult to find a place to put the new ones that I acquire!

Here's another simple truth. Simplicity requires space and a willingness to part with that which cannot possibly be parted with. Earlier, in "Faith," I described a potential flood threat that caused me to look at which of my treasures I would take if I had to evacuate my home. The final list was very small, and did *not* include any of the treasures I mentioned above. What it *did* include was the stuff that is irreplaceable: the photo negatives of my treks in Nepal, musical audio tapes made by the Piano Player and me, my mother playing her organ, and the Songteller, certain photographs and letters, and only a few mementos. That was all. But as yet, I have not chosen to simplify by disposing of the rest of my stuff. Eventually, my planned relocation to Quadra Island or some other guided move will require me to do just that.

Simplicity applies to emotions as well. Go to the heart of all negative emotions, and the root emotion is fear. Go to the heart of all positive emotions, and the root emotion is love. Love and fear—very simple concepts, complicated by layer after layer of complex emotional variations. To further simplify things, since love and fear cannot coexist simultaneously, if I surrender to love, see my world through God's eyes, I eliminate the whole spectrum of fear-based emotions. How simple that sounds, and how difficult it is to do.

Certainly, simplicity may be applied both creatively and spiritually. Creative arts—music, poetry, prose, drama, art, and all the rest—may be either complex or simple, but the physical laws of creation are very simple, and so are basic spiritual laws. Dissect all the complex physical laws, and they reduce to some very simple equations. Newton's laws and Einstein's theories are not at all complicated. Strip all the complicated rules, regulations, and rituals away from our religions, and they are reduced to some very simple spiritual truths. To love God and my fellow travelers is not a complicated concept.

Of all the applications, however, mental simplicity seems to be the hardest to achieve, at least for me. I personally can take the simplest concept, the simplest idea, the simplest question, and thoroughly complicate things by analyzing it to death. I do not know how many times I have taken a problem to my spiritual mentor in Al-Anon after having turned it over and over in my mind, analyzing it from every conceivable angle, and still stymied for a solution. I present the problem to her, and with a very few words, she strips it down to the core issue and a solution magically emerges. Mental simplicity is one of her gifts, and she uses it well. I am barely beginning to master the art.

While the Songteller and I were creating my musical gift of love, he asked me a question about the sound intensity of the master. It was a simple question that required a simple yes or no answer. But, I proceeded to give him a complicated dissertation on how the sound intensity varied on different sound systems, and any number of other variables that could affect my response. He finally got frustrated and said, "Just give me an answer—yes or no!" So I did, whereupon he looked at me, obviously irritated, and said, "Now, wasn't that simple?" It *was* simple. I was the one that had chosen to make it difficult.

I have also spent much of my life analyzing the lives of others, so that I could help them straighten out themselves. When I first met the Piano Player, I analyzed his excessive drinking and outrageous behavior as to cause and effect. The effect was very self-destructive, so what in his past created the guilt he was punishing himself for? I had all sorts of theories based on what he had told me about his life, which included physical and sexual abuse, a dishonorable discharge from the army for theft, and six months in prison. All of these events, plus a hundred more, were the cause of his drinking. All I had to do to cure his drinking problem was to love him enough and help him feel good about himself again. Right? Wrong! To be sure, all of this did have an effect on him. But the simple truth was that he had a disease that caused him to drink uncontrollably, and there is no cure for this disease. The only effective treatment of symptoms is to abstain from using alcohol. No further analysis required.

Simplicity is a principle that I am still learning how to practice after many years of experience in making my life more complicated than was necessary. Writing this spiritual autobiography has required me to simplify my socio-spiritual life, to pick and choose which events and activities are absolutely essential to walking my unique path, and eliminate the rest. Over time, my choices have shifted as my guide has directed me, but my guidance has been to always simplify and focus on my creative assignment. Over time, I have simplified my home environment by de-cluttering it, removing the unneeded, unused, and no longer meaningful objects, sorting and clearing out outdated stuff, reclaiming my basement by removing the ghosts of the past.

De-cluttering or simplifying my home paralleled the de-cluttering of my heart, the clearing out of old and outdated emotions and purging and healing of old wounds. De-cluttering my mind through simplifying my thought processes has also paralleled my spiritual growth. Walking with my guide really is a very simple process. None of the principles I use to help me do this are complex. The twelve steps contain simple, but not easy, concepts. They are not easy especially for someone like me who keeps on wanting to complicate my life by making being my true self and walking my unique path much harder than God ever intended it to be. I still have this tendency to clutter, as one look at my dining room table can attest. (I believe this is a genetic defect, since both my mother and her mother exhibited the same characteristics.) And I still want to analyze everyone's behavior, including my own, and speculate as to the reasons why, rather than simply accepting and dealing with the end result. My Al-Anon sponsor has told me many times that it did not matter *why* the Piano Player drank. What mattered was that he did, and that was the reality I had to live with, accept, and deal with.

I have told myself the same thing over and over—that it does not matter *why* people do the things they do. What matters is how I respond to what they do. In fact, sometimes knowing *why* can complicate things even more. Some time ago, I became angry because one of my soul sisters, who has called and connected with me almost every night for well over a year, had not called in four days. I knew *why* she has not called. She had a new man in her life, and she had given him the time previously reserved for me. If I did not know why she had not called, I would have called her myself to connect and make sure that she was okay, a very simple act sourced in love. But because I did know why, I felt hurt and angry, and I complicated the situation even further by refusing to call her. Beneath the anger and hurt lay fear, fear of losing her as a friend. And the pain came from the denial of love to this special person in my life. Knowing *why* took me out of love and into fear, where I could have, if I chose to, created exactly what I feared by my own actions, or lack of them. I could have easily complicated this situation to the point where it got really ugly. Thanks to the wisdom of my guide, however, I did not do that. I worked through my fears, accepted the reality of the situation, forgave both her and myself, and reconnected. God's wisdom, the wisdom of love, is very simply grounded in simplicity.

~ Order

Order is the principle that makes and keeps my life manageable. Without order, there is chaos, and chaos leads to insanity. Order eliminates chaos and restores sanity, giving peace and serenity a chance to develop and grow. Order in the court quiets a disruptive courtroom. Order in my life in the physical world quiets a disruptive environment. Order in my mind quiets disruptive thoughts. Order in my heart quiets disruptive emotions. Order in my soul quiets all disruption and helps me to be my true self and follow my unique path. Order in my mind, heart, and soul simultaneously quiets a disruptive life.

So order, too, can and should be used in all aspects of my life. Another Al-Anon slogan is "First Things First." Using this slogan is a way to practice order by priority. The most immediate activities, events, problems, or challenges are attended to first. Chaos results when there are no priorities and all things are considered or attempted at once. Chaos creates crisis, since the likelihood is that nothing, or very little, will be accomplished. But crisis does not necessarily create chaos. Crisis can be dealt with in an orderly manner. Emergency medical technicians and others who deal with medical emergencies are trained to be orderly. Fire drills and emergency evacuations bring order to potentially chaotic situations.

In our physical world, order in society is achieved through adherence to laws, rules, regulations, and prescribed processes to deal with violations. Order in my home, especially where there are children, may require a similar process. Order in my mind requires both a logical thought process and mental discipline (otherwise known as judgment or wisdom). Order in my heart requires that I feel and release my feelings as they happen and not bury them alive in the dark recesses of my heart. Order in my soul requires that I allow myself to be guided along a spiritual path, whether it is the twelve steps of Alcoholics Anonymous, other paths prescribed by organized religion, or more metaphysical and mystical approaches.

Creative order is perhaps the simplest to understand. There usually is an orderly process used to create a painting, compose a musical score, write a book, prepare a gourmet meal, bake a cake, cut hair, or sew a dress. To be sure, the resulting art form may not be orderly, but the process of creation is—first things first and one step at a time. When I began to write this book, I first created an outline and an order of presentation of the gifts, principles, practices, and road hazards. Then I created an orderly process for filling in the outline—the tools (pen, notebook, computer, word processor), the time for creation (variable), and the schedule (also variable, but somewhat determined by my guide). Certainly, God gave me my marching orders. ("It's time to write.") He also nudged me along by suggesting a deadline for completing the first draft and defining the focus required to meet it (writing and relationship). It was then my task to order my life in such a way as to meet this deadline.

Orderliness of this kind is one of my gifts, and one I have used for many years in my professional and personal life. Planning work tasks and other projects and activities has always come easy for me. Ordering tasks is a mental process, as is ordering thoughts in general, and I normally do this very well. Mine is a logical mind with an aptitude for mathematics and other forms of symbolic translation. I have a talent for reading music, learning foreign languages, working crossword puzzles, taking and transcribing shorthand, and writing computer code. I also can (and will) attempt to analyze just about anything of interest, but more specifically all of my problems (and others'). I am not content simply knowing *what*. I also want to know *why*.

All of this requires orderly mental processes, but it does not necessarily lead to an orderly mind. Remember, an orderly mind also requires mental discipline. Conclusions reached using an orderly mental process may be used in a highly disorderly way, especially when disruptive emotions are present. Fear, anger, jealousy, envy, and a host of related fear-based emotions can turn mental order into chaos very quickly. Mental discipline provides the willingness to move through and beyond disruptive emotions in an orderly and positive way.

Unfortunately, mental discipline is not one of my gifts, so the results of my orderly thought processes have not always been applied in an orderly way. Analyzing others' problems and personality quirks may be an exciting and challenging logical pursuit and nothing more, creating no mental disruption or chaos. If

I use these conclusions and my understanding to help me relate to others in a more accepting, loving, and compassionate way, I am exercising good judgment or mental discipline. But, if I take these conclusions and use them to try to fix, save, or otherwise interfere with the rights of others to choose their own paths, order gives way to chaos and insanity because I am attempting the impossible. Too many times in my life I did exactly that, especially with the Piano Player, and the result was anything but mental order. Neither was there mental order when I turned my logical thought processes loose on my own problems and used the conclusions to condemn myself or validate false negative beliefs. Mental order thus requires both technique and wisdom. When either is lacking, order is difficult to maintain.

Order in my heart has been even more elusive for most of my life. Emotional order requires me to feel and release my feelings *as they are felt*, not thirty, forty, or fifty years later! A wounded heart with many unhealed breaks or festering sores of anger or resentment is not orderly, and mine was a very wounded heart. After all, I medicated and stuffed my feelings with food and other addictive substances and behaviors for a very long time. How could my heart be anything but wounded? Order in my soul was also nonexistent for all the years that I had neither a God to guide me nor a spiritual road map to follow. Spiritual order requires both, and with them my soul becomes content.

It should come as no surprise that spiritual order had to come to me before I could even begin to apply the principle of order to my mind and heart. Mental discipline and emotional healing are grounded in spiritual truth. The ability to use my orderly thought processes wisely comes from allowing God to guide me and using love as the basis for my choices. The courage to open and cleanse the multiple breaks in my heart, to unbury and expose emotional land mines, is not self-generated. That courage came directly from a loving, caring, supportive God who was right there with me, applying massive doses of love to my raw and bleeding wounds as they were unearthed and exposed. And the courage and strength to feel all my feelings as they arise and let them go comes from God as well.

Before I began walking with my guide, my life appeared

orderly, but was not in order. It was, in many important ways, unmanageable and chaotic. External order in my physical world was an illusion I carefully orchestrated through control and caretaking, and did not come from my internal self. Now, the order I feel in my mind, heart, and soul extends outward and creates order in my physical world without the need for control and caretaking. It just sort of happens. External orderliness manifests from internal order. An ordered heart, cleared of buried feelings and unhealed wounds, opens, and as it does, I become more open, loving, and generous in my interactions with others. An ordered mind manifests as ordered behavior and a more meaningful and productive life. An ordered soul manifests in my relationships as love, kindness, gentleness, compassion, and wisdom. All impact my environment and the way in which I live my life, and the effect is not forced. It is natural and spontaneous. Internal order creates external order. Internal chaos creates external chaos. Internal chaos forced to conform to the illusion of order through control and coercion is a volcano ready to erupt.

My outdoor life with the Skier/Climber was a very orderly life, externally. Ours was an orderly physical and mental world, what I now refer to as a head trip. I molded myself to fit this orderly, logical life, and my orderly, logical thought processes fit in very well. But my heart and soul were in chaos and forced to conform by controlling and caretaking. And every so often, under the influence of too much gin during Happy Hour or too much stress on a steep ski hill, the volcano erupted in a violent display of tantrums and tears. The Skier/Climber would patiently weather the eruption, the pressure would be temporarily relieved, and I would resume my orderly, controlled life—until the next eruption.

This scene was repeated many times during ten years of marriage and, although not terribly pleasant, it was not physically harmful to either of us. We were the lucky ones; others are not so fortunate. Inner chaos forced into the illusion of order through control and coercion more often manifests as rage, battering, drive-by shootings, lynchings, torture, murder, rape, incest, and all other variations of physical violence. As with everything else, the cure for much societal disorder is an internal cure, not an external one. Naturally orderly people create naturally orderly societies which, in turn, could create a naturally orderly world. Order is the principle, and the source is love. And the Al-Anon slogan that fits here is "Let It Begin with Me."

~ Balance

Balance is the principle that brings harmony into my life. Balance can be applied to two or more complementary aspects of being or doing to create a harmonious blend. A weighted scale visually represents balance between two objects when each weighted side is equal. A mobile visually represents balance among several objects when the distribution of weight among all the objects is equal. In both cases, imbalance is caused when one object is either much heavier or much lighter than the others—when one aspect is overdeveloped or underdeveloped. Imbalance is created through extremism. Balance is created through moderation.

When applied to my true self, balance ensures that no one single aspect of my being overshadows or overpowers any other—that my mental, physical, emotional, spiritual, and creative selves have equal importance and equal expression. If I visualize my true self as a pie cut into five distinct pieces, balance assures that the pieces are the same size and the whole is circular, not tilted or lopsided. When my true self and my life are in balance, walking my unique path becomes much steadier and less prone to slips and falls. Just as an unbalanced load puts stress on a washing machine, an unbalanced load puts stress on my life.

Balance may be applied not only to all major aspects of my true self but also to every part and subpart. And again, balance may be applied to the relationship among the subparts or to each individual component. If I subdivided my physical life into such categories as social events, solitude, sex, sleeping, eating, traveling, working, and so on, then balance assures that none of these is either overindulged or under-indulged in. If I single out one specific thing, such as solitude, balance assures that I have neither too much nor too little. Balance may also be applied to opposites—work and play, heart and head, being and doing. Opposites may be found in any or all aspects of my true self—opposite character traits, emotions, beliefs, attitudes, thoughts, behaviors. In short, the principle of balance may be applied anywhere that imbalance may create disharmony and a loss of serenity.

Maintaining balance in my life is not one of my personal gifts. Addicts are extremists in the use of their drug (or drugs) of choice, and I am a recovering addict. Too much is the key here—too much food, too many cigarettes, too much emotional need. For most of my life, my aspects of self were gravely out of balance; the pieces of my pie were all different sizes and shapes. To be sure, the sizes and shapes changed as I moved through my various lives, but they were never balanced. In my outdoor life, mental and physical dominated; in my musical life, physical and creative took precedence. Through both lives, and the one before, the spiritual and emotional parts of Nadine were very small and undeveloped compared to the rest. My creative self was relatively constant, although the form of creativity changed over time, from music and art to photography and writing, then to music and writing. There was never balance or harmony within myself, nor was there balance in the specifics of my life. Aside from the imbalance caused by my addictions, I was too serious, too responsible, too controlling, too caretaking, too organized, too isolated, too insecure, too much in my head. Again, as with so many of the principles, I did not begin to achieve balance in my life until I rediscovered and began to develop my spiritual self. Walking with my guide easily and effectively requires balance, and in doing so I have begun to acquire it.

Ever so slowly, over time, the major components of my true self have been brought into a more balanced relationship among each other. I say *more* balanced because I am a work in progress. Because my mobile had been tilted so heavily toward the mental/physical and away from the spiritual/emotional, I have concentrated on the undeveloped parts and ignored the others. Even now, after many years of walking with my guide, I am still heavily into spiritual, emotional, and creative growth. Eventually, I hope to achieve better balance among all parts of my true self and then expand them equally. Each aspect is important, especially as I grow older. No aspect can be ignored if I am to live a healthy, happy, balanced life in service to God.

I also still have difficulty balancing specific events in my life.

There, too, the pendulum swings from one extreme to the other before it settles down into balance somewhere in the middle. This has been particularly true with the extremes experienced in my outdoor and musical lives, where those extremes were part of my spouse's life, not mine. In my outdoor life, the extremes were physical and mental. We skied, backpacked, climbed, or kayaked nearly every weekend for nine and a half years. Now, years later, I still resist physical activity except for my daily walking. Also in my outdoor life, mental stimulation came through scientific and secular reading, work-related learning experiences, and other heady pursuits. Today, I rarely read a secular magazine or newspaper, never read anything scientific or technical, and have not chosen to learn a new skill, take a course, or otherwise stretch my brain in a very long time. I read a lot, but my reading is spiritually based. This is *not* balanced.

In my musical life, the Piano Player liked background music, usually country/western. He also liked to watch television—sports, movies, and news. So for fifteen and a half years, either the radio, television, or stereo was playing during his (and mine when we were together) every waking hour. When he died, I turned off everything. Now, more than ten years later, the radio and TV are still off. I have watched only five or six movies during that time and am possibly the only person in the country who hasn't seen *Titanic*. Eventually, I responded to a music-starved soul and began listening to tapes and CD's—soothing background music, romantic piano, the songs created by the Songteller. But, so far, that is it. Again, no news, no sports, no current events, nothing secular, which is definitely not balanced. I keep thinking I should change my ways, but so far I have not, except when national crisis compels me to. On September 11, 2001, I joined the rest of the world in observing and grieving the World Trade Center tragedy. But even then my television viewing was minimal. Instead, I followed it through the CNN Web site on the Internet.

There are other areas of my life where I actively and continuously strive for balance. When I do not, when I get skewed in these areas of my life, I get crazy. One of these important areas is balance between relationship and solitude. Walking my unique path under the direction of my guide and serving him creatively through writing and music requires a lot of alone time. But, I was isolated and cut off from meaningful relationships for most of my life, so I also need continual interaction with my soul friends. Finding the proper balance between alone time and shared time is a constant challenge for me, and too much of either really disturbs my serenity. One recent Christmas season, I overbooked social events and shared time, and by Christmas day I could not face another dinner. I was done. On the other hand, when I travel alone, which I usually do, I need to be out among people to maintain my sense of connection. Going out for dinner, visiting a shopping center or mall, chatting with motel clerks and maids—these are ways that I keep my balance and my serenity.

Still, the single most important area is balance between my heart and my head, between being and doing, intuition and action, female and male, yin and yang. Remember, I have been a head person, a doer, most of my life. Quieting my mind and listening to my heart, allowing my guide to be heard, is relatively new to me. Again, the pendulum had to swing to the other extreme before I could hope to settle into a balanced position. Finding my way to my true self and unique path required me to shift from being a self-willed, head-guided doer to a God-willed, heart-guided be-er, and neither extreme is a good place to be. Self-willed doers act without guidance; God-willed beers have guidance but do not act on it. So the two must be integrated. The way it works now (or is supposed to work) is that my guide speaks through my heart, and my head listens and responds. God and I work together as a partnership. God's part is to give me the guidance I need, and my part is to act upon this guidance. But there must be balance between the two partners—balance and cooperation.

This autobiography is the result of the integration and balance of heart and head. For several years, I wanted to write a book of this nature and just could not get started on it. This was the time when I was working very hard to establish a relationship with God, to learn how to follow his direction, to find my true self, to open my heart to love, and heal my wounds. The doer was immobilized. Then, one day many months ago, God spoke to me through my heart and said, "It's time to write." It took me five more months of mental preparation before I could begin, but eventually my mind began to respond. The spiritual principles and the self-disclosure come from my heart. The words are formed and positioned into sentences by my mind; and the interpretation and presentation of the meaning of the principles often come from a source of understanding that brings clarity to me as I present it to you. Source, heart, and head, working in balance and harmony, are creating these words to be shared with you.

I have mentioned my power animals before—the deer influences my heart and the eagle influences my mind (see "Freedom"). The deer is my gentleness and compassion, and the eagle is my free spirit. The deer is very loving and grounded, while the eagle still tends to want to fly too high and too far. But, with time and experience, the eagle has learned to connect with the deer, to follow the deer's guidance before taking off, and to reconnect with the deer through frequent landings. I need them both with me for a successful flight. Without the deer, the eagle has no spiritual support. Without the eagle, the deer has no spiritual freedom. Together, we can all fly—safely, successfully, and on a course charted and supported by God. And again, the key to a successful flight is balance.

~ HUMOR

Humor is the principle that allows me to travel the road home lighter and freer. Humor lightens both my load and my disposition and makes me a much more desirable traveling companion. Being able to see humor in all situations, no matter how painful and tragic, is a gift, but it is also a quality that can be acquired. Seeing through the eyes of humor is akin to seeing through the eyes of love. Both are a matter of perception. I can just as easily see the humorous, as I can see the bleak. What I perceive is a matter of choice.

A true sense of humor is an internal quality that is also, I believe, sourced in love. Comedians and joke tellers create humor from the outside in. They say or do something I perceive as funny, and I laugh. Laughter sourced in love comes from the inside out. It is spontaneous and natural and springs from the sheer joy of being or thinking loving, but humorous, thoughts about someone I care about. Sadly, too few of us are able to laugh from the inside out.

We wait for some external event or person to make us laugh. Thus, comedians and comedies and other funny events are very popular entertainment.

Even more sadly, too many of us laugh at humor that is not humor at all, but ridicule. Ridicule is sourced in fear. Black humor, racist humor, sexist humor, sexual humor, any kind of humor that belittles or downgrades a certain group of people or the life force of sexuality is not humor at all because it is not sourced in love. There are a few wonderfully gifted comedians and comediennes who can talk about themselves and their humanness in a very loving and funny way, and that is humor. But these are few and far between. Much of what we consider to be humor is ridicule.

Laughter is an expression of humor, but it is not humor itself. Laughter can be very forced, very surface, and very external. Laughter can be used as a wall to keep me isolated from others, to avert the possibility of openness and true intimacy. I know several women who do this, who go into what I call flit mode where everything is happy-happy and nobody ever reveals anything of substance to anyone else. Laughter is also a ruse to create the illusion that all is well when it really is not, the laughing-on-the-outside, crying-on-the-inside syndrome. The Piano Player was an absolute master of this when he was drinking. He was a happy, funny drunk, the life of the bar or the party, always laughing and telling raunchy jokes. I could always tell when he was in the bar because his unique laugh rang out above all the background chatter. And the more he hurt inside, the louder he laughed.

A true sense of humor comes from being able to see the big picture through eyes sourced in love. Having vision, being able to see beyond the immediate, reduces the events of my life to their proper size and importance. Those of us who practice humor use the Al-Anon slogan, "How important is it?" Humor simply does not take life too seriously, no matter how serious life tries to be.

As with all things, the key with humor is balance. Practicing humor requires me to strive to stay somewhere in the middle between taking life too seriously and not seriously enough. The bleak picture of life seen by humorless people and the always cheerful view seen by those in flit mode are equally self-destructive. The humorless are too despondent and defeated to look at and work on their own issues, to follow the twelve-step road map or any other path to God, while the ever-cheery ones are too busy avoiding their issues.

People who work twelve-step programs laugh a lot. Sometimes the laughter is forced and a form of avoidance, but mostly it is not. The bottoming-out process that brought me first to my knees and then to God is as close to a near-death experience as I hope to have. And near-death experiences usually change one's perspective, making "How important is it?" very easy to grasp. So we laugh a lot. I hadn't been in program very long at all when I discovered something very disturbing about myself. I laughed more in the hour and a half I spent at my Al-Anon meeting than I did all the rest of the week! The years I spent with the Piano Player had cost me many things, and my sense of humor was one of them.

You see, I do have a sense of humor, or at least I thought I did. To be sure, as a perfectionist, I took myself too seriously most of the time. And before I rediscovered my lovable true self, I took what others said and thought much too seriously and personally. But, remember, I am an optimist by nature, and optimism is usually evidenced by a sense of humor and a reasonably happy disposition. So I smiled a lot, not always from the inside, but I still smiled. The Skier/Climber nicknamed me Smiley when we were first married. However, in time, my nickname was changed from Smiley to Grumpy, and his nickname became Meany, so obviously my sense of humor had deteriorated, but not disappeared. Freedom from my self-inflicted bondage brought my sense of humor back, and again I smiled and laughed a lot and viewed my life in a fairly balanced way. When I first met the Piano Player, we laughed a lot. And the dreams I had for our life together did not include the reality of living with alcoholism and alcoholic behaviors.

Over time, as the disease progressed, the laughter disappeared for both of us and whatever sense of humor I had disappeared as well. The Piano Player, when he was drinking, took nothing seriously, so I had to compensate and take everything seriously. That was the shape I was in when I came into my programs. And the loss of my humor had occurred so gradually that I did not even know it was gone.

One of the first things my guide taught me when I began

walking with him was to lighten up, to reclaim my misplaced sense of humor and place it on a firmer foundation. And he did this by example. God has a wonderful sense of humor. He should have, for he definitely knows the big picture and that my attempts to change it really do not change anything. They may alter the route but never the destination. And he has placed me in some pretty funny situations in order to bring me the healing required to open my heart or to show me how far I have progressed. One such situation involved a woman I used to work with that I really disliked. Something about her grated on me, and being around her or anywhere near her affected me like fingernails scratching across a blackboard. Then, one day, I ran into her quite by accident while walking. The next day, I met her again. I had not seen her in years, and why God chose to cross our paths twice is not clear, except that I possibly did not get the message the first time. And the message, of course, is that I no longer find her irritating. In fact, I find her quite lovable. So whatever emotional wound she brought to the surface has apparently been healed. And, after I left her, I thought of another woman I intensely disliked many years ago, and jokingly asked God if he was going to bring her back into my life as well!

Anyway, I am pleased to report that God's example has gradually rubbed off on me and I view my life from a broader and less serious perspective. I do smile now, from the inside out and much more often, and I laugh a lot more, too, spontaneously and lovingly. Opening my heart and surrendering to love has connected me more strongly to the source of humor, and the more I see myself and my life through his eyes, the easier it becomes to see humor in both. I still sometimes take myself too seriously and others too personally, but both of these traits are diminishing.

Some time ago, I had a somewhat unexpected visit from the Songteller. Now, I thoroughly enjoy this man's company, but, I have been, in the past, leery of him when he gets too physically close. I would take his sometimes defensive words personally and our time together much too seriously. Fear has kept me from being totally open to him and to seeing him—and us—from the broader view required to see the humor in the way we relate. That was not so this time, and I got a very different picture. He is, when viewed from a more loving and detached perspective, a delightfully funny man, and how we relate is even funnier! Going shopping with him is funny because he can never make up his mind about what to buy, and watching the twenty-something salesgirls trying to entice my sixty-something friend into buying is hilarious! And then there is the bantering that goes on between these two people who are both "always right"—this comes close to being a comedy routine! There was the vanity license plate bearing his name that I distinctly remember and he denies ever having, and the color of his new coat (he said maroon, I said brown, and it could be either). But the best part was when he tried to convince me that my dream is impossible (something he periodically does when he feels threatened). What he says comes from his head, not his heart, and is designed to push me away—but not *too* far away. I have never taken what I call Canned Lecture No. 3 seriously, but I have taken it personally, and started to again this time. But I stopped and regained my perspective, my sense of what my truth is, and my sense of humor. He went through his routine, I stood my ground, and we parted as friends (which is one of the things we do not argue about). I smiled at the time, and still smile when I think about our visit. Seeing both the man and our relationship from a more humorous perspective has given me a much more pleasant and comfortable point of view.

~ Maturity

Maturity is sometimes defined as the state or quality of being fully developed or complete. Maturity, to me, is a quality most of us aspire to, but it is a journey, not a destination. Maturity, like spiritual recovery, is a process, and the quality can always be refined and enhanced. Plants reach maturity, but people do not, not as long as we are alive. Maturity is complete only at the time of my death, and then only relative to my current lifetime.

Maturity is thus not truly a principle, but it is so closely related to the principles that I chose to include it with them. Maturity is also a quality that, when properly developed, makes it much easier and more pleasant to walk with my guide along my unique path home. Immature travelers are much more prone to want to chart their own course, and they often do not have the degree of commitment required to follow a prescribed path, no matter what the path may be. Immature travelers tend to look for the softer, easier way, which makes their path longer and more difficult in the long run. Immature travelers behave in immature ways and are thus more susceptible to being caught up and stuck in the road hazards. I know that, in my case, I had to reach a certain level of maturity before I was even willing to connect with my guide, let alone walk with him and follow his direction. For me, maturity is a very important quality indeed.

What is maturity, as it relates to being my true self and following my unique path? Maturity is, first and foremost, the willingness to take personal responsibility for the quality of my life—for my thoughts, my attitudes, my behaviors, my actions, my beliefs, my desires, and my hopes and dreams. Maturity is also evidenced by the acquisition and application of wisdom to my life experiences. Mature people are both responsible and wise. They understand the meaning of the Al-Anon slogan, "Let it begin with me" because they know that "me" is the only person they can change. They understand that no matter how bizarre, erratic, painful, or frustrating other people's actions and behaviors may be, it is still never about them and *always* about me. They understand the meaning of the Serenity Prayer, say it often, and use the principles frequently. Mature people are willing to do the work required to improve the quality of their lives.

Mature people also practice, through self-discipline, those principles that enhance the quality of their journey down the road home, that make the trip easier, happier, freer, more joyous, and more rewarding in all ways. Maturity relies heavily on all the principles, but is most strongly connected to willingness, trust, humility, patience, commitment, courage, acceptance, tolerance, and gratitude. Spiritual maturity is required in order for me to love unconditionally and thus is also a basis for compassion, forgiveness, generosity, and gentleness.

As with many of the principles, maturity is a quality that affects every aspect of my being—mental, physical, emotional, spiritual, and creative. Physical maturity accepts the responsibility for the quality of all aspects of my life in a physical world—my body, my environment, my country, and my world. Mental maturity accepts the responsibility for the quality of all aspects of my mind—

thoughts, beliefs, attitudes, and the actions and consequences that spring from them. Emotional maturity accepts the responsibility for my emotions and the actions and consequences of actions caused by them. Spiritual maturity accepts the responsibility for the quality of my spiritual life and the development of all of my God-given gifts and rewards. Creative maturity accepts the responsibility for the development and use of my creative gifts. Maturity, by definition, is accepting the responsibility for self-care and self-development (or the lack of it) in all aspects of my life, as well as caregiving when caregiving is required.

Maturity is often linked with chronological age, but in truth it is not related at all. Although physical maturity is often defined by sexual development, physical maturity extends far beyond puberty (as does sexual maturity, for that matter). Although maturity may increase as I journey through life, aging does not guarantee it. Nor does youth necessarily equate with immaturity. One of my soul sisters has a teenaged daughter who she refers to as having an "old soul" because she consistently displays a spiritual wisdom far beyond her years. On the other hand, the Piano Player was very immature and always said he never wanted to get old. When he died, at fifty-nine, his father described him as "a little boy who never grew up."

In the case of the Piano Player, his immaturity had nothing to do with age but rather with his unwillingness to accept the normal responsibilities of life (including the responsibility for treatment of his disease). For most of us, the normal events of life bring increased responsibility and we accept it, maturing in the process. Making my own living, getting married, having children, raising and educating them, preparing for retirement, all these natural events of life bring responsibilities that, when accepted, develop maturity, at least the aspects of maturity required to function in our physical world. Thus, mental, physical, and emotional maturity will probably (but not always) develop. Ideally, spiritual maturity will develop as well, but that is an ideal, not the norm, in our decidedly non-spiritual society. Spiritual maturity may not develop until we reach the final stages of our lives, or it may not develop at all.

As for me, I always thought of myself as being very mature. Actually, I was, in my physical world—I was very responsible. I claim to have been born with a giant R stamped on my forehead because I cannot recall a time when I have not been responsible for my physical self. I behaved responsibly, acted responsibly, studied responsibly, played responsibly, worked responsibly, kept appointments responsibly and always on time, handled money responsibly, shopped responsibly, organized treks responsibly, played road gigs responsibly, ran a business responsibly, and was more than happy to take on other people's responsibilities as well as my own. With the Piano Player, that included the responsibility for his life and recovery from his disease, and that was not very wise. So, the wisdom of maturity was not always there, even in my supposedly mature physical life.

However, my story as already shared makes it very clear that maturity was grossly undeveloped for many years in all other aspects of myself. Unquestioning acceptance of other people's beliefs as my own is not mental maturity. Neither is mental laziness and apathy. Stuffing and anaesthetizing emotional pain and other unwanted feelings, and throwing tantrums and venting my anger in inappropriate ways are certainly not examples of emotional maturity. Disregarding and discarding my creative gifts when they did not happen to fit my current lifestyle was not creative maturity. And disregarding and discarding God certainly was not spiritual maturity. My life and others' were run on self-will, and self-will is not mature. Willfulness is childishness; and I was, in most ways, like the Piano Player, a child who had not grown up. I just was not as open about it as he was. And it was not so much that I did not want to grow up, but rather that I did not know that I *needed* to grow up. I willfully and falsely believed that I was already there, when my truth was that I had barely even begun. I thought I was mature and thus was not open to the need for change.

Maturity is coming to me as a byproduct of finding and owning my true self and walking with God down my unique path. The first and most obvious step was reclaiming my lost spirituality. That aspect of my true self could hardly mature while it was disowned and rejected. From there, piece by piece and part by part, I have accepted the responsibility for the quality of the other aspects of myself that had been ignored or disowned, and I am doing the work required to upgrade the quality of my being and life. Following my personal road map, the twelve steps, and working with my spiritual mentors has gradually helped me to mature, not only spiritually, but physically, mentally, emotionally, and creatively.

I finally understand that the only person I can change is me, and the quality of my relationships with my fellow travelers is determined by my level of maturity, not theirs. And, with time and experience, I have come to understand that the wisdom of maturity comes from God. I am responsible for doing the footwork, for practicing the principles that develop maturity. But the wisdom of maturity is a gift that comes from him and comes only when I am ready to receive it. The key that truly has opened the door to my becoming ready to receive the gift of wisdom, that has prepared and readied me, is humility. Releasing false pride and setting aside the "I think I knows," becoming truly teachable, has opened my mind to the wisdom found in my heart and is bringing me the maturity to become compassionate, forgiving, and generous with others and with myself. One of my soul sisters told me not too long ago that I have gotten older, and I understood this to be a complement. What she was saying was not that I have aged, but that I have matured. And, oddly, as I have matured, I feel my age less. I am younger in heart but wiser in spirit.

~ SYNCHRONICITY

Synchronicity is the principle my guide uses to do his part in manifesting my dreams or otherwise co-creating my life. Synchronicity refers to those odd quirks of life that some call luck, fate, chance, or coincidence. Synchronicity puts me in the right place at the right time in events where perfect timing and perfect sequencing of events are required to make it happen. Orchestrating such events is beyond the scope of human capabilities, at least in my opinion. Synchronicity is involved in unlikely or chance encounters and in winning the lottery, again what most would attribute to luck or chance. But I do not believe in luck or chance. I believe in synchronicity. And I call these events God shots, because God is the director who makes them happen. His timing is perfect, but mine is not. He has proved that to me over and over.

Synchronicity can also keep me from being in the wrong place at the wrong time through intuitive warnings, those gut feelings that warn me to change course or direction. Every time there is a plane crash, there are always stories of those who either were delayed at the last minute and missed the flight or were otherwise guided to change their plans. And there are those who, for reasons known only to themselves and God, are flying on standby and make the flight. Synchronicity does not always create a pleasant result by the world's standards, but it is always the correct spiritual result. My highest good does not always come in a form that is easily recognized as such.

Synchronicity works best when I am in close contact with my guide, walking close to him and listening carefully. And the more synchronicity is recognized and appreciated, the more often it will occur. Sometimes a God shot occurs like a bolt out of the blue; other times it is somewhat more anticipated. Doors unexpectedly open that were either not apparently there or were firmly closed. Hearts and minds open that were firmly and rigidly closed. Or what I call the domino effect takes us from place to place and ultimately to God's intended destination.

One of my soul friends, a member of the hospice team who administered both to the Piano Player and my mother, tells the story of how she made her way from South Dakota to Idaho and then to her present life. Shortly before graduating from college, the funding for the job she had accepted in South Dakota vanished. She found herself a soon-to-be graduate with no job and many expenses. Desperate, she sent out resumes to every potential job site she could think of, including the hospice in the Idaho city where I lived for many years. The hospice director set up an interview with her in a city where she had a friend she had not seen in years. The night before the interview, my friend was up late visiting with her friend and went for the interview tired and emotionally vulnerable. Because she was tired and emotionally vulnerable, her emotions were very visible. Because her emotions were very visible, she was offered a job, which she accepted. Had she known the full scope of the job, she wouldn't have accepted it, but she did not. She accepted the job and came to Idaho single, alone, and scared.

My friend is the daughter of a Methodist minister and very sincere in her religious faith, so one of the first things she did after settling into her job was look for a church home. The first

Methodist church she went to had a reputation for being open and friendly, but when she went, no one even talked to her. At the other Methodist church that was *not* reputed to be friendly, she was greeted and welcomed warmly. Because she was welcomed, she chose it as her church home; and because she chose it as her church home, she met her husband-to-be. They are now married, have a combined family of four, and her husband has subsequently been called to be a Methodist minister.

I have already shared that my path was charted indirectly through relationships because God knew that in those cases I would follow my heart (and him). My path has not been as obviously synchronous as my soul friend's path, but there have been plenty of synchronous events along the way. To be sure, I did not call them God shots back in the days when God and I were not on speaking terms, but that does not mean that they were not.

One of these was a career God shot. After I graduated from college at thirty-five with a bachelor's degree in mathematics, I went back to work for the scientific laboratory I had worked for before college. But there were no technical jobs available, so I worked first as a secretary and then as a reactor operations scheduler, which is unquestionably the most boring job in the world. Eventually, I got so bored and desperate that I went to my supervisor and volunteered to do typing for anyone who needed typing done. The man who brought me his typing was a young Ph.D. nuclear engineer who was also assigned to my supervisor but was about to become the head of a newly formed reactor safety analysis group. He found out about my degree, asked me why I was doing typing, and I told him—because I was bored and desperate. He then went to our supervisor and asked if I could be assigned to him, and I became the first member of his group. This man was my first, and greatest, professional mentor and a spiritual mentor as well, back when I had no spirituality. I recognized much later that he was the first man I had ever met that lived his Christian faith and practiced unconditional love. A chance circumstance? I think not. I desperately needed both a professional and a spiritual mentor, so God graciously arranged to put the teacher and student together. Unfortunately, the student responded very well to the professional mentoring but not at all to the spiritual mentoring; I simply was not open to it. But the seeds were planted and would begin to grow many years later.

Now that I recognize the source and give him credit where credit is due, God shots are much more apparent and are greeted with awe and gratitude. And, since I am actively seeking his guidance, being in the right place at the right time, for me, seems to happen more often these days. Teachers come into my life, deliver and receive their gifts, then leave again. The events of my life sequence in exactly the right way, and I have the sense of being in rhythm with the flow of the river of life, just sort of moving along with the current. The most obvious God shots are those that either bring partial validation of a dream or a direct and highly improbable response to a prayer. These events say to me, “Be patient. You are on the right track, and your desires will manifest in the proper time.”

One summer, I spent four weeks on a pilgrimage to and from the center of the labyrinth on Quadra Island in British Columbia. Now, one of the things I miss when I travel alone is hugs and other forms of touch. (I compensate by petting a lot of dogs; they are much more receptive to a stranger's touch than people are!) A couple of days before I was scheduled to catch the ferry back to the U.S., I wrote about missing my hugs in my morning pages and then promptly forgot about it.

The morning I was to ferry back to the U. S., I drove down from Sidney to the ferry terminal in Victoria at what I thought was an early hour, and ended up eighteenth on the standby list. I was given a number and told to park behind a sport utility vehicle with an Idaho license plate. (I took note of this because it was only the second Idaho car I had seen in three weeks!) There was about an hour and a half before the initial Custom's check, so I wandered around the inner harbor, taking pictures. Then, as I was coming back to my car, I heard a woman's voice call out, "I know you." I looked up and saw a lady with sunglasses on who looked vaguely familiar. She said again, "I know you. You spoke at the Overeaters Anonymous workshop in Twin Falls, and you gave me a tape." It turns out that the woman, who belonged to the car parked ahead of me, was Liz from Boise, Idaho, who had also spoken at the same workshop. She and her husband were vacationing in Victoria. What is the first thing program people do when they meet? Why, they hug, of course! God had provided me with some needed hugs and a mini-meeting in the Black Ball ferry waiting line in Victoria, British Columbia! Ultimately, we got into our cars, got onto the ferry, and never connected again.

Coincidence? I don't think so. The probability of meeting a program person I knew at that time and in that place is astronomically small. The event required perfect sequencing and perfect timing, and that is synchronicity.

Chapter IX

THE PRACTICES

THE practices are specific actions and behaviors that support the principles and make them a part of my everyday life. The practices are both mental and physical activities that manifest spiritual truth and promote emotional well-being. The practices are designed to strengthen my connection to my guide, to keep me sourced in love, and to express that loving connection to myself and my fellow travelers. The practices also provide the means to affirm my true self and co-create my life, to do my part in the creative process. Where the principles are the "whats," the practices are the "how tos."

Prayer and meditation strengthen and deepen my relationship with God through making conscious contact with him, and mindfulness, or living in the moment, keeps me close to God. Self-care and self-discipline are the ways I take loving care of my true self—body, mind, and spirit. Courtesy, gentleness, and service are the ways I express love, compassion, and generosity to my fellow travelers. The choices I make and the boundaries I set affirm who I am and serve to define my unique path and create the essence of my journey through life. Visualization and affirmations can be used to enhance the quality of my life, to make the journey more pleasant.

The practices are all tools for spiritual growth that I personally use on my journey. Some of them I use often, and some of them I use only occasionally. But I have used all of them often enough to know that they, like my program, work when I work them. There are other practices specifically suggested to support recovery in twelve-step programs that I have not written about, so I will mention them briefly here.

- **Reading** - all literature approved and issued by specific twelve-step programs, daily meditation books, and anything else that is pertinent and appealing. I have been reading books that relate to the various aspects of my spiritual journey voraciously for over ten years now, so my library of reference materials is pretty awesome (as evidenced by the appended bibliography). My guide routinely takes me by the hand in bookstores and leads me to whatever I need to read in order to move along my spiritual path.
- **Writing** - the twelve steps, journaling, processing emotions and other bothersome issues, morning pages, a daily step ten review, amend letters to those who have left, and anything else that helps me to work through my issues. My library of written materials is also pretty extensive.
- **Using the Telephone** - to reach out for support from my fellow travelers when the path gets rocky and rough, to give support to others, or simply to connect with another soul friend. This is a practice that I use more incoming than outgoing.
- **Attending Meetings** - a continuous and essential source of love and support for those of us who are active in twelve-step programs. Meetings provide mutual support and keep me spiritually connected with the fellow travelers who share my compulsions.
- **Sponsorship** - connecting with a spiritual mentor who has what I want (serenity and/or abstinence from my drug of choice) and can help me maintain the same conditions. Getting a sponsor was my first step towards establishing intimacy with a fellow traveler.

These practices, too, work when I work them. All of the practices have been, and are, an important part of my personal process, that which keep my true self following the direction of my guide and walking my unique path.

~ Prayer

Prayer is talking to the God of my understanding. It is one of the two ways in which I connect with my guide, meditation being the other. Prayer is something I now do every morning of every day of my life. It is also something I do anytime during the day or night when I feel the need to communicate with God. Frequent communication with God serves to strengthen our relationship, to bring us closer to each other. And, as with any relationship, the more open and honest I am with him, the closer and more intimate our relationship becomes.

Prayer is an individual practice, one that each of us approaches in a different way. Prayer may be communal or singular, public or private, and each has a slightly different effect. Communal prayer, as practiced in religious ritual or as used in the closing of twelve-step meetings, brings me closer to God through others. Communal prayer connects me spiritually with my fellow travelers. I once attended an Alcoholics Anonymous meeting at an international conference in San Diego, and the spiritual force of 65,000 people saying the Lord's Prayer in unison was totally awesome. So is the spiritual force of ten people, standing in a circle and holding hands, saying the Serenity Prayer. Communal prayer connects us to God through each other in a way that must be experienced to be understood.

Singular, or private, prayer is a direct line, not a party line, to God, and there are possibly as many ways to talk to God privately as there are people who do it. It may be a formal, down-on-my-knees conversation, or it may be an informal, hi-how-ya-doing-type chat. Also, there is no prescribed time to pray. It may be done first thing in the morning, the last thing at night, or any time in between. Whatever is comfortable for you works best. Talking to God should become a very comfortable action. If it is not comfortable, the chances are that you will not do it very often. Informal and often is better than formal and infrequent. The God of my understanding likes to hear from me often so he knows that I know where I am. Remember, I tend to either run ahead or lag behind. Prayer keeps me close so I do not stray too far off course.

Although there is no prescribed or suggested time or place to pray, there are suggested ways to pray. First of all, prayer is asking for God's guidance, not telling him what to do. As the eleventh step suggests, prayer is "praying only for God's will for us and the power to carry that out." That does not mean that I should not tell God what my wants, needs, and desires are. After all, that is how I co-create my life in partnership with God. What it does mean is that it is up to God to decide how my prayers are to be answered. I tell him my desires, but allow him to create the outcome. If what I want, need, or desire leads to my highest good and/or the highest good of someone else, my desires will be fulfilled. God's will for me is always directed toward the highest good of all. If what I want, need, or desire does not lead to my highest good or the highest good of someone else, my prayers will still be answered but probably not in the way I expect them to be. All prayers are answered, but the form is not always recognized. Ultimately, all of life's events, no matter how unpleasant or uncomfortable, move me forward toward my highest good, and move others there as well.

Prayer is how I transmit love—to myself, to my special soul friends, to anyone, anywhere, in the world and in the universe. Thus, prayer is a powerful healing medium, for love is the greatest healer there is of all wounds—physical, mental, emotional, spiritual, and creative. Sending out love through prayer can melt walls and open hearts and minds. Sending out love through prayer for our enemies or those who live and act through fear, not love, is a tremendously important healing action. If done often enough by enough of us, sending out love through prayer can ultimately heal the world.

Prayer is how I attain self-forgiveness and forgiveness of others. Since the God of my understanding is not a judgmental God, I cannot seek his forgiveness, for in his eyes I am perfect. But I am not perfectly forgiving of myself, so I often need to pray to him for forgiveness so that I may, in turn, forgive myself for my imperfect human behavior. Prayer is a powerful tool to use in forgiving others as well. The most effective way to turn hate into love and to free myself from the bondage of resentment is to pray for the persons I hate or resent. Remember, prayer sends love and is healing, both to them and to myself. And it works even when my heart is not in it.

Prayer is also how I ask for help, but empowerment can only be received if I am in a position of humility. That means that I understand that God is my source of power, that I am being empowered by him to do whatever it is I am asking his help to do. It means that I understand in my mind and believe in my heart that I cannot do this thing without his help, that I am powerless in that area of my life. An alcoholic who cries out to God to help him quit drinking without first admitting powerlessness will usually not be empowered until he or she surrenders. God will not feed my ego, he only feeds my spirit. Humility comes from the spirit, not the ego.

Once surrender is complete and humility brings the sense of absolute knowing that God is my source in all matters, I no longer have to ask for help. I can then allow God to do for me what I cannot do for myself, simply knowing that it is so. Prayer then becomes how I affirm this through positive words and statements. Affirmative prayer is the most powerful form of prayer, for it relies on God's power to create the miracles in my life.

Finally, prayer is how I say thank you, how I express my gratitude for the blessings of my life. (It is also suggested that I express my gratitude for the challenges of my life, but I am not always able to reach that level of enlightenment!) God likes to know that I appreciate his many gifts and will gladly provide me with more of the same when he is recognized as the source of these gifts. As I graciously and humbly accept his gifts, he will graciously and humbly send me more or energize and strengthen the gifts that are inherently mine. Again, the key is the awareness and acceptance of God as the source of all the good that comes to me.

My personal prayers are both semiformal and very informal. I talk to my guide informally whenever the need arises, but my semiformal prayer is a daily ritual, begun and ended by playing my God music box for him. (The God of my understanding loves music!) The song my God music box plays is "Wind beneath My Wings," and the words fit him very well. When I first began talking to my guide each morning, my semiformal prayers were long and complex, and took about ten minutes of fast talking to complete. Paradoxically, as my relationship with God has become deeper, more intimate, and more continuous, the need for a lengthy semiformal prayer time has become less and less. Not that I stay centered in God's presence and call on him often, my morning prayers are short and to the point and go something like this:

"Good morning, God. Thank you for giving me another day. Thank you for giving me all the days of my life and all the gifts of my life, the greatest of which is the awareness and acceptance of your presence within me. I am the perfect expression of all that you are, and I shine our light and love into the world. I allow that perfect expression to manifest in my body as perfect health and freedom from physical pain. I allow that perfect expression to manifest in all of my relationships, making them unconditionally loving, God-centered, and healed. I release the past and joyously look forward to this new day."

This prayer is then followed by my step three dedication (see "Step Eleven"), a period of silence specifically dedicated to those experiencing severe life challenges, and my quiet time with God (see "Meditation").

As you can see, my personal morning prayer is primarily a prayer of gratitude and love. I say "thank you, God" every day of my life for the blessings of my life and send out love to my special soul friends and to the world. My personal spiritual dedication reaffirms my commitment to allow God to guide me in all aspects of my life. The prayer to God that I sometimes end my morning pages with affirms love, guidance, strength, wisdom, and courage relative to whatever challenges were processed through the pages that day.

The very informal chats I have with God whenever the need arises usually are prayers asking for help or guidance, or questioning my understanding of his guidance. They are often brief pleas for self-forgiveness when doubt overpowers faith and pain and fear disconnects me from love. My morning pages contain both conversations with God and specific prayers, as well as my daily step ten review. Prayer, talking to my guide, is an integral part of my life now, as natural as breathing. Together, prayer and meditation create the lifeline between me and God that allows him to guide me down my unique path, the road home.

~ MEDITATION

Meditation is listening to and experiencing God, and it is the second way that I connect with my guide. Meditation is also something I do daily, but in ways that are somewhat non-traditional.

Besides quietly sitting and stilling my mind for an extended period of time, I meditate while writing, walking, and reading, and anytime during the day or night when there is a break in the action, a time to clear my mind for a few moments. Again, what is important is that I take the time to slow down, quiet my mind, and connect with God. Communication is always a two-way street. It does me little good to pray for guidance if I am unwilling to be quiet enough to hear it. Again, as with any human relationship, there are two aspects of relationships that lead to intimacy: sharing and listening. To relate to my guide, I share myself through prayer and listen for his guidance, experience his presence, and receive his gifts through meditation.

Meditation is also an individual practice, and it, too, may be either communal or singular. In Buddhist tradition, meditation is often communal and provides the same sense of connection through others that communal prayer conveys. I personally have not experienced this form of meditation. My meditation practices have been almost exclusively singular. As with prayer, the key word here is comfort. I must do what is comfortable, do what works for me. Otherwise, as with prayer, I will find myself not doing it. I once took a course in eastern meditation, and I found it very difficult at that place in my spiritual recovery to sit very still, concentrate on my breathing or an object, still my mind, and be absolutely quiet. Consequently, when the course ended, so did my meditation practice. Many years passed before I incorporated formal meditation as a part of my daily spiritual practice.

When I first began to meditate formally, I focused my gaze on an object of spiritual significance, then used a word that signified my intention to connect with God's presence whenever my mind began to wander (as it always did). (This form of meditation is sometimes referred to as centering prayer.) My word of intention was namaste, a Hindu and Buddhist greeting that means "The God within me greets the God within you." Ironically, I first heard and used this greeting with our Sherpa guides on my first trip to Nepal many years ago, during the time when all aspects of God had been disowned by me. I did not, at that time, have a clue as to what the greeting meant!

Today, I spend an hour each morning in the silence with my

guide, simply experiencing his presence without external distractions. The candle I light reminds me that his light is within me, as it is in all of us. I now consider meditation, or resting in the silence, the highest and most intimate form of prayer. I rest in the quiet and experience God's love, strength, power, and peace, then carry the sense of that presence with me out into my world.

Now that I am in tune with the God within, I find quieting my mind much easier, something that has become a semi-automatic process. Besides practicing formal meditation, I also practice the art of listening and watching for the messages my guide sends me. The messages are always there. As I said earlier, there are no unanswered prayers. I may not hear or see the message my guide sends me, or I may choose to ignore it or misinterpret its meaning, but that is *my* error, not God's. God's messages are my truth; it's his job to send them and my job to receive them. And the more I learn to receive them with an open mind and listen with an open heart, the more accurate my reception will be. In fact, true and accurate reception requires that I listen with my heart, not my head. Meditation teaches me how to do that, to discern the difference between mind talk and heart talk, to quiet my mind so that my heart can be heard. Meditation helps me to experience my connection to the God within, to universal wisdom and truth. Meditation calms and centers me as I become more in tune with the presence of God. Meditation enhances and expands my gift of intuition and makes it much easier for me to follow my unique path under the guidance of God.

My second most important form of meditation is writing. I have shared that I write three pages in longhand daily, usually (but not always) in the morning. I began this practice exactly one year after the Piano Player died, and more of God's truth has been given to me through this writing than through any other medium. I cannot write with a cluttered mind, at least not in longhand. All the words you are reading here were written first in longhand, then transcribed and refined on my computer. Writing by hand seems to slow me down enough to get the heart connection and allows God to bring in the words, ideas, and insights that he wants me to share with you. But before I could do this, I had to be prepared, to heal emotionally, to evolve and grow spiritually to the place where I would be willing to write these words. That evolution and growth came primarily through my morning pages. In pages, I process grief, work through anger, face my fears, open and heal old wounds, break through denial into reality, and monitor my feelings and my interactions in relationships. In pages, God gives me spiritual insights and personal truths, clarity, wisdom, understanding, encouragement, and love. In pages, I first talked of him, then to him, and now with him. My conversations with God are sometimes indirect musings and sometimes very direct discussions. I ask a specific question, and he answers. Sometimes his answers are clouded by my own desires, but usually they are not. The answers are always there if I choose to interpret them correctly.

Interestingly, before I reconnected with God, I used to hate writing in longhand and always typed personal letters or, in fact, any writing. Longhand was too slow—I could not keep up with my racing mind. And that, of course, is exactly the point of writing in longhand—to quiet or slow my racing mind and give God a chance to be heard. Obviously, back in those days, I did not want to hear him!

My third most important form of meditation is walking. Remember, I was a hiker/backpacker in my outdoor life, although I certainly did not meditate then. I was usually so preoccupied with getting from point A to point B that I hardly saw anything in between! I quit walking in my musical life because it hardly fit our nomadic musician's lifestyle. Still, after we settled down in one place, after the Piano Player began drinking again, and before my insanity had hit bottom, I began to walk again as a way to relieve some of the tension in my life. My work location was near the municipal airport, and I love flying, so the route I walked was a spiritual place for me. Part of my route followed a quiet, little-used back road leading to the "old" airport. It was serene, peaceful, and seasonally gifted with wildflowers and meadowlarks. The entire route was without the bustle of the popular walking/biking paths and had minimum vehicle traffic. Walking clears my mind, nurtures my soul, and sometimes just allows me to feel connected, grounded, and centered to the earth and the God that created it all. Naturally, I walk alone. As I said earlier, meditation for me is not communal or conversational. Meditation is a solo gig.

Reading is also a form of meditation for me, used in a slightly different way. I read several meditation books daily by various authors, and the messages contained therein are very often exactly the messages I need to bring clarity to an issue I am struggling with. Or the messages reinforce a truth or remind me of some principle I have temporarily forgotten to use. Guidance from God may come to me through my reading. And, as always, the key is being willing and open to receiving it.

When what I need and desire from my guide is love and healing, I often use music as a form of meditation. Music is more than just background for me. My soul is so attuned to music that I listen to it, focus on it, which forces me to quiet my mind and receive the love it contains. For me, soft piano or guitar music, with nature sounds interwoven amongst the quiet melodies, is particularly soothing. My own piano tape, entitled "A Gift of Love," is exactly that and is very quiet, loving, and healing. I have used this tape many times in this way, and others have shared with me that they have done the same thing.

Some time ago, I over-trained while exercising and aggravated a fairly painful neck problem and nerve irritation that I had first experienced twenty years earlier. Treatment included using a neck traction device I affectionately call my hanging tree. When the problem reappeared, stayed, and was painful enough to keep me from writing and playing the piano, I got out my twenty-year-old hanging tree and began using it again, twice a day, thirty minutes each session. Now, hanging myself involves sitting very still with my face supported by the traction device, a system of pulleys and weight. It is not possible to talk, read, or write while doing it. But I can listen, so that is what I do. I allow God to send me love and healing through the very loving guitar and piano music given to me by the Songteller, a gift of love that happens to be exactly thirty minutes long.

These forms of meditation help me quiet my mind and listen to what God has to tell me, experience his presence, and receive his gifts of love. Besides these somewhat formal ways to meditate, I habitually pause just long enough to be given the guidance I need to walk with my guide along my unique path or to intuitively handle some difficult situation that requires divine assistance. Meditation, like prayer, is also an integral part of my life now, as natural as breathing. The intimate relationship I have today with the God of my understanding has been created through practicing prayer and meditation.

~ MINDFULNESS

My first title for this practice was "Living in the Present." Then I thought, there must be a word that describes this, and there is. The word is mindfulness, and it comes from Buddhist teachings. Only, mindfulness uses a finer time increment. Mindfulness lives in the moment and is fully mindful, or aware, of what is happening in the moment. Mindfulness knows that the moment, right now, this instant, is really all there is. The past is gone, and the future is, by definition, undefined. All I have, all I can count on having, in terms of my life experience, is now. My life is not past, present, and future, although we categorize it as such for convenience in a world that functions in linear time. My life is a very long string of successive moments. Now is all there is.

Now is also eternal. In the moment, linear time stands still for an instant—the past and future do not exist. In the moment, all is well and all is love. Fear lives in the future and is based on past experience. Worry lives in the future and is based on projection. Resentment, regret, anger, guilt, and shame live in the past; pain and sadness may live in either place. I may be experiencing the pain of losing what was or the pain of losing what could be. Expectations also live in the future and are based on past experience. "What ifs" live in the future; "if onlys" live in the past. In fact, all of the road hazards, those principles that make being my true self and following my unique path much more difficult than intended, live in either the past or the future. In the present, in this moment, there is nothing to fear. There is only love. And since God is love, that is where I find him. God lives in the moment, not in the past or in the future. God is here with me in the now.

Mindfulness, or living in the present moment, is a practice that keeps me firmly connected to my guide. It is a practice because I have to consciously discipline my mind to do this. Mindfulness is not an automatic process for me. My mind has been flitting back and forth between past and future for so long that it does not know how to stay in the present. Staying in the moment seems odd and unnatural, and even uncomfortable. Being totally aware of my surroundings and being present in what I am doing also feels unnatural and uncomfortable. Most of us pride ourselves on being able to do more than one thing at a time. We eat and read or eat and converse, or we drive while talking on a cellular phone. Mindfulness does not approve of such behavior. Mindfulness concentrates on every action exclusively. God may not object to my saying my prayers while showering and drying my hair (which I did for many years), but this is not being mindful. Which action do I fully concentrate on? Ideally, my prayers, but that was not always the case.

Twelve-step program participants practice mindfulness one day at a time, the idea being that I can do for one day what would seemingly be impossible when viewed over a longer time span. So those of us who are recovering addicts give up our drug of choice one day at a time for as long as we live (or recovering). If anyone had told me before program that I would be willing and able to abstain from eating ice cream and chocolate for any significant length of time, I would have said they were crazy. But I have done that now, one day at a time (actually one moment at a time), for over eleven years. The sobriety countdown at an international convention of Alcoholics Anonymous is particularly impressive. Some of the AA's have as many years of sobriety as AA has been in existence (nearly sixty years). And they have done it, as I have, one day at a time. In the present, in the moment, walking hand in hand with God, the compulsion is relieved. That is mindfulness.

Still, mindfulness is perhaps easier to practice with compulsive behavior than with the other aspects of my life. As hard as it was, giving up sugar was infinitely easier than giving up my need to control, which is based on fear. When I am being mindful, living in the moment, God is in charge of my life and directs my participation in it. When I take things back that I have turned over to God, I have moved out of the present, away from my guide, and into the future or the past.

The present is where the past has its meaning and the future is shaped. In the moment, I have the gift of being able to reshape my life. If the past derives its meaning in the present, then I can choose to give it any meaning I like. I can choose, in the moment, to replace anger and resentment with forgiveness; guilt, regret, and shame with acceptance and self-forgiveness; negative memories with positive memories. I can choose, in the moment, to let go of any part of my past that I do not wish to take with me into my future. My thoughts, beliefs, and actions in the present will create my future experience, that what I do or do not choose in the moment shapes my future. This has become very obviously true for me, in the physical sense, as I age. The choices I made twenty years ago, when I traveled the road, ignoring God's direction, have certainly created my present. Twenty years ago I did not practice preventive body maintenance, and now I am paying the price in body repairs. Still, I know that the body maintenance and rebuilding that I do now will shape a more physically fit and healthier body twenty years from now.

There is another aspect of mindfulness that is vital to intimacy in relationships with my fellow travelers, and that is what I call being present. Being present means that all my attention is focused on our interaction. All aspects of my being are present, alert, and paying attention. My eyes are on you, I am talking directly to you, or I am listening intently to you. My mind is not racing ahead to formulate a reply or rebuttal, nor is it daydreaming or distracted by other thoughts. I strive for this degree of involvement with all my soul friends, and most of them are present as well. In fact, I am so used to their being fully present that when they are not, I get flustered.

Not long ago, I was having lunch with one of my soul friends in our favorite restaurant. We were sitting across from one another, very present and connected, and it was my turn to share. Suddenly, my friend turned away from me and began looking intently across the room behind me. I found myself stammering, unable to finish my sentences, and wanting to look around to see what the distraction was. I became confused and frustrated and totally mystified as to what was causing her to be so inattentive. After several minutes, the mystery was solved when my soul friend excused herself and headed for the one-person restroom located across the room. She had been watching a line of women go in and out, waiting for her turn to use it!

As I write this, I am present and living in the moment. I am practicing mindfulness by default because that is the only way I can write. When I begin to struggle for words, it means that it is time to take a break, that either God is tired of channeling me or I am tired of receiving. (Guess which one it is!) Creating involves mindfulness. Anytime I do something without a sense of time, I am living in the moment. Anytime I am so absorbed in what I am doing that I cannot be distracted, I am being mindful. Anytime that I have the sense that I am walking hand in hand with my guide, that all is well and on schedule, that I am free and happy and blissfully serene, I am being mindful, living in the present with God.

I wish I could say that this was usually the case, but it is not. I still spend a lot of time charting the details of a future that is not mine to detail. And I still get stuck at times in the past. Revisiting the past to open and cleanse old emotional wounds is essential for healing, but I am to stay only long enough to release the pain. As the Songteller has said in song, "It's good to seek old times again and visit with the past. But don't try and stay too long, your welcome may not last." If I were more enlightened and more mindful, I could do that from the present without having to go back and feel the pain. I could simply choose to reframe the past through choosing to remember only loving experiences, forgiving and forgetting all else. But, I am not that enlightened yet, so I have to do it the hard way.

Still, I have come far with this practice since I began walking with my guide. Maintaining my serenity requires it, and I value my serenity more and more each passing day. Staying close to God requires it. I get lost, separated, and scared when I move too far out into the future or stay too long in the past. So I have to come closer again, by consciously bringing myself back into the present, into the moment. When fear comes or I find myself in a pit of emotional pain, I need only move back into the present with God to find relief from my emotions.

I will have to admit that sometimes the present is not very much fun, such as when I was up all night nursing an abscessed tooth. But, if I move too far away from the present, I lose touch with both my reality and God, and the pain is, after all, a signal that my body needs attention. So I do what I have to do to lessen the pain: stay mindful and call my dentist in the morning.

~ Self-Care

Self-care is the practice that cares about me. Self-care is sourced in unconditional love and expressed through compassion, forgiveness, and generosity. Self-care is directed toward myself and is a prerequisite for compassion, forgiveness, and generosity toward others. Implicit in the directive to love my neighbor as myself is loving myself as well, and self-care is an expression of self-love.

Self-care is self-nurturing. It is the act of giving the very best to myself. Caregivers understand this principle very well and practice it continuously. When they do not practice self-care, which connects them to and draws from the source of all love, caregiving becomes subject to burnout in whatever aspect of self that is being neglected. Caretakers, on the other hand, do not know how to practice self-care and often believe that to do so is selfish. Caretakers are thus parasites, because their source is the one they are taking care of. They get what they need to keep on caretaking, not from God, but from the caretakee (also known as the victim). When the victim does not give enough back to sustain the caretaker, anger and resentment soon begin to grow.

For many of us, myself included, either one or both of our parents, our primary childhood nurturers, was a caretaker, not a caregiver. Since caretakers do not love us unconditionally, we left childhood with a sense of deprivation and have gone through life starved for the love and nurturing we did not receive as children. For us, practicing self-care as an adult can be a form of re-parenting. We can learn to give ourselves the nurturing and loving care we so desperately need by identifying what was not given to us freely as children and providing it to ourselves. For example, I am touch-deprived. Apparently, I was not held and touched enough beyond my dependent early years. For sure, I do not recall being hugged or held as a young child or teenager, as healthy touch was not a part of our family life. Later, I reached out for touch through dancing and sexual contact, but often what I really needed from a man was not sex, but simply to be held. So my personal self-care includes lots of healthy touch—hugs from both male and female friends, regular therapeutic massage, and a lot of self-massage. In that way, I am giving Little Nadine what she missed, and her needs are being met. Again, the key here is *self*-care. Nurturing Little Nadine is my job, not someone else's, unless I wish to find myself emotionally dependent on another person for my well-being. That is a place I have been far too often in my life, and I choose not to go there again.

Self-care is caring for all aspects of self—physical, mental, emotional, spiritual, and creative. Self-care varies from person to person. What I perceive as self-care may be very different from what you perceive as self-care, but the principle is the same no matter how I choose to practice it. Caring for myself requires me to identify my own personal needs and satisfy them as best I can, in ways that are loving and disciplined, not self-destructive or harmful. Satisfying a need for my drug of choice is self-destructive and harmful, and is definitely not a part of self-care.

Physical self-care nurtures my body and its environment. Physical self-care includes such things as a balanced, nutritional diet, adequate sleep, a comfortable, clean, pleasant home, body maintenance (dental exams, physicals, exercise, vitamins, hair and skin care), and balance between work and play. Physical self-care allows me to rest when I am ill and be active when I am not. Physical self-care does not tolerate abuse in any form, whether it is violence, sexual abuse, or the use of drugs or chemicals that are harmful to my body. Self-care is a principle of balance and moderation; excesses and extremes are usually not considered to be caring and loving. I was not practicing physical self-care when I abused my body by eating compulsively and bingeing, smoking three packs of cigarettes a day, pushing my body beyond its natural limits or not exercising at all, being sexually promiscuous, drinking alcohol to the point of being drunk, neglecting dental and physical maintenance, or not maintaining a clean body or clean house, all of which I did at various stages of my life.

Mental self-care nurtures my mind and requires stimulation, discretion, and selectivity. Cluttering my mind with irrelevant, meaningless, or negative thoughts is not good mental self-care. Neither is working it to death trying to analyze everything in my life nor anaesthetizing it through inertia. Television can be a great anaesthetizer. The Piano Player and I spent hours on end in front of another of his drugs of choice. Television can also be a great educator. It depends on how it is used.

Quieting the mind through meditation is a form of mental self-care. So is stimulation and stretching of the mind by learning new skills or considering new ideas and philosophies. Reading my spiritual autobiography may be a form of mental self-care for others; writing it has definitely been mental self-care for me. So is learning how to play new and different music, working crossword puzzles, or reading *A Course in Miracles.*

Spiritual self-care nurtures my soul and comes in as many forms as there are spiritual practices. Prayer and meditation are the most obvious forms of spiritual self-care, but so is attending church or synagogue, practicing mindfulness and loving kindness, waving a prayer flag, fasting, or even lying on a bed of nails. Spiritual self-care is whatever nurtures my spirit. For some, spiritual self-care may be listening to a great symphony, watching a brilliant sunset, climbing Mt. Everest, or riding a Harley. For me, spiritual self-care includes feeling the energy of a giant redwood, watching the tide come in along the Oregon coast, walking the paths of Rebecca Spit on Quadra, my island home, listening to Giovanni's brilliant piano arrangements, reading my daily meditation books, or spending a quiet afternoon around the square table with my Al-Anon sponsor and soul friend. For others, it may be visiting a great cathedral or mosque, feeding the needy at a food bank or soup kitchen, taking Holy Communion, saying the rosary, or reading the bible. Spiritual self-care is simply doing whatever works.

Creative self-care is nurturing my creative spirit. Creative self-care is the act of creating whatever it is that I have been gifted to create. Writing these words is part of my creative self-care. So are playing the piano, singing, and photographing. Creative self-care for two of my soul friends is painting. For another, it is writing, singing, gourmet cooking, and raising roses and orchids. For still another it is singing, playing the guitar, and writing songs. For someone else, it may be any number of things. Whatever the gift, creative self-care requires that I use it to create.

Emotional self-care is nurturing my heart, and is possibly the most difficult area of self-care for most of us. Emotional self-care could be subtitled emotional management, and most of us do not do it very well. Managing an emotion requires me to, first, feel it, be aware of what it is when it occurs. Then I must own or accept it, choose how or whether to act on it, and then release it. For me, emotional self-care means that I also learn from the presence of an emotion so that I can minimize or eliminate undesirable emotions, the road hazards that destroy my serenity. And, where emotional self-care has not been practiced in the past, there is a lot of clearing-out of emotional baggage to do before self-care can be effectively practiced. As the book title says, feelings buried alive never die. They must be exorcised through whatever means works for me, and the exorcism is usually a long, painful process. Nurturing my heart involves healing unhealed wounds and minimizing new wounds through practicing unconditional love, forgiveness, compassion, humility, and self-care. To be sure, God can heal my wounds if I allow him to, and the true healing of a wounded heart is, I believe, a gift from God. But there is footwork to be done first, and the path is arduous and demanding for those of us who have not practiced emotional self-care.

It should be clear from this section that self-care is a principle I have only begun to practice seriously since I started walking with my guide. I aspire to live a long life, beyond 100 years, if possible, so all aspects of self-care are very important to me now. Unfortunately, too much of my physical self-care regimen is needed to undo the damage done through too many years of abuse and neglect. My hope is that what I do today will create a better future twenty years hence, but some things seem to be irreversible. Arthritis has begun to twist my fingers noticeably, cataracts are forming in my eyes, and there are days when my joints feel like the rusty joints of the Tin Woodman in the *Wizard of Oz*. My knees would be happier if I weighed less, but I don't seem to be able to accomplish that weight loss. Mental self-care is somewhat lacking in that I have not been doing enough mind-stretching by learning new skills. I do very well with spiritual self-care and have made great progress in emotional and creative self-care, especially considering where I started from in all three. So I hope that if I keep improving, I will be able to keep on doing God's work and he will let me stick around for awhile longer. I rather like my current life. It is a quality life and I have been blessed in many ways. And the only way to maintain a quality life is through self-care—physical, mental, emotional, spiritual, and creative.

~ Self-Discipline

Self-discipline is the practice that keeps me on task and on track when distractions come and challenge my dedication. Self-discipline upholds my integrity and authenticity when I am tempted to pretend to be someone I am not. Self-discipline keeps me walking my unique path with my guide when his direction is unclear or unwelcome. Self-discipline keeps me going when my unique path becomes rocky and difficult, and a seemingly smoother path beckons temptingly. Self-discipline helps me do the things that are beneficial for me even as I resist doing them. Self-discipline keeps me on time, on schedule, and on the job when I would rather be doing something else. Self-discipline gets me to a dental appointment when I hate going to the dentist, gets me to work on time when I hate getting up early, gets me to mow the lawn when I would rather be hiking or golfing. Self-discipline keeps me working the twelve steps when I am tempted to quit, gets me to meetings when I do not want to go, and reminds me to pray and meditate when I am prone to forget.

Self-discipline walks arm in arm with maturity. They are so directly intertwined that it is not clear to me which comes first, the chicken or the egg. Without a certain degree of maturity, self-discipline is difficult at best, impossible at worst. But self-discipline is also one of the defining practices of maturity, an action that evidences maturity, so each is obviously very dependent on the other.

Self-discipline is discipline without an external enforcer. Discipline is usually a three-part process. Guidelines are given for conduct or performance, consequences are defined for deviations from the guidelines, and the consequences are enforced when deviations occur. The one for whom the guidelines are set always has the choice of following them or not; but if he or she chooses not to follow the guidelines, he or she is subject to the consequences.

The person for whom the guidelines are set is usually held accountable by another person or group of persons. Self-discipline is discipline administered to myself by myself and, as such, I am responsible for setting both the guidelines and the consequences and enforcing them when I deviate from the guidelines. There is no one else involved. I am accountable only to myself or to God, if he is the one who has inspired the guidelines.

And therein lies the difficulty with self-discipline. When the guidelines are set for me by someone else, and someone else enforces the consequences, I usually pay attention to them and do my best to adhere to them. But when the person who sets the guidelines and consequences and to whom I am accountable is *me*, it is very easy to ignore them or change them to accommodate the deviations. My definition of self-discipline is that which I have very little of. Like patience, self-discipline is something I have struggled with all of my life.

You see, I am very good at discipline, at following guidelines defined by *others*—but not at all good at following my own. Remember, I have spent most of my life being and doing what I perceived others wanted because I believed I had to earn their love and approval. Rebellion was not my style—the imagined consequences were too dire to even consider! But, left to my own devices, when the only person I was accountable to was me, the outcome was very different. For sure, self-discipline did not work with my food addiction, nor did other-discipline, for that matter. The forces of addiction do not respond well to self-imposed control devices. But non-addictive behaviors can respond if and when I choose to practice self-discipline. Unfortunately, too often, I do not choose to do that. Self-discipline does not inspire me to exercise when I do not want to exercise, get up early when I do not want to get up early, or spend time every day writing when I would rather do something else.

Self-discipline is automatic with those things I want to do or where the consequences of my not doing them are totally unacceptable. My self-discipline in working my two twelve-step programs is firmly in place, because I choose not to risk the consequences of not working my programs. My self-discipline in doing the healing work required to open my heart and maintain my true self and unique path in an intimate relationship has also been very dedicated. So I guess the guiding force here is the desire to act and the severity of the consequences. The consequences of losing myself or my abstinence are too serious to risk. The consequences of not exercising enough or sleeping late are not severe enough to keep me in line. At least not yet. The time is probably coming when they will be.

The one area of my life where self-discipline is absolutely required is in following the direction of my guide. To be sure, he provides the guidelines, but the consequences are usually not obvious or defined and it is totally up to me whether or not I choose to follow them. So this is where he chooses to test my resolve, and I have been tested in this way many times.

While completing the first draft of this book, I got the message from my guide that I was to focus on writing and relationships for the remainder of the year. I interpreted relationships to be one-on-one connections with my soul friends and began evaluating and eliminating other events that involve more people. I stopped volunteering for extra Al-Anon service, dropped out of choir, ended my hospice volunteer work, put any musical activities aside for now, and concentrated a bit more on my writing. Then, around the end of October, the guidance became more specific. The first draft of this autobiography, which is a part of my healing, was to be finished by year's end, some two months away. So I got a little more serious about it, but apparently not serious enough.

Then my marching orders became even more specific. My guidance was that I was to concentrate on my writing seriously enough to finish the first draft, do a read-through and edit, and make copies to give to my two soul sisters for Christmas. I had shared my writing (and thus myself) with my other soul friends, but not with them, and it was now time for me to give them that gift as well. I was also gently informed that the relationship I was to concentrate on now was, in fact, the relationship between myself and God, and doing both of these things required a degree of isolation from my fellow travelers that I was neither used to nor comfortable with. This was the first time, since I have been walking with my guide, that he asked me to do something apparently contrary to program principles, and I didn't quite know how to handle it!

But, I did it. I went into what I call monastic mode and stayed cloistered until the draft was completed. I turned off the phone bells and advised my soul friends that their calls would ring through and be returned when convenient unless it was a crisis. I eliminated all of my twelve-step meetings, going to church, and all other group events, keeping only my weekly one-on-one scheduled luncheon dates and telephone contact with my soul friends. I concentrated on my writing and on prayer, meditation (with and without music), walking, reading, and connecting with God. I called it a living eleventh step, and it was definitely an exercise in self-discipline. God may have given me the guidelines, but I was the enforcer, and the consequences for deviation were spiritual and undefined. I still do not know what they would have been because I finished the draft and distributed it as I was guided to do.

A year later, I went through a similar exercise in self-discipline. I was guided to update and expand my draft, this time in isolation from my programs and my soul friends during the Christmas season, another living eleventh step. I went "home" to Quadra Island to do this because "home" is where I will ultimately be doing what writing God has planned for me beyond this book. Another year passed and I found myself in a motel room in the Carson Valley of Nevada, working on the third draft while waiting for the Songteller to have an aneurism surgically repaired. Once again, I was in relative isolation, apart from my soul friends at Christmas, and once again, self-discipline was required to get the task completed.

During my first period of self-imposed isolation, I referred to a meditation on discipline, and my comments are still pertinent. This is what I wrote:

One of my daily meditations for today is on discipline and ends with this thought: "The task during a time of spiritual discipline is simple: listen, trust, and obey because something is being worked out in you." And I know that is truth because I can feel it. Something is shifting within, and I am being moved in a different direction. The writing is part of my healing, and the cocooning is part of a transformation that is required for me to move into the next phase of my life, to do whatever it is that walking with my guide requires me to do now. Going into voluntary isolation, moving away from my fellow travelers, is a prerequisite to moving closer to them again in a different way, from a different place, bearing different spiritual gifts. What they are, what spiritual gifts I am being given during this time of transformation, has not been revealed yet. But something is coming, and the preparation for receiving it is an exercise in self-discipline.

~ COURTESY

Courtesy is the practice that acknowledges and validates the intrinsic value of myself and my fellow travelers. Courtesy is the outer expression of a basic inner truth, which is that the God presence within each of is always worthy of being treated with dignity and respect. Courtesy is thus a manifestation of unconditional love, an action that expresses and demonstrates unconditional love to myself and to others. Courtesy includes the qualities of politeness, good manners, considerateness, kindness, thoughtfulness, gentleness, respect, and dignity. Courtesy considers and honors the desires, needs, feelings, and well-being of others. Courtesy is other-centered, not ego-centered.

Courtesy is one of the cornerstones of relationships and can be offered to anyone and everyone, no matter how close or casual the interaction may be. The extension of courtesy is as appropriate with total strangers as it is with soul friends and intimate loves. Courtesy smoothes the rough edges of relationships and makes my life and the lives of others much more pleasant. Courtesy respects boundaries, honors thoughts and feelings, and remembers birthdays and anniversaries. Courtesy honors and respects the rights of others even when their rights conflict with mine. Courtesy follows the rules of the road and the rules of society when not following them would be harmful to another or to myself. Courtesy does not react to rude and inconsiderate behavior with rudeness and inconsiderateness. Courtesy instead acts in a way that agrees with a sense of value and self-worth.

The Golden Rule—"Do unto others as you would have them do unto you"—is an exercise in courtesy. If the principle of courtesy were practiced by all of us all the time, all forms of abuse—mental, emotional, physical, sexual, spiritual—would no longer exist. There would be no more drive-by shootings, road rage, battered women, racial persecution, or suicides. If I value another person as a human being, if I view them through the eyes of love, if I look beyond the outer persona to the God-person within, then I would not or could not harm them. If I value myself as a human being, if I view myself through the eyes of love, if I have found and am connected to the God within myself, then I could not or would not harm myself. If I believe myself to be worthless and others validate that belief by treating me as if I am worthless, the cycle of self-hate and abuse is perpetuated. That is one reason why our penal institutions do such a great job teaching criminals how to be better criminals.

Courtesy does not restrict feelings, but rather determines how I act on my feelings. I can be hurt, angry, frustrated, doubting, or fearful and still treat you with courtesy and respect. Courtesy does not require me to never be angry, but it does require me to deal with my anger in a way that is not directly harmful to you. Screaming at you or hitting you is certainly not courteous; pounding a pillow or a punching bag and then talking to you about my angry feelings is courteous. Courtesy requires maturity, self-discipline, self-love, forgiveness, compassion, awareness, acceptance, and humility. In fact, courtesy is directly related to many of the principles and gifts I have written about.

As with many of the other principles, such as honesty and trust, I have always considered myself to be a courteous person when, in reality, I was not. My personality is neither aggressive nor abrasive. I was taught to obey rules and respect authority figures, and my role as a people-pleaser required me to always consider and accede to the desires of those I cared about. I was certainly not overtly rude, thoughtless, or inconsiderate; thus, rude, thoughtless, and inconsiderate people really bothered me and I was not at all tolerant of their behavior. Yet, at the same time, my own behavior was covertly discourteous. Remember, for many years I was a controller and caretaker who kept people around using emotional hooks, deception, and other forms of emotional blackmail. The love I gave was conditional, at best, and I never honestly shared myself with anyone. Controllers, caretakers, and those who love conditionally are not courteous because their actions restrict the rights of others to live their lives in freedom and dignity. And none of these roles reflects the intrinsic value of my fellow travelers or myself. Of course, during the years when I held my relationships together by controlling and caretaking, I had no sense of the intrinsic value of anyone. I could hardly recognize the presence of the God within us all when I had turned my back on him. My intrinsic value, and that of others, was based on what each of us did and how we did it. Then love, trust, and respect were all earned. Whether or not it was earned depended on how closely others (or I) came to meeting my standards. I was anything but courteous. Polite, congenial, well-mannered, self-sacrificing, yes, but courteous, I was not.

So courtesy, too, is a principle I have learned to use properly only after walking with my guide and rediscovering my truth as I have defined it, which is that we are all human beings, not human doings, and deserving of love, respect, trust, and courtesy on that basis alone. It is only when our behaviors are viewed through the eyes of love that courtesy can be extended to all people under all circumstances. To be sure, being courteous to a child molester, a rapist, or a murderer is not an easy thing to do, but it is the God-like thing to do. True compassion requires me to love the perpetrator even as I minister to the victim. Fortunately, in my life I have not been faced with such extreme tests of unconditional love. I have a hard enough time extending courtesy to those I love that I still want to save or protect from themselves.

Oddly, it often seems that it is easier to be courteous to those persons who are not close to me than it is to be courteous to those who are. Familiarity may or may not breed contempt, but it definitely breeds the tendency to be discourteous, especially when personal boundaries are weak or nonexistent. The more emotionally enmeshed I am with you, the less courteous I may be. Remember, courtesy is an expression of unconditional love. Emotional dependence or need and unconditional love cannot coexist in a close physical relationship. In those areas where I perceive that I need you, I cannot risk losing you by allowing you to be free. There, courtesy gives way to control and manipulation. Also, the closer I am to you, the greater the tendency will be for me to want to protect you from the challenges of life, to save you from your own learning and growth experiences. To attempt to do so is grossly discourteous.

I have two very special soul sisters, and the three of us refer to our connection as "the sisterhood." When the connection was formed, we were all recovering from relationship losses and just beginning our journey of spiritual and emotional growth from the place where living with alcoholism had stopped it. All of us had been humbled by our experiences, all of us were open and teachable, and for a time we walked our unique paths side by side, using the road map of the twelve steps, both learning from and teaching each other. Then, over time, our paths began to change. I am the oldest sister and, as such, had the most experience in dysfunctional behavior and possibly the greatest motivation to heal and grow. And, although we all began with the same spiritual mentor, I worked with her and learned from her regularly and they did not. So while I continued to move ahead on my chosen path, the other two began to lag behind and veer off in diverse directions, onto paths similar to those that I had traveled, unsuccessfully, years before. Concerned for their well-being, and hoping to spare them the pain I had endured, I shared my experiences with them, trying to get them to listen and change course. But they could not seem to hear me, so I talked louder and more incessantly, saying the same things over and over to ears that became increasingly more deaf. First one, then the other, closed their minds to what I was sharing with them and are now walking the paths they have chosen without any unsolicited guidance from me. Now, although our hearts are still connected, our paths are not, and the openness and teachability are gone. Whatever spiritual work we were to do together is finished for the time being.

With more time, this may again change. The potential for teaching and learning will always be there as long as our hearts are open to each other. But, for now, it is gone. The lessons for me are lessons of detaching with love, acceptance, humility, and surrender. The practice I forgot to use until it was too late was courtesy.

~ Gentleness

Gentleness is the physical expression of unconditional love. Gentleness is soft and softens whatever it touches, whether it is the rough edges of a relationship or a hardened heart. Gentleness is recorded by all the senses—it can be seen, heard, felt, and even tasted and smelled. Gentleness can be seen in my eyes, heard in the tone and intensity of my voice, felt in my touch. A taste sensation or scent can be either gentle or overpowering. Gentleness is kind, delicate, and unobtrusive. Gentleness soothes the disturbed, wipes away tears, mends broken wings and broken hearts, and cleanses all wounds. Gentleness makes every challenge of life and the harshest discipline much more bearable. Tiny babies, puppies, kittens, chicks, bunnies, all small and fragile creatures, require gentleness. Anything or anyone, big or small, that is fragile and delicate requires gentleness. Anything or anyone, big or small, strong or weak, sturdy or fragile, coarse or delicate, can benefit from gentleness. Most of us are much more fragile and delicate than we are willing to reveal. Often, harshness, rudeness, gruffness, and a generally bad disposition can be effectively treated with gentleness.

Gentleness is always sourced in love, but love is not always gentle. Sometimes love has to be tough, as required in dealing with rebellious teenagers and practicing addicts. Tough love sets boundaries. It says, "I love you, but your behaviors are unacceptable." But even tough love can be administered gently and perhaps more willingly accepted.

In the medicine card description of the qualities of the deer, my heart's animal guide, this story is told. The deer was called to visit the Great Spirit. On her way, she met a horrible demon who blocked the trail. The demon tried very hard to frighten the deer, but she was not afraid. She spoke gently to him, asked him to let her pass, and looked at him with eyes filled with compassion and love. Her gentleness and love melted his heart, and his fearsome body shrank to nothing. The deer's gentleness cleared the path for others to visit Great Spirit without fear. The deer's medicine is gentleness, and this story clearly demonstrates its power. Gentleness is no wimp. It can get results that no amount of force could ever achieve. Closed and wounded hearts and minds do not respond to force. They respond to love and gentleness.

Gentleness is a manifestation of strength, not weakness, particularly in those from whom it is unexpected. My soul sister who initiated the sword attack ("Optimism") has a very gentle heart, and therein lies her true strength if and when she allows us to see it and chooses to use it. Gentleness in a man is particularly attractive to me. A man who is not afraid to show his gentle, loving, caring side is a man of integrity who knows who he is and stands firm in his truth. For the truth is that all of us, male or female, have the ability to be gentle human beings because of the love that we share as God's children. Unfortunately, too many of us do not recognize the love that lies within nor make any attempt to display that love as gentleness.

I have always had a loving heart. That is the first and most important of God's gifts to each of us. But I have not always revealed my truth to you as gentleness. In fact, for most of my life, I have kept that truth carefully hidden, from you and even from myself. To be sure, sometimes it came out in unexpected ways. The music I play, the romantic, soft music that appeals to me, requires a very gentle touch, and that is one of my greatest musical gifts. Kawai, my marvelous piano, responds to gentle touch as no piano I have ever played has. So my music revealed my gentleness even as I chose to hide it. Possibly, that is why I chose not to play it for all those years. Through my music, others would have sensed the gentle, vulnerable side of Nadine that I sought to hide behind my analytical mind and busy life. I equated gentleness and vulnerability with weakness, not strength, and weakness, the inability to take care of myself emotionally, led to intense pain. I also considered gentleness and vulnerability to be feminine qualities, and for years I rejected my own femininity. I was a woman who worked and played in a masculine world. I had few female friends and was always more comfortable with men than with women. Vulnerability and softness simply did not fit my persona.

So I kept my loving nature a secret and forgot how to express it through gentleness. Not that I was harsh or mean. I was not, at least most of the time. Certainly, there were times, particularly with the Piano Player, when I was. But, most of the time, I functioned in some neutral zone between harshness and gentleness, a zone with hardly any feelings at all. My persona was bright and efficient, not soft, feminine, caring, and gentle. I may have looked like I had loving feelings, but it was all external, a wonderful show of confidence and having it all together. Without love and its expressers, forgiveness, compassion, and generosity, the facade had no substance, and it certainly was not an expression of my truth.

What I expressed to the world as love was not, in fact, love at all. I may have taken care of others, but that is not the same thing as being gentle. Caretaking is sourced in need, not love; so any gentleness I may have shown while doing it was not sincere. And anyone who is in touch with their feelings would sense this lack of sincerity.

Even the Piano Player, who knew me as well as anyone, did not see the softer, gentler Nadine because I did not reveal it to him. During his last days, when he was too weak to get out of bed, I helped him take care of his waning bodily functions and was his primary caregiver. During one of her visits, a hospice nurse asked him if he was surprised that I did these things. His answer was, "I didn't think she would do it."

Since I have begun to walk with my guide, I have rediscovered and accepted my truth. I not only have the gift of love that all of us are given, but I have an inherently loving nature. It is one of my personal gifts and the reason that I have the deer as an animal guide. I am basically a loving, peaceful person, a flower child, if you will. I am not competitive, I dislike confrontation. I am not a fighter, but a lover. The feminine qualities I suppressed effectively for so long are all very much a part of me. My challenge is to let them come out in appropriate ways because I am not a feminine woman in the traditional sense. I am not beautiful, curvy, or the bosomy motherly type. I am neither glamorous nor soft and cuddly, and I tend to come on too strong. So mine has been a process I would describe as softening the rough edges, allowing my loving nature to shine through and soften what is already there, of tempering strength with softness.

Gentleness is one of the many qualities that I have been cultivating for some time now, a quality I strive to put into practice. Allowing the love that is inside to show on the outside has been a long, gradual process. Here, too, I am a work in progress, with much room for further improvement. Changes have come in every aspect of my life, changes that reflect my true loving self and integrate that self into my outer persona. My hair style is softer and more feminine, but still casual. I own and wear dresses again that are longer, more flowing and feminine, in softer colors. My casual clothes, which I wear the most, are softer and more feminine as well. My sweatshirts and T-shirts are decorated with flowers, country, and mountain scenes, and my jeans are looser. I speak in a lower, quieter voice and swear less. I also am more expressive, and my feelings and emotions are much more visible. I laugh more and I cry more, and it has become much easier for me to allow others to see me do both.

But, more importantly, the process has been internally created, not simply external. Now that I have opened my heart and surrendered to love, now that I can feel the presence of God as love within me, it is easier and more natural to gently express it. But it is still not effortless; the love in my heart still comes out filtered through my head, and gentleness is not an automatic result. I have had to discover and set aside the "I think I knows," those prideful places where I thought I already knew how to express love gently and thus wasn't open to change. Certainly, the most important of those was playing my piano music, where my true gift was masked behind false pride. The Songteller gave me a magnificent gift of love when he shattered that mask ("Passion"), and the learning to love curriculum has manifested most quickly and effectively in my music. Now, my music expresses gentleness as honestly as anything else I do. That is the gift I share now with those who are open to receiving it. Gentle, loving music from a gentle, loving heart: music inspired by the deer.

I hope that, with more time and a closer and more constant connection with God, my external self will more closely match my true self and I will express strength and gentleness in a more consistent way. I know women in-program who have this quality, and one day I hope to join their ranks. Gentleness in my voice comes when I speak from my heart, not my head. I know what that feels like now; it happens when I share at meetings, when I write, and when I speak to my soul friends. Gentleness in my eyes comes when I feel compassion for others, or when I send love to others without any thought of getting it back. I know, too, what that feels like, and I believe others can see and feel it now as well. Gentleness manifests in my whole being when my mind and my heart are in total agreement and when I know my truth and am not afraid to share it with others, even when challenged. Gentleness comes with faith, trust, surrender to love, compassion, forgiveness, generosity, and humility, which is a place I visit more and more often.

Fortunately, God is infinitely patient and is content with progress, not perfection.

~ SERVICE

Service is, quite simply, doing what I love to do. Service is also doing what I do with love. Either way, it is a spiritual practice because it is an action sourced in love. Adding love transforms any action, no matter how ordinary, into an act of service. Service is thus another way to strengthen my connection to God, to follow his guidance and direction. We are all doers—the secret of service is to add the love component, to ground our actions firmly in spiritual truth, allowing God to express through us. Adding the love component is an art that can be acquired through conscious awareness and desire. The motto when doing anything is, "Be love."

Loyalty and service walk arm in arm and are pointers to those persons, places, and things that are near and dear to my heart. Service is the action phase of loyalty. Since service is sourced in love, it is loving action that expresses and demonstrates my faithfulness—to you, to myself, and to my guide. Service is, by definition, an action being done with God, since God is love. But, service may also be done for God. Certainly, those who are called to the ministry, or are otherwise connected to religious practice, are doing service for God. So are those of us who use our creative gifts to sing, write, or speak about spiritual truths. But we are also doing service for ourselves. What I give away, I get to keep; and what I teach, I also learn. I have received and learned much since I began to write in service to God. In fact, the Songteller told me that I was writing this for myself, and in many ways that is truth.

Still, I am primarily writing for others. Sharing my insights, beliefs, thoughts, experiences, and spiritual journey along the road home is one of the ways I fulfill the mission my guide has given me to fulfill. It is how I walk my unique path, and it is my gift of love to my readers. If any part of my experience strikes a familiar chord, a been there, done that response in my readers, my mission has been fulfilled. If something I believe challenges others to question and solidify their beliefs, my mission has been fulfilled. Whether others agree or disagree doesn't matter. If I have reached someone else in any way with any of the words I write, my mission has been fulfilled. I have offered them a gift of love, and they have chosen to receive it.

All acts of service are gifts of love. Remember, that is the title I was given for my first tape of classical piano music, and the title truly fits. Playing the piano is something I love to do, and sharing my gift through the tape is an act of service, another gift of love. Anything I do for others in service is a gift of love, because love is freely given without expectation or attachment to outcomes. If I do something for someone else with the expectation of a specific response, that is neither service nor a gift. It is not service because the love component is not unconditional. It is not a gift because a gift has no strings attached. Gifts with strings attached are barters or trades, not gifts. A true gift is given in love for the sheer joy of sharing something with someone.

Service is something I have only learned how to do since I began walking with my guide. Before that, I viewed service as many people still do. Service was something I did to support someone or something, not necessarily because I wanted to, but because it was expected of me. Or because if I did it, I might gain the love and approval of others. Doing something for the sheer joy of doing it was not service; sharing my creative gifts was not service. Service was often a have-to, not a want-to, and I did it for what it could get me. I took courses and joined organizations, espoused causes, not out of love, but for personal gain. Joining the local mountaineering club got me a husband; joining a professional society got me better performance reviews at work and looked good on a resume. Volunteering for professional society committees got me company-paid trips to Washington and San Francisco. None of my so-called service work was either a gift or sourced in love.

I also did a lot of things for a lot of people, but not in joy or love and usually not without expectation. Remember, I believed that I had to earn love. So if I worked really hard to please others, I expected them to love me! If I was nice to them, they would be nice to me. Right? Not always. I did do service, in a sense, when I did things I liked to do, but never without expectation or attachment to outcomes. I liked to hike, write, photograph, and play music, but I always was concerned about people's opinions of what I did. The result was more important than the action, and that is not true service. Until I learned how to love unconditionally and give without expectation, I could not do true service to anyone. And that did not come until I knew and walked with my guide, the God of my understanding.

Now, as I grow more confident in God and the path that he is guiding me down, my desire is to offer more and more of my life as service, to be able to stay sourced in love in all actions, not just a part of them. That is my desire, but I am a long way from achieving it. To be sure, I follow the direction of my guide, but that does not mean I am in a loving place at all times. I am far from being either enlightened or awake. Still, more and more of my actions and personal interactions are sourced in love, and more and more of my actions and interactions involve doing the things I love to do, sharing my passions with others, doing loving service to those people, groups, places, and things that my heart has led me to embrace.

What are some of the ways I practice service? I offer service to myself by taking loving care of my body, mind, and soul. Healthy eating, moderation, and balance are forms of service, as is brushing my teeth. Prayer and meditation are a form of service, to myself and to God. Things that stimulate my mind, force me to stretch and grow mentally, are a form of service. Using my creative gifts, whatever they may be, is a form of service to myself; sharing them is service to others; and both serve the master creator. Driving my car, nurturing my house, tending my yard—these are all forms of service to myself. Treating people, places, and things that I love with loving care is service. Extending this care and concern to the earth and beyond is compassionate service to all mankind.

Service to others can be just about anything as well, provided it is offered lovingly. Service to others nurtures friendships, strengthens the spiritual connection among people, enhances community, and creates strong bonds sourced in love. Service is love in action. Any time I give unconditionally, without expectation or attachment to outcome, I am deepening the bonds of love. Service is calling a friend, being present and attentive, staying up all night with a sick child, rekindling an old friendship, being a hospice volunteer. Service is also working in any one of a zillion different professions dedicated to serving others. To be sure, I can be paid for doing what I love to do, as long as I continue to do it for love, not money. The adage is, "Do what you love to do, and the money will follow."

Doing things that fulfill my spiritual purpose and mission is service to myself, my fellow travelers, and my guide. This is the service that creates my unique path and determines the actions and interactions that chart the course of my life. Staying on my unique path requires me to stay focused on my mission and purpose and not get distracted, to concentrate on making my unique contribution to the big picture. How do I choose which actions and interactions to take? I use two criteria. First, I ask, "Does doing this fit my purpose and mission?" Second, I ask, "Does this task or action require one of my unique talents, or could someone else do this equally as well or better?"

Remember, my purpose is to share God's love with others through sharing my true self and my creative gifts with them. And again, my mission is to heal with love and guide with words. My unique talents include writing, singing, playing the piano, speaking or sharing, and certain other personal strengths. So any time I am asked to play the piano, I will say yes. Any time I can share through writing or speaking or sharing with a soul friend, I will do it, voluntarily or when asked. Anytime that I can share love by being loving, kind, considerate, friendly, open, honest, courteous, forgiving, compassionate, helpful, or generous, I will do that too. And to those people and groups that my heart has called me to support, I will do service in areas where I can uniquely contribute. I have supported my twelve-step groups by being there, going to meetings, chairing the meetings, and doing money-handling, but I do not do garage sales or table decorations. Others can do that as well or better than I can. I can make different contributions than others because we walk different paths and have different unique gifts. The common thread for doing this, however, is service.

~ BOUNDARIES

Boundaries define both my personal space and the parameters of my relationships. Boundaries are the outer perimeters of my comfort zone. My boundaries tell others which of their behaviors and actions are acceptable to me and which are not. Their boundaries tell me which of my behaviors and actions are acceptable to them and which are not. Setting and upholding boundaries allows me to take responsibility for my life, speak my truth, and follow my unique path with integrity and honesty. My personal boundaries are part of my true self and my expression of that self through the way I conduct my life.

Setting and upholding boundaries is the action that defines detachment with love. Without clearly defined boundaries, detachment is very difficult, if not impossible. Emotional dependence is virtually guaranteed in the absence of clearly defined boundaries. Without boundaries, personal definition becomes confused and muddled, and my individuality, my true self, is easily lost or confused with that of others. With boundaries, I cannot lose myself in another person, either by choice or by default. With proper boundaries, the emotional hooks of others have no place to land. Controllers, fixers, and people-pleasers hate boundaries until they learn how to set their own.

Boundaries are often confused with walls, but they are very different. Walls are rigid and do not allow others to come close to me, to be intimate. Thus, walls encourage emotional dependence because without intimacy, I need emotional hooks to keep others near me. Boundaries, on the other hand, work with, not against, intimacy. Boundaries are flexible and may change depending on circumstances. Boundaries allow others to come close to me, but within established guidelines. Boundaries are the rules of the road for intimate relationships.

As a teenager, I could not understand why my parents, so obviously and vocally unhappy about their lives and displeased with each other, stayed together. Many years later, the answer was quite clear. They were totally enmeshed, totally emotionally dependent upon each other, and in a tremendous amount of emotional pain. Their boundaries were walls, and behind those walls, they lived together, very alone and separated, for fifty-six years.

Boundaries apply to the physical, mental, emotional, and spiritual aspects of my life. Boundaries define both my personal space and what constitutes physical, mental, emotional, and spiritual abuse for me. Boundaries are directly related to my personal beliefs and values and are as unique and individual as I am. What is acceptable to me may not be acceptable to everyone. The boundaries I set (or setting them at all, for that matter) are linked to my personal experience and my core feelings about myself. When I love, value, and care for myself, my boundaries will reflect this and will serve to protect me from abuse of all kinds. When I do not love, value, and care for myself, my boundaries (or lack of them) will reflect this as well. Boundaries can, thus, be healthy or unhealthy, constructive or destructive, depending on my past experience and sense of self-worth. Furthermore, boundaries will shift and change as I do. The more I learn to love myself and trust and follow the direction of my guide, the stronger and healthier my boundaries will be. Healthy boundaries will always protect me from abuse and serve the interests of my highest good.

Those who perceive themselves as victims do not know how to set boundaries, or they would not perceive themselves as victims. A person without boundaries allows everyone and everything to "do it" to them. I have also learned that people without boundaries act as if no one else has any either. I recall a time when I was standing in line waiting for the next available bank teller. A woman came up behind me and stood so close that I could almost feel her breath on the back of my neck. This was a violation of the boundary of my personal space, my comfort zone for physical closeness. When I asked her to step back, she looked at me as if I were insane. Obviously, it didn't bother her, but it definitely bothered me!

Since I was, for most of my life, one who either purposely or unintentionally lost my true self in others, setting boundaries was not something I either understood or practiced. Still, there were certain boundaries that were inherent to me, based on my own life experiences and core beliefs. Physical abuse was not a part of my personal experience; neither of my parents either practiced it or believed in it, though they did practice mental, emotional, and verbal abuse. Based on this experience, any form of abusive physical violence is simply not acceptable to me. When I was exposed to the potential for it with the Piano Player, he understood very quickly that I would not accept that behavior from him. To be sure, I did accept much unacceptable mental, emotional, and verbal abuse from him, but not physical abuse. That boundary was tested and held firm at a time when I did not even know what a boundary was. I knew what walls were, but not boundaries. I had lived with a wall around my heart for most of my life, a wall that was vulnerable to only two things: music and words, my two primary creative gifts. The Marlboro Man, who was not whole, was a writer and penetrated the wall with his words. The Songteller and the Piano Player penetrated the wall with their music. And it has been through music that the last traces of the wall are finally being removed, allowing me to fully open my heart to love.

As I have learned to walk with my guide, honor and value my true self, and follow my unique path, as I have opened my mind and my heart to love and to others, I have also learned to set boundaries that reflect and protect my true self. Over time, unhealthy boundaries, those that were either too permissive or too restrictive, are being changed to uphold the integrity of who I am. Of all my boundaries, the mental ones have changed the least. Mental boundaries have been in place most of my adult life, and abuse typified by coercion, domination, intimidation, belittling, cynicism, prejudice, bigotry, manipulation, deliberate dishonesty, and other overt methods of control was not, and is still not, acceptable. To be sure, for a long time I did not always uphold these boundaries by openly challenging these behaviors. I simply avoided confrontation with mental abusers by keeping out of their way.

Physical boundaries were in place, but have shifted and changed as I have become more and more aware and accepting of who I am and what I believe. As a people-pleaser, I was overly generous with my personal possessions, then resented it when someone took advantage of my generosity. Later, I became overly possessive and very selective of who shared my personal space—who came to my house, rode in my car, shared my life. Now, as my heart has opened to love, I am becoming more generous and less selective. I will openly and generously share myself, my love, and my possessions with others—within limits. I still do not lend anything to anyone that I am not willing to lose. Only my soul friends have permission to come to my home uninvited.

Sexual boundaries, too, have changed drastically over time. My sexual boundary was monogamy until I violated it in my first marriage, and I was not celibate as a single person. The one-man woman became a multi-man woman between my outdoor and musical lives, when sex was strictly physical, fun and games, and sexual promiscuity was totally acceptable. With the Piano Player, I was again faithful, even though I was continually being accused of being otherwise. Now, as an unmarried woman who finally knows that God, not sex or food, is my sole source of love, I am celibate by choice. Physical sex, sex without an emotional and spiritual component, simply does not interest me anymore, even though I am a very sexual woman. As I have learned to love myself, respect my body, and walk with my guide, my sexual boundaries have shifted to reflect this. When it is time again for me to be in a committed and holy love relationship, I will be both sexual and monogamous.

Still, the most drastic changes have occurred with spiritual and emotional boundaries. This is where I had no boundaries—only walls—so I have had to start from scratch. Spiritually, the walls that separated me from God and religion did not begin to come down until my beliefs relative to God began to be defined. So, again, my boundaries have shifted as my beliefs have shifted and as my heart has opened to God and to love. Today, since my spiritual beliefs do not match the stated creed of any religion found in my area, my participation in religious practice is bounded by my ability to take what I like and leave the rest. Another spiritual boundary has to do with relationships. The willingness and ability to connect on a spiritual level is a nonnegotiable requirement for special friends and intimate relationships. By definition, intimacy includes the spiritual component, but I still maintain friendships with those who do not own their spiritual selves. I keep them because we have a long history of friendship, but I would not choose them today. Nor would I choose a mate, a life partner, without this gift, for a holy relationship based on unconditional love would be impossible.

I have left emotional boundaries for last, because these boundaries are still being defined. With walls, I kept others at a distance and used emotional hooks to keep them from getting too far away. Without walls, I allow others to come close and no longer need emotional hooks to assure their continued presence. But those who have come close have, for the most part, come to me from a position of love and thus I have not had to protect myself from any form of negativity or attack. The most serious exception I can think of was the sword attack by my soul sister who lashed out at me in retaliation for pain I had inadvertently caused her ("Optimism"). At that time, emotional hooks were still in place and my boundaries were not yet defined. I did not protect myself, and the result was very wounding. Now, I believe that the strongest boundary I can present against emotional attack and negativity is to keep my mind and my heart open, keep myself close to my guide, and radiate and transmit love and forgiveness, tempered by compassion and humility. As I view the sword attack through the eyes of humility, I see that my false pride caused it and my insensitivity to her pain escalated it. Humility and compassion would have prevented it, and both are expressions of love.

This is what I believed when I first wrote this section, but it had not been tested by anyone who is very close to me and thus in a position to wound deeply. Then, when I was ready, I was given the ultimate test from the one I have let come the closest to me, the Songteller. He was found to have an aneurism, a life-threatening condition, and I was guided to go to Nevada and be present to provide love and support both before and after the surgery. When I arrived, I was greeted warmly and invited to share his life on a daily basis. But then, over time, I overstepped my bounds, something shifted, and my presence became very threatening to him and a perceived threat to his relationship.

When the Songteller feels threatened, he tries to push me away. This time, he pushed very hard, not once but several times, lashing out from behind a wall of fear. Before, I have hidden behind my own walls, but this time I was open and undefended. Before, as I have written, I have simply ignored his words, but this time I heard them and reacted to them. My walls were down, but my boundaries were not yet in place. I had neglected to ask God for help, and I was not viewing my friend through the eyes of love. As a result, my open heart was sorely wounded before I was able to move out of the line of fire. And move I did. I honored his request and stayed away from him during the surgery and after. I tried to close my heart to him, but couldn't, and I was very afraid of letting him come close to me again. Part of me wanted to leave, but I couldn't do that either. I knew I had to stay and face my fear; otherwise, our friendship could have been lost forever.

Then, when he was recovered enough to do it, I asked him to meet me to talk this out. I courageously invited him back into my space and he came, with wall in place and guns blazing. But this time I was prepared. This time I humbly invited God to sit with me and do the talking, and this time my open mind and heart were protected by a strong shield of unconditional love. This time I saw through the wall of fear to the sensitive, caring man hidden behind the wall. I faced my fear, moved through it, stood firm in my truth, moved back far enough to give him emotional breathing room, and suddenly the wall disappeared and we were friends again. It took several tries but I finally got it right. And I know now, without a doubt, that with God as my partner and love as my protective shield, my emotional boundaries are solid and strong.

~ CHOICES

Choices define my personal freedom. The choices I make either validate or negate my true self, or cause me to follow or deviate from my unique path. Whether my journey, the road home, is smooth, happy, joyous, and free or rocky, painful, and limiting depends primarily on my choices. Walking with my guide is a choice, and so is striking out on my own, separating from God. Everything I do, say, and believe—my attitudes, thoughts, feelings, and behaviors—is determined by choice. I can choose to be happy or sad, calm or angry, forgiving or resentful, loving or hateful, grateful or ungrateful, positive or negative, active or passive, flexible or rigid, accepting or rejecting. I can choose to own my own personal power or I can choose to give it away to you. I can choose to satisfy my needs from within or look for others to satisfy them for me. Through my thoughts, attitudes, and behaviors, I can choose to be healthy or sick, rich or poor, married or single, content or lonely.

Choices are the building blocks with which I co-create my life, the way I confirm and reinforce my personal commitments and uphold my personal truth. Choices can build or tear down, uplift or demoralize, lead me to my highest good or lead me down a path of wanton self-destruction. Used wisely and as my guide directs, choices keep me in step and in line with him. Used unwisely, as my willful mind directs me, choices may take me on some highly challenging detours that teach me some very interesting lessons. Guided choices require both an open mind and heart; an open mind gathers all the pertinent information so my open heart can make an informed choice. Choices guided by an open mind and heart are always in my best interests, but I am not always wise enough to see that.

Those of us who see ourselves as victims do not know we have choices. In fact, it is that lack of knowledge that allows us to be victimized. Earlier, I told the story of my Al-Anon friend who stayed in a physically abusive marriage for many years before choosing to leave under threat of death. The choice to leave was always there, but she couldn't see it. No matter how desperate a situation is, there are always choices. Where physical choices are not possible, mental, spiritual, and emotional choices are. If I have been imprisoned, I do not have the choice of leaving prison. But I do have a choice as to how I react to my experience. I can hate it and make every moment miserable, or I can accept it and perhaps even learn from it. There are always choices.

Even as a child, I had choices, although I probably did not understand this. Young children who are abused physically, sexually, mentally, emotionally, or spiritually unconsciously make the choices necessary for their survival or, if they do not, they do not survive. Those who do survive childhood trauma either recover and heal from their trauma or perpetuate the cycle of abuse through the choices they make. Those who choose to blame and refuse to take responsibility for their lives often find themselves repeating the same pattern of abuse over and over, either with themselves or with their children. Those who choose to accept, forgive, and take responsibility for their lives can heal and move beyond the pattern of abuse. For sure, none of this is easy and requires massive doses of love from God, self, and others. But the process is begun, the footwork done, through the choices I make.

As an addict, I also have choices. I have the choice of using or not using my drug of choice in a self-destructive way. Once I choose to use in a self-destructive, compulsive way, I give up my choices about that which I am powerless over, be it alcohol, narcotics, sugar, sex, gambling, whatever. But no matter how cunning, baffling, and powerful my particular drug of choice is, I always have the choice to abstain. I may not see that I have this choice or I may not be willing to do whatever it takes to abstain, but I still have a choice.

When I was living with the Piano Player, I maintained strict control over certain aspects of our lives, even after I knew doing so was enabling him to drink, because I had "no choice." I had no choice but to support us both financially, no way to make him financially responsible and accountable for his actions, because to do so would jeopardize my own financial well being. When we worked as road musicians, I had no choice but to make sure that he was fed, napped, bathed, and sober enough to make it through a five-hour gig. Choices I viewed as unacceptable were always shot down by statements beginning with, "Yeah, but..." So the cycle continues until hidden or unacceptable choices become acceptable and visible.

Making uninformed choices without a spiritual guide is a scary proposition. I know, because I've done it that way for most of my life, and doing so was a choice. I chose to turn my back on God, to push him out of my life, and I chose to let him back in again. I chose to let false pride close my mind to certain truths, and I chose to humbly allow him to replace false pride with the humility that opened my mind again. I chose to reject my true self as a married woman, and I chose to reclaim my true self as an unmarried woman. I choose now to be my true self in any relationship state. Before, I shifted identities when I married and shifted back when I was divorced or widowed. Before, in order to reclaim my identity, I had to reclaim my birth name. I have changed surnames six times in my adult life. Now I know that it does not matter what last name I carry—Nadine is Nadine. I am who I am. That, too, is a choice.

I have already written about the wisdom of walking with my guide down my unique path by following my heart. That, too, is a choice, and it is always the correct one. Any other path is a detour. It may be a necessary detour, but it is a detour nonetheless. Sometimes, detours are required to allow me time to heal and find my true self and get ready to move onto my unique path again. Sometimes the uninformed choices my heart makes when my mind is closed to certain truths lead to a path that feels like a detour because the road is so rough and full of unexpected twists and turns. Still, deliberately choosing to follow my head and not my heart is usually a painful choice, at least until my heart can be subdued. When I married the Skier/Climber, it was a choice of head over heart. The outdoor man who had gently touched my soul one glorious summer day in the shadow of the Sawtooth Mountains of Central Idaho was unavailable and unwilling to establish a relationship with me. I was, at the time, nearly thirty, single, and tired of being alone, and my head said, "Give it up and find someone to marry." So I followed my head, chose the outdoor man I knew was available and willing, and talked him into marrying me. Because these two men skied and backpacked together, we were all three often together on weekends. And for awhile, my heart made me painfully aware that I had not followed its direction. With time, my heart closed, the pain was subdued, and I settled into my chosen relationship. Ten years later, when the Skier/Climber and I separated, my first thought was, "Well, now maybe I can get something going with my heart's choice." My heart had not forgotten, but it did not happen and I chose to move on.

Two years later, because I had not learned my lesson, I repeated the same scenario but with a slightly different twist. This time, both my heart's first choice (the Songteller) and the man I would choose to marry (the Piano Player) touched my soul with their music. But, the first man was married and unavailable at the time, so my heart grudgingly stifled its desires and moved me on to the second man. Again, I was single and tired of being alone, and again I talked him into marrying me. This marriage also kept me in contact with my heart's preferred choice, through their music. Only this time my heart closed immediately to him out of loyalty to the Piano Player, and I defended it fiercely with a solid wall of fear and hostility. Since my mind was closed to the realities of living with alcoholism, my heart-guided path was full of potholes, boulders, and crashes. I have often wondered if an informed heart would have chosen that path. I certainly would not knowingly choose it again now, and I won't have to. The choice and the path got me where I was supposed to go. It reunited me with God.

Seventeen years later, after the Piano Player had died, my heart surprised me with the truth that it still cared about its first choice.

Several more years passed before I was healed enough to open my heart to him. More time passed before my mind fully opened to our reality and gave my heart the input it needed to make an informed choice. Loving this man is a choice that is guided by both an open mind and heart, and the result is a much smoother ride for us both, wherever our paths lead us.

Today, I choose to follow my informed heart, and thus God, wherever it/he may lead me. I know that, even though my unique path may not always be smooth and free of challenges, it is always the right path for me. I try not to take too many detours, but I still make unwise choices and get lost occasionally, just a little off track. Doing whatever it takes to find my way back is a choice as well. I humbly pray daily for help from my guide through the gift of discernment—to be able to recognize whose talking, my head or my heart. More and more, I have learned which is which so that I can make wise, informed choices, choices guided by love. Choices guided by love are always choices that lead to my highest good, for that is God's desire for me. Choices guided by love honor my true self, keep me on my unique path, and bring me the gifts from God that were always mine. Choices guided by love cause me to follow the principles that enhance and uphold my newly rediscovered gifts and negate or nullify the road hazards that would steal them from me again. Choices guided by love protect me and lead me safely along the road home.

~ VISUALIZATION

Visualization is a creative practice, one that helps to manifest my God-inspired dreams into my physical reality. Visualization concretizes imagination, which is the origin of all creativity. Visualization puts form and substance to my hopes and desires and tells my guide, "This is what I want, this or something better." And, since my dreams come from him in the first place, he generally works with me to create them, or something better.

The soul friend who does my tarot readings suggests creating a treasure map, and this is a form of creative visualization. A treasure map is a collage of desires—it might contain pictures of a new car, a new or improved house, or a new relationship. My treasure map for relationships includes the qualities desired in the other person—spirituality, gentleness, honesty, openness, presence, courtesy, affection, love, whatever. My soul friend always cautions to be specific, to tell my guide exactly what is important if it is important. Otherwise, God will not have all the information needed to fulfill my desires.

Visualization does not have to be a collage or in art form or writing. Visualization can be a mental process, but only if I am a very visual person and I am able to focus in my vision at will. That is the key to creative visualization—being able to focus on the desired result. When I created my tape, *A Gift of Love*, I knew what result I wanted and worked toward that, but I did not visualize it, at least not consciously. The end product was there, however, somewhere in my mind or I would not have known when we achieved it.

Visualization is not a practice that I consciously choose to use very often. However, at some level of my mind, I must have some sort of a creative image, because I know, I absolutely *know* when something (or someone) fits my true self. Obviously this was not true before I came to know my true self, but it definitely is now. And this may be another key to successful visualization. When I know myself well and accept what I know, then I can more easily visualize the life experiences that will fit.

When I first saw Saraswati, my wonderful house, from the outside, I had the sense that it could be my house. When I walked inside, both my realtor soul sister and I knew immediately that it was indeed my house. Even though I had no conscious vision of what my house looked like, I knew it when I saw it. I knew when I saw my first Mitsubishi Eclipse that it was my car, again without a conscious vision. I just knew I desired a little, sporty, fun-to-drive car. My conscious visualization of a piano was not a baby grand, but I knew when I sat down and played Kawai that it was my piano.

Perhaps I have been visualizing all this time and just not consciously putting in the details. The room in my home that I call my Quadra Room was created in that way, one piece at a time. All I knew when I started was that I wanted a bedroom big enough to hold all three pieces of my bedroom set. So I hired a contractor to knock out a wall between two smaller rooms and refinish the walls and floor. I matched the wall color with the bluish-green of my bedding, and from there it took on a life of its own. I found sheer panels and draped valances for the windows, curtain rods that fit the sheers, and a Persian-ish carpet that pulled all the colors—forest green, sea blue-green, and some pink—all together. I loved the room, and I did not know why. Not until my soul led me to my island and I realized that the colors of the room are the colors of sea and forest. I have since added art and glass treasures that fit as well. Again, I did not consciously visualize this room as it exists today. But I absolutely knew what was right.

I have already shared with you my desire to co-create an intimate love relationship, a holy relationship sourced in love and guided by God. I also believe that such a relationship deserves to be honored by the formal holy commitment of marriage. I have, in three tries, never had a wedding with a special dress, music, and friends and family in attendance. I have had one small ceremony with a minister and three witnesses and two Nevada elopements. I created this dream of a marriage with a special dress, music, and my soul friends. When I first walked out into the back yard of Saraswati, I had this weird sense that I was going to be married in one corner of the yard, so that became the foundation of the dream. I have since added the music, who will sing and play it, the person who will perform the ceremony, and the friends and family I hope will be there. None of this has, of course, manifested because I lack one very important component—a willing male participant, whose input has to be factored in as well. But, one item has manifested, and that is the one item that is totally mine to choose and conceivably fits any form the dream may take. That item is the dress. As I visualized it, it was to be the pearl-white color of the Audi I walked past every day, cocktail length, soft, feminine, and flowing.

One late winter day, several years ago, I decided to mall-walk, something I rarely do. I was prompted to walk through the stores, something I also never do. While walking through this one department store, I was prompted to make a pass through the women's dress section, another something I never do—and there, resting idly on a sale rack, was the dress: pearl white, cocktail length, soft, feminine, and flowing, and in a size I could conceivably fit into with a little body sculpturing. I tried it on, the fit was close enough to risk the investment, and I bought it. The salesclerk who took my money commented that it would be a great dress to wear on a cruise. I didn't tell her that I had other plans for it! Since then, I have been led to the accessories for the dress—jewelry, undergarments, and shoes—and have pared my body down to the correct size to wear it. All that's still missing is the willing male participant!

The other manifestation of a visualization is a part of my dream to move to Quadra Island, my future home. I now own five acres of mossy rocks and trees on Quadra (not previously visualized), and soon after I bought it, I began speculating about what kind of a house I would like to build there. I thought that what I would really like to do is move Saraswati, but that is impossible. The next best thing would be to recreate it, modified to match the climate and terrain. Saraswati is a plain, rectangular, ranch-style house, single-story with a basement, attached garage, and family room. So I sketched out a similar plan, but made it two stories with the main living quarters upstairs, the balcony and deck between the two floors, and I took off the family room, opened up the living room, moved the bedroom across the end of the house, and put the garage underneath on the ground floor with the studio/gallery. Then I promptly forgot about it.

That next summer, while I was staying on Quadra, I met a couple who had retired and were building a house there. The wife mentioned that she had found her house plan in a house plan magazine, so when I got home I decided to buy some magazines and see what was there. Most of the plans in these magazines are either very elaborate or very simple; there is not much in between. I looked through one magazine, marked a few prospects, picked up the second one, opened it at random, and there it was. The house plan: a two-story version of Saraswati, with the balcony and deck between floors and a garage underneath. The interior design is close enough to what I sketched to be absolutely scary. And it was the only such design in all three magazines, which prompted me to order it. This may or may not end up being Saraswati II, but it definitely fits my visualization.

Possibly, if I used creative visualization more, I would have more positive results to report, but so far that is it. It is enough for me to believe that creative visualization is a practice that can be used to create a more positive life. Knowing my true self is, I believe, the key to success. The other requirement is letting go and allowing my guide to make the final decisions. I can strongly suggest, but he has the final word on what is for my highest good, with or without visualization.

~ AFFIRMATIONS

An affirmation is a form of positive self-talk. For those of us who are programmed or otherwise inclined to think, believe, and speak negatively about others and ourselves, the use of affirmations can negate the negative. Affirmations quiet the doubter that tells me I cannot or that I am silly even to try ("I am capable of doing the work that I have been assigned.") or that things just are not going to work out the way I want them to. ("I have faith that God will bring me the desires of my heart or something better.") Affirmations also quiet the critical parent who says I am stupid, dumb, fat, lazy, or just not good enough. ("I am bright, capable, slim, and energetic.") Affirmations can transform false core negative beliefs, such as, I am unlovable or intrinsically flawed, into a sense of my real truth. ("I am a lovable, worthwhile child of God.") Affirmations can heal the mental and emotional components of physical illness and contribute to better health. Affirmations are repeated often and out loud in order to get their message firmly implanted in both my mind and my heart.

Using affirmations is a practice that can be used to do my part in the co-creation of my life. They are, or can be, a form of commitment to my dreams as offered to me by God. Consider my dream of co-creating a tape to celebrate the resurrection of my musical gifts (see "Divine Order"). When I was given the dream, and accepted it through commitment to doing it, I could have used an affirmation to help create it. (I did not.) One such affirmation could have been, "I am creating a wonderful tape of classical music to share with my friends." Or, "I am listening to a professionally produced tape of classical music that I have co-created." Either one would have been appropriate had I chosen to use affirmations. In this case, my commitment and the Songteller's cooperation were all that was needed. In most cases, God takes a more active role, and affirmations serve to continually reconfirm my commitment.

Affirmations may be used singly or preceded by a release of my error thoughts or feelings to God before affirming positive ones. Using an affirmation cited in the first paragraph, I would add, “I release to God my false belief that I am unlovable,” before, “I am a lovable, worthwhile child of God.” Used in this way, affirmations are useful aids in the twelve-step process designed to remove character defects or shortcomings. When I humbly ask God to remove my shortcomings, as required by step seven, an affirmation can and does acknowledge the release of a negative behavior and allow its replacement with a positive one. For example, suppose I have released the negative character trait of gossiping about people. My affirmation could be something like, "I speak only kind, loving, gentle words about others." This reinforces my commitment to release negative behavior and allow its replacement with something more positive. This is, to me, the most effective way to use affirmations. One that I use daily is designed to begin each day with a clean slate relative to the past. It is “I release the past and joyously look forward to this new day.”

Notice that I form my affirmations in the present tense even though that which is affirmed is not apparent in the present moment. My affirmations begin with "I am," not "I will be." Remember, God is found only in the present, not in the future. And also remember that it is in the present that I shape my future. Even though it may sound a little odd to affirm that "I am calm, confident, and serene" while experiencing anxiety, insecurity, and chaos, that is the only way the affirmation can work for me. If I release my fear to God and keep on repeating the affirmation, I will ultimately find myself responding to it. I will become calm, confident, and serene. My guide will help me to create whatever positive life situation I desire, but always on his schedule. Affirmations do not usually transform overnight. Some of them take a very long time to manifest in my reality.

Affirmations can be applied to any aspect of myself where positive change is desired. My affirmation that "I am strong, healthy, and free of pain," is a positive affirmation that affects my physical well-being. The affirmation, "I am calm, confident, and serene," is primarily an affirmation that affects my emotions. "I am loving, gentle, kind, compassionate, and wise," enhances and strengthens spiritual qualities that I wish to develop. "I am co-creating a spiritual autobiography to share with others," affirms my commitment to writing this book. "I am clear-headed, articulate, and logical," affirms a desire to enhance mental qualities. There are as many ways to use affirmations as there are things to affirm.

Notice, too, that my affirmations are more general and less specific. It is usually wise to give my guide as much room to work in as possible, particularly when what I perceive I want may not be exactly what he has in mind. To affirm that, "I am married and co-creating a holy relationship with the one you have chosen for me," leaves the field wide open. Even when I am pretty sure who "the one you have chosen for me" is, it is best not to call him or her by name on the off-chance that I am wrong.

Affirmations designed to heal physical challenges do not specifically call for direct healing; rather, they negate the mental or emotional conditions that relate to the physical condition. For example, one of my sources contains a very extensive list of physical challenges, together with related mental or emotional conditions and appropriate affirmations. For the relatively benign, but somewhat aggravating, condition of snoring, the related mental/emotional condition is given as the stubborn refusal to let go of old patterns. The corresponding affirmation is, "I release all that is unlike love and joy in my mind. I move from the past into the new, fresh, and vital."

As is the case with visualizations, using affirmations is not a practice that I have routinely followed. So I do not have a lot of experience in their use, mostly because I do not normally experience a lot of negative self-talk to positively counteract. At least, that is the case now. Back when I still believed myself to be unlovable and lived with much fear and doubt, I did not know anything about positive affirmations, so I could hardly use them. Now that I know what they are and how to use them, there are fewer things to use them on. My affirmations, when I do use them, are designed to enhance positive qualities rather than counteract negative ones. For example, when I affirm that, "I am lovable, kind, gentle, compassionate, humble, generous, forgiving, and wise," these are spiritual qualities that I know I have but wish to strengthen. It is not because I believe that I am unloving, harsh, mean, uncaring, arrogant, stingy, resentful, and stupid. And when I affirm good health, it is because I want to keep my good health, physical strength, and relatively pain-free body.

But, even though I do not personally use a lot of affirmations, I do believe in them. I certainly believe that I am responsible for doing my part to co-create my life, and I would prefer to co-create a life sourced in love, not fear. Any practice that counteracts negativity has to have a positive result. My perceptions create the world I experience, and negative thoughts create negative perceptions. If I falsely believe that I am unlovable, I will (and did) create experiences that confirm that belief. If I believe the world is evil, I will see only that evil behavior which confirms my belief. If I am continually telling myself that I am stupid, lazy, clumsy, or afraid, my experience will validate those beliefs. All of this must somehow be undone if I am to find my true self, walk my unique path, and willingly follow the direction of my guide. Negative thought is a tremendous road hazard for anyone striving to find their way guided by one who is expressed as love. Negativity causes me to doubt, to despair, to whine, to argue, to challenge, to balk, to hesitate, to procrastinate, to waffle, to do all sorts of weird things that make the journey anything but happy, joyous, and free. The "I can'ts" and "yeah, buts" do not make God's task any easier. It is pretty difficult to follow my heart when it is closed by fear and my head wants to go in a different direction. Affirmations can help me to deal with the ego-gremlins inside my head. For best results, use them generously and as often as needed. Their application is limitless.

Chapter X

THE ROAD HAZARDS

THE road hazards are those principles that, when practiced, make connecting with my guide, following his direction, knowing and being my true self, and walking my unique path difficult at best and impossible at worst. The road hazards may cause me to separate from or renounce my guide or willfully ignore or disregard his guidance. Some of the road hazards force me to carry a heavy load while walking my unique path, a load I was never intended to carry. Some of the road hazards tie me to other fellow travelers and thus hamper my freedom to walk with my guide. All of the road hazards are unneeded and unnecessary hindrances to my progress, my spiritual growth. Without the road hazards, my road home is truly happy, joyous, and free. The smallest dose of any one of them can drastically change these conditions and steal my God-given gifts and rewards from me. Road hazards are challenges to be felt or acknowledged, accepted, learned from, and then released to God for healing through love and forgiveness. Holding on to any one of them can make the road home dark, bleak, and frightening.

Fear is the basis for all of the road hazards and can only be replaced by love. Fear, addictions, and false pride separate me from my God, knowledge of my true self, and the guidance I need to walk my unique path. Anger and resentment tie me to the objects of my anger or resentment and destroy my freedom to walk my path without restrictions. Guilt, shame, regret, and suffering are heavy burdens I carry with me on my journey, burdens that weigh me down and can cause me to falter, stumble, and lose my way.

Negativity makes my path unpleasant, dismal, and depressing. Denial, complacency, and resistance hamper my ability to be myself and find my unique path. Expectations destroy joy and serenity and put stumbling blocks in my path. All of the road hazards affect my relationships—with my God, myself, and my fellow travelers. All of the road hazards are also great teachers. They uncover wounds that need to be healed and point to actions that need to be taken. The way I deal with them is a vital part of finding my true self and walking my unique path. And the closer I walk with God, the fewer road hazards there will be to deal with and learn from.

There are, of course, many more hazards than I have chosen to write about—but these have been the major blocks to my personal journey home. These are the principles that work to separate me from God and negate my use of his gifts. The only way to free myself from their destructive influence is to live in the moment, close to my God and sourced in his love, and humbly allow his help in removing them. The road hazards live in the past and future, never in the present. The pits that they create are pits I create for myself when I willfully leave the safety of the moment.

~ Fear

Fear is the antithesis of love and is the underlying source of all of the road hazards. Fear and love cannot coexist; I cannot love and fear in the same moment. Fear, like love, is a state of being as well as an emotion. Thus, all thoughts, beliefs, attitudes, behaviors, and actions are either sourced in fear or sourced in love. There is no other choice.

Fear expresses itself in many ways. Fear is the basis for all of the road hazards that follow, plus hatred, distrust, doubt, despair, sadness, loneliness, confusion, apathy, disappointment, meanness, arrogance, deceit, grandiosity, egotism, self-centeredness, intolerance, impatience, aggressiveness, submissiveness, violence, worry, anxiety, panic, pessimism, and a host of other similar traits, none of which lead to joy and serenity. Following a course of action motivated by fear never leads me to my highest good. Recognizing a potentially dangerous situation, accepting its reality, and acting on that reality is not a course of action motivated by fear. Panic is a feeling motivated by fear, and panic only makes whatever it is worse, not better.

If love is connection to my God and my fellow travelers, fear is separation and isolation. Fear is a loner and demands that I be a loner as well, cut off from love and God. Fear does not allow others to come close to me, or vice versa. In fact, that is how fear exerts its power over me, by keeping me separated and isolated, suspicious and mistrustful. That is how fear managed to rule my life for so many years without my even knowing it consciously. My belief system was not consciously fear-based, but my behaviors were, and my behaviors define my true state of being. My various and sundry fears guided me down a false path for a very long time. It was only when I became desperate for a different way that I reached out to love and began to recognize and deal with my fears.

Love and God live in the present; fear lives in the past and in the future. Fear projects past experience onto future events and thus can recreate them. If loving someone has created a painful wound in the past and I project that into the future, I will subconsciously recreate that experience. If I have been abandoned in the past and project that fear into my future, I will create life experiences to support abandonment. Sometimes, a healthy dose of unconditional love can break the cycle. That and consciously choosing to move from fear into love, from past and future into the present, are the only options available.

Fear created by physical danger often appears to be in the present, but really it is not. Think about it. Horror movies create fear through anticipation of what could happen or what did happen, not what is happening. The events leading up to the axe murder are much more frightening than the axe murder itself. And the fear that builds before the next bloody scene depends on our recollection of the first. My fear of being attacked by a bear while hiking alone is based on what could happen, should I surprise one, and what has happened to others who have had bear encounters. In the moment, I am safe. And as long as I follow the suggested course of action while hiking in bear territory, I will most likely stay that way.

One time, while vacationing, I was driving my car, Mitsu, on an unfamiliar, two-lane highway, moving along with a steady stream of traffic. My mind was more on the scenery than on driving, and suddenly I realized that the traffic was not moving anymore. It was stopped for a red light about a quarter of a mile ahead. I slammed on my brakes, knew that I could not stop in time to keep from hitting the car in front of me, and swerved off the road to the right. The car behind me also could not stop and rear-ended the car I had barely missed, slightly sideswiping Mitsu in the process. I got out, surveyed the damage (a paint smudge for me, a smashed front end for the other car), gave the other drivers my name and address, and since there was no disabling damage, we all drove away. While all this was happening, I was present in the moment and quite calm. By the time I got to a gas station, I was shaking so badly that I could barely hold the gas pump. I had gone back into the experience, which was past, and projected a different outcome, the serious accident that could have happened. While it was happening in the present, there was no fear. Fear only came when I chose to go back into the past and create a different future.

Fear comes in all sizes and varieties. There are minor fears that are irritating and inconvenient, and there are major fears that immobilize and control my life. I have already shared three of my major fears—public speaking, solo performing, and intimacy. I also have suffered from fear of abandonment, fear of falling, fear of water, fear of confinement, fear of failure, fear of success, fear of self-disclosure, fear of death or physical pain (to myself or others), fear of emotional pain, fear of losing myself in someone else, fear of danger, fear of change, fear of the unknown, and fear of fear itself. There are, of course, many other fears—spiders, snakes, flying, heights, crowds, germs, dark places, loss, fire, earthquakes, tornadoes, floods, whatever. These and a host of other fears all have two things in common. They are all based on the projection of something that could happen (future) based on something that did happen (past). What was and what could be unite together to create fear.

I have seen many definitions of fear as an acronym. FEAR = False Evidence Appearing Real, Feelings Experienced As Real, even Forget Everything And Run! But the definition I like the best and am using now is Feeling Excited And Ready. This is the definition I concentrate on when I choose to do something that I used to avoid doing because I was afraid, like telling my story at an

Al-Anon brunch or providing the special music at church. Or inviting the Songteller to come closer. These are all actions that can still take me out of love and into fear. But not as often and not as deeply as before I connected with my guide and ultimately surrendered to love. You see, where I am is a choice. I can choose to be sourced in love, or I can choose to be sourced in fear. And I am continually moving back and forth between the two states of being. My desire is to stay sourced in love, to walk closely beside my loving guide in the present, where there is no fear. That is my desire, but it is not always my choice. Sometimes, fear sneaks up on me when I am not looking and takes hold unexpectedly. Sometimes, fear lurks in the places I have found it before, and I know it is there waiting for me. Always, when I find fear, it is because I have temporarily left my God and wandered off into either the past or the future. When I release the fear, return to the present, and let God take over again, fear dissolves and is healed by the light of love.

Sometimes, the fear that surfaces is old fear, fear that has been repressed and buried for years, fear that bursts out uncontrolled so it can be owned and healed. That, too, is the result of my choosing love over fear. Twice recently I have experienced fear as an uncontrollable shaking of my hands and even my entire body while doing something before a group. In one instance, I was at an Al-Anon meeting where we were asked to choose a principle (mine was hope) and share on it while standing up in front of the group. In the other, I was attempting to play Clair de Lune, one of my mother's favorites, as the special music in church on Mother's Day (see "Power"). In both cases, I became immobilized by fear, unable to do what I was supposed to do. In both cases, I came to understand that the fear that surfaced was fear that originated many, many years earlier, when I was performing as a teenager, fear that the need to excel simply numbed out. In both cases, when I was able to release the fear (and my activity) to my God and stay in the moment, I was able to resume doing what I was supposed to do—not well, mind you, but we got through it. In both cases, the physical expression and release of fear was an important part of healing it.

As I look back down the path I have traveled, I see that I am making much better choices between fear and love than I used to. Too often in the past, my fears dictated my thoughts, behaviors, and actions, and nowhere was this more true than in my relationships. My fear of intimacy kept me from experiencing that which I have still not experienced—an intimate relationship, sourced in love, with a male soul friend. My opportunities for love were too often overcome by fear, and the relationships never had a chance to develop.

Between my outdoor and musical lives, when the eagle and I were flying very high and free, I met the man I called my Marlboro Man (see "Reality"). A mutual friend referred to him as the "gentle cowboy"—he was tall, dark, blue-eyed, boyishly handsome, very bright, wonderfully creative, and very sexual. He called me his Neat Lady, and at that time we fit about as well as any two people could. Neither of us wanted a love relationship, or so we said, but both of us *needed* a love relationship, and that need soon took us to an emotional place that neither of us knew how to handle. He was terrified of love, and I was terrified of intimacy. He had begun to care too much, and I had let him come much too close—a writer, he had touched my soul with his words. So fear took over for us both. I tried to push him away by pulling him too close, and I succeeded. He ended the relationship, broke my heart, and sent the eagle crashing to the ground in a devastated heap of broken feathers and dreams. The crash was so severe that, for the first time ever, I became willing to look at my part in creating it. And I did. The next two years were an important time for me, a time of self-analysis and self-discovery. To be sure, it was all a head trip, but at least I had begun to look.

I also spent the next two years trying to get him back through establishing a friendship that could perhaps lead to something deeper. He would not see me, so I wrote him letters and tried to convince him that I wanted a friendship and could handle it. He would answer eventually, and every so often he would agree to see me, to check me out. And, as soon as he got close again, fear took over, I repeated my odd behavior, and he left again. Friendship was impossible for us; we were both too consumed by fear. Yet when the fears subsided, I really did care about him and I know he cared about me, love in the form I believe in today. He was a very special person in my life.

Eventually, the Marlboro Man remarried and so did I, to the

Piano Player. Occasionally he would stop in at our tavern to see how I was doing, but we never did reestablish a relationship. Six months after the Piano Player died, the Marlboro Man also died, and my grief for him was as real and intense as my grief for my husband. Our love affair was short-lived, but very real. A happy ending (or any ending at all) was made impossible because of our fears.

~ ADDICTIONS

Addictions are a means of filling a spiritual void, a need for divine love, with a substance, activity, or emotion. My drug of choice thus becomes a substitute or replacement for God, for the love I desperately seek, but cannot find. Paradoxically, even as my addiction separates me from God, it can also lead me to him. When the consequences of using my drug of choice become unbearable, when my will is beaten into submission by a compulsion it cannot control, the path back to sanity is a path that leads to God. That is the path I took to find him and to connect with him in a way I was not able to before, even when I recognized and owned his existence. While I was using, my drugs of choice *were* my Gods, but they were false Gods. It was only when I put them down that the real God could take his proper place in my mind and my heart.

It is true that alcoholism and other addictions are diseases. It is also true that those of us who are the children of addicts are much more likely to contract the disease. This is particularly true of alcoholics, drug addicts, and compulsive overeaters. But, when the void is already filled with a spiritual sense of a kind and loving God, the desire to begin use of the drug that triggers the disease is greatly lessened. To be sure, the tendencies may be there, but the need is not.

One of my soul friends has had a strong sense of spiritual connection for much of her life. As a young girl, she renounced a dogmatic religion that keeps score and punishes and found and began walking a different spiritual path. She knows she is genetically predisposed to alcoholism and chooses not to use alcohol. She sometimes uses food as a temporary substitute for love, but her usage is not compulsive. Most of the time, the void is filled. Another soul friend, too, is very connected to a kind and loving God and has been all of her life. For her, too, food sometimes becomes a substitute, but only when she is spiritually depleted and mentally, physically, and emotionally exhausted. As soon as she strengthens her spiritual connection and replenishes herself through self-care, God fills the void and food is no longer a problem.

For me, food became a substitute for God at such an early age that my spiritual self had no chance to emerge. As I have shared before, my equation was food equals love. If food equals love and love equals God, then food equals God is a logical conclusion. There was always plenty of food available, so there was no reason to go looking for love elsewhere. But food also equals fat, and fat did become a problem; at the age of ten, I was five foot four and wore a size seventeen dress. So at thirteen, I starved myself into a twenty-three-inch waist, anemia, and borderline anorexia. Where was love to come from then? Why, from boyfriends, of course! But boys and sex were too scary at thirteen, so food became my lover and my God again until I was brave enough to begin to use my second drug of choice.

Interestingly, while I was compulsively eating, I did not understand that I used food and sex interchangeably as substitutes for God and love. Since coming into program and hearing other addicts share their stories, it has become clear that multiple addictions are common. Some use food and spending interchangeably. My Piano Player used alcohol and gambling. Oftentimes, alcoholics recovering in AA will find themselves compulsively eating. Food is, after all, the most readily available and socially acceptable drug of choice. So is sex, for that matter, in a committed relationship, so something odd happened to me when I was married. I got thin. I had lots of sex during my first two marriages, and I was thinner then than during any other time in my pre-God life. In between these marriages, when I did not have a regular sex partner, I got fat again. In between my outdoor and musical lives, in the days of the Marlboro Man and sexual promiscuity, I stayed thin. I stayed thin with the Piano Player as well, until the disease virtually wiped out our sex life. Then—guess what happened—I got fat. Food equals love. And with my self-esteem at an all-time low, I got really fat, as heavy as I have been as an adult. I have photos to prove it.

Also interestingly, after I reunited with the God of my earliest understanding, but before I began working my programs, I was able to diet successfully and lost about twenty pounds. But then I began to struggle again. There was still a void to fill because God and I were still separated. To be sure, I was talking to him, but we were not connected as yet. That connection did not occur until I broke my isolation and began working the programs of Al-Anon and Overeaters Anonymous. Through that connection, the understanding that God equals love, and the willingness to abstain from my binge foods, my food compulsion has been lifted, one day at a time, for many years. Through Al-Anon, the damage done to my body, mind, and soul due to living with an addiction (his *and* mine) is also being repaired, one day at a time.

I now have a loving God who fills the spiritual void as long as I choose to stay close to him. If I stray too far away, I can be tempted and the compulsion could return. So I choose not to stray far away, and I choose to abstain from my proven drugs of choice, sugar and purely physical sex. I do not work a program for sexual addiction. I willingly choose celibacy because I know that purely physical sex is dangerous for me.

Fortunately for me, my drugs of choice did not lead me down a life-altering path. But they could have. Both my father and his mother were diabetics, and had I continued to abuse sugar, I would be as well. For those that are diabetic, addiction to sugar is life-threatening. The mother of one of my soul sisters is an insulin-taking diabetic, and her sugar binges have shortened her life. Obesity has also been shown to shorten life expectancy. The obese and morbidly obese are maiming and killing their bodies.

And then there is sexual addiction. Back in my promiscuous days, sexually transmitted diseases were a risk, but not one I took seriously. Then, the sexually transmitted diseases were all curable; now, they are not. Today, sexual addiction is a very dangerous game of Russian roulette. And many people still choose to play it.

Addictions do not only alter my unique path—they may also shorten the journey home considerably. Drug overdose deaths are far too common to ignore. Even a socially approved addiction like workaholism can lead to a drastically shortened path. But, again, as I said at the beginning, it can also lead people like me, who have scorned more traditional paths to God, to come to him in a prostrate and humble position. And that is, after all, where I needed to be to begin to follow his direction and reclaim both my true self and find my unique path.

Not surprisingly, the more humbled I have become, the easier and more pleasant the journey with him is. Other paths may be easier and more clearly defined, but they are possibly less challenging and, for me, the softer, easier way does not work. I have always enjoyed being challenged, so I am grateful to have been given the road map I have to follow. The spiritual foundation for everything I will ever need for my journey down the road home can be found in the twelve steps. With them, God is my drug of choice, and I use him willingly, enthusiastically, and joyfully. I also work to share the benefits of using him with others. Love should be the drug of choice for all of us. The supply is infinite, and the rewards for usage are tremendous. All the gifts of God and none of the road hazards—those are the promises offered to us by love. And, as always, the choice to use or not use is mine.

~ PRIDE

Pride, like love, is a principle that is misunderstood and misused. We are taught that pride in ourselves, our accomplishments, our country, and our heritage is a good thing that increases self-worth. We are also taught that pride is one of the seven deadly sins and the basis for much pain and suffering. So which is it? I believe that it depends on whether pride is based on truth or false thought. Pride based on truth is paradoxically sourced in humility, in absolutely knowing that those gifts and accomplishments of which I am proud are sourced not by me but by God. When I fully accept and understand that what I am is the essence of God and all that I do is the expression of God working through that essence, then pride encourages me to allow that expression and become the very best I can be. Pride sourced in truth is thus a reward, not a road hazard, and includes the recognition that with God as our source and essence, we are inherently equal and equally loved.

Pride based on false thought believes in inequality, that we are either less than or better than others based on our actions and behaviors. Price thus becomes a road hazard when it strives to replace the false belief of being less than with the equally false belief of being greater than. This brand of pride, which I will call false pride, continually compares and competes to maintain the illusion of being better than. False pride is conceit, and those of us who don't think we have it suffer from it the most. I know because I was one of those who did not understand or acknowledge my own conceit or pridefulness. In fact, the first draft of my spiritual autobiography did not even have a section on pride—true or false! It wasn't a subject I even wanted to discuss!

At that time, I had completed three fourth steps, was working on a fourth, and had identified a rather large assortment of character defects and fears. I mentioned many of them when I wrote about humility—arrogance, judgmentalism, perfectionism, self-righteousness, grandiosity, intolerance, dishonesty, self-deception, and pridefulness. I have mentioned other undesirable character traits in other places—my need to control and caretake, my wanting to fix and save others, my reluctance to ask for help from others or from God. What I did not understand was that these are all symptoms of a deeper malady, one that I listed, but not as a root cause. All of these character defects, all of these traits that make my journey more difficult, are rooted in false pride. All of the fears I refuse to let go of are fears grounded in false pride. And my God could not and would not remove the symptoms until the root cause was discovered by me, accepted, and released to him. Until false pride is replaced by humility, I cannot know my true self. And once I know my true self, that my essence is love and perfection, I no longer need to hide behind the mask of false pride, and I am rewarded with pride based on the truth that who I am is good enough. In fact, who I am is marvelous, as is everyone! I no longer have to build myself up by tearing others down. My sense of worth does not have to be created at someone else's expense—it simply is. Knowing this truth leads to the expression of it, followed by true pride.

False pride keeps me separate and isolated from my God

because I'm comparing myself to and competing with him. False pride tells me I'm wiser and smarter than God, but deep down I know it's a lie. Without exception, every struggle I have shared in working the steps, in walking with my guide, and in creating and maintaining my relationship with him has been the direct result of my false pride. Also without exception, every problem that I can think of that I have had in my relationships with myself and others has also been rooted in false pride. Ironically, I eventually came to recognize the need for humility, but not the need to let go of my false pride in order to keep it. And, as with fear, God cannot remove from me what I refuse to let go of. I humbly asked him to remove all the corollaries to false pride, but not the false pride itself.

False pride is, of course, based on fear and the false belief that who I am simply isn't good enough. The need for false pride stems from a self-imposed separation from God, and false pride then perpetuates that separation. The path back to God requires the relinquishment of false pride, either voluntarily or involuntarily. Reconciliation through religion may or may not be voluntary. Reconciliation as the result of the ravages of addiction is usually involuntary. The forces of addiction literally drive us to our knees. When my guide suggests that I get up and walk with him, I can only do so consistently and successfully by releasing my false pride.

False pride is quite obviously a tremendous road hazard. Where false pride closes my mind and/or my heart, it becomes impossible to either see my true self or find my unique path. Until the Songteller shattered my mask of musical false pride, I was not free to let my heart direct my fingers. My closed mind would not allow it. False pride closed my mind to many other things as well. False pride expects and requires me to be right, perfect, in control, self-sufficient, strong, virtuous, honest, successful, smart—in short, whatever it takes to be better than others. False pride says I have a right to be arrogant, judgmental, and critical, and to tell others how they should walk their paths because false pride tells me I am wiser and smarter than they are. False pride keeps me unforgiving, angry, and resentful, justifies attack, fuels denial and resistance, and is very attached to outcomes. If I am competing and comparing, winning becomes much more important than how I play the game.

False pride also may enhance needless suffering. If I am to remain better-than, I must negate guilt, shame, and regret through self-imposed punishment. False pride, like fear, underlies all the road hazards I have written about. Even negativity is enhanced by a peculiar distortion of false pride. When my dad proclaimed that this world had seen its best days, it somehow made him feel wiser than those of us who did not share his perception and judgment. Or maybe it just made him feel *right*!

False pride steals the accomplishments of others and thus robs them of their sense of accomplishment. This is a particularly common malady between parents and children, but it also is found between siblings, spouses, and even best friends. My parents were always very openly proud of my musical and intellectual achievements, almost embarrassingly so. They kept on bragging about my piano playing long after I had quit doing it! They bolstered their sense of worth through me, and I ended up without any because I was expected to do these things to make them "proud." False pride gets its strokes through assumed ownership—because I am *your* child or spouse or sibling or friend, what *you* do reflects back on me. In order for me to be better than, my child, spouse, parent, or friend has to be better than as well. When the Piano Player would (in my opinion) get too drunk to play well while we were working, I got furious with him. After all, I was up there on stage with him and he was embarrassing us both! Oddly, it never seemed to bother our audience, but it sure bothered me!

False pride also plays havoc with twelve-step recovery because false pride refuses to recognize character flaws or mistakes. To be sure, I have lost my false pride relative to my drugs of choice or I would not be working the steps, but if I haven't lost it with anything else, I soon find myself in trouble. I can make it through step one, and hardly through steps two and three, but then I get stuck on step four. I know several people in both my programs who have been coming to meetings for a very long time and have never completed the fourth step, thus keeping themselves from moving on into true emotional healing.

My awareness of the true extent of my false pride has only come recently through a commitment to acquiring humility. A wonderful woman in my Al-Anon group, who personifies humility for me, shared this prayer with us: "God, please help me to set aside all that I think I know about you, about me, about this program, and about these steps, so that I may be open to a new understanding of you, of me, of this program, and of these steps."

False pride cannot say this prayer sincerely, and I could not have said it sincerely even a few months ago. To set aside all the "I think I knows" would have been unthinkable, if not impossible because one of the things that I thought I knew was how to work a program better than others. Even my recovery itself was a victim of my false pride.

I remember the first time someone in-program suggested that I had a problem with false pride. It was at an Al-Anon meeting, a few months into my recovery. I remember it because I was so wounded by the remark that my first impulse was to leave, to go home and never return. Of course, I didn't—actually, I couldn't. I was still on my knees, and crawling away was not an option. My false pride wouldn't let me!

~ Anger

Anger is an emotional reaction that reflects displeasure or disapproval of an action or behavior. Anger is not about whom you are, it is about what you do or do not do. Anger may be triggered by a sense of injustice or wrongful action directed either toward myself or someone else. Anger is often fueled by a sense of powerlessness. Those of us who perceive ourselves as victims are often very angry people. Anger can also be used by those who victimize as a way to control their victims. Tyrants use anger to intimidate; victims use anger to shock. To invoke anger in another, for someone else to deliberately try to make me angry, is also a form of control, and alcoholics know how to do this very well. If I allow someone else to dictate my moods and feelings, I have in fact given them all my personal power and, hence, my freedom. That is why we Al-Anon's practice the principle of detaching with love.

Anger is something that all of us feel, but few of us know how to manage. Many words have been written and spoken on anger management, because unmanaged anger, anger suppressed or anger out of control, is a most damaging and destructive road hazard. Anger separates me from my guide and negatively affects all of my God-given gifts. Anger is a form of attack, either of a fellow traveler or of me. Suppressed anger, anger turned inward, manifests itself as a covertly violent attack on myself or others. Suppressed anger may manifest as passive-aggressive behavior, depression, cancer, and any number of other physical afflictions. Uncontrolled anger or rage, anger turned outward, manifests as an overtly violent attack on myself or others. Anger is expressed as rage, murder, battering, rape, self-mutilation, torture, and all kinds of abusive acts. Once created, anger can only be released through acceptance and forgiveness. If not released, anger becomes resentment.

Anger itself is simply an emotion, one that is sourced in fear, not love. And, as with any other emotion, when anger is simply felt and released, it loses its power to disrupt and destroy. It is my angry actions that can be damaging and destructive. I say "can be" because they do not have to be. Anger can be managed, but to do so requires maturity, self-discipline, and the willingness to change attitudes and beliefs. Anger management does not simply involve appropriately dealing with anger once it appears. The most effective anger management gets to the root of the problem. The easiest way to deal with anger is to minimize it by eliminating the source. And that requires some drastic attitude adjustments.

Look far enough beneath anger, and you will find fear. In fact, when I am exposed to intense anger or hatred, I immediately know that the one who is angry and full of hate is motivated by intense fear. And since fear lives only in the past and future, anger lives there as well. Most anger is a reactionary device. Someone says or does something I do not like, and I become angry. The action provokes the anger, and it is already part of the past when I react. Or I may become angry because someone has not yet acted as I expect them to, which is in the future. Right now, in this moment, I am not angry about anything. To become angry, I have to move out of the present, leaving love and my God behind.

There is another prerequisite to anger, and it is its primary cause. *Anger requires a judgment call.* Anger does not appear out of the blue. For it to manifest, I have to have made some sort of a judgment about the object of my anger. When I swear at an inept driver, I have judged their driving skills against my personal standards and found them to be inferior. When inept driving causes a near-miss, I judge and am afraid. When I became furious with the Piano Player because of his behavior while drinking, I judged his behavior by my personal standards and beliefs. I was also very afraid that I would lose him.

Which brings up another interesting facet of anger, the "you always hurt the one you love" syndrome. The people I get the angriest at are the ones who are the most important to me and thus have the most potential impact on me and my life. If someone I barely know has an accident after drinking too much and totals his car, I will probably be compassionately concerned, but not angry. If the Piano Player had done the same thing, I would probably have been madder than hell. I would have been angry at him for a zillion different reasons, angry at me for being married to him, and, underneath all the anger, terrified because of what could have happened. The stronger my emotional investment is in someone, the more angry and fearful I will be. Thus, another aspect of anger management is detachment with love.

When I was a child being raised on a farm, I had a real talent for coming into contact with barbed wire. And, since human skin is no match for barbed wire, I was usually cut fairly badly. Every time I hurt myself with barbed wire (or anything else), my dad would get very angry and yell at me. I could never understand why he did that. I was already hurt and needed nurturing, not scolding. It was many years later before I understood that his anger was triggered by his fear and his inability to keep his precious daughter from being hurt.

There is another secret about anger that I have learned through observing my own behavior. Most of the time when I am angry at someone, it is not about them at all. It is really about me. I am not really angry at their action, but rather at my reaction (or lack of reaction) to it. In my musical life, when I was responsible for operating our tavern, I used to get really angry at customers when they got rowdy or belligerent to the point where someone had to step in. Usually the someone was the bartender, but I was still ultimately responsible and I am not comfortable with confrontation. So what I was really angry about was my own discomfort and lack of assertiveness, based on my fear of physical violence. It was not about them at all; it was about me.

Anger is not a road hazard that has caused me a lot of problems, either before or after reconnection with my guide. Even though I had buried a lot of feelings, anger was not one of them. I have searched long and hard to see if it was suppressed, buried so deep that I was unaware of its existence, and so far I have not found any huge pockets of festering anger. Neither have I been passive-aggressive or depressed for any length of time. I can recognize both forms of behavior and understand them, but I don't relate to them because I have not been there.

I have, of course, been angry; and when I was angry, I acted on it inappropriately. I snapped at the Rescuer, threw temper tantrums with the Skier/Climber, and screamed like a fishwife at the Piano Player. Back in those days, I did not know about dammit dolls and punching pillows. When I got angry, I vented it through others, the supposed objects of my anger. It was not until I began walking with my guide and going through the grief process, following the Piano Player's death, that I learned about anger management. Anger is, after all, a part of the grief process, and I was angry that he had died and taken our music with him. I got my first dammit doll from the hospice bereavement counselor, used it, then gave it to a friend who needed it more than I did. Dammit dolls are plain little stuffed dolls that can be punched, thrown, and cursed at. They give the bereaved an acceptable outlet for what many believe to be unacceptable behavior. How can I allow myself to be angry at one I love for leaving? Easily. He left, didn't he? And took all of "our" dreams with him.

Dealing with anger as it arises in a way that is not damaging and destructive is the first component of anger management. My soul sister that wields a sword (see "Optimism") attributed her childhood bulimia to anger-stuffing and believes that venting anger is part of her self-care. And she's right. Except that she has, in the past, vented it directly and then wondered why the ventee reacted unfavorably and refused to discuss the problem. Anger management requires me to vent, certainly, but not directly. Talking about anger, not talking from anger, is a much kinder and productive way to deal with my fellow travelers. Remember, anger/fear and love cannot coexist in the same moment. Sword attacks are not sourced in love, and relationships are not strengthened by anger and fear.

My desire to keep my God-given rewards of serenity and joy has caused me to embrace the second and most important component of anger management—eliminating anger triggers. It is impossible to be serene and joyous when I am angry. The Al-Anon slogan, "How important is it?" helps me to focus on what is really worth causing me to lose my serenity and joy (which, it turns out, is not much). I am also eliminating as best I can my personal anger triggers, which means I have to surrender my judgmentalism. To be sure, much of my judging led to grandiosity and arrogance, not anger. But none of these traits contributes to serenity and joy, so judgmentalism had to go. It, too, lives in the past and in the future, so living in the moment is another key to anger management. So is giving up righteousness, expectations, perfectionism, and other negative behaviors. Self-attack is as, or more, destructive as other-attack; and I am still harder on myself than on anyone else. Righteous anger depends on my point of view, and it is still sourced in fear, not in love. Anger of any kind separates me from my God, who is expressed as love. And staying close to him, mindfully in the moment, is the ultimate form of anger management.

~ Resentment

Resentment is anger that is suppressed, unforgiven, and held over time. Anger, too, can be held over time. I have a soul friend who is very angry, not simply resentful, toward her parents. But usually the fire of anger, over time, is converted to the smoldering ashes of resentment.

Resentment is another terribly destructive road hazard, since it can steal serenity, joy, and freedom over a very long time period. When I participated in an experiential self-discovery workshop called Life Training, one of the things our small group was asked to do was list all those we held resentments against, together with how long we had held the resentments, and then total the times. The facilitator then added up all our times, and came up with something like 2,540 years, ten months, and twenty days of total resentment time, a long time to be without serenity, joy, and freedom!

Resentment is an emotional hook that binds me to the person or group of persons I hold the resentment against. Holding resentment means that every time I think about the action that fueled the original anger, I get angry again. I thus am doomed to relive the event and feel the same anger over and over. There is a movie titled *Groundhog Day* whose plot is about a man caught in a time warp. He relives Groundhog Day over and over until he learns his lesson and is free to move on. Resentment operates the same way. I get to relive the same old anger over and over until I learn my lesson—acceptance and forgiveness—and am free to move on.

So why do I hold on to resentment? Often, it is simply a matter of false pride. Being wounded and right maintains the illusion of being better than. Resentment always carries a hidden payoff. If it did not, I would not choose to keep it because holding on to it really isn't very much fun. Often the payoff is that I do not have to look at something within myself or take responsibility for doing something different. While I maintain resentment against you, I am not required to do my part to improve the quality of our relationship by dealing with whatever caused my resentment in the first place. Resentment keeps the focus and blame on you, not me. I don't have to become accountable for my part.

For years, I held major resentment against my parents because they took me out of the Chicago public school system, where my gift of intelligence was recognized and would have been nurtured and developed. Instead of staying in the city, they moved me to the farm and into a one-room schoolhouse. I further resented the fact that they did not program or encourage me to go to college. Blaming them took the responsibility off me. I could have educated myself if I had wanted to, especially after I got into a professional world filled with college graduates, but I did not. If it had not been for the Skier/Climber, I probably would not have ever gone to college. And, to this day, I still do not take the responsibility for self-education that I should. It's as if part of me still believes that because *they* made what I perceive to be a bad choice, I am stuck with the result. I am not. I won't ever be a Quiz Kid, but I can still develop my intelligence to its highest potential.

Resentment clearly lives in the past and ties me to it. It also serves to create a similar future, as my story above indicates. Resentment has all the other characteristics of anger as well, since it is built upon anger. Resentment is based on fear and definitely requires a judgment call. My major resentment will be toward those who are closest to me—parents, in-laws, spouses, siblings, and children. And oftentimes, my resentment, like the anger that created it, is really directed toward myself.

The key to release from resentment is forgiveness, and it is a two-sided process. I must not only forgive those I have judged and condemned, but I must also forgive myself for judging and condemning them. For me, self-forgiveness has been the hardest part and has taken the longest time. It is much easier for me to forgive others for their part in whatever created the resentment than to forgive me for holding onto my anger. After all, in most cases, resentment does not harm the other person directly. Most of the time, I am not honest enough or courageous enough to discuss it with others, so they may not even know I hold the resentment. My parents never knew how I felt about my education because I never told them. So, the person that was harmed the most was me.

Those of us recovering from addictions in twelve-step programs understand how dangerous resentments are. In fact, the fourth step outlined in the *Big Book of Alcoholics Anonymous* begins with a listing of resentments. Resentment can take me away from God and back into my addiction. Remember, fear and love cannot coexist in a single moment. And anything that separates me from love separates me from God.

For me, since anger is not a major road hazard and resentment is built from anger, neither is resentment a major road hazard. Understand, too, that since I let very few people close to me and come from a small family, there were very few people who qualified for major resentment. Still, the resentment I had was deep-seated and very hard to eliminate, especially since my mind so quickly intellectualizes things away. As soon as I discovered resentment, I would talk myself into forgiveness. In other words, my head would forgive but it never got to my heart. My major resentment, which was directed at my parents, took many passes before it was completely forgiven and healed. I have already described my healing from the most serious and painful one, which was the one incident of sexual abuse by my dad ("Forgiveness"). I don't know how many times I thought I was done with that one, only to have it reappear one more time. And I don't know how many times I have forgiven myself for holding the resentment, only to find that there was more to release and forgive.

None of my resentments, either toward others or myself, were released before I began walking with my guide. Forgiveness is rooted in unconditional love, which requires a solid connection to the source of all love. And my work with anger, described previously, has been work on resentment as well. Anger management includes acceptance and forgiveness, which eliminates the source of resentment. Minimizing anger also minimizes the potential for resentment. For the most part, now I am free of both.

I say, for the most part, because there is one trap I still fall into that leads to the formation of resentment. It has to do with caretaking versus caregiving. Remember, caregiving is selfless giving, whereas caretaking is based on an expectation of a payback. Caregiving also requires a foundation of self-care, and sometimes when I do not care for myself adequately I begin to expect things from others who may be unable to give them. Caregiving then is transformed into caretaking, and caretaking is a primary creator of resentment. A wise woman in one of my Al-Anon groups put it this way: "When I find myself with resentment, it is usually because I am doing something for someone that they should be doing for themselves." That is caretaking, or enabling, and some sort of expectation is always involved. When I "took care of" the Piano Player by making sure he was fed and napped before a gig, my expectation was that he would stay sober enough to finish the last set. Sometimes he was able to meet my expectation, and sometimes he was not.

There is a passage in one of my daily meditation books that says, "Expectations are premeditated resentments." And they are. When caregiving becomes caretaking and expectations are present but not met, resentment quickly forms. And when they do, it is my cue to look at my part in their formation and to act accordingly. Resentment of this kind is a signal that I have moved from love to fear and left my guide behind. In fact, all the road hazards provide the same message. The antidote is always the same: Surrender once more to love and stay close to my God in the moment. Freedom from resentment comes through acceptance, forgiveness, and compassion, and acceptance, forgiveness, and compassion come through surrender to love.

~ GUILT

Guilt is the emotion that tells me I have made a mistake that I have judged and condemned myself for making. Guilt says that I have failed in some aspect of my life. Guilt may result from wrongful thoughts, beliefs, attitudes, or behaviors, anything I perceive as a violation of my own (or someone else's) personal belief system. Guilt is a burden that may be carried for an instant or for a lifetime. The burden of guilt may be picked up immediately or assumed many years after the action that precipitates it. Guilt may lead to self-punishment, both consciously and subconsciously. Like its base emotion, fear, guilt lives in the past and in the future, never in the present with God. As is true with all of the negative emotions, guilt is an unnecessary burden that separates me from my guide, keeps me from recognizing and using my God-given gifts, and makes walking my unique path weary and difficult instead of happy, joyous, and free.

Guilt requires both a trial and conviction. For me to feel guilty, I have to not only judge that I have violated a personal truth, but condemn myself for it as well. Guilt is never objective. Guilt does not simply observe that I have made a mistake. Guilt takes it one step further and says I am a bad person because I have made a mistake. Guilt thus merits punishment or sentencing, self-inflicted or other-inflicted. Both are a form of attack, and the methods of attack are simultaneously direct and indirect, conscious and subconscious. Unresolved guilt fuels addictions and contributes to all forms of physical, mental, emotional, and spiritual illness. The antidote for guilt is, of course, forgiveness, but often, forgiveness cannot be accepted until the sentence has been served, the self- or other-imposed punishment is complete. I know people who have literally sentenced themselves to years of hard labor or self-imposed exile because of guilt. The Piano Player drank partly to escape guilt, and his behaviors while drinking simply piled on more guilt. So the guilt/punishment negative spiral continued for most of his life.

Guilt may be earned or unearned, valid or invalid. Earned guilt is guilt I feel because I have deviated from either my own value system or a value system established by others that I have accepted as my own. With earned guilt, I have judged and condemned myself. With unearned guilt, someone else has judged and condemned me according to their value system, and I have accepted their judgment as being correct. Children are often burdened with a lot of unearned guilt because they have no way to discern what their truth is and is not. As a child, if I am told I have erred, that I have done something I should feel guilty about, I will probably believe it. As an adult, I may do the same thing if I am not aware of my truth, my values, and my beliefs. Unearned guilt is often based on the words, "I should," "You should, "I should not," "You should not." In program, we tell each other not to "should" on ourselves. When I do "should" on myself, what I should do is often based on values I do not really agree with, not values that reflect my true self, my personal truth.

I have shared that my mother chose to have several abortions before she gave me life ("Perseverance"). At the time, what she did was not in conflict with her personal value system, so she assumed no guilt for her actions. Fifty years later, late in her life, she came to believe that abortion was sinful; and, being either unwilling or unable to confess her "sin," began to carry a huge burden of unearned guilt. Over time, her body began to sag and curl up into a little, shrunken ball and her mind gradually began to lose its ability to function. Now, her official diagnoses were osteoporosis and dementia, but I believe that the burden of guilt has a lot to do with her physical and mental decline. It was only when her mind digressed to a place where she was free of guilt that she was able to let go of her body and leave this life.

While writing this section on guilt, I mentioned to my Al-Anon sponsor and spiritual guide that my topic for the day was guilt and that it was a road hazard. She expressed a different opinion. She said that guilt was a signal that I have gotten off course, deviated from my own personal value system, and that without guilt I might not know and be motivated to change my behavior. Sort of a learn-through-pain principle. I thought about this for awhile before beginning to write, and I finally came to terms with it. Yes, it is true that guilt is a signal, but it is a signal that includes not only judgment, but condemnation. When I do my fourth step inventory, I am to do it impartially, not to judge or condemn, but merely to observe, to list my behaviors. It is neither necessary nor desirable for me to feel guilty about my character defects to humbly ask God to remove them, as required by steps six and seven. In fact, my experience was that as long as I felt guilty about what I had done, I wanted to keep it a secret from God and thus could not go on to steps five, six, and seven. Doing my inventory without a sense of guilt has been essential for my spiritual recovery. And the reason for this is that guilt keeps me separated from God; fear and love cannot coexist. If I am dedicated to following the direction of my guide, to walking my path sourced in love, then I do not need guilt to maintain my integrity. I will correct myself when I get off course without the need to punish myself.

Guilt is a road hazard I know all too well. I have lived with it most of my life, even as I told myself intellectually that I did not believe in guilt. Earlier, I shared the story of how my first husband chose to leave this life (“Hope”). When he died, part of me believed that he died of a broken heart and that I was somehow responsible. I remember thinking at the time, “Boy, I'm glad I don't do guilt!” It would be years before I could go back into that event, accurately reframe it, and release the buried guilt.

The same situation occurred when I divorced the Skier/Climber. After a very logical and unemotional property settlement and uncontested divorce, he said to me, "You know, I felt really bad when you left." He threw me a rock of guilt, I picked it up, and immediately stuffed it into my pack without feeling a thing. Again, it would be years later before I unburied it and tossed it away.

But the most obvious and most tragic evidence of the guilt I carried is in the story of how I came to turn my back on God. It was, after all, guilt over my inability to maintain the sexual abstinence required by my chosen religion that created that schism. The priest and the Catholic Church may have forgiven me through the sacrament of penance, but I had not. I was still guilty in my own eyes because I could not follow the moral requirements of this religion perfectly. I had judged and condemned myself and projected that judgment and condemnation onto a God who I now know does neither. The guilt I carried kept me separated from God for over thirty years, and I am not sure exactly why I was finally able to call on him again. Possibly, the pain associated with living with and loving the Piano Player had been enough penance to earn forgiveness. Perhaps the desperation I felt was greater than my guilt at that point. Whatever the cause, I am eternally grateful for the result.

Since God and I have reconnected and I have been walking with him, I have struggled to rid myself of unresolved guilt, to throw away the contents of my bag of rocks ("Forgiveness") one by one and accept forgiveness. Making my ninth step amends removed part of the guilt, but not all. Coming to know that my "sins" were never sins in God's eyes, but merely learning experiences has been a long time coming.

Once obtained, freedom from guilt is a precious gift and one I truly want to keep. So I monitor my actions carefully, and when I stray from either my truth or my path, I make an immediate course correction. Notice, I said monitor, not judge or condemn. Beating myself up when I make a mistake is not acceptable behavior any more. Beating myself up when I make a mistake is what turns slips into full-blown relapses. As a recovering food addict, I simply cannot allow myself to accept guilt when I slip with my food, nor can I allow myself to accept it in any other area of my life. So I observe and act accordingly and do not choose to pick up any new rocks of guilt. I do not pick up rocks from anyone else that are not mine to carry, nor do I knowingly act in such a way as to contribute to another person's bag of rocks. None of this is acceptable behavior for me today.

When I was backpacking during my outdoor life, I routinely carried a thirty-five- to forty-pound pack over rough and difficult terrain. Carrying that heavy a physical load was very hard on me, but it was nothing compared to the emotional load of guilt that I carried every day of my life. I no longer choose to do that. I choose to walk with my guide, in the present, leaving guilt behind in the past. I am much lighter now, and my path is much easier to walk. And that is the way it was always intended to be.

~ SHAME

Shame is the false belief that I am a mistake. Shame says that there is something intrinsically wrong with my true self. Shame says that I am flawed, that somehow I arrived here in damaged condition. Shame says that I am not whole, that a vital piece of my self is either very flawed or totally missing. Shame thus encourages me to cover my flawed self, to keep it hidden behind the mask of false pride, even from the eyes of God.

Shame, too, lives in my past (where it was created) and in my future, never in the present with God. Shame first comes to me as a child and is then reinforced through life experiences. Guilt feeds shame, but for shame to grow it has to already be present. I once heard a soul friend share that she did not understand why God had put such an insignificant person as her on earth. That is a declaration of shame. Shame says, "I am unlovable, worthless, not good enough, flawed, stupid, clumsy, helpless, incapable, ugly, or always to blame." Such beliefs are false core negative beliefs, and most of us have at least one. I am not born with shame. I am born a perfectly lovable child of God. God does not create imperfection; I do, by my mistaken perceptions of what I am. And those mistaken perceptions are what create shame.

If I have been blessed with wise parents who love me unconditionally, see me as a perfectly lovable child of God, and see themselves as perfectly lovable children of God as well, then there would be no reason for me to take up the burden of shame. However, very few families are this enlightened, so shame becomes an almost inevitable addition to my essence, an extra burden I carry until my life experiences lead me to put it down. Parents who carry shame give it to their children. This is not intentional; it simply happens. If I perceive that I am flawed, I will transmit that sense to my children. As a child growing up, one of my soul friends was continually told by her mother, "Don't have kids, they ruin your life." Her bag of shame bore the label, "It's all my fault."

Shame is often a silent companion in that I may not know it is there. I may continually experience the effects of shame but not relate them to shame or understand the cause. My shame was that I was flawed in such a way as to make me unlovable. As a child, I continually had to earn what love I could feel and accept. Now, this sense was there probably in infancy, but it was strongly reinforced in my childhood years. When I became the scapegoat for the resident grade school bullies, I knew I had not done anything to invoke their cruelty. So it had to be that there was something very wrong, very unlovable, very awful about me to inspire such harsh treatment. That is shame, and it points out a truth about shame that sets it apart from guilt. Shame is always unearned. I do not create shame for myself—it always comes from an external source. I do not believe that there is something wrong with my essence until you tell me so through your words or actions.

Shame worked in my life continually until it was brought out of the darkness and exposed to the light of truth. I hid my true self from others (and from myself) because I was ashamed of what we would find if we looked too closely. I constructed and hid behind a false self, a mask based on doing, not being, and used false pride to maintain it. My shame kept me isolated and apart from my fellow travelers and from my God. The guilt I carried for not doing things perfectly united with the shame I carried for not being perfect, and the combination was lethal. It was lethal because it killed my spirit, my passion, my joy, everything but my physical existence. I was cut off from God and my God-given gifts. Cut off and still unaware of the truth because the truth was hidden behind the mask in the darkness of shame.

In the very earliest days of my recovery, I was counseled for codependency. That was when I began to read, voraciously, everything I could find on alcoholism, codependency, and adult child issues. One of the first books I read was John Bradshaw's early work on toxic shame, *Healing the Shame That Binds You*. I remember thinking, as I read it, that I could not relate to it, did not quite understand what it was all about. The cloak of denial was heavy back then. I did not have a clue that I was a victim of unearned shame, that I had been carrying a burden of shame since childhood. To be sure, there had been shame connected to excess weight, but that was an external means to mask the internal shame. The guilt of overeating created the shame of being fat, but the true shame lay far beneath the surface, hidden and disowned. Being fat was a way to keep others from getting close enough to see it.

So shame stayed with me, through the Piano Player's death, through two fourth steps, and through nearly three years of recovery in Al-Anon and Overeaters Anonymous. By this time, I knew I had a problem with self-love, but I had intellectualized it away. In other words, I knew in my head that I was lovable, but I did not believe it in my heart. My Al-Anon fourth step inventory includes a section on love and several questions intended to reveal a sense of whether a person believes he or she is lovable. I answered them all, "I think so," and that was my truth at that time. I did not yet know about my hidden shame.

Then, when I was ready, a mentor appeared with the gift that brought my awareness of and the beginning of release from shame. I had known this woman for a long time, but we had never connected. When we did, it was clear to me that I was supposed to follow her guidance, so I did. Her gifts were the book that started me writing morning pages and Life Training, a very intense, experiential self-discovery weekend.

All I knew about Life Training before I went was that my mentor said I needed to be there. When the sessions began, it soon became clear to me that this was a very intense and direct way to get at those issues most of us do not want to get at. The sessions were long and emotionally draining, and I was very afraid that something was going to be pulled out of me that I did not want to see. At noon on the second day, I almost left. But something said, “No, you have to go through this.” So I did, and that afternoon, something was pulled out of me that I did not want to see. That something was my hidden shame, my false core negative belief that I was unlovable. And guess what. Once in the light of reason, it was shown to be what it had always been—a lie, an illusion, the bogeyman in the closet. By the end of the weekend, I had cried buckets of tears and was emotionally exhausted, but I was also on the road to freedom from shame. Later, I understood the miracle that I had been given. I am lovable. I do not have to hide any parts of myself from others anymore. To be sure, I still carried my guilt and the mask, but the reason for the mask was gone.

One of my soul friends asked me what I had gotten out of Life Training, and I told her, excitedly, "I found out that I am lovable!"

She smiled and said, "I already knew that." Ah, but I didn't! Shame had kept me from seeing my truth.

Now, as I walk my unique path with my guide, I walk it without the burden of shame. I know who I am, I know my truth, and I am learning how to better project that inner truth through my outer persona. Removing all aspects of the mask, my false self, is a process, but they are gradually falling away. False pride does not give up its hold easily, but I am making much progress toward integrity between my soul and personality, the inner and outer me. The one thing I absolutely do know is that beneath the mask lies an essence that is love. Shame itself is no longer a road hazard for me, and I am very grateful that it is gone. Without it, I can accept the challenges of life and not take them personally. Before, when faced with rejection, hostility, indifference, or even loss, it was somehow a validation of my own intrinsic unlovability. Now I understand that all of these challenges are simply that—challenges—and that it's not about my core being at all. This is tremendously freeing and is especially useful to me now as I risk sharing my creative gifts with others.

Years ago, I wrote a book about the summer the Skier/Climber and I spent camping, backpacking, kayaking, and climbing in Western Canada. It was a typical outdoor book, a narrative with black-and-white photos, and I submitted it to several Canadian publishers. When the rejections came, I gave up and have not, since then, submitted anything I have written for formal publication. Now, some thirty years later, I am writing another book of a very different sort. This one contains my essence—my heart, soul, and personality are here for all to see, woven throughout the principles that have helped to shape the person I am today. But, I am no longer ashamed of my true self or too falsely proud to share it with others. So any rejections I receive when I submit this for publication will be about my writing, not me. And I will not give up. The marvelous book that gave me morning pages, a book that has touched many lives, was self-published. I am writing this spiritual autobiography for and with my guide, and he will provide his desired outcome. And shame will not keep me from doing my part in creating it.

~ Regret

Regret is the road hazard that refuses to accept reality, that wants to change an outcome by changing the past. Regret is not happy with the present and fantasizes a different outcome based on "if only." "If only" I had done something different, made a different choice, married a different man, taken a different job, lost weight, gained weight, whatever. "If only" I had done the thing I did or did not do, life would be better. Regret wants to go back and rewrite my story with a different, happier, or more pleasant ending. Regret has not accepted the ending as lived or chosen to learn the lesson in the event and move on.

Regret quite obviously not only lives in the past, but is stuck there. Regret is immobilized and unable (or unwilling) to take responsibility for whatever can be done now (if anything) to correct past mistakes or reverse choices. While I was growing up, my mother continually played the regret game. Her version was, "If only I hadn't married your father, then (blank)." "Blank" would be whatever she believed would have been different had she made a different choice, and she was free to fill in the blanks any way she wanted to. "If only I hadn't married your father, I would be…" richer, thinner, have a nice house, or would not have to stoke up the coal furnace every morning. Regret allowed her to fantasize any kind of a future she wanted. But it also kept her from taking any responsibility for making changes to her life in the present.

My soul friend's mother who felt that having children had ruined her life ("Shame") obviously regretted having them. She also obviously was neither willing nor able to make the best of her choice in the present. Regret puts the blame for my present situation on something that cannot be changed. Regret thus makes me a victim of circumstances and powerless over my own life.

Regret walks arm in arm with guilt. It is often those actions I feel guilty about that also create regret. And the degree and depth of guilt and regret are directly proportional to the degree and depth of my emotional investment in the outcome. When I was attending grief support groups after the Piano Player's death, regret was a commonly shared condition. "If only I had insisted (or not insisted) on a certain treatment, then my loved one would have lived or not suffered as much." Some regret is probably a natural aspect of any major loss, but wallowing in regret and refusing to let go of it is not. Again, regret keeps me stuck in the past and unable to move forward, to learn and grow from my experience. Regret can thus keep me separated from God and unwilling and unable to follow him. Whereas most of the other road hazards make the journey more difficult or less pleasant, regret stops me in my tracks.

The antidote for regret is acceptance and forgiveness. I must accept, first, that I am human and human beings are prone to make mistakes. In fact, making mistakes is part of being human. Making mistakes is one of the ways that I learn and grow. Next, I must accept the reality that I perceive has resulted from the action I regret. Wishing it to be something different will not make it so. Accepting what is is the first step to either changing it or my perception of it. Any situation can be as bad or as good as I choose to perceive it. And correct choices can only be made in the light of reality.

My life, as is true with most of our lives, has had several major forks in the road to negotiate, the kinds where the choices made really did drastically alter the course of my life. For me, moving from Illinois to Idaho was a major fork, as was choosing not to follow a traditional path by marrying one of the Catholic men who would have married me. Not having children and running off with the Piano Player were others. A fork with the most serious consequences was when both the Piano Player and I were given the tools for spiritual recovery from our addictions and neither of us chose to use them. All of these forks in the road were chosen without any direct help from my guide, so certainly, if I were so inclined, I could have had plenty of reason for regret. But unlike guilt, I do not practice regret. Once a choice is made, informed or not (see "Choices"), it is made and the result is accepted by me. If it is not acceptable, then I can choose again.

I really do not know what to attribute this to—my responsible nature, my optimism, or possibly a conscious choice *not* to do what Mother did. And I guess it really does not matter what has created this desirable position. The fact is that I simply do not second-guess my choices. Once a decision is made, that's it. I don't wish I had bought a different car or a different house or a different whatever, nor do I go around checking all the dealers to see if I could have bought it cheaper somewhere else. I accept the outcome, and if I am not pleased with the outcome, I do whatever I can do to change it.

The one area of my life where I have felt regret is in my personal relationships. I have, in the past, regretted those actions and behaviors that have been unknowingly or knowingly hurtful to others. But, even in those cases, I have not usually held on to regret. Once I have become aware of my error, I have made my amends, made an effort to change my behavior or actions, forgiven myself, and moved on. Mentally, I have not clung to the past. Emotionally, the past has clung to me.

The one exception to this, a regret that I held onto for many years, involved not a human, but a pet. When the Piano Player and I were working as road musicians, we were adopted by a part-Siamese cat we named Misty. Misty had apparently belonged to someone who moved around a lot, like a construction worker, because she loved to travel (something most cats do not like to do). Misty also loved to climb—shower curtains, drapes, and very tall trees. She was an independent, free-wheeling, passionate animal, and we both grew very attached to her. Too attached, it turns out.

After a particularly disastrous road trip, the three of us went back to Las Vegas to recover and took up residency in a cheap motel near the strip. Misty was street-wise and always seemed to be able to take care of herself, so we never tried to restrain her. One night, we heard a pitiful meow, opened the door, and there she was, dragging her hind legs behind her. She had obviously been hit by a car and was seriously injured. So I called a 24-hour veterinary clinic (they have 24-an-hour everything in Las Vegas), put her in a basket, and took her in.

The diagnosis was a broken pelvis. The vet told me that it was possible that she might survive with surgery, but that her recuperation time would be long and difficult and she probably would not be able to climb anymore. The kindest thing I could have done at that point would have been to euthanize her, but I just wasn't ready to let her go. So I told the vet to do what he could, paid him some money, and left her. About a day later, he called and said she had died, which was undoubtedly the best for her. My regret was that I had made a choice that had caused her an extra day of pain and suffering. I lived with that regret for many years until I was finally able to grieve her loss, forgive myself, and let it go.

Not regretting my choices certainly does not mean that all my choices have brought me joy, prosperity, and peace—they obviously have not. Living with the Piano Player and his disease was not joyous, prosperous, or peaceful. But the choices I made and the experiences they provided have brought me to the place where I am today, and I am eternally grateful to be here. Had I chosen a different path, I might have eventually ended up in this same place, but I don't know that. It's not part of my experience. I am a composite of all my choices and all my life experiences. Changing any of it would change me, and I like who I am and where I am today. And, possibly, that is the key to not holding on to regret—liking who I am and where I am and understanding that the choices I made, mistakes and all, are what created that happy result. (This also holds true for choices made for us as children, which helps turn resentment into acceptance and forgiveness.)

Making behavioral choices not sourced in love that affect my soul friends is a source of regret for me, especially when the outcome is not exactly as I had hoped for. But even in those cases, I have learned to let go, make my amends, if required, forgive myself, and move on. I have finally figured out that I do not have the power to alter God's plan for my life or the lives of those I care about. I may affect the schedule or timing, but not the outcome. If the relationship is meant to continue, it will survive my improper choices. If it is not meant to continue, it won't and it wasn't supposed to. "If onlys" will not create a different outcome, and neither will regret.

~ Suffering

Suffering is a condition caused by my refusing to alleviate or let go of pain. Suffering may be involuntary, as in the case of other-inflicted physical torture, but usually it is a choice. Suffering can be physical, mental, emotional, spiritual, or creative. Any aspect of my self where pain can be felt is a potential area for suffering.

Contrary to some beliefs, suffering is not noble. God neither asks nor expects us to endure unnecessary pain in his name or in any other name. God is expressed as love, and love wants only the best for us. And the best does not include self-torture or self-punishment for any cause.

Notice that I said *unnecessary* pain, not pain *per se.* Actually, God would prefer that I have no pain at all, but most of us insist on creating it for ourselves. Most of us also insist on creating much more pain than is required for any given situation, and that excess pain is suffering. Refusing to take available medication for physical pain is a form of suffering. Refusing to get treatment for addiction to my drug of choice is a form of suffering. Allowing myself to be terrorized by anxiety and fear is a form of suffering. Refusing professional help when required to help me climb out of an emotional pit is a form of suffering. Martyrdom and self-sacrifice are forms of suffering. Anything I do or do not do to prolong the agony is a form of suffering.

Pain is a necessary part of life as most of us choose to live it today. Wounds of all types must be healed, and healing is painful. Physical recovery, as from surgery or accidental injury, hurts. Emotional recovery, digging out and purging buried emotional pain, hurts. Mental recovery, the purging of fears and other mental demons, hurts. Spiritual recovery, the process of coming to a place of love, forgiveness, humility, generosity, and compassion, can be a very painful journey. So I am not advocating the elimination or medicating of all pain with substances—that is what I used to do when I was using my drugs of choice. What I am advocating is the elimination of excess pain, or suffering.

The only true healer of pain is love, but most of us are not open to allowing love to completely heal all wounds, all forms of attack, all of the sources of pain in our physical world. To be completely open would be to see all fear-based perceptions as illusion, all actions sourced in fear as a call for love, and to be detached with love from all worldly occupants. Emotional attachment, or need, is what creates the pain of loss. As long as I am emotionally attached to anything or anyone, I will experience the pain of loss when it or they are no longer here. So pain is an expected part of my life. Without total detachment, it can be minimized, but not totally avoided. I believe the saying goes, "Pain is inevitable, suffering is optional."

Suffering due to a loss is stuck in both the past and the future simultaneously, because most personal losses also involve the loss of their associated dreams. The suffering of martyrdom or self-sacrifice is stuck in the future, a quest for some sort of future reward, an "if, then" situation. Suffering may be a form of self-punishment related to guilt, a somewhat skewed declaration of love, a way to get attention and sympathy, or a pit I fall into that I choose not to come out of. Suffering is a choice. It is self-inflicted. As the book title says, *You Don't Have to Suffer*. The antidote for suffering is humility, the willingness to let go, detachment with love, acceptance, forgiveness, and surrender. There is no suffering with the God of my understanding in the present moment.

People who live stuck in the past with regret do martyrdom and suffering well. My mother's often-vocalized regret for marrying my father, coupled with her unwillingness to do anything to correct her perceived error in judgment, created martyrdom and thus much suffering—fifty-six years worth, to be exact. My mother suffered until the day my dad died, whereupon he miraculously turned into Saint Clifford, this perfect man she always loved. Then she proceeded to suffer because he had left, and the mantra changed to, "I'll never love another man like I loved your father." And she didn't.

The Piano Player, too, because of his disease, became an expert in physical suffering, which may have been self-punishment associated with his guilt. Although this had always been true to some degree, his last years were particularly awful in that regard. The house we lived in bore the marks of his physical suffering—dried blood stains and dents in the walls where he had fallen into them and injured himself. He was forever falling, was covered with bruises, and suffered a broken finger and ankle (which he walked on for a month before having it treated). And I can only imagine how awful he felt when he was jaundiced and bloated with ascites after his liver began to shut down. I had hepatitis for three weeks, and I know how indescribably awful I felt. His pain lasted for months.

As for me, I may not have done regret, but I did do suffering. That theme runs throughout my marriages and beyond. Sometimes it was physical, sometimes mental, sometimes emotional, and always spiritual. The pain of my self-imposed separation from God was a constant but unacknowledged companion, so for more than thirty years, I suffered spiritually. I suffered physically, emotionally, and mentally for fifty-seven years of my life from the consequences of misusing food, my drug of choice. I suffered physically in my outdoor life every time I chose to push my body beyond its natural limits of physical endurance, something I did routinely. I suffered mentally with the Rescuer because I refused to accept his financial obligation to his mother. After all, I worked so that she did not have to, like any good martyr would. And I obviously suffered emotionally during the fifteen and a half years I was with the Piano Player. I was a wonderful enabler, and enablers become martyrs by default. Enablers take on not only their responsibilities, but the responsibilities of the alcoholic as well, and that's the stuff that martyrdom is made of. I took care of everything. I managed our tavern so that it would support itself, worked full time to support us, played music on weekends, and maintained a semblance of a household. Strangely, I did not feel like a martyr. I just felt tired!

Most of my suffering was emotional, and I kept on suffering long after the pain of staying in the relationship far outweighed the rewards. That is, by the way, one definition of addiction. Addicts keep on using their drug of choice long after the pain caused by using it has begun to outweigh the benefits or rewards. In Al-Anon, I came to understand that I, too, was addicted, not to alcohol, but to the alcoholic.

My suffering continued after his death, but it was not the pain of losing the Piano Player that I refused to let go of. I had detached with love from him, but I had not detached with love from our music, which ended when he left. Most of the pain I experienced during the first years following his death was because I chose not to let go of the music. A part of me still feels that loss, at times, and is drawn toward stage performing, long after the rest of me has chosen to put it behind me. So part of me has not reached acceptance and is still suffering.

Walking with my guide did not end my suffering. However, continuing to walk with him is minimizing it. As I learn to live more and more in the present with God, as I learn to stay sourced in love and emotionally detached from my soul friends and other meaningful enhancements to my life, I am quite naturally beginning to experience less pain in my life. And the pain I do experience is not being held onto. Certainly, I have no more desire to feel the pain of separation from God that comes when I try to emotionally detach without love from any one of my fellow travelers. I am not at all interested in staying in an emotional pit created by such an attempt at separation. So when I find myself there, I do the things I need to do to quickly leave the pit: surrender, allow God to help me, detach with love from the one to whom I have become emotionally attached, and accept the reality that created the desire to separate. And the sooner I choose to do these things, the less pain I experience.

~ NEGATIVITY

Negativity is the condition that results from allowing negative thoughts, beliefs, attitudes, and feelings to create my life experiences. Negativity is diametrically opposed to my truth and negates many of my God-given gifts and rewards. It is very difficult to be joyous, serene, free, loving, or passionate when immersed in negativity. It is even more difficult to walk with my guide in any kind of consistent manner. Staying close to him, sourced in love, while practicing negativity, is impossible.

Negativity is a downward spiral that leads me into a mental and emotional pit, farther and farther away from my God. Negative thoughts, beliefs, attitudes, and feelings create negative experiences, which serve to validate and reinforce my negative thoughts, beliefs, attitudes, and feelings. For those caught up in this vicious circle of gloom and doom, life can be a frightful and dismal experience; and the road home can be long, hard, dark, dangerous, and extremely unpleasant. Truly negative people get lost in their self-created darkness until they choose to become willing to allow the light to come in. The light is, of course, love, and it casts out all darkness. God is always there, waiting to shine his healing light into the darkness, but I have to invite and allow him to do that.

Negativity comes in many various forms, all of which are sourced in fear. One of my soul sisters has what she calls fear movies, scenarios of fear, doubt, and despair that she plays out in her mind. I have what I call doubter attacks, those times when I doubt that I am good enough, smart enough, or strong enough to do whatever it is that I am supposed to do. The doubter also says that my dreams are foolish, that nothing is going to work out as I would like it to, or that by the time they do I will be too old to care! The doubter says my writing is worthless if it isn't accepted by a publisher or my music is worthless if it's not appreciated and applauded. The doubter takes rejection personally and says, "See? I told you that you were worthless." Negativity accepts her false conclusion as truth.

Negativity can find a flaw in every experience, a reason why the best of ideas cannot possibly work, a blemish on the most perfect work of art. Negativity is a perfectionist, and anything short of perfection is hopelessly flawed. Negativity projects economic collapse, bank failures, natural catastrophes, even the end of the world. Negativity supports a lot of sensationalist tabloids and legal and illegal exploitation. Negativity promotes fear and often profits from it.

Negativity lives in the past and creates a future that reinforces itself. Negative beliefs create experiences to support them. When I believed myself to be unlovable, I chose emotionally unavailable partners who validated that belief. When I believed that anyone I loved would leave me, they did. And if *they* did not, I did. I will, in some way, manage to create the experiences I need to validate my negative belief. If I believe that all men are liars and cheaters, all the men I am attracted to will be liars and cheaters. Or I will behave in such a way as to induce them to lie and be unfaithful. If I believe that everyone is out to get me, they will be. If I believe that my body is weak and vulnerable to illness and injury, illness and injury will be a major part of my experience. If I believe that I am old, I will begin to feel old, act old, and be old. (Believing myself to be young may not totally reverse the aging process, but it certainly makes it a lot more pleasant!)

Negative beliefs also create negative perceptions. What I believe is what I will see, hear, and sense. If I believe the world is evil and sinful, then evil and sin are what I will see and hear. If I believe that flying is dangerous, every plane crash will validate my fear-based belief. Never mind the 8,700,454 previous flights that arrived safely at their destinations. One crashed; therefore, flying is dangerous.

Negative thoughts create negative feelings. Negative thoughts are what put me into what I call the pit, a place of intense emotional pain. Going into the pit requires a trip back into the past, where I create a negative thought based on a past experience. Let us say that someone close to me makes an unkind or untrue comment to me while sourced in fear. At the time the comment is made, I am sourced in love, know it is not truth, and disregard it. Later, I have an attack of doubt and start to believe that the remark is truth or was intended to hurt me. This negative thought can, if I allow it to, put me into a pit of sadness, anger, despair, and pain. I can make this pit just as deep and unpleasant as I want simply by going back, finding more reasons to create negative thoughts, and piling in more sadness, anger, pain, and despair. Or I can choose to move back into the present, back into a loving place, where all was well to begin with. Nothing about the event itself has changed except my perception of it.

Negativity breeds negativity. Your negative energy can invade my personal space and affect my positive energy if I allow it to, if I do not protect myself from invasion. My protective armor is love, and I keep it in place by staying very close to my guide. Unfortunately, not many of us seem to know how to do this. Negativity is invasive, and it has permeated much of our modern society. We are, as a nation, very negative, and we seem to thrive on negativity. The news we all watch is filled with negativity. Plane crashes are news. Near-misses are news. Uneventful flights are not news. The devastation caused by earthquakes, tornadoes, and hurricanes is news. Serial killers, mass murders, and drive-by shootings are news. Train wrecks, wars, and persecution are news. Never mind that most of us will go through our lives without experiencing any of these tragic events firsthand. Never mind that most schools are not host to crazed killers, that most planes, trains, and buses do make it safely, that most of us do not make a habit of shooting our husbands or deserting our children. Positive events are not news.

I have already shared enough about myself for you to know that negativity is not my style. It is in direct conflict with two of my personal gifts, optimism and hope. So I cannot personally relate to those who habitually see, and thus create, a life experience filled with gloom and apprehension. But I can relate to those of us who have allowed negativity to keep us from finding and being our true selves and walking our unique paths because that is what I did. I did not view my world negatively, but I viewed myself negatively. My true self lay hidden behind my negative perceptions, and the path I walked was too often guided by fear, not love. Fear movies and doubter attacks were a routine and accepted part of my life. Emotional pits were created, wallowed in, and ultimately escaped from. But, once free, I usually managed to create another one and jump in again.

Since I have started walking with my guide, my personal negativity has decreased as my faith and trust in God have increased. With God, I am rediscovering my truth, reclaiming his gifts, and learning how to walk with him in the present moment. And that is the antidote to negativity. It is what makes that particular condition no longer appealing. My gifts are precious, and I want to keep them and develop them. Walking with God, serving him in the ways he would have me serve him now, demands that I honor my truth, honestly appraise my gifts, and release all negative perceptions of myself. Walking with him joyfully demands that I release all negative perceptions of my world. Every negative moment I experience is a moment separate from him and from love, and that is not where I choose to be today. Not that I don't still experience negativity—I do. The doubter still attacks, and the pit still beckons. But when I find myself heading that way, when I cry the first tears or feel the first pangs of anger, I stop, take note of where I am, feel and release my feelings to God, and move as quickly as I can back to the present. My path is leading me to open my mind and my heart, surrender to love, replace false pride with humility, and express gentleness, forgiveness, compassion, and generosity to myself and my fellow travelers. And those conditions do not coexist well with negativity.

~ Denial

Denial is the inability or unwillingness to acknowledge reality as it relates either to myself or my fellow travelers. Denial does not see the obvious or hear the words that describe the obvious. Denial is blind, deaf, unfeeling, and lives in a world of fantasy. Denial is not aware of reality and thus neither accepts reality nor can make any attempt to change it. Denial lives in the past, the way things were, or in the future, the way I wish things would be. Denial never lives in the present with God and truth.

Denial is often used as a shield, a protective device, a security blanket that I cling to until I am ready to face my reality. Denial often minimizes truth, says that things are not as bad or as destructive as they really are. Denial says I don't *really* have an eating or a drinking problem; I can quit or control it anytime. Denial says this relationship isn't really *that* unhealthy for us; I'll stay in it a little while longer. Denial couples easily with procrastination, which puts off dealing with a problem. Either or both merely serve to postpone the inevitable. Truth and reality will ultimately prevail. Either the problem will resolve itself or it will begin to destroy those who are affected by it. In the face of obvious self- or other-destruction, denial usually gives way to reality or truth.

Attempts to penetrate denial or to rip off the protective blanket are usually a waste of time. I will cling tightly to denial until I am ready to see the truth of my situation. Everyone that knows me well will see my reality long before I do. And any attempts I make to force you to see your reality before you are ready will either be ignored or actively rejected. Should you try to break through my denial, the same result will occur.

I have already shared the unpleasant consequences of my attempt to rip the protective blanket away from the Songteller ("Loyalty"). All other attempts I have made with others to rudely and uncaringly penetrate denial have had similarly unpleasant results. Force does not work. What does work, over time, is healing love, personal pain, or a combination of both. If I am loved enough, or if I or someone else hurts badly enough because of my denial, I will ultimately drop the blanket and face my reality or truth.

The only possible exception to this that I can think of is an intervention for chemical addiction. In an intervention, a trained counselor and a cadre of concerned and caring family members and/or friends confront the addict with their feelings about the consequences of his using, and strongly suggest that he choose formal treatment for his disease. Interventions must be sourced in love, and the interveners must be willing to accept any outcome. As with treatment itself, sometimes they work and sometimes they do not. Sometimes the addict accepts his reality and attempts to act on it. Sometimes he does not, stays in denial, and keeps on playing his deadly game.

Addicts are masters of denial, and many have a very high threshold for pain. Certainly, the Piano Player did, and I have known others with an even higher pain tolerance. Owning a bar gave me many examples of how strong denial can be in alcoholics. I have seen customers wreck their cars, injure themselves (or others), be court-ordered into treatment, put on Antabuse, get multiple drunken driving convictions and the accompanying fines and jail sentences, lose their jobs, wives, and children, ruin their health, and endure countless other consequences that would have broken through the denial of any person not consumed with self-hate. Still, these folks just go merrily along, unwilling to acknowledge their truth. Again, I will stay in denial of my reality, no matter how damaging and destructive my truth may be, until I am willing to accept it and do something to change it. And that willingness, that surrender, is a long time coming for some of us. The Piano Player never made it, not in this lifetime. Denial can have some very serious consequences.

Of course, there are many other things I can deny besides the reality that I am addicted, especially if I choose not to take responsibility for my life. I can become a victim and deny that I have choices and the power to co-create my life. I can deny that a relationship or a job has grown lifeless and stagnant and it is time to move on. I can deny that it all begins with me, that changes in my life experience require changes in me, not my spouse, children, or friends. I can deny that there is anything wrong with my life or that things are as bad as they are. The list goes on and on. All of us use or have used denial as a coping mechanism, some of us just more than others.

How have I used denial? Ah, let me count the ways! I have denied the reality of emotional pain by either stuffing it or medicating it with food. I have denied the true value of my intelligence, musical, and artistic gifts. I have denied the true value of who I am, of my own self-worth. I have denied the emptiness and pain of a life without a spiritual foundation, a life cut off from God, love, and meaning. I have denied the emptiness of personal relationships with myself and my fellow travelers. I have denied the loneliness of isolation and the frustration of doing it all myself, of not asking for help when I needed it. I have denied the self-abuse aspect of excesses—sexual promiscuity, food, cigarettes, alcohol, physical activity. I have denied my role in creating unhealthy relationships—it was always about them, never about me. I have denied my own humanness, my vulnerabilities and imperfections. I have denied the humanness of others by expecting invulnerability and perfection in them.

With the Piano Player, I denied the severity of his disease and the most obvious consequences. I denied any responsibility for my role as an enabler or for educating myself about alcoholism. He was the one with the problem, not me. I denied the very real physical danger inherent in traveling with someone who drank continually. I denied the affect of the disease on me mentally, emotionally, sexually, and financially. I denied my own insanity in accepting unacceptable behavior. When our relationship began to deteriorate, I denied the very obvious signs that it was time to let go and move on. When his health began to fail, I denied the seriousness of his condition even as his body deteriorated before my eyes. When he was dying, I denied that too (as did he) until his liver began to shut down. After he died, I denied the depth of my pain and the length of time it would take to reach acceptance.

But perhaps the time when I was in the deepest denial was not when the Piano Player drank, but when he didn't. While he was drinking, I convinced myself that the only problem in our relationship was that, and if he ever quit, my life would be perfect. So when he did quit, my life became perfect. It had to be; that was my illusion. "And they lived happily ever after." So I had, for nearly three and a half years, a perfect marriage and was very happy because that was the way I was supposed to feel. To be sure, it was better because the physical affects of his disease were removed. My irresponsible husband became much more responsible. He was home when I got home, we ate regular meals together, the lawn got mowed, the cars got washed, things that broke got repaired. We played a lot of golf and took two marvelous camping vacations to Western Canada. He woodworked, built some fabulous furniture, and his piano playing was better than it had ever sounded before. Life in my physical world was perfect.

Or was it? Seeing it from a more distant perspective gives a somewhat different view. At that time, I still had a God I had only talked to once since we had married, so the relationship had no spiritual connection. The sober Piano Player was very quiet and emotionally withdrawn, so we did not really talk very much. We watched a lot of TV together in those days, and when we did talk it was usually about the bar. We never talked about feelings, so there was no emotional connection. I had hoped that our waning sex life would improve without alcohol, but it didn't, so it should be no surprise that I began to gain weight. I was also managing the bar and working full time during this sober period, so it could be that I did not have time to realize that my perfect life was not perfect. Or it just could be that I was in denial about the reality of the situation. And, because I was tripping along, happy as a clam in my denial, I assumed that he was happy too and that his sobriety would last for the rest of our lives, even though he had quit going to Alcoholics Anonymous as soon as he was off probation. That, too, was denial—he wasn't and it didn't. End of the perfect marriage, end of that phase of denial.

Now that I walk with my guide and have rediscovered my truth, denial has become less and less of a road hazard. But, in those areas of my life where false pride still operates, denial still operates as well. In fact, false pride and denial work together very well—to be better than (or even as good as) requires denial of any circumstance or trait that doesn't fit that perception. Denial keeps me unaware of the extent of my pridefulness and how closed my mind has been to new and different points of view and ways of doing things. Denial also still operates in my relationships when I choose to see only my version of reality and not compassionately and courteously honor the other person's position. In that sense, although I can recognize what I perceive to be their denial, I fail to recognize my own. When I base my words and actions on my perception of their reality and don't consider what is really going on with them, I am in denial. I continually did this with the Piano Player, and I have done it with the Songteller.

With the Piano Player, I could see how alcohol was affecting his life and spoke and acted as if he could too, and wanted to change. His truth was that he could see it and wasn't ready for change, but I denied that reality, so my words and actions were hurtful to us both. With the Songteller, I could see how not following his heart in his work and his personal relationships was affecting his life and, again, spoke and acted as if he could see it too and wanted to change. His reality is that, although he can see it, he is neither ready nor willing to change, and my denial of that reality has also caused me to speak and act in ways that are inappropriate, given that he is in a relationship and thus hurtful to us both. But, as he put it recently, "You're getting better." So maybe there's hope. I'm getting tired of having to make amends!

~ COMPLACENCY

Complacency is the road hazard that takes things for granted and denies the potential for change. Complacency assumes that what was true about my life yesterday and is true today will also be true tomorrow. Complacency does not appreciate the gifts of daily life, but instead naively expects that those same gifts will continue to be present in the future as they have been in the past. Complacency thus lives in the past and the future with fear, not in the present with God.

Complacency assumes that my spouse, my soul friends, my children, my house, my car, my job, my health, my money, my personal belongings, my favorite restaurants, anything that is a part of my life today will also be a part of my life tomorrow and the next day in the same way they are a part of my life today. Complacency thus assumes a continuum of experience rather than being grateful for the experience in the present moment. Complacency is then shocked when life "lifes" us and the unexpected happens. Certainly, we all know these things can and do happen, but complacency lulls us into thinking it won't happen to us. Usually it doesn't, but when it does, complacency leaves us unprepared to deal with the life challenge.

Complacency forgets that there are no guarantees beyond the moment in any of our life experiences. Some life experiences may seem to be relatively dependable, but all are subject to radical and sudden change. Water lines break, wind takes down power poles, sewer lines clog, tires go flat, batteries go dead, jobs are eliminated. People we care about get sick, leave, or die. Accidents happen—tornadoes, hurricanes, earthquakes, and wild fires. That which we have depended on suddenly becomes undependable or nonexistent. Complacency becomes shocked, angry, or indignant when expectations are no longer met, when the expected becomes the unexpected. Complacency simply refuses to accept the impermanence of life and life experiences and thus cannot appreciate its gifts as they are experienced.

Possibly the best example of complacency that I can think of is the attitude that most of us had relative to internal security before September 11, 2001. Those of us not involved directly in intelligence gathering or national security naively assumed that we were safe from terrorist action on home ground. I'm not sure why we thought that when terrorist acts have been committed in every other part of the world and are, by their very nature, nearly impossible to either predict or prevent. Certainly, the Oklahoma City bombing was an act of terrorism, even though the perpetrator was a U.S. citizen. But, that was Oklahoma City and it affected a relatively small number of innocent people. It would, and did, take a much larger catastrophe to jolt us out of our complacency.

Note that I used the word "jolt." Unfortunately, complacency is the one form of denial that is not usually gently removed. Most of us do not recognize the onset of complacency and replace it with gratitude without some sort of a catastrophic catalyst. Also unfortunately, the usual reaction to whatever it is that shattered our complacency is to attempt to prevent the unpreventable, to protect or defend ourselves against the shattering event. This is a reaction rooted in fear and does nothing to solve the problem. The vagaries of life cannot be defended against. We can prepare for them, certainly, but not eliminate them. And the best preparation I know of is the recognition and acceptance of the transitory nature of life. What is true today relative to my life may be true tomorrow… or not. There are absolutely no guarantees in my physical world. It is only in the spiritual realm that life never ends.

The antidote for complacency is, of course, gratitude, which is an important byproduct of love. When I have a realistic view of life, an understanding of and belief in divine order, a close relationship with God, and an attitude of gratitude toward every aspect of my life, even the most mundane, there is no longer any room for complacency. In fact, I first mentioned complacency in "Gratitude," which was written before I decided to include complacency as a road hazard. Complacency was added when I realized that it continues to be a very present failing of mine. No matter how hard I focus on gratitude, I still tend to take too much of my life for granted.

I am, however, better than I used to be. (It's called progress, not perfection.) I have shared with you that my intellectual and creative gifts were taken for granted and devalued for years ("The Path"), and I have described how I was jolted out of complacency with my musical gift ("Creativity"). Certainly, my life itself was taken for granted for most of it. What has happened as I have begun walking my unique path with my guide is a gradual recognition and acceptance of life's transitory nature, coupled with gratitude for its many blessings and gifts.

I have, however, been complacent about my normally good health, and deviations from that condition, whether it be laryngitis that lasts a few days or a back problem that lasts a few months, are usually jolts to my complacency and challenges to my attitude of gratitude. I have also been complacent about my abstinence from compulsive eating. It has been so many years since I've had a real problem with food that I tend to forget I have one, and that's not a good place to be. Members of Alcoholics Anonymous are cautioned not to forget their last drink, and I am wise not to forget my last binge. It is that memory that inspires me to stay connected to God so that I am not tempted to do it again. To be sure, occasionally, I am jolted a bit by a box of chocolates that calls to me from a friend's kitchen counter, or a display of brownies that I run into unexpectedly next to the meat counter in a grocery store. But for the most part, my abstinence goes unchallenged by my previous binge foods and I become complacent again.

As I look back at my life, it becomes clearer why complacency has been a problem for me. I have had no major jolts—no life-threatening health challenges, no car accidents, no house fires, no near misses in planes, no floods, tornadoes, or earthquakes, no unexpected sudden losses of loved ones. During my outdoor life, when I continually did things beyond my physical abilities that had life-threatening potential, I came out of them unharmed and unjolted. During my musical life, when I was habitually riding cross-country with an active drinker, I also came out of it unharmed and unjolted. For whatever reason, life has been very gentle with me, and I do appreciate that. But I also tend to take it for granted.

The only real complacency jolt I can think of involves the Piano Player, not me, and it was his first relapse after not drinking for about three years. Back then, I did not know that alcoholism was a disease. He had been through a treatment program, he was seemingly happy as a sober man, I was happy he was a sober man, and we now had a "perfect" life. The problem had been cured. Besides, who in their right mind would start drinking again after being sober for three years? Why would anyone *want* to start drinking again when it was so obviously self-destructive? The answer, of course, is any non-recovering person with the disease of alcoholism, and that was the Piano Player. I became complacent about his addiction and was jolted out of it. Of course, my first reaction was to try to "fix" it. I eventually learned that the only thing I could fix was my attitude and swore that if (or when) he sobered up again, I would be very grateful and not take it for granted. He did stop drinking again, I was grateful, and did not become complacent. In fact, I saw the signs of relapse at least a year before it happened, so when he relapsed again I wasn't jolted because I saw it coming!

The one area of my life where I am not complacent, at least since I've been walking my unique path partnered with my guide, is my spirituality. I am eternally grateful for my spiritual gifts and ever aware of what must be done to continue my spiritual growth. I do not take my relationship with God for granted and continue to follow on a daily basis all of the practices designed to strengthen and deepen our relationship. Improving my conscious contact with the God of my understanding, as suggested by step eleven, is a never ending and top priority process. I neither expect this relationship to remain the same nor do I want it to remain the same. My relationship with God is constantly evolving as I become more and more in tune with the God presence within me, and every change brings me closer to being able to consistently express and experience love to myself, to you, and to all of God's other creations. And as I become more able to express and experience love, I become more grateful and less inclined to be complacent in all aspects of my life.

~ Expectations

An expectation is an attachment to a specific outcome determined by my own personal value system. I may have an expectation of myself, my fellow travelers, even of God. My expectations may be realistic or unrealistic, attainable or impossible, valid or invalid, but they are always my personal desires. Other people's expectations of me are not mine unless I choose to accept them as mine.

Expectations demand a judgment call. I must judge whether or not someone has satisfactorily achieved the desired outcome. If others expect me to be an A student (and I accept that as my expectation as well), then a B disappoints us both. If I expect you to always be on time and you are late for an appointment with me, then I am disappointed. When I decide to take my will and my life back from my God, it is because he has not met my expectations of results and I am disappointed. Thankfully, he does not return like for like. Unconditional love does not expect anything of anyone.

One of my daily meditation books calls expectations premeditated resentments, and that is certainly true. Any time I expect others to act, believe, or generally live their lives according to my personal standards, I am setting myself up for anger and resentment against them. Any time I expect myself to perfectly live up to my own (or someone else's) value system, I am setting myself up for anger, guilt, regret, and resentment against myself. Any time I expect God to provide me with a specific and definite outcome and he does not come through, I set myself up for anger and resentment against him.

Expectations live in a future based on the past. My personal standards and values are based on past experience and are extended to the future. If my favorite baseball team has won ten games in a row, I expect them to win the eleventh. If their pitchers have pitched brilliantly in the past, I expect them to pitch brilliantly in the future. If the team has a history of not being able to win in post-season games, I will expect that as well.

Expectations destroy serenity faster than anything else I can think of. And the higher my expectations are, or the more expectations I cling to, the faster and farther I can fall into the pit of disappointment and despair. Accepting the expectations of someone else as my own is a especially deadly trap, particularly if the expectations are excessively demanding. Perfection in anything is excessively demanding—perfect grades, perfect performance, perfect whatever. Zero defects is a goal to strive for, but not a goal to expect.

I have, of course, had my share of expectations, mostly about myself but also of those I cared about. Many of my expectations of myself were accepted from someone else. My parents expected me to get good grades, to be the top of the class, so I took that expectation and held it for many years. They also expected me to excel in music, so I assumed that one as well. Part of my fear of solo performing comes from the expectation that I should play as perfectly as I did years ago. I expected myself to achieve and be successful in my various professions, and I was. However, my perfectionism, which is an unrealistic expectation, kept me from doing new, unusual, or overly difficult and challenging tasks. I pretty much stayed with what I was comfortable with, rather than risking not meeting my own expectations for myself.

My perfectionism extended to others as well. I imposed my particular set of standards on the Piano Player and expected him to always play his best so that we would always sound our best. He always did play the best he could at the time, but sometimes the best he could do was pretty awful. And I would get very angry because he did not live up to my expectations. Not his, mind you, mine. Oddly, when I was playing music with him, I had few expectations for my own performance. I was a neophyte in that area of music, and since he put no expectations on my performance, neither did I.

I also had a whole set of expectations about his behavior and actions, but only when he was sober. When he was sober, I expected him to do what I call "man" stuff, those activities that are traditionally performed by men, and he did. When he was using, I did not expect him to do anything (except play the piano), and that is about all he did do.

But perhaps the one area where I have had the most unrealistic expectations of both myself and others has been in working my twelve-step programs, walking my spiritual path of recovery. Once a character defect was unearthed and owned, I expected it to magically disappear immediately. Never mind that it took me sixty years to perfect it, I expected instant relief. Once my head got the hang of a particular principle or concept, I expected to be able to apply it perfectly from then on. And if I expected this of myself and someone else was in-program too, I expected it of them. I have spent a lot of time taking not only my own inventory but others' as well. I have held expectations about how meetings should be conducted and have become very disturbed when my expectations were not met. I have created expectations of what your path should be and how you should walk it. This has been particularly true with the soul sisters, who have both chosen different paths than I expected them to. And despite my concerns and expectations of dire consequences, God is working in their lives very well. And will continue to without any further help from me. Love is all that is required here. Love and acceptance, for that is the antidote for expectations. Again, unconditional love accepts rather than expects. Unconditional love does not judge, so how could it have expectations? The God I know today never did have a list of rules and regulations that he expected me or anyone else to live up to. I may have believed that at one time, but today I know better. To be sure, he has suggested certain standards of conduct that, when followed, lead us to our highest good, but he does not judge or condemn us for our mistakes. Guilt and punishment are human creations, not related to divinity. Guilt and punishment are sourced in fear, and my God is pure love. There is no connection at all.

As I have learned to walk with my guide, to be more and more sourced in love, I am also eventually learning to rid myself of most of my expectations. I am less harsh on myself and others, and much more accepting and loving. I am also much more serene as a result of giving up my expectations. This does not mean that I no longer strive to do my best. What it does mean is that I accept whatever my best is at any given time and move on to the next event. I try very diligently to not let expectations, good or bad, based on past events create future events. I try to stay as much as possible in the present with God and let go of expectations. I say "try" because I still can get pulled into expectations relative to my soul friends, especially the ones I care deeply about. Often, this happens when a blanket of denial drops and a window of truth opens momentarily. I then build false expectations based on that moment of truth, not realizing that the window has since slammed shut and is covered again by the blanket.

I should know better than this because I lived through it many times with the Piano Player when he was drinking. Often, he would offer me just enough of a glimpse of truth or a hint of action based on that truth to keep me around, and I would form an expectation of an imminent return to sobriety and sanity based on that glimpse of truth. Then, after too many disappointments and some wise counsel in Al-Anon, I learned not to expect anything until it happened, no matter what he said or how desperately he said it.

That was some years ago, however, and I recently had to learn the same lesson over again—and over and over. True, it was a different soul friend and slightly different circumstances, but the result was the same. A window of truth opened, I formed an expectation, I overreacted based on that expectation, and the window of truth closed again. Or a pattern of behavior was established, I formed the expectation that it would continue, and when it did not I was very unaccepting and unforgiving. Same stuff, different person. Now my memory has been refreshed and I will, I hope, not repeat the same mistake again. Hope is appropriate in such cases, love and acceptance are always appropriate, but expectations are not. Living in the present with God will spare me the pain of unmet expectations based on past experience. And the next time the window of truth opens, I will patiently wait for my soul friend to come through it, not try and help him along.

~ RESISTANCE

Resistance is opposition, and it can be sourced either in love or in fear. Resistance sourced in love says, lovingly and peacefully, that in order to stand in my truth, I must oppose your position. Resistance sourced in love is a statement of integrity and not a road hazard. Resistance sourced in fear is the road hazard. Resistance sourced in fear opposes a call for action, a course correction, a thought or feeling that is sourced in love. Resistance sourced in fear says, "I don't want to," "I don't think so," "You want me to do *what*?" Resistance sourced in fear lives in the past with, "Yeah, but," and in the future with, "What if?" Resistance may either refuse or stall and is thus manifested through procrastination and stubbornness. Resistance drags its feet and digs in its heels.

When I did not want our road cat, Misty, to run free, I would put a collar and leash on her and take her outside. Now, this cat was not about to let anyone tell her where and when to move. She dug in with all four paws and multiple claws and refused to move at all. I have seen people dig in just the same way when they felt either threatened or were being coerced. That is resistance.

Resistance can be very painful and harmful. When my cat resisted being led on a leash, the collar choked her and caused physical pain. If she had resisted hard enough and long enough, or if I had not given in, she could have choked to death. When the Piano Player resisted treatment for his alcoholism after his physical health had obviously deteriorated, the result was not only painful, but, ultimately, fatal. Resistance can be damaging, not only physically, but also emotionally, mentally, and spiritually.

Still, of all of the road hazards, resistance is one of the best teachers. Resistance tells me to take a look at the thought, feeling, or action that I am resisting and ask myself why I am resisting it. An honest answer can reveal a hidden fear and, once revealed, the fear becomes much less ominous and usually can be released. My fear of public speaking was supported for years by my resistance to doing anything that might involve getting up in front of a group. Had I looked into the reason for my resistance sooner, perhaps I could have faced that fear and made the choice to move through it long before I did.

Resistance is usually a head trip. My heart only resists when my head tells it to do something that is not my truth. When I followed my head and not my heart and married the Skier/Climber, my heart resisted for a time before it closed and buried the pain. Heart resistance usually manifests in closure, shutting down. Head resistance is an unwillingness to surrender to an external or internal stimulus. It may be a request or demand from a fellow traveler or a prompting from my heart. Resistance to a prompting from my heart is an unwillingness to surrender to love, to God's will, and such resistance makes it very difficult to find and follow my unique path. If I choose to let my resistance chart my course of action or inaction, then following my unique path becomes impossible. My path becomes a detour until such time as I move through my resistance and begin to follow my heart once more.

When my resistance is to an external urging, it may be loved-based resistance, a flag that signals when my integrity is being challenged. Or it may be based on false pride, a dislike of other people telling me what to do, say, or believe. Some of us will resist simply to resist, and that can be either fear- or love-based. When the Songteller tries to talk me out of loving him, I resist because loving him is my truth. Standing firm in my truth, not allowing other people to cause me to deviate from my truth, is a principle that I have only recently begun to practice, so I am very aware when my integrity is challenged. In those cases, resistance is simply saying, "No, that is not my truth," and is usually quiet and unshakable. Should I resist or protest too loudly and too insistently, the truth I am defending may not, in fact, be my truth at all. Or it may be a truth that has not yet been confirmed by my heart.

In the process of sharing me and my life with you, I have already given many examples of resistance. Certainly, my resistance to coming out of the closet about my addictions was a major one, at least in terms of time. I began educating myself about alcoholism and codependency in 1989, about food addiction in 1991, and everything I read that was influenced by the twelve-step philosophy told me to go to Al-Anon and Overeaters Anonymous. But I resisted doing that until 1993. When God answered my first prayer for help for the Piano Player, I knew he was still there for me, but I resisted calling him back into my life for another five years. The Piano Player resisted treatment for his disease long after he knew it was a disease and could kill him. He resisted all forms of loving self-care, as did the Skier/Climber, who never visited either doctors or dentists. Obviously, denial and resistance are closely related because when denial leaves, resistance often takes its place. And both are intimate partners with false pride; in fact, false pride is often the creator of resistance when denial is replaced by awareness.

The linear time line that flows with awareness, acceptance, and action is often lengthened dramatically by resistance. Certainly, the linear time line between my awareness of the need to surrender to God's will and actually doing it has been greatly lengthened by resistance. My resistance has made following the direction of my guide and walking my unique path much more difficult than it had to be, and my resistance to specific actions makes it more unpleasant than it needs to be. Resisting God changes the course of my path, but resisting others may just make my journey less fun. The Al-Anon slogan, "How important is it?" also directly applies to resistance. When resistance delays acceptance of reality, or of my truth, it is course-altering. When resistance needlessly disturbs my serenity through inaction or procrastination, it is always undesirable.

So resistance may be a pointer that tells me exactly what my heart (and thus my guide) wants me to do or where he wants me to go. Usually, when I feel myself resisting something internally, I understand that the something is a wound that needs to be healed. Some time ago, I was urged by my heart to return to the Catholic diocese where my separation from God occurred more than thirty-five years ago. I had not, in all that time, ever been back in that building, and I knew it was time to go back, feel the pain, and be released from it. My resistance was high, and I was afraid of what I would feel there. I eventually did go, and what I found was that same sense of spirituality in the ritual that I had experienced originally. Yes, there was pain, but the pain was soon replaced by an inner peace. Still, I chose not to continue going to Mass because the teachings of the Catholic Church are not compatible with my untraditional belief system.

A year later, I found myself resisting once more. What I was resisting was both Jesus and Christianity. I had been struggling to come to terms with my relationship with Jesus and to reconcile his message of love with my understanding of Christian doctrine. I had, it seems, rejected Jesus and his teachings along with the exclusivist interpretation of the same. I had, in effect, reconciled with God, but not with Jesus or with the belief system that carries his name. Now,

I have no such problem with Buddha and Buddhism, Mohammed and the Muslims, or any other of the world's great religions, so obviously I had a wound that required healing.

Then I was given a gift of love by the Methodist pastor whose church I used to attend—a nondenominational book on Christian theology and doctrine, and it presents a somewhat less restrictive view of Christianity and Christian philosophy. Without all the varied assortment of "Thou shalts" and "shalt nots," the philosophies and principles bear a striking similarity to those of my twelve-step programs. Unconditional love, humility, surrender, hope, faith, charity, forgiveness, compassionate concern for others, even service—they're all there. The only difference seems to be that the twelve steps connect directly with God and don't require a belief in the need for an intermediary. Now, for traditional Christians, this is a very big difference indeed, but that's not what's important here. What is important is that I was given the gift of clarity, and clarity led to reconciliation with both Christ and Christianity. I embraced Jesus, or, rather, allowed him to embrace me. My resistance to his loving presence was gone, as was my resistance to those who honor the doctrine of traditional Christian churches. But I still resisted participating in Christian ritual and myth that was not compatible with my personal belief system. That resistance was based on my truth and thus an expression of personal integrity.

Then, after much searching, the circle finally closed. I followed an Internet path from the site of my primary spiritual validator through her Unity church to the Unity School of Christianity. Reading their mission statement, I thought "Yes! This is where I fit!" But that's as far as it went, for the closest Unity church was over two hundred miles away. The path down which I was being led came to an apparent dead end.

Now, a year later, the path has reopened and I find myself resisting again. While I was in Nevada to give love and support to the Songteller, in the tiny town of Genoa, nestled beneath the Sierra Nevada Mountains, I found the Unity Church of Today. The moment I walked into my first service, I knew I had found my church home. Nellie, the pastor, invited us all to go on a spiritual pilgrimage through Advent, and that's what I did. My stay in the

Carson Valley was extended through Christmas, so that I could have that experience with Unity, and the tiny blue star that I brought home with me continually reminds me to follow my heart. Now I have experienced the fit—the love and forgiveness of Jesus and the wisdom of his teachings combined with glorious music and the freedom to chart my own spiritual course. There's no question about it—I have been called to serve Unity. But how, and why? I live in Idaho. I have program service commitments, a wonderful house, and wonderful friends in Idaho, and my ultimate destination is Quadra Island. Surely the path from Idaho to Quadra is a straight line… or is it? My head says this is ridiculous, but my heart says something very different.

So as I write this, I am conflicted, stuck in resistance between awareness and acceptance. There are many fears attached to my resistance, but eventually, with some gentle nudges from my guide, I will move through the pain of resistance to acceptance and appropriate action. But today, I am resisting the call of my heart and ignoring the lesson that resistance is teaching me. Today, I am stubbornly refusing to surrender to God's will for me now, even though I know what the outcome will be. Resistance is a strange creature. Often, it has to run a specific course or a certain level of awareness must be reached before I am willing to act. Sometimes God gets tired of waiting for me and intervenes. And his timing is always perfect. Acting too soon is painful, as is waiting too long to act. I hope that this time I will move myself to act before he has to do it for me.

Chapter XI

AFTERTHOUGHTS

THE words I am to share with you to put closure on this gift of love are not coming easily to me. How do I conclude something that has no conclusion? How do I end a work that has no ending, only a never-ending progression of endings and beginnings? I am a work in progress, and my road home is a process that is continuously evolving. Change is the only constant in my progression through life. To be sure, the goal does not change, and that is, of course, to become more perfectly one with my God and with love. But my path, the way through which I work towards attaining that goal, is ever changing; and this creation, this gift of love, is but a small segment of my unique path. So whatever ending I write is not really an ending at all, but rather the beginning of the next phase of my journey.

And since walking my unique path is a process, there are, throughout this sharing, a number of "to be continueds," areas or aspects of my life that are either still being scripted or where I was made aware of some prescribed action I had not yet taken. Most of these have been resolved, but some have not. Since writing my first draft, many changes have occurred, all designed to move me closer to my guide and to integrity, to a harmonious blending of inner beliefs and outer behaviors. My course work in Learning to Love has shown me the value of and need for forgiveness, compassion, generosity, and humility. And false pride has been acknowledged and added as a major road hazard, especially for me. As my false pride has been released and replaced by humility and true pride, so have my major fears been released and replaced by God's love. My sense of community has been expanding and growing as I have been expanding and growing in love, as has my ability to feel and express compassion for others. That is a process within a process.

Also, as predicted, my guide has helped me move through my resistance to answer his call to serve Unity. With the loving support of the deer, the eagle has flown to the Carson Valley of Western Nevada and has landed and nested in the spiritual shadow of the Sierra Nevada. There, I have begun a new and exciting segment of my unique path, one that begins in the Carson Valley and ultimately ends on Quadra, with points in between undefined at this time. I have left my house, my friends, and my service positions in Idaho to follow my star, and I now have a new house, new friends, and new service opportunities with the Unity Church of Today. I also have a new mission—to express and experience divine love to all creation—and a vision to define it that includes sharing my authentic self through sharing my unique gifts as an expression of that mission. One of those unique gifts is my music, and it too has expanded, beyond the boundaries of written notes to free expression through improvisation. Finally, now that the Songteller is no longer 643 miles away, our relationship has changed and continues to change to fit the current reality of our respective life situations. This, too, is a process within a process, one that is being scripted and directed exclusively by God.

When I asked my guide how to conclude our gift of love to you, he suggested that I end it the same way I often end my morning pages, and that is with a prayer that talks to what has been written. So, here is my prayer as I finish this phase of my journey down the road home:

> Dear God,
>
> Thank you for all the gifts you have given me during our co-creation of *The Road Home*, the greatest of which is the experience of your divine presence within me and the awareness of the inherent gifts that spring from that presence. Other gifts include an open mind and heart, trust, surrender, humility, patience,

inspiration, understanding, forgiveness, compassion, generosity, insight, clarity, vision, and the willingness to finish that which we had begun. Please offer these gifts and many more to anyone who reads our words. I know that if any part of what we have written touches anyone in a way that will bring him or her closer to love and to you, my mission and your desires will have been fulfilled. Thank you for your guidance and for allowing me to serve you in this way. Your will is love; may it be done at all times and in all ways. Thank you. I love you. Amen.

Chapter XII

APPENDIX

TRAVELING the road home is an individual experience, unique to each of us. This book is intended to be a companion on the journey, a spiritual tool that may be used in many different ways. It is suitable both for individual study and group discussion, and it has been suggested that a workbook or study guide be created to accompany it. It may be read continuously from cover to cover or taken in smaller doses as a daily reader, one section or subsection at a time. The spiritual essays categorized as gifts, rewards, principles, practices, and road hazards may be selected by simply opening the book at random or by purposely choosing an essay to study in more depth. For those who wish to choose purposely, here is an alphabetical listing of the spiritual essays and their corresponding page numbers:

Chapter XIII

BIBLIOGRAPHY

SINCE the time I began walking with my guide and following the map that he gave me to follow, I have enhanced my twelve-step recovery with both program-approved and outside reading materials. I describe myself as a voracious reader and a compulsive book buyer, and my library mirrors the stages of my spiritual growth. I am including in this bibliography only some of the many books that I have been guided to along the way, books that provided me information, guidance, inspiration, new concepts, or validation of those concepts that were already a part of my personal belief system. Those texts or authors that have been the most influential and helpful to me on my journey are marked with an asterisk. And, since their works fall into many different categories, I am listing them that way for ease of reference. With this listing, as with everything else in this book, take what you like and leave the rest.

ADDICTION

*Alcoholics Anonymous World Service, *Alcoholics Anonymous* (The Big Book), NY: Alcoholics Anonymous, 1976

*Brady, Tom, Jr., *Thirsting for Wholeness, the Spiritual Journal of Addiction and Recovery,* FL: Health Communications, Inc., 1992

*Covington, Stephanie and Beckett, Liana, *Leaving the Enchanted Forest: The Path from Relationship Addiction to Intimacy*, CA: Harper San Francisco, 1988

Drews, Toby Rice, *Getting Them Sober*, NJ: Bridge Publishing, 1980

*Greeson, Janet, *It's Not What You're Eating, It's What's Eating You*, NY: Simon & Schuster, 1990

Maxwell, Ruth, *The Booze Battle*, NY: Ballantine Books, 1976

Melody, Pia, with Andrea Wells Miller and J. Keith Miller, *Facing Love Addiction*, CA: HarperSan Francisco, 1992

Milam, Dr. James R. and Ketcham, Katherine, *Under the Influence*, NY: Bantam Books, 1981

Norwood, Robin, *Women Who Love Too Much*, NY: Simon & Schuster, 1985

Schaef, Anne Wilson, *When Society Becomes an Addict*, NY: Harper & Row, 1987

CODEPENDENCY

*Beatty, Melody, *Codependant No More*, NY:Harper/Hazelden, 1987

Beatty, Melody, *Beyond Codependency,* NY: Harper/Hazelden, 1989

Beatty, Melody, *Playing It by Heart*, MN: Hazelden, 1999

Bradshaw, John: *Bradshaw On: The Family*, FL: Health Communications, Inc., 1988

Melody, Pia, with Andrea Wells Miller and J. Keith Miller, *Facing Codependence: What It Is, Where It Comes From and How It Sabotages Your Life*, CA: Harper San Francisco, 1989

Melody, Pia, and Andrea Wells Miller, *Breaking Free: A Workbook for Facing Codependence,* CA: Harper San Francisco, 1989

*Miller, Angelyn, *The Enabler—When Helping Harms the Ones You Love*, NY: Random House, 1988

Schaef, Anne Wilson, *Co-Dependence: Misunderstood-Mistreated*, NY: Harper Row, 1986

COMMUNITY

Peck, M. Scott, *A World Waiting to be Born*, NY: Bantam Books, 1993

Williamson, Marianne, *The Healing of America*, NY: Simon & Schuster, 1997

COMPASSION

Salzberg, Sharon, *A Heart as Wide as the World*, MA: Shambhala, 1997

Skog, Susan, *Radical Acts of Love: How Compassion Is Transforming Our World*, MN: Hazelden, 2001.

Stefaniak, Jerome, *Compassionate Living—Everyday Spirituality*, TX: Brockton Publishing, 1994

*Straub, Gail, *The Rhythm of Compassion*, VT: Tuttle Publishing, 2000

DAILY READERS

_______, *Each Day a New Beginning*, CA: Harper San Francisco, 1982

*Al-Anon Family Group Headquarters, Inc., *One Day at a Time in Al-Anon*, NY: Al-Anon Family Groups, 1968

*Al-Anon Family Group Headquarters, Inc., *Courage to Change*, NY: Al-Anon Family Groups, 1992

*Ban Breathnach, Sarah, *Simple Abundance: A Daybook of Comfort and Joy*, NY: Warner Books, 1995

*Beattie, Melody, *The Language of Letting Go*, NY: Harper/Hazelden, 1990

*Beattie, Melody, *Journey to the Heart*, CA: Harper San Francisco, 1996

Beattie, Melody, *More Language of Letting Go*, MN: Hazelden, 2000

Gawain, Shakti, *Reflections in the Light*, CA: New World Library, 1988

*Overeaters Anonymous, *For Today*, CA: Overeaters Anonymous, 1982

*Rosemergy, Jim, *A Daily Guide to Spiritual Living*, MO: Unity Books, 1991

*UNITY, *Daily Word*, MO: Unity School of Christianity, annual publication.

*Vanzant, Iyanla, *Until Today*, NY: Simon & Schuster, 2000

FORGIVENESS

*Ferrini, Paul, *The 12 Steps of Forgiveness*, MA: Heartways Press, 1991

Jampolsky, Gerald G., *Forgiveness—the Greatest Healer of All*, OR: Beyond Words Publishing, 1999

*Nerburn, Kent, *Calm Surrender, Walking the Hard Road of Forgiveness*, CA: New World Library, 2000

HEALING

*Anderson, Susan, *The Journey from Abandonment to Healing*, NY: Penguin Putnam, 2000

Bodine, Echo, *Passion to Heal*, CA: Nataraj Publishing, 1993

*Bourne, Edmund, *Healing Fear*, CA: New Harbinger Publications, 1998

*Bradshaw, John, *Healing the Shame That Binds You*, FL: Health

Communications, Inc., 1988

Bradshaw, John, *Home Coming: Reclaiming and Championing Your Inner Child*, NY: Bantam Books, 1992

Gawain, Shakti, *The Path for Transformation*, CA: Nataraj Publishing, 1993

*Gawain, Shakti, *The Four Levels of Healing*, CA: Nataraj Publishing, 1997

*Hay, Louise L., *You Can Heal Your Life*, CA: Hay House, 1984

Hay, Louise L., *The Power Is Within You*, CA: Hay House, 1991

*Myss, Caroline, *Anatomy of the Spirit*, NY: Three Rivers Press, 1996

Roth, Ron, *The Healing Path of Prayer*, NY: Crown Publishers, 1997

*Taylor, Cathryn L., *The Inner Child Workbook*, NY: Penguin Putnam, 1991

*Truman, Karol, *Feelings Buried Alive Never Die*, NV: Olympus Distributing, 1991

Truman, Karol, *Healing Feelings...From Your Heart*, NV: Olympus Distributing, 2000

Whitfield, Charles L., *Healing the Child Within*, FL: Health Communications, Inc., 1989

LOVE

Ferrini, Paul, *Love without Conditions*, MA: Heartways Press, 1994

*Foundation for Inner Peace, *A Course in Miracles, Text, Workbook for Students, Manual for Teachers*, Ca: Foundation for Inner Peace, 1975

*Jampolsky, Gerald G., *Love is Letting Go of Fear*,

Jampolsky, Gerald G., *Teach Only Love*, OR: Beyond Words Publishing, 2000

Roman, Sanaya, *Soul Love*, CA: HJKramer, 1997

Ruiz, Don Miguel, *Beyond Fear*, OK: Council Oak Books, 1997

*Williamson, Marianne, *A Return to Love*, NY: HarperCollins, 1992

MEDITATION

Fishel, Ruth, *The Journey Within*, FL: Health Communications, 1987

Fontana, David, *Learn to Meditate*, London: Duncan Baird, 1999

Goldstein, Joan, and Soares, Manuela, *The Joy Within*, NY: Simon & Schuster, 1990

*Rathbun, Ron, *The Silent Miracle, Awakening Your True Spiritual Nature by Stilling Your Mind*, NY: Penguin Putnam, 1999

PRAYER

*Cameron, Julia, *Heart Steps—Prayers and Declarations for a Creative Life*, NY: Penguin Putnam, 1997

*Cameron, Julia, *Blessings—Prayers and Declarations for a Heartful Life*, NY: Penguin Putnam, 1998

*Cameron, Julia, *Transitions—Prayers and Declarations for a Changing Life*, NY: Penguin Putnam, 1999

*Williamson, Marianne, *Illuminata, A Return to Prayer*, NY: Riverhead Books, 1994

*Williamson, Marianne, *Illuminated Prayers*, NY: Simon & Schuster, 1997

RELATIONSHIPS

Bradshaw, John, *Creating Love*, NY: Bantam Books, 1992

Chopra, Deepak, *The Path to Love*, NY: Harmony Books, 1997

*Gattuso, Joan, *A Course in Love*, NY: HarperCollins, 1996

Ruiz, Don Miguel, *The Mastery of Love*, CA: Amber-Allen Publishing, 1999

Roman, Sanaya, *Spiritual Growth*, CA: HJKramer, 1989

*Vanzant, Iyanla, *In The Meantime—Finding Yourself and the Love You Want*, NY: Simon & Schuster, 1998

*Vanzant, Iyanla, *Living Through the Meantime*, NY: Simon & Schuster, 2001

*Williamson, Marianne, *Enchanted Love—The Mystical Power of Intimate Relationships*, NY: Simon & Schuster, 1999

RELIGION

Boorstein, Sylvia, *It's Easier Than You Think, The Buddhist Way to Happiness*, NY: HarperCollins, 1995

Fox, Matthew, *One River, Many Wells*, NY: Penguin Putnam, 2000

Huyler, Stephen P., *Meeting God, Elements of Hindu Devotion*, CT: Yale University Press, 1999

Khan, Pir Vilayat Inayat, *Awakening, a Sufi Experience*, NY: Penguin Putnam, 1999

*Lewis, C. S., *Mere Christianity*, NY: Macmillan Publishing, 1943

Mitchell, Stephen, *Tao te Ching*, NY: HarperCollins, 1988

Newell, J. Philip, *The Book of Creation, An Introduction to Celtic Spirituality*, NJ: Paulist Press, 1999

*O'Donohue, John, *Anam Cara, A Book of Celtic Wisdom*, NY: HarperCollins, 1997

*Smith, Huston, *The Illustrated World's Religions*, A Guide to Our Wisdom Traditions, NY: HarperCollins, 1994

SELF-CARE AND SELF-DISCOVERY

*Ban Breathnach, Sarah, *Something More, Excavating Your Authentic Self*, NY: Warner Books, 1998

*Beatty, Melody, *Finding Your Way Home*, NY: HarperCollins, 1998

Beatty, Melody, *Stop Being So Mean to Yourself,* SF: Harper San Francisco, 1997

*Cameron, Julia, *The Artist's Way, a Spiritual Path to Higher Creativity*, NY: G. P. Putnam's, 1992

Cameron, Julia, *The Vein of Gold*, NY: G. P. Putnam's, 1996

*Gafni, Marc, *Soul Prints*, NY: Simon & Schuster, 2001

Muller, Wayne, *How, Then, Shall We Live? Four Simple Questions That Reveal the Beauty and Meaning of Our Lives,* NY: Bantam Books, 1997.

Myss, Caroline, *Sacred Contracts, Awakening Your Divine Potential*, NY: Harmony Books, 2001.

Roman, Sanaya, *Living with Joy*, CA: HJKramer, 1986

Roman, Sanaya, *Personal Power through Awareness*, CA: HJKramer, 1986

Roman, Sanaya, *Spiritual Growth*, CA: HJKramer, 1989

SPIRITUALITY AND MYSTICISM

*Borysenko, Joan, *A Woman's Journey to God*, NY: Penguin Putnam, 1999

*Borysenko, Joan, *7 Paths to God*, CA: Hay House, 1997

Chopra, Deepak, *How to Know God*, NY: Harmony Books, 2000

Fischer, William L., *Alternatives*, MO: Unity Books, 1980

*Goldsmith, Joel, *Practicing the Presence*, CA: HarperCollins, 1991

Hausman, Winifred Wilkinson, *Your God-Given Potential*, MO: Unity Books, 1999

Jampolsky, Gerald G., *Shortcuts to God*, CA: Celestial Arts, 2000

*Kelly, Elizabeth, *Spiritual Journey*, OH: Cimarron Books, 1997

Monahan, Sister Molly, *Seeds of Grace: A Nun's Reflections on the Spirituality of Alcoholics Anonymous*, NY: Riverhead Books, 2001

Nerburn, Kent, *The Wisdom of the Great Chiefs*, CA: Classic Wisdom Library, 1994

Rathbun, Ron, *The Way Is Within*, NY: Penguin Putnam, 1994

*Rosemergy, Jim, *A Closer Walk with God*, CO: Acropolis Books, 1997

*Rosemergy, Jim, *The Sacred Human*, MO: Inner Journey, 1996

*Ruiz, Don Miguel, *The Four Agreements*, CA: Amber-Allen Publishing, 1997

*Vanzant, Iyanla, *Faith in the Valley*, NY: Simon & Schuster, 1996

*Vanzant, Iyanla, *One Day My Soul Just Opened Up*, NY: Simon & Schuster, 1998

Walsch, Neale Donald, *Conversations with God, book 1*, NY: G. P. Putnam's, 1995

Walsch, Neale Donald, *Conversations with God, book 2*, VA: Hampton

Roads Publishing, 1997

Walsch, Neale Donald, *Conversations with God, book 3*, VA: Hampton Roads Publishing, 1998

Walsch, Neale Donald, *Friendship with God*, NY: G. P. Putnam's, 1999

Walsch, Neale Donald, *Communion with God*, NY: G. P. Putnam's, 2000

*Zukav, Gary, *The Seat of the Soul*, NY: Simon & Schuster, 1989

Zukav, Gary, *Soul Stories*, NY: Simon & Schuster, 2000

TRANSITION AND LOSS

*Albom, Mitch, *Tuesdays with Morrie*, NY: Bantam Doubleday, 1997

Beatty, Melody, *The Lessons of Love*, SF: Harper San Francisco, 1994

*Brumet, Robert, *Finding Yourself in Transition*, MO: Unity Books, 1995

Childs-Gowell, Elaine, *Good Grief Rituals*, NY: Station Hill Press, 1992

*Deits, Bob, *Life after Loss*, AZ: Fisher Books, 1992

*Kubler-Ross, Elizabeth, *On Death and Dying*, NY: Macmillan Publishing, 1969

*Tatelbaum, Judy, *You Don't Have to Suffer, A Handbook for Moving Beyond Life's Crises*, NY: Harper & Row, 1989

TWELVE STEPS

______, *Twelve Steps and Twelve Traditions*, NY: Alcoholics Anonymous World Services, 1988

______, *The Twelve Steps of Alcoholics Anonymous*, NY: Harper/Hazelsen, 1987

*Al-Anon Family Groups, *Paths to Recovery—Al-Anon's Steps, Traditions, and Concepts*, VA: Al-Anon Family Group Headquarters, 1997

Al-Anon Family Groups, *Al-Anon's Twelve Steps and Twelve Traditions*, NY: Al-Anon Family Groups, Inc., 1988

Beatty, Melody, *Codependents' Guide to the Twelve Steps*, NY: Prentice Hall, 1990

Covington, Stephanie S., *A Woman's Way through the Twelve Steps*, MN: Hazelden, 1994

Friends in Recovery, *The 12 Steps, A Way Out*, CA: Recovery Publications, 1989

L, Elizabeth, *Twelve Steps for Overeaters*, NY: Harper/Hazelden, 1988

*Overeaters Anonymous, *The Twelve Steps and Twelve Traditions of Overeaters Anonymous*, CA: Overeaters Anonymous, Inc., 1993